THE EFFICACY OF JUDICIAL REVIEW

Over the past century, countries around the globe have empowered constitutional courts to safeguard the rule of law. But when can courts effectively perform this vital task? Drawing upon a series of survey experiments fielded in the United States, Germany, Hungary, and Poland, this book demonstrates that judicial independence is critical for judicial efficacy. Independent courts can empower citizens to punish executives who flout the bounds of constitutional rule; weak courts are unable to generate public costs for transgressing the law. Although judicial efficacy is neither universal nor automatic, courts – so long as they are viewed by the public as independent – can provide an effective check on executives and promote the rule of law.

Amanda Driscoll is an Associate Professor of Political Science at Florida State University and an Associate Professor of Law (by courtesy) at the Florida State College of Law. Her research, which considers comparative courts and the rule of law, has been funded by the National Science Foundation and was awarded best conference paper on law and courts by the American Political Science Association and the Southern Political Science Association.

Jay N. Krehbiel is an Associate Professor of Political Science at the University at Buffalo. He studies how public support for courts – both international and domestic – affects judicial behavior. Krehbiel is a former Fulbright Scholar at the University of Oslo.

Michael J. Nelson is a Professor of Political Science and Affiliate Law Faculty at the Pennsylvania State University. His most recent books, *Judging Inequality* and *The Elevator Effect*, won the Pritchett Award for best book from the Law and Courts Section of the American Political Science Association.

The Efficacy of Judicial Review

THE RULE OF LAW AND THE PROMISE OF INDEPENDENT COURTS

AMANDA DRISCOLL
Florida State University

JAY N. KREHBIEL
University at Buffalo

MICHAEL J. NELSON
Pennsylvania State University

CAMBRIDGE
UNIVERSITY PRESS

CAMBRIDGE
UNIVERSITY PRESS

Shaftesbury Road, Cambridge CB2 8EA, United Kingdom

One Liberty Plaza, 20th Floor, New York, NY 10006, USA

477 Williamstown Road, Port Melbourne, VIC 3207, Australia

314–321, 3rd Floor, Plot 3, Splendor Forum, Jasola District Centre, New Delhi – 110025, India

103 Penang Road, #05-06/07, Visioncrest Commercial, Singapore 238467

Cambridge University Press is part of Cambridge University Press & Assessment, a department of the University of Cambridge.

We share the University's mission to contribute to society through the pursuit of education, learning and research at the highest international levels of excellence.

www.cambridge.org
Information on this title: www.cambridge.org/9781009388924

DOI: 10.1017/9781009388948

When citing this work, please include a reference to the DOI 10.1017/9781009388948

First published 2025

A catalogue record for this publication is available from the British Library

A Cataloging-in-Publication data record for this book is available from the Library of Congress

ISBN 978-1-009-38892-4 Hardback

AD: *To my parents, and in memory of Rosemary;*

JK: *To Nash and Walker, for challenging the rule of law at home every day;*

MJN: *To Jim Gibson, who showed me what it is like to love the research process.*

Contents

List of Figures — *page* ix
List of Tables — xi
Preface — xiii
Acknowledgments — xvii

1 **The Promise of Judicial Review** — 1

2 **Theorizing Judicial Efficacy** — 28

3 **How, When, and Where to Evaluate Judicial Efficacy** — 59

4 **Measuring Public Support for the Rule of Law** — 99

5 **How Judicial Independence Facilitates State Constraint** — 136

6 **Citizens' Convictions and Judicial Review** — 158

7 **Judicial Review Amid Partisan Publics** — 185

8 **Do Partisan Litigants Weaken Judicial Efficacy?** — 207

9 **The Prospects of Judicial Review** — 239

References — 255
Index — 283

Figures

1.1 The rise of judicial review and constitutional courts *page* 4
2.1 Typology of executive–judicial interactions 41
3.1 Global distribution of judicial independence and judicial constraints on the executive in 2021 65
3.2 Temporal trends in judicial independence and judicial constraints on the executive in four countries 66
3.3 Perceptions of constitutional court independence from the executive and legislative branches 68
3.4 Perceived level of executive influence on constitutional court decisions 69
3.5 Perceived appropriateness of executive influence over the constitutional court 70
3.6 Perceptions of judicial and public efficacy in the face of executive overreach 71
3.7 Public judgments of the normative desirability of judicial independence 72
3.8 Comparing expert and public judgments of judicial independence 74
4.1 Distribution of support for the rule of law, by country 113
4.2 Bivariate correlations between support for the rule of law and respondents' demographic and political characteristics 120
4.A1 Difference in average support for the rule of law, by demographic and political characteristics 134
5.1 Illustration of executive–judicial interactions in the treatment conditions in the Vaccine Approval and Lockdown Experiments 141
5.2 Direct effects of the Vaccine Approval Experiment 144
5.3 Direct effects of the Lockdown Experiment 149
5.4 Direct effects of the Lockdown Experiment (with Compliant condition) 154

6.1 Conditional effects from the Vaccine Approval Experiment (Support for the Rule of Law) 165
6.2 Conditional effects from the Lockdown Experiment (Support for the Rule of Law) 167
6.3 Conditional effects from the Lockdown Experiment (Executive Approval) 171
6.A1 Direct effects of the Lockdown Experiment (Legislature Treatments) 180
6.A2 Conditional effects from the Lockdown Experiment (Legislature Treatments) 182
7.1 Typology of responses to contravention and clearance by a copartisan and outpartisan executive 190
7.2 Direct effects of the Mandatory Vaccine Experiment 197
7.3 Conditional effects from the Mandatory Vaccine Experiment 201
8.1 Typology of responses to contravention and clearance according to the partisanship of an abstract review challenger 211
8.2 Direct effects of the Abstract Review Experiment 220
8.3 Conditional effects from the Abstract Review Experiment 224
8.A1 Direct effects of the Abstract Review Experiment (with Control condition) 233
8.A2 Conditional effects from the Abstract Review Experiment (with Control condition) 234

Tables

4.1 Respondents' descriptions of with strong commitments to the rule of law *page* 107
4.2 Distribution of support for the rule of law indicators, by country 111
4.3 Psychometric properties of support for the rule of law indicators 112
4.4 The stability of support for the rule of law in Germany 115
4.5 The stability of support for the rule of law in the United States 116
4.6 Correlates of support for the rule of law 124
4.7 Logistic regression results, 2021 question wording experiment 128
4.A1 Distribution of support for the rule of law indicators, alternative country selection 130
4.A2 Psychometric properties of support for the rule of law indicators, alternative country selection 131
4.A3 Item selection table: March 2020 MTurk Survey 132
6.A1 Linear regression results: Vaccine Approval Experiment 176
6.A2 Linear regression results: Lockdown Experiment (United States and Germany) 177
6.A3 Linear regression results: Lockdown Experiment (Hungary and Poland) 178
6.A4 Linear regression results: Lockdown Experiment (Legislature Treatments) 183
7.A1 Linear regression results: Mandatory Vaccine Experiment (United States) 204
7.A2 Linear regression results: Mandatory Vaccine Experiment (Germany) 205
8.A1 Linear regression results: Abstract Review Experiment (Germany) 229
8.A2 Linear regression results: Abstract Review Experiment (Hungary) 230

8.A3 Linear regression results: Abstract Review Experiment (Poland) 231
8.A4 Linear regression results: Abstract Review Experiment (Germany, including control condition) 235
8.A5 Linear regression results: Abstract Review Experiment (Hungary, including control condition) 236
8.A6 Linear regression results: Abstract Review Experiment (Poland, including control condition) 237

Preface

In the second full week of March 2020, we bid farewell to our students for spring break with the expectation that we'd see them in a week, or maybe two. News reports documented that a novel virus, called COVID-19, had made its way to the United States and threatened the health and welfare of citizens around the globe. The mood on our campuses was tense, but attitudes varied. Some students had hurried home in abject panic and fearful for the lives of their loved ones while others were convinced this virus was nothing more than a cold or a flu (and were elated at the prospect of an extra week of vacation). An extended spring break turned into a full suspension of in-person classes for the remainder of the academic year and the cancellation of all commencement ceremonies. We wouldn't see most of our students again. Many of them would graduate without ever returning to campus. This book is also dedicated to them and to the graduating class of 2020.

We watched on the news as governments – the US federal government, our state governments, and governments worldwide – sought to respond to the emerging crisis. We saw politicians starting to discuss major infringements on citizens' rights and liberties, most notably freedoms of association and movement. We suspected that some of these politicians might try to use the pandemic for their own political gain, and we were struck by the idea that the pandemic presented a rare opportunity to understand the public's support for the rule of law at a time when citizens faced an overwhelming threat to law and order and the upheaval of seemingly every facet of everyday life. When we saw an email from the National Science Foundation (NSF) advertising a special call "to conduct non-medical, non-clinical-care research that can be used immediately to explore how to model and understand the spread of COVID-19, to inform and educate about the science of virus transmission and prevention, and to encourage the development of processes and actions to address this global challenge," we saw an opportunity to leverage the pandemic to learn about the public's support for the rule of law.

We envisioned a study where we would measure public support for the rule of law in a handful of countries and field a panel study in Germany. We proposed to study how proximity to crisis – real or perceived – might bolster or undermine the public's support for the rule of law. By the time we fielded our first survey two weeks later, our own daily routines barely resembled what they had been just weeks before. Jay was trying to decide whether or not groceries needed to be cleaned with Clorox wipes, Amanda was trying to keep a preschooler busy long enough to jump on a call, and Michael had driven halfway across the country (with a couple of shirts and two pairs of pants . . . because, of course, the pandemic would only last a week or two) to live in his friends' basement.

We were naive about so many things. As we designed our first experimental vignette that centered around state-mandated lockdowns, we thought we were crazy to suggest that the state would require people to stay in their homes for a week, much less a month. We fretted that it might be a violation of research ethics to suggest to our survey respondents that the COVID-19 crisis might last for more than a few weeks, much less from May until July. It was *inconceivable* that we would be living with COVID-19 at the end of summer: Surely ("*surely!*"), it would all be in the rearview mirror by the start of the next academic year. And, when we applied for the grant, we were naive enough to ask for a year-long panel survey to be able to examine "whether citizens' attitudes change after a crisis has dissipated." How wrong were we as the COVID-19 virus continued to wreak havoc long after the NSF money was spent.

As we submit the final manuscript of this book almost exactly four years later (testing the limit of the word "immediately" in the NSF's original call), we reflect on how far we and this project have come, in ways that we did not (indeed could have never) imagine or foresee. Writing this book has taken a lot of grit; there were many times when this project, much like the global crisis from whence it originated, was unwieldy, chaotic, overwhelming, and confusing. It is no small miracle that while we each had our episodic doubts and misgivings along the way, our crises of confidence never coincided enough to derail the project entirely. While there are, of course, many advantages to collaborative research, this "division of doubt" proved to be an invaluable one as we forged ahead.

We can now reflect with clearer eyes on the path we took to get to this finished product. There are a great many research projects that start from a well-conceptualized research question, then move to a carefully selected research design, and culminate in a paper or manuscript that executes that design. As it might be clear now (and will certainly be obvious by the time one has finished reading this book), this is not one of those projects. Just as the pandemic presented us with a unique opportunity to do this research, so too did it present unique challenges to our "standard" research process. The best we could do was try to roll with the changes and adapt as best we could. Despite our best efforts, there are, of course, decisions we look back on now with a mix of confusion, frustration, and – on occasion – humor.

All research projects have some degree of "ugh, I wish I had done X differently." This book has it in spades.

Through the ups and downs the research process inevitably entails, we were encouraged bit by bit by our discoveries. The public's support for the rule of law is high and unwavering, even in the face of abject crisis. We had not been optimistic about this at the outset of our work, so to see such resilience was as much a psychological boost as it was an interesting finding. Likewise, that judicial review by independent courts can animate the public to constrain the state gave us hope that perhaps democracy's prospects are not as gloomy as they may sometimes seem. This finding also let us reorient this research and ourselves in a base of knowledge that was both well-grounded and comfortingly familiar. In a time that was punctuated by bad news and doomsday predictions, on more than one occasion, the project's findings – both expected and unexpected – gave us reason to take heart.

So many projects end with a solemn promise to "never go through this again." Never has this rung truer than when thinking about the trials of doing research during – and about – a worldwide crisis. We look forward to continuing our collaboration in not with a less weighty context. We cannot help but reflect on what a privilege it has been, and it continues to be, to be empowered to collaborate so closely with one's friends, especially in these extraordinary times.

Acknowledgments

All books incur debts as they come to fruition; ours is no exception. We have been so lucky to have the benefit of careful feedback from the community of law and courts scholars in the United States and Europe as we've worked on this book. Two people, in particular, deserve special thanks. First, Jeff Staton suffered through drafts of every chapter of this book – multiple times – as a discussant and conference organizer. We presented the first paper in this project at the Global Law and Politics online workshop he hosted with Dan Brinks and Rachel Cichowski in the fall of 2020, in what would be the first virtual academic conference of many to come. Jeff would later give us some tough love at our book conference, which led us to cull a whole facet of the original project, greatly focusing and strengthening the manuscript as a whole (may our chapter on legislative oversight RIP). Second, it was in that online workshop that Georg Vanberg told us that it seemed that we were particularly interested in "institutional guardrails" to the rule of law, a phrase that helped to keep us on track when YouGov questionnaire deadlines were looming every six weeks and the project had become diffuse and unwieldy. He graciously agreed to read early versions of Chapters 2 and 5 and Zoomed with us to provide some very incisive comments. We are indebted to both Georg and Jeff for their insights and for their mentorship.

We are indebted to the editors of this series – Zach Elkins, Tom Ginsburg, and Ran Hirschl – who provided us with the opportunity and encouragement to bring out this research in its best form. That they saw potential in the project even in its early stages gave us much needed confidence and inspiration to keep going. And once we had draft materials to share with them, their feedback and comments provided us invaluable direction that helped shape the project into a (hopefully) more compelling book. It is an honor and a privilege to have our work included here.

We likewise benefited from the process at Cambridge University Press. The three anonymous reviewers of our proposal and draft chapter gave us incisive comments and suggestions that resulted in profound improvements to the project. We are fortunate to have received such insightful feedback at such an early stage of our work. Additionally, we would be remiss if we did not express our thanks to Marianne Nield at Cambridge University Press, who helped shepherd us through the process.

We also owe a special debt of gratitude to the other commentators at our book manuscript conference: Ryan Carlin, Christopher Reenock, and Dino Christenson. The book that you hold in your hands is very different from the draft they read and their thoughts – about how to emphasize the role of partisanship and the contextual factors of COVID-19, how to connect our argument to the literature on executive unilateral action, and how to frame our research design and measurement strategy (among so many other things) – gave us both the encouragement we needed to slog to the finish line and a roadmap for how to make the book (we hope) worth the readers' time. Many others at Florida State University (FSU), including Andy Ballard, Olga Gasparyan, and Quintin Beazer, offered thoughts on parts of the book, and Martín Gandur and Giulia Venturini participated as notetakers that would help us reflect on critical advice we received.

We have also benefited from the feedback of audience members and discussants at meetings of the Southern Political Science Association and the American Political Science Association, the European Consortium for Political Research's Joint Sessions, the Global Law and Politics Workshop (and Conference), and faculty workshops at the University of Texas at Dallas, Penn State Law, and the University at Buffalo and its Baldy Center. Terrified (but resigned to the fact) that we are certainly missing someone, we are particularly thankful for the comments we received from Sara Benesh, Matt Hitt, Josh Boston, Ben Engst, Øyvind Stiansen, Campbell MacGillivray, Lydia Tiede, Katarina Šipulová, Joep Boonekamp-van Lit, Yulia Khalikova, Igor Logvinenko, Rachael Hinkle, Abby Matthews, Dara Purvis, Jud Mathews, Adam Nye, and Ben Johnson. The book also benefited tremendously from conversations with Jim Gibson, Morgan Hazelton, Christy Boyd, Keith Schnakenberg, Dan Tavana, Chris Zorn, Chris Witko, Sivaram Cheruvu, Mason Moseley, Erik Herron, Trey Thomas, Matt Gabel, Chris Reenock, Aylin Aydin-Cakir, Quintin Beazer, and Martín Gandur.

We have been so lucky to work on this project with a cadre of exceptional research assistants, many of whom became the coauthors of various papers that spun out of this project. Sangyeon Kim painstakingly assembled data on COVID case counts and deaths at the subnational level for all of the countries we surveyed (and then, at prospectus reviewers' request, cut from the book), wrangled the Germany panel data, and assisted on a paper about the role of partisanship in democratic norms violations (Driscoll et al. 2024). Taran Samarth was a true rock star helping us proofread questionnaires, analyze data, and begin to put the pieces of the book together. They singlehandedly resurrected an experiment we had left for dead, resulting in Driscoll et al. (2023). Taylor Kinsley Chewning and Bailey (Johnson) Boldt compiled and pretested the materials for our COVID-19 teaching modules just in time for the semester's start in the fall of 2020, which allowed innumerable (un)lucky undergraduates an opportunity to engage with some of our early data from the Germany panel survey (Chewning et al. 2020). Martín Gandur and Taylor Chewning were early in their graduate careers when they provided meticulous proofreading of survey instruments and early drafts of manuscripts; by the time this book had come to fruition, they were full coauthors on not one but two standalone journal manuscripts from this project (Gandur, Chewning & Driscoll 2025; Chewning et al. 2025). Teresa Ousey, Maddie Hindman, Nicholas Riebel, Mike Burnham, Morrgan Herlihy, Danielle Beavers, Josefina Carcamo Vergara, Bailey Johnson Boldt, Kwabena Fynn Fletcher, Vivienne Butera, Chandler Campbell, Colin Fuller, Andrea Gann, Miranda Garcia, Andje Louis, and Gabriella Porter provided stellar research assistance throughout the process, and were critical in documenting a myriad of aspects of rule-of-law violations in the COVID-19 pandemic era. We owe Harley Roe a special debt of gratitude for his assistance in taking the penultimate versions of this book manuscript well across the finish line.

An array of generous funding made our research possible. The project began as a National Science Foundation RAPID project (Grant Nos. SES-2027653, SES-2027671, and SES-2027664). Of course, any opinions, findings, and conclusions or recommendations expressed in this material are those of the author(s) and do not necessarily reflect the views of the National Science Foundation. Erik Herron (West Virginia University [WVU]) was a gracious and generous early reader of the RAPID grant proposal, helping us center the core of the proposal's argument. Lea Herron and the staff in the Eberly College Research Office at WVU, Laura Katari Kitchens at FSU, and Carol Mellott and Rocco Zinoble at Penn State were all instrumental in helping get the proposal put together and submitted just as the pandemic began so drastically changing every facet of everyday life; it is no small task to coordinate three university bureaucracies to move in the same direction, much less during a time when everyone everywhere was being directed to work from home. Reggie Sheehan at the National Science Foundation was exceptionally helpful as we navigated the RAPID process and throughout the lifespan of the grant. We are indebted to the Institute for Humane Studies for two separate grants, grant no. IHS008667 and IHS017151, which provided funding for our US pilot studies that was critical for item selection of our rule-of-law battery, while grant no. IHS017151 funded our book conference that we hosted at FSU in the fall of 2023.

WEST VIRGINIA HUMANITIES COUNCIL

As Krehbiel's work on this book mostly came while he was at WVU, he has a long list of Mountaineers to thank for their support. The project benefited from funding from the Jim and Gail Woolwine Political Science Faculty Travel Fund at WVU – our surveys in Poland and Hungary, in particular, would not have been possible without the Woolwine's generous support amid the pandemic. In addition, the Department of Political Science at WVU and funding from WVU's Research and Scholarship Advancement (RSA) Grant program provided generous support. A particular thanks goes to John Kilwein, who as chair was always supportive of the project even as he deftly navigated the department through a series of challenges. Additionally, this project is presented with financial assistance from the West Virginia Humanities Council, a state affiliate of the National Endowment for the Humanities. Any views, findings, conclusions, or recommendations do not necessarily represent those of the West Virginia Humanities Council or the National Endowment for the Humanities. In addition, Krehbiel wants to extend his appreciation for his new colleagues in Buffalo, who have given him a warm welcome to the department and the city. Listing all the people who contributed with their encouragement, thoughts, and advice would push us far beyond our page limit, but Krehbiel would like to give heartfelt thanks to his family, especially Rebecca who helped him persevere through the peaks and valleys of the research process. That he was able to somehow make it through writing a book while navigating both the pandemic and their entry into the world of parenthood is a testament to just how amazing a partner she is.

Driscoll acknowledges the broad and varied sorts of support she received that enabled her to write this book. Financial support was provided by both the Institute of Politics (IOP) at Florida State University (FSU) as well as the Council for Research and Creativity (CRC) Grant Program: the CRC grant supported the extension of the Germany panel survey from four to six waves, while the support from the IOP allowed for several surveys to be fielded in the United States. Driscoll benefited immensely from the resources made available to her from the Department of Political Science and the College of Social Sciences and Public Policy at Florida State University, more broadly, and from the advocacy and mentorship of Brad Gomez and Tim Chapin, in particular. The Political Science department at FSU hosted a terrific book conference that empowered us to take a pretty good book manuscript and make it immeasurably better. Beyond FSU, she is grateful to her local and extended network of friends and family whose friendship and support are as steadfast as they are manifest. Her husband and daughter are endless fonts of diversion, engagement, inspiration, and joy. Special gratitude is reserved for Driscoll's parents, Mary and Wally, who not only taught reading and cupcake arithmetic to a COVID-19 home-schooled kindergartener but picked all of us up when we took an occasional (but inevitable) spill. This would not have been possible without them.

At Penn State, the project could not have happened without the support of Michael Berkman and the McCourtney Institute for Democracy, Lee Ann Banaszak and the Department of Political Science, and Scott Bennett and Clarence Lang in the College of the Liberal Arts. We appreciate the staff of the Political Science department, especially Kristy Boob and Michelle Ilgen who were incredibly helpful with an untold number of administrative details and their general good humor and telling Nelson to stop talking to them and get back to writing. Nelson owes debts of gratitude to Matt, Ellen, and James Schill (in whose basement he was living, sheltering from the pandemic, when we wrote the NSF grant and started the book in the spring of 2020), Naomi Barasch and Jeremy DeFoe (whose taste for takeout and video games made the first year of the pandemic much less lonely), Johnny Gallagher (who endured him answering emails about this project from Wi-Fi hotspots in Pittsburgh, Luxor, Munich, La Paz, and everywhere in between), his parents, and too many friends to risk forgetting to list someone. He is lucky to have such a great support system.

1

The Promise of Judicial Review

From the ashes of the Nazi regime in Germany rose a new constitutional order designed to prevent the horrors of fascism from returning to German politics. Having experienced the consequences of a political system that lacked effective constraints on state power, the legal scholars and political leaders tasked with writing Germany's new constitution – what would become known as the "Basic Law" (*Grundgesetz*) – set about constructing a new constellation of political institutions that would act to limit any future attempts at pushing state power beyond constitutional boundaries (Brecht 1949; Collings 2015; Friedrich 1949). As an expression of this foundational goal, the first article of the Basic Law set out three core tenets of the new German democracy: human dignity, human rights, and the obligation of the political system to respect the rights enshrined in the Basic Law.[1] And throughout, one theme in particular permeated as a priority: the rule of law (Grote 2014).

Yet ensuring that state respect for these rights and the rule of law posed the true challenge. After all, the Weimar Constitution had similarly provided for individual rights (Maier 2019), yet it had failed to prevent the Nazis' ascent to power. Learning from the lessons of the Weimar Constitution's shortcomings while building on past German experience with judicial review (Kommers and Miller 2012), the designers of Germany's new constitution turned a newly established constitutional court to serve as the "Hüter des Grundgesetzes": the guardian of the Basic Law. This new Federal Constitutional Court (*Bundesverfassungsgericht*), empowered to nullify government actions, was thus born to "ensure respect for and give effect to Germany's free democratic basic order" and "to limit state power" (German Constitutional Court 2024).

The Court has since flourished in this role. Scholars and practitioners alike frequently refer to it as one of the most consequential institutions in German politics

[1] Specifically, Article 1 states: (1) Human dignity shall be inviolable. To respect and protect it shall be the duty of all state authority; (2) The German people therefore acknowledge inviolable and inalienable human rights as the basis of every community, of peace and of justice in the world; (3) The following basic rights shall bind the legislature, the executive and the judiciary as directly applicable law.

and influential constitutional courts in the world (Kommers 1994; Vanberg 2005). Indeed, so immediately clear was the court's capacity to constrain executive power that Germany's first post-war Chancellor, Konrad Adenauer, went so far as to describe the court as "the dictator of Germany" (Vanberg 2000).[2] Similarly, when the Court celebrated its fiftieth anniversary on September 28, 2001, the keynote speaker, Gerhard Casper, declared that "If cities are to define German republics, then please allow me – at least for today and on this occasion – to choose the city of Karlsruhe, where the Federal Constitutional Court is located" (Casper 2001). And if imitation is a reflection of success, the replication of the German court's design and structure in new democracies from post-Soviet Europe to East Asia reflects the court's consistent position as an effective bulwark against those who would challenge the constitutional bounds of state power.

Such continued success does not arise by virtue of the mere existence of judicial review. Rather, the capacity of a court such as the *Bundesverfassungsgericht* to effectively impose constraints requires, as Vanberg (2005, 121) quotes a German member of parliament describing it, the ability to give elected officials "a bloody nose" if necessary. This need to translate judicial review's promise into reality raises important questions. How is it that a court can effectively harness the power of judicial review to compel executives to remain with in the constitutional limits of their authority? What allows judicial review to be transformed from a legal proceeding into a politically relevant exercise of judicial authority? Under what conditions is this efficacy likely to flourish – or to wilt? And how can courts fulfill such a role as "defenders of the constitution" in the face of powerful political forces like partisanship? Answering these questions is the central goal of this book.

THE RISE OF CONSTITUTIONAL COURTS AND JUDICIAL REVIEW

Judicial review was once considered an anomaly of the North American experience, but it has since expanded remarkably such that it is now considered a hallmark of modern liberal democracy.[3] Germany was not alone in its transformation to a

[2] In a similar turn of phrase, a German newspaper in 2012 described the Court's president as Germany's "true head of state" (Collings 2015).

[3] We use the term judicial review with a focus on the evaluation of an executive or legislative action for its conformity with constitutional norms and standards. While we acknowledge that judicial review can be more expansive than this – for example the assessment of whether administrative actions are consistent with legislation – our focus here on state constraint leads us to emphasize its application as the enforcement of constitutional limits on state authority. In this sense, our focus on this specific form of judicial review makes it conceptually identical to the term constitutional review. Likewise, our use of the word "courts" throughout the book refers to those judicial institutions – supreme courts, constitutional tribunals, etc. – that are endowed with this authority to evaluate the conformity of state actions with constitutional norms and obligations. As such, we use terms like "constitutional courts" and "apex courts" interchangeably. For an excellent overview of different types of constitutional review, see Ginsburg and Versteeg (2024).

constitutional system guarded by judicial review. As the world emerged from World War II, the importance of state constraint was a topic of great concern. Across Europe, parliamentary supremacy had been the dominant form of government; the war demonstrated its deficiencies in a terrifying way (Gardbaum 2014; Lutig and Weiler 2018). As a result, states across Europe adjusted their systems of government in the years after the war. Whereas granting courts – or a single court – the constitutional authority to nullify the actions of duly elected officials had been anathema to many legal thinkers, such judicial power quickly became a staple of a renewed form of liberal democracy. Just as the Germans had integrated a constitutional court into their new post-war political system, so too did the Italians (Volcansek 1994) and, a few decades later, the French (Stone 1992) in the form of the *Conseil Constitutionnel*. Likewise, democratizing countries from South Korea (Ginsburg 2003), to Poland (Schwartz 2000), to Spain (Garoupa, Gomez-Pomar, and Grembi 2013) made the adoption of judicial review a central component of their refounded democratic systems. These and many other countries empowered judiciaries as a failsafe against executive or legislative aggrandizement (Cappelletti 1971). As Ginsburg (2008) explains, "constitutional review was seen as an important bulwark against arbitrary governments, and courts were able to draw on this legitimacy in constraining the state" (87).

Of course, judicial review was not a new constitutional invention in the 1940s nor did it "spring new and fully developed from the head of John Marshall" (Cappelletti 1971, 25; see also Rakove 1997). Made famous by John Marshall's opinion for the US Supreme Court in *Marbury v. Madison*, judicial review was viewed as a natural consequence of Judeo-Christian notions of higher and lower spheres of legal authority: if lower laws come into conflict with some higher sphere of authority, the lower must yield to the higher (Cappelletti 1971; Ginsburg 2008). In the century after *Marbury*, judicial review remained (in Tocqueville's words) "peculiar to the American magistrate": few constitutions around the globe explicitly provided courts with the power of judicial review (de Tocqueville 1835). But, this changed rapidly in the first half of the twentieth century (Ginsburg 2008). The top panel of Figure 1.1 uses data from the Comparative Constitutions Project to plot the percentage of constitutions establishing judicial review, by year. While less than 20 percent of constitutions provided for judicial review in 1900, around 80 percent of constitutions did so by the century's end. Today, judicial review has "become a hallmark of the rule of law" such that "[a] democracy without some form of judicial review is considered deficient" (Lutig and Weiler 2018, 316).

A variety of theoretical explanations have emerged to explain the rise and proliferation of judicial review, yet central to them all is the sense that judicial review serves as a powerful mechanism of state constraint. In addition to the *catastrophic* account we describe in the opening pages of this book, *federalist* accounts emphasize the importance of state constraints across levels and branches of government; judicial

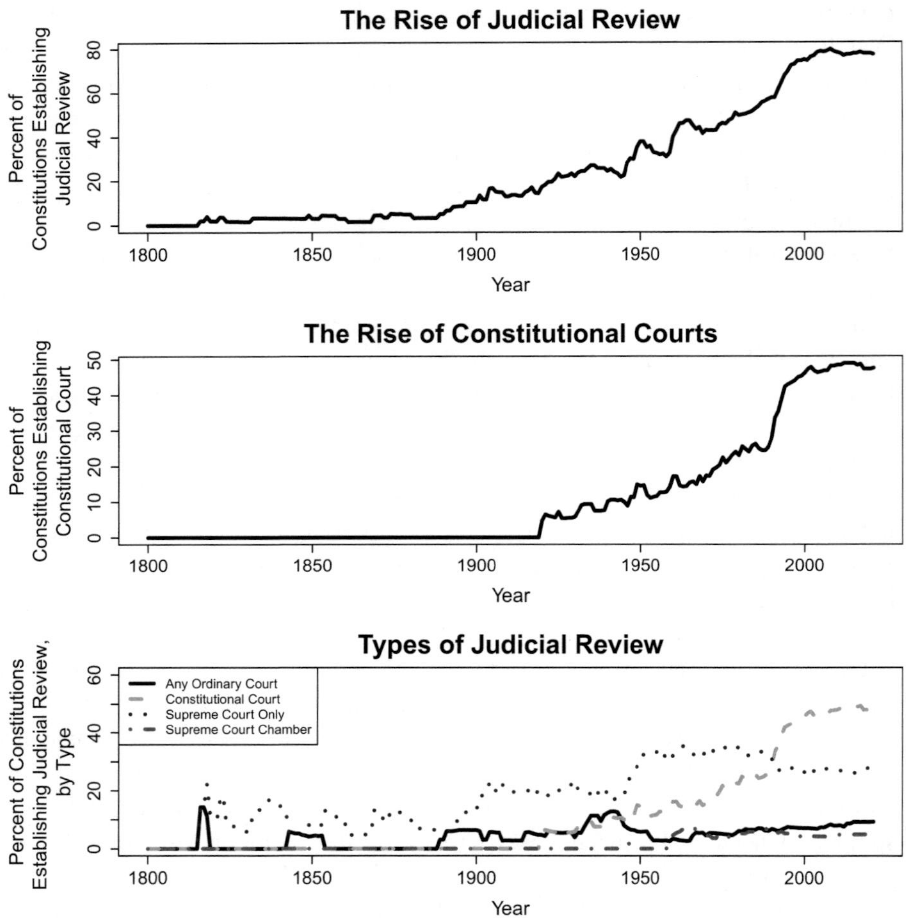

FIGURE 1.1 The rise of judicial review and constitutional courts. The top panel plots the percent of constitutions in each year that formally establish judicial review. The middle panel plots the percentage of constitutions that establish a constitutional court. The bottom panel plots the percentage of constitutions that establish each type of constitutional review. The data, which range from 1800 to 2021, come from Elkins and Ginsburg (2022).

review helps to ensure that elites respect complex governmental structures and their constitutionally authorized spheres of authority (e.g., Ackerman 1997; Shapiro 1999). *Ideational* accounts prioritize the usefulness of judicial review for the protection of individual rights, suggesting that judicial review might safeguard against human rights violations and threats to citizens' constitutionally guaranteed rights and liberties (e.g., Cappelletti 1971). In the past few decades, a set of *strategic* explanations has suggested that judicial review is useful not only for citizens but also elites: as those drafting constitutions think ahead, they see judicial review by independent courts as useful insurance in the face of electoral uncertainty to ensure that the constitution's core values are respected (Ginsburg 2003; Hirschl 2004; Stephenson 2003). While no single one of these accounts can fully explain the global rise of judicial review (Ginsburg 2008), that it has increased in frequency and expanded in scope is incontrovertible.[4]

The second and third panels of Figure 1.1 use data from the Comparative Constitutions Project to illustrate the sharp rise in the percentage of constitutions that establish a specialized constitutional court (middle panel) and the distribution of types of constitutionally endorsed judicial review worldwide. While constitutional courts became increasingly popular throughout the twentieth century, their popularity skyrocketed following the fall of the Berlin Wall in 1989.[5] Today, about half of constitutions worldwide provide for a specialized constitutional court, and judicial review by a centralized constitutional court is much more popular than the decentralized model of judicial review.

How is judicial review exercised in practice? Judicial review can vary on a number of dimensions that define its various modalities.[6] First, scholars distinguish the power of judicial review in the extent to which it is centralized in a single court or constitutional chamber. The "Centralized," "European," or "Kelsenian" (after its founder) versions of constitutional review vest the power of judicial review in a specialized constitutional court that is structurally removed from the rest of the judiciary (Harding, Leyland, and Groppi 2008; Horowitz 2006). Jurisdictional rules for these courts vary, but generally questions concerning the constitutionality of legislation are referred – by ordinary court judges or litigants – to a specialized constitutional court that is situated apart from the formal judicial hierarchy and is empowered to make a final ruling on the constitutionality of legislation, executive actions, or governmental proposals. This form of judicial review was first used in Austria and has been adopted in countries like Germany, Italy, and Spain; variants abound throughout the democratizing world. The alternative modality, often called a "decentralized" or "American" model, distributes the power of judicial review diffusely throughout the judicial hierarchy. Any judge confronted with a statute or action that violates the constitution is empowered to use judicial review to strike the statute as unconstitutional. This decentralized form of judicial review is found throughout the separation of powers systems of Latin America, as well as many British colonies in the Western Hemisphere, Africa, and Southeast Asia.

4 For fuller reviews of these theories, see Ginsburg (2008). For empirical tests – which provide particular support for strategic accounts – see Ginsburg and Versteeg (2014).

5 For more on the adoption of constitutional courts worldwide, see Romeu (2006) and Kim and Nolette (2024).

6 For an excellent primer on the differences and empirical distribution of these different modalities of constitutional review, see Mavčič (2018).

In addition to variation in *who* can conduct judicial review, countries also vary according to *when* laws can be reviewed.[7] On the one hand, courts like the US Supreme Court exclusively exercise "concrete" judicial review, only deciding actual cases or controversies that come about after a law has been enacted and when the legal or constitutional controversy has been challenged in a specific instance or case. In other systems, constitutional courts are empowered to exercise "abstract" judicial review, which allows courts to decide on the constitutionality of laws or administrative actions without the need for a concrete case or harm to litigants. Notably, this form of judicial review has the potential, in some systems, to take place prior to promulgation or enactment of a challenged statute or regulation, allowing the court to serve as an ancillary legislative chamber as opposed to an adjudicatory body. Data from the Comparative Constitutions Project documents that, as of 2021, a majority of constitutions do not specify at what stage of the legislative process legislation is reviewed for its constitutionality. But, of those constitutions that specify, 24 percent allow for review pre-promulgation (*ex ante* review), 35 percent allow for *ex post* review, and 42 percent allow for constitutional review at either stage (Elkins and Ginsburg 2022).

Judicial review also varies in the scope of a constitutional or judicial ruling, a feature which often covaries with the timing and centralization of judicial review. The (often abstract review) decisions rendered by centralized constitutional authorities often carry with them *erga omnes* effects, meaning the decisions are binding to any and all parties involved in a constitutional controversy, whether they are parties to a particular case or not, and direct harm need not be empirically substantiated. Where judicial review is exercised with reference to concrete cases, judicial decisions are said to be binding *inter partes*, such that they are only for the plaintiffs litigating in a particular case. The exception to this general rule is when the norm of *stare decisis* applies, which implies that future judicial decision-making is bound to adhere to the legal standards set out in a particular case or settlement. Such is the case with Supreme Court decision-making in the United States, where the pinnacle court's adjudications are viewed as binding and informative for all future judicial decisions throughout the judicial hierarchy.

Scholars have observed that this dramatic expansion of judicial review and constitutional authority has coincided with the rise of rights-related litigation and the increased involvement of judicial authorities in all manner of policymaking arenas (Bricker 2016; Hirschl 2008; Vallinder and Tate 1995). Not only has the formal authority and autonomy of high courts expanded (Brinks and Blass 2018; Hirschl 2024), so too has the constitutionalization of the rights of citizens, creating both the opportunity and the venue for expanded claims of constitutionality (Botero 2023; Epp 1998; Hirschl 2004). Courts and the judicial authorities that operate within

7 We discuss these differences in more detail and summarize the empirical literature on abstract judicial review more fully in Chapter 8.

them have been featured prominently in many of these accounts, sometimes playing the protagonists to rights-claimants, while in other instances revealing pronounced reluctance to involve themselves in such questions or controversies (Botero, Brinks, and Gonzalez-Ocantos 2022; Bricker 2016).

In short, the presence and exercise of judicial review has proliferated over the course of the past century, in all parts of the globe. States worldwide have put their faith in independent courts as tools to police the boundaries of state authority, ensuring that executives and legislatures do not overstep their constitutionally authorized powers. But, has this worked? Theorizing and identifying the conditions under which the use of judicial review by constitutional courts might be an effective tool of state constraint is the aim to which we now turn.

UNDERSTANDING JUDICIAL EFFICACY

Answering our research question – when are courts effective tools of state constraint? – requires us to clarify what we mean by *judicial efficacy*. At first glance, the idea that constitutional courts might constrain the state seems obvious. After all, that governments must adhere to the rules that structure the political process is a commonsense foundation of the rule of law. Constitutions and legal statutes represent a stated commitment to designated powers and formalized procedures. They delineate the process by which preferences become policy, the prerequisites for ambitious citizens to enter the class of political elites, and the process by which disputes are adjudicated when the interests of actors with legitimate claims come into conflict. Irrespective of one's power or prestige, that both governments and common citizens are equally bound by the law is a premise which has long stood at the foundation of democratic systems of governance. Judicial review, then, is a tool that constitutions can use to ensure the rule of law is respected.

Moreover, scholars frequently highlight the global expansion of judicial power, noting that many governments today represent juristocracy or "rule by judges" (e.g., Hirschl 2004, 2008). In many cases, it is now unelected judges rather than elected representatives that have the final say on many of the pressing political and policy issues affecting citizens and governments around the globe. These accounts suggest that courts – particularly those formally empowered to exercise judicial review – have become so politically formidable that they have the potential to be *the most* influential branch of government.

In practice, achieving this ideal is easier said than done. Compliance and enforcement of the rule of law are challenges that every political regime must face. For reasons ranging from resource constraints to ideological judgments, not all legal violations face commensurate legal consequences. These challenges only increase in scope and difficulty when the person or entity pushing the boundaries of the law is vested with political power. The practicalities of trying or punishing elected officials for illegal actions – the traditional consequences for breaking the law – are complex, especially if those officials are to be investigated or tried while they are in office. In many places, elected officials are protected from prosecution for the duration of time they serve in office, incentivizing efforts to sustain their control on power. If those in power feel that they are able to defy the law with impunity, abuse of power may run rampant, and state constraint may prove impossible. James Madison, in Federalist Paper No. 51, summarized this challenge well: "In framing a government which is to be administered by men over men, the great difficulty lies in this: you must first enable the government to control the governed; *and in the next place oblige it to control itself*" (emphasis added).

There are good reasons to be skeptical that constitutional courts will necessarily be an automatic agent of state constraint. While courts worldwide have been imbued with the power of judicial review, they are – paradoxically but indisputably – incredibly *weak*. Unlike executives who command armies or legislators who can oversee and discipline the bureaucrats who implement the laws they pass, courts must depend on others to implement their policies. As Alexander Hamilton famously wrote in Federalist #78 (Hamilton, Madison, and Jay 1787/1788):

> Whoever attentively considers the different departments of power must perceive, that, in a government in which they are separated from each other, the judiciary, from the nature of its functions, will always be the least dangerous to the political rights of the Constitution; because it will be least in a capacity to annoy or injure them. The Executive not only dispenses the honors, but holds the sword of the community. The legislature not only commands the purse, but prescribes the rules by which the duties and rights of every citizen are to be regulated. The judiciary, on the contrary, has no influence over either the sword or the purse; no direction either of the strength or of the wealth of the society; and can take no active resolution whatever. It may truly be said to have neither FORCE nor WILL, but merely judgment; and must ultimately depend upon the aid of the executive arm even for the efficacy of its judgments.

This lack of implementation authority and the accompanying threat of noncompliance presents a fundamental challenge for judicial efficacy: if courts speak but no one listens, they are ineffective.

Given the challenges to compliance and implementation, purely legal solutions to legal violations – in other words, the mere establishment of judicial review – are insufficient to ensure a stable system of the rule of law. However, other potential consequences exist. For centuries, societies have supplemented legal consequences for illegal actions with political consequences:

> The threat of excommunication (which had political implications) was the means by which popes enforced divine law against kings; the threat of revolt was the mode of enforcement for Germanic customary law; against some monarchs it was the looming threat of being deposed or beheaded. Allegations about violations of the law were a rhetorical resource that helped rally support for those who opposed

> regal actions. In such cases, then, the sanction that served to enforce the law against the sovereign – the source of the law – was not a legal sanction, but a political one (Tamanaha 2004, 117).

Where elected officials know they are likely to face robust political consequences for illegal action, they may exercise self-constraint not because they fear legal repercussions, but rather because they know illegal actions will undermine their own political self-interest. Conversely, if incumbents are sufficiently confident they will face no real political consequences for crossing the line of constitutional or statutory law, they might have few incentives to adhere to the written rule of law. Perhaps because they have co-opted courts, stacked the deck of institutional players, or believe the public will overlook the transgression, incumbents in such a position may see no reason to refrain from using their office to advance their own political interests.

Our argument in this book is that judicial review can provide both legal *and political* penalties for incumbents who violate the rule of law, thereby helping to constrain the state. Courts with the power of judicial review are, almost by definition, able to levy legal penalties on incumbents who violate the rule of law. But critically, not all courts have the ability to create *political* damages for incumbents.

This latter idea forms our definition of judicial efficacy: *courts are effective when they are able to create political penalties for elites who fail to abide by the constitutional limits on their authority.*[8] When courts strike down a law through the power of judicial review, they are merely putting their thoughts about the congruence between a policy and a constitution down on paper. Judicial decisions are neither self-enforcing nor self-implementing. For judicial review to be effective, judicial decisions must have meaningful, impactful consequences. It is this political force – in addition to the legal force – of decisions that defines judicial efficacy. Effective courts are able to inflict *both* legal and political penalties on incumbents. When those consequences are diffuse or nonexistent, a court lacks efficacy.

Before moving forward, it is helpful to compare our definition of judicial efficacy with those others have suggested. This term has been widely used, albeit with varying definitions. Stone Sweet (2012) provides a procedural conceptualization of efficacy:

> Constitutional review can be said to be effective to the extent that the important constitutional disputes arising in the policy are brought to the [constitutional court] on a regular basis, that the judges who resolve these disputes give reasons

[8] Our focus in this book is theorizing the context whereby judicial review enables state constraint, focusing on the constraint of elites who are positioned to otherwise abuse state power. We acknowledge there are other ways in which courts' influences might be felt. For instance, in an ideal world, courts' decisions are binding also on litigants, on corporations, and the mass public. Achieving those other forms of influence, however, still require the state's cooperation (whether passive or active), which may not be forthcoming without an incentive to do so.

> for their rulings, and those who are governed by the constitutional law accept that the court's ruling have some precedential effect... Where review systems are relatively effective, constitutional judges manage the evolution of the polity through their decisions (825).[9]

Harding, Leyland, and Groppi (2008) provide a more normative conceptualization: "whether the court's interventions are consistent with the norms set out in the constitution and whether these norms are consistent with principles of 'good governance'" (18).[10] And, on a more empirical front, Magalhães and Garoupa (2020) equate efficacy with efficiency, using a measure of case processing time.

None of these definitions serve our purpose well. Stone Sweet's definition centers litigants in their decisions to bring disputes to courts and accept judicial rulings. While we agree that acceptance of rulings is an important outcome, we argue that efficacy is more about responses to decisions than a willingness to use the legal system in the first place.[11] Likewise, our primary interest is in the ability of judicial review to promote state constraint, so Harding, Leyland, and Groppi's normative definition is not particularly appropriate for our purposes. Moreover, their definition focuses more on the propriety of a judicial opinion than any effects it might have on litigants or implementing populations. And, while we appreciate Magalhães and Garoupa's (2020) more empirical approach, we take a broader view of efficacy: it matters not just how quickly courts decide cases but whether those decisions "matter."

Other conceptualizations of efficacy relate the concept directly to judicial independence. Fariss and Dancy (2017) suggest efficacy is synonymous with de facto judicial independence, although Ríos-Figueroa (2007) disagrees:

> Formal guarantees of judicial review and independence, however, are not enough to make the judiciary an effective power. In many countries, judges do not exercise their legal capacities, or they simply defer to those in power when making decisions. Hence, for those constitutional provisions to become more than "pieces of paper," the gap between institutional design and the institution's effectiveness must be filled (31).

Judicial independence and efficacy may be related, but they are not synonymous. As Ríos-Figueroa (2007) writes, judicial independence may enhance judicial efficacy (a hypothesis we test repeatedly throughout this book), but judicial independence does not necessarily imply the presence of an efficacious court. Independence is, in a broad sense, the freedom of judges to decide cases as they see fit. Efficacy – as

9 Stone Sweet (2012) writes that per this definition (at the time he was writing), Germany, Hungary, and Poland are all examples of effective courts.

10 The authors also articulate a second criteria closer to our conceptualization: "whether the court's pronouncements are then actually embedded in practice, that is, whether they are followed."

11 Of course, courts whose decisions have no teeth are impotent dispute resolvers. As such, a hesitance by litigants to turn to a judicial system would be an empirical implication of a court with extraordinarily low efficacy.

we explain in further detail below – relates to the *consequences* of those decisions: are there penalties for ignoring courts?[12]

Still more conceptualizations directly link efficacy and implementation (e.g., Clark 2010, 67). Epstein and Knight (2018) write that "efficacious decisions" are "those that relevant external actors will respect and with which they will comply" (272) and Vanberg (2020) argues that "Courts are influential if executive branch officials cannot easily evade decisions or refuse to comply with them" (570). Ríos-Figueroa (2007) defines an effective judiciary "as one that is able to rule against the interests of power holders without being systematically overruled, challenged with noncompliance, or punished with more aggressive policies, such as court packing, impeachment of judges, or budgetary cuts" (31–2).

Our conceptualization of efficacy is closer to these definitions. At its core, efficacy is about the consequences that judicial decisions bring to bear outside of the courtroom, and nonimplementation of a judicial decision is an important indicator that a court may be lacking in efficacy. But, for our purposes, while nonimplementation is one possible way that a court might lack influence, it is not necessarily a sign that a court lacks efficacy. Courts may strategically enable noncompliance (e.g., Staton, Reenock, and Holsinger 2022; Staton and Vanberg 2008). Moreover, as executives respond to judicial decisions with an expectation regarding the presence and magnitude of a penalty for disregarding a court, there is a potential for miscalculations resulting in nonimplementation that is subsequently met with an unanticipated public outcry and corresponding political penalty (Vanberg 2000). Conversely, that executives abide by a court's decision does not necessarily imply judicial efficacy because governments might comply for strategic reasons that are unrelated to the threat of a noncompliance penalty (Whittington 2005). As a result, observing judicial efficacy is not as straightforward as observing (non)implementation, and treating the two as synonymous risks misidentifying judicial (in)efficacy. For this reason, our conception of efficacy is broader than a single-minded focus on nonimplementation and instead takes a broad view of the political penalties associated with challenging an efficacious court.

It is important to note here that our conceptualization of efficacy is fundamentally *negative*: courts with efficacy are those who can successfully impose political penalties on incumbents. But there is another, more expansive, conceptualization of efficacy that would envision a court's ability to fully legitimize executive actions (e.g., Johnson and Whittington 2018). Dating back at least to Dahl's (1957) suggestion that "[t]he main task of the Court is to confer legitimacy on the fundamental policies of the successful coalition," dozens of studies have sought to understand the conditions under which citizens might change their views of policies in response to a judicial decision (294). By this account, a judicial decision in favor of a policy might inspire confidence in the government's action and thereby foster acceptance from an otherwise suspicious or unsupportive public. In this way, "effective" courts

[12] We discuss conceptualizations of judicial independence in more detail in Chapter 2.

might be able to *lessen* the political penalties of rule of law violations by ruling in an incumbent's favor, thus rallying public support for an incumbent's policy.

This suggestion that courts might be able to shape public opinion has important implications. In particular, it makes the prospect of court capture even more tantalizing. Not only does such capture lower the risk of unfavorable decisions and thus create increased opportunities to entrench preferred policies, but it might also provide incumbents with a tool to shape public opinion toward their preferred policies. If courts bring with their decisions enhanced public acquiescence or acceptance on controversial policies, then deck stacking or court co-optation is not just a matter of skirting accountability. Institutional capture could actually bolster regime support.

We are profoundly skeptical that courts, including even the most independent ones, have this power. As we elaborate in Chapter 2 and go on to demonstrate throughout this book, we see limited theoretical reasoning and no empirical evidence to support Dahl's suggestion that courts might legitimate governmental policy. Instead our findings show that following a court's explicit endorsement of a policy (which we term "clearance"), citizens accept the policy just as they would have had the court not acted at all. This asymmetry – that courts' decisions against the government can elicit a response from citizens while declaring a policy constitutional does not – reflects the centrality of state constraint as a fundamental function of courts and judicial review.

POLITICAL PENALTIES FOR RULE OF LAW VIOLATIONS

We have suggested that courts are effective when they can impose political penalties for rule of law violations. What sorts of political penalties exist? In modern democracies, executives may face an array of political penalties for their violation of the law. Transgressing the written rule of the law may be costly in terms of elite bargaining, as a demonstrated willingness to abandon the "rules of the game" may undermine trust that bargaining is occurring in good faith. Alternatively, it may be that the citizens themselves can impose penalties on the government by withdrawing their electoral or political support. The credible threat of this punishment, in theory, will incentivize "good" behavior. These two types of political ramifications correspond to two different explanations for the emergence and perpetuation of the rule of law, which we address in turn.

Elite-Driven Penalties

In an elite-based account of the rule of law, political consequences may be borne with the loss of good faith among competing or bargaining elites.[13]

[13] Competition need not be present for political penalties to be felt; political penalties may also manifest as a loss of support from one's own coalition partners. Insofar as bargaining partners

A longstanding theoretical explanation of judicial independence describes the utility of judicial review as a useful tool to mitigate the risks inherent in political competition, where sufficiently friendly courts might serve as an "insurance" policy for when an incumbent faces the inevitable loss of electoral access to office (Ginsburg 2003; Ramseyer 1994). Subsequent theoretical work clarifies the institutional and informational conditions where the government's (and the opposition's) adherence to the rule of law comes about from an intraelite agreement about the "rules of the game," in exchange for a peaceable alternation and transfer of power (e.g., Chávez, Ferejohn, and Weingast 2011; Epperly 2019; Finkel 2008; Stephenson 2003; Yadav and Mukherjee 2014). Provided that elites are sufficiently risk-averse and forward-looking, and the environment is sufficiently competitive, elite adherence to constitutional principles can emerge as an equilibrium solution to an iterated prisoner's dilemma. In this transitory solution space, all parties voluntarily accept constraints when in power and commit to political temperance more generally with the expectation that this same constraint and temperance will be observed by their opponents when they lose access to office.[14]

Subsequent elite-centric models incorporate the role of judicial review in facilitating elite bargaining and compromise by theorizing review as a means of information transmission between opposed, and sometimes mistrustful, political elites (Carrubba 2005; Staton, Reenock, and Holsinger 2022). By these accounts, institutional oversight works to monitor the bargain and to serve as an informational clearinghouse that allows opposing parties to credibly signal why their defections from a pre-agreed upon commitment may be palatable to all parties involved (Carrubba 2005; Reenock, Staton, and Radean 2013). In Staton, Reenock, and Holsinger's (2022) most recent contribution to this class of models, independent judicial review gives opposing elites the opportunity to credibly convey their rationale for taking the sort of extra-constitutional steps that we explore here, and to prove their resolve by ignoring a court that rules that action unconstitutional. Although these sort of governmental transgressions can pose a threat to an entire political regime, Staton, Reenock, and Holsinger's (2022) work makes clear the conditions under which the mere act of judicial review can allow competing elites to convey information, turn down the temperature of political conflict, and to steer competing

are also motivated by electoral or other considerations that connect them to the public's opinion, precipitous loss of public support can cause them to abandon political leaders for the sake of their own electoral prospects (Fiedler 2022). The fall of multiple governments over the Brexit controversy is but one example.

14 Staton, Reenock, and Holsinger (2022) characterize this forbearance in terms of generalized "prudence," where the government abstains from abusing office to stymie the political opposition, and the opposition moderates its policing of objectionable policies in the interest of long-term stability and perpetuation of democratic competition (26).

parties away from the precipice that devolves into autocratization or democratic breakdown.[15]

Citizen-Driven Penalties

A second sort of political repercussion is the one that citizens themselves impose and is at the center of public-centric explanations for the rule of law. By these accounts, the credible threat of a loss of public support incentivizes governmental elites' adherence to the rules, such that executives might exercise self-restraint and a stable rule of law regime will prevail (e.g., Christenson and Kriner 2020a; Weingast 1997). The public may impose a variety of penalties on incumbents as they update their opinions about the executive, her policies, and the procedural implementation of her political agenda (Christenson and Kriner 2019; Braman 2016). Citizens may withhold their support for the executive or decrease their support for the policy issue at hand when an executive chooses to ignore the court. This public support matters for policymaking, as squandering the public's support in one area of governance might compromise the support required for other priorities on the political agenda. Public buy-in is consequential not only for the legitimacy of policymaking and institutions, but also for compliance (Carlin et al. 2022; Gibson 1991). Moreover, research documents a widespread public preference for "routine" governmental policymaking (Singh and Carlin 2015). As such, to the extent that the public must adhere to and respect a policy for it to have "teeth," deviations from legal norms and routine procedures of implementation can undermine the public's willingness to follow the law.

Executive transgressions may well prove costly beyond the sense they are associated with a loss of public acceptance. The democratic context typically provides multiple types of opportunities for citizens to express their displeasure. Citizens can mobilize in opposition by using their financial resources to support an alternative candidate or cause, their time to volunteer with a political campaign or to attend a civic meeting, and their civic skills to persuade other voters or organize a protest (Brady, Verba, and Schlozman 1995). The electoral connection provides the most severe form of punishment: politicians who overreach could find themselves voted out of office.[16] Where the public will collectively punish incumbents for their failure to adhere to the law, elites' political survival hinges on their respect for legal

[15] The Staton, Reenock, and Holsinger (2022) account requires that the parties must be sufficiently committed to democratic compromise, that courts be independent from both the government and the opposition, that noncompliance be costly by virtue of some sort of broader public backlash, and that judges must be sufficiently tolerant of said incumbent noncompliance (28–9).

[16] Irrespective of its form, though, such threats represent *political* penalties. These penalties that can be imposed only by a concerted effort and action of the public is of particular importance in democratic contexts.

boundaries, leading self-interested and ambitious political leaders to observe and comply with legal obligations (Weingast 1997). In sum, beyond the immediate loss of position an electoral defeat represents, the consequences of a loss of public support that can stem from the transgressions we investigate are varied and far-reaching.

Our focus in this book is on the possibility that the public might be positioned to constrain the state with the help of judicial review and sufficiently widespread commitment to the rule of law. Yet we dialog directly with many of the elite-centric bargaining models in at least two critical ways. First, our own theoretical account emphasizes the ability of institutions – and specifically judicial review – to facilitate monitoring and information transmission about the constitutional appropriateness of state action. Second, it is often the case in elite-bargaining models that the public's support – most often for the judicial institution itself, but also sometimes for the regime or for the policy in dispute – is a characteristic of the environment that enables or prohibits a particular equilibrium to obtain. Often, this parameter of public support is critical insofar as it defines a space for efficacious institutional oversight: provided public support for a court is sufficiently high, or provided that noncompliance is sufficiently costly by virtue of the penalties the public might impose, then elites' information conveyance through judicial proceedings is credible.

Despite the centrality of public support in these theoretical models and their power to help understand the conditions by which the rule of law might be self-enforcing, the opinions and attitudes of democratic citizens are rarely the focus of direct inquiry. With regard to public responses to noncompliance or nonimplementation, a burgeoning field of research has established that incumbents who fail to obey courts face consequences from their constituents (e.g., Carlin et al. 2022; Driscoll, Çakir, and Schorpp 2024; Driscoll et al. 2023; Krehbiel 2021c). While this research fills an important void, the observational research is plagued by inescapable endogeneity while the experimental work considers the public's reaction to only one sort of executive response to a high court directives.[17] Here, by contrast, we consider a more complete portfolio of possible combinations of judicial behavior and governmental response to obtain a holistic view of public responses to judicial review.

A Focus on the Public's Acceptance

The attitudinal response we consider in this book is the public's *acceptance* of a policy proposal or government action.[18] We make this decision for two major

[17] For example, the work of Driscoll et al. (2023) presents respondents with differing rationales for government noncompliance, while Carlin et al. (2022) report the results of experiments where subjects learn of noncompliance with judicial decisions but the specifics of the substantive judicial order are not specified.

[18] In Chapter 5, we discuss the technical details about our measure of acceptance. Briefly, we follow previous studies that conceptualize acceptance as a combination of attitudes regarding

reasons. First, attitudinal responses to policies are a prerequisite to all collective action. Before an individual can withdraw his vote in response to a policy he dislikes, he has to dislike the policy: an attitudinal response. Before someone chooses to attend a protest, she has to have an opinion about the cause she is protesting for or against. That opinion, again, is an attitude. For this reason, understanding attitudinal responses to potential violations lies at the heart of understanding larger processes of political accountability.

Of course, the electoral penalties the public might inflict are undoubtedly persuasive: these costs are the decisive mechanism of democratic accountability. Yet we view the public's acceptance and acquiescence as a critical precursor to electoral action. Without the initial attitudinal response, neither electoral remuneration nor retribution is possible.

Second, these larger processes of electoral accountability raise additional, more complicated concerns about voter mobilization and behavior, candidate emergence, campaigning, and vote choice that complicate any attempt to study the electoral side of state constraint. While much democratic theory suggests that citizens will use the ballot box to retaliate against executive encroachment, the practicalities of electoral punishment imply that it might be more likely in theory than in practice (e.g., Driscoll and Nelson 2023b). Compounded with omnipresent concerns about voter sophistication (Achen and Bartels 2016), there is good reason to doubt whether the public provides a realistic constraint on ambitious politicians. Even with such constraints on accountability – of which politicians are likely aware – the threat of even a hindered punishment has the capacity to influence officials' behavior. As such, because these attitudinal responses are a prerequisite to electoral behavior, we choose to emphasize the first point in this chain of actions – the attitudinal response to a rule of law violation.

PUBLIC EVALUATIONS OF EXECUTIVE ACTION

We are far from the first to suggest that the public might impose political penalties for rule of law violations. Indeed, a rich literature on state constraint has long emphasized the importance of cultural values, particularly democratic norms and values, for sustaining the rule of law and democratic governance (Almond and Verba 1963; Claassen 2020; Easton 1953; Lipset 1959; Putnam 1993). Likewise, another expansive strand of research has focused on the capacity of institutions to structure political outcomes (Huber 1996; North 1990; Tsebelis 2011), including those related to core democratic principles like accountability (Tavits 2007) and responsiveness (Powell 2004), as well as citizens' attachment to the state (Elkins and

citizens' support for an executive action, their view that the action was legitimate (or appropriate), and their willingness to comply with the government's action (e.g., Gibson, Caldeira, and Spence 2005).

Sides 2007) and ultimately the survival of constitutions and democracy itself (Elkins 2010; Elkins, Ginsburg, and Melton 2009; Linz 1990; Maeda 2010). Our approach here combines insights from both accounts to evaluate the interaction between system-level institutional features – for us, judicial independence – and individual-level attitudes, specifically support for the rule of law.

Studies of the public's response to executive unilateral action in the United States provide a useful point of comparison (e.g., Braman 2023; Christenson and Kriner 2020b; Reeves and Rogowski 2022a). Like us, scholars working in this vein are seeking to understand the conditions under which the public might serve as an efficacious check on executive action. As Christenson and Kriner (2020b, 6) explain, "the president's standing among the public is perhaps the most ubiquitous and salient measure of a president's political capital and thus ability to advance his or her agenda in Washington." As the public withdraws its support from the president, it is difficult for the president to accomplish his or her policy goals. In contrast, strong public backing translates into effective political capital for policy-minded executives (Barrett and Eshbaugh-Soha 2007; Canes-Wrone and De Marchi 2002).

From this literature, two points are particularly relevant for our purposes. The first concerns how the public evaluates unilateral executive actions. On the one hand, Reeves and Rogowski (2016) describe that the public generally disapproves of presidential unilateral action, with variation in evaluations of these executive actions inexorably linked to the public's commitment to the rule of law (see also Reeves and Rogowski 2022a). On the other hand, Christenson and Kriner (2017a) contend that concerns such as partisanship are the primary driving forces behind the public's responses to executive unilateral action (see also Christenson and Kriner 2020b). Relatedly, Braman (2021) finds that approval of the executive plays an outsized role when the public evaluates executive action while constitutional considerations – here, as judged by "experts" – have no effect on respondents' policy support (see also Braman 2016, 2023).

Yet these studies have important differences from our own. For instance, Reeves and Rogowski rely on generic questions about particular types of unilateral actions, while Christenson and Kriner, as well as Braman, deploy questions that tap reactions to pressing real-world controversies. And, although all three sets of authors acknowledge the potential for a partisanship-versus-democratic values debate, they do not test these competing considerations head-to-head. Our ability to concisely weigh these contrasting claims is further complicated by these authors' near-exclusive focus on the public's reaction to executive unilateral authority in United States (but see Reeves and Rogowski 2023). This limitation leaves us less sure about how other citizenries respond to unilateral executive actions where these sorts of actions are more commonplace, such as contexts where executives have broader constitutional mandates to wield this particular sort of power (but see Chu and Williamson 2025). Although this lack of evidence leaves us agnostic about which account presents the more persuasive set of evidence about the factors shaping the public's response to executive action, it sets the stage for these dueling considerations – support for the rule of law and partisanship – to play a prominent role in our investigation.

Second, Christenson and Kriner's studies investigate the extent to which legislatures and courts might affect the public's response to executive action. Interestingly, though, their research designs focus on extra-institutional actions rather than the formal system of checks and balances. They write: "Even when they cannot block or overturn a unilateral action, other political actors remain relevant through their special capacity to mobilize the public and bring popular pressure to bear on the White House" (Christenson and Kriner 2020b, 7). They demonstrate that both congressional criticism of an executive action and the threat of litigation both detract from the public's support for executive actions. (Christenson and Kriner 2017c, 2019). As they conclude in one study, "[p]ublic opinion – not formal checks by Congress and the courts – serves as the primary check on the unilateral executive" (Christenson and Kriner 2020b, 8).

If strategic political communication by legislators or potential litigants can shape the public's response to executive action, then it stands to reason that democratic institutions themselves, especially courts, might play a particularly important role in channeling public opinion as their decisions provide credible signals to their constituents that an executive is overreaching. After all, there is a chasm of difference between an interest group saying they might sue the executive or a legislator taking to the lectern to disparage a policy they do not like, and a pinnacle court summarily striking down an executive action. When courts exercise their power of judicial review, they harness both a powerful legal tool and the trappings of judicial office to inform the public about whether an executive is overstepping their constitutional authority. This possibility – left unaddressed in existing studies – forms the foundation for this book.

OTHER THEORIES OF JUDICIAL EFFICACY

How have others thought about the conditions under which courts become powerful and effective partners in governance? We contribute to a rich set of studies that have sought to understand the conditions under which powerful judiciaries emerge and persist.[19] The classic separation of powers models position courts as an additional veto player in the policymaking process whose assent is required to enact or implement policy (Ferejohn and Shipan 1990; Tsebelis 2011). Subsequent innovations on these models underscore how the mere presence of judicial review can shift the strategic landscape of policy-motivated incumbents and change the scope of viable policy that might reasonably displace a status quo (Shipan 2000). Although an instructive approach to mapping judicial review's effect on the scope of bargains struck in the policymaking process, these veto player models make judicial efficacy a

[19] For a helpful review of these theories, see Vanberg (2015).

fait accompli, as questions of compliance are set aside and courts' decisions are presumed to be binding.

Perhaps the most prominent of these alternative theories of judicial efficacy emphasizes judicial legitimacy and the public's support for courts. As Gibson, Caldeira, and Baird (1998) write, courts that lack legitimacy can "find it difficult to serve as effective and consequential partners in governance" (343). When citizens hold a court in high regard and expect officials to uphold the integrity of the judiciary by faithfully implementing judicial rulings, the threat of punishment at the ballot box for noncompliance can compel officials to comply with decisions, including those with which they disagree (Krehbiel 2021c; Staton 2004; Vanberg 2001). This electoral threat, coupled with public awareness of a government's failure to comply, can exert considerable influence on the bounds of judicial authority (but see Driscoll and Nelson 2023a, 2023b; Nelson and Driscoll 2023). The public support theories of judicial efficacy and power suggest that courts need to be careful stewards of their public standing: without it, there is no reason for legislators or executives to listen to their decisions and obey their opinions. By this logic, courts might be expected to exhibit self-restraint in the face of declining public standing (Clark 2009).

An empirical implication of these legitimacy-based accounts is that they envision broadly supportive courts as having the power to impose both political penalties on incumbents for rule of law violations but also the ability to legitimate constitutionally suspect policies, thereby weakening constraints on the state. Empirically, the evidence that courts have this power to legitimize is both mixed and conflicting. Some suggest that courts can lend an air of authorization to otherwise suspect policies (Bartels and Mutz 2009; Clawson, Kegler, and Waltenburg 2001; Gibson, Caldeira, and Spence 2005), while other studies suggest that judicial decisions polarize public sentiment (Adams-Cohen 2020; Clark et al. 2018; Franklin and Kosaki 1989; Woodson 2019). And an even larger set of studies suggests that a court's ability to change public opinion is either conditional or limited (Bishin et al. 2021; Christenson and Glick 2015b; Fontana and Krewson 2023; Stoutenborough, Haider-Markel, and Allen 2006; Zilis 2015).[20] Nearly all of these studies focus on the ability of a single court – the US Supreme Court – to affect public attitudes (but see Woodson 2019; Baird and Javeline 2007; Bentsen 2019; Kreitzer, Hamilton, and Tolbert 2014). As a result, we know little about how different types of courts, political contexts, or other factors condition the ability of courts to shape public opinion. Further, these studies tend to focus on changing citizens' minds on particular issues, rather than on the overarching issue of state constraint: to what extent can judicial

[20] For other studies on this topic, see Brickman and Peterson (2006), Clark et al. (2023), Fontana and Braman (2012), Gash and Murakami (2015), Grosskopf and Mondak (1998), Hanley, Salamone, and Wright (2012), Hume (2012), Johnson and Martin (1998), Mondak (1992), Nicholson and Hansford (2014), Thompson (2022), Ura (2014), Zink, Spriggs, and Scott (2009).

decisions shape citizens' attitudes toward the policymakers whose decisions the court is reviewing? Or, put differently, can courts shape public opinion in ways that can constrain or embolden executives?

A second set of theories, known as *nonmajoritarian accounts*, suggests that compliance with judicial decisions – and allowing a powerful judiciary to emerge – provides direct benefits to policymakers. By this logic, many issues on which executives or legislatures must make policy are unsavory for elected officials to act upon because the issue divides their constituents (e.g., many social policies). In these situations, a strong judiciary can provide political cover to other policymakers by providing the final say on issues where legislators or executives may prefer to not act (Graber 1993; Rogers 2001; Stephenson 2004; Whittington 2005). As Graber (1993) puts it, policymakers "encourage or tacitly support judicial policymaking both as a means of avoiding political responsibility for making tough decisions and as a means of pursuing controversial policy goals that they cannot publicly advance through open legislative and electoral politics" (37).

These nonmajoritarian theories imply that courts are powerful because of the distribution of public support for other branches of government. Thus, courts derive their power from other politicians' strategic calculi vis-à-vis the electorate: they provide a useful way for incumbents to avoid or deflect public ire or evade direct political accountability entirely. Moreover, the very political disagreements that make courts useful foils for incumbents also make it difficult for citizens to coordinate a campaign against the court to reduce its power or independence, further emphasizing their usefulness to incumbents on controversial issues.

A final class of explanations suggests that strong judiciaries provide insurance for policymakers who know they may someday find themselves out of power (Boudreaux and Pritchard 1994; Ginsburg 2003; Landes and Posner 1975; Ramseyer 1994; Stephenson 2003). These theories suggest that judicial efficacy is tied to political competition. When competition between political factions in a country is high and partisan control of the elected branches of government is variable, those currently in power can benefit from independent courts that are less likely to overturn their policies when the other faction comes into power. By this logic, incumbents may tolerate a sometimes pesky independent court in the short term, knowing they will benefit from its protection when they are in the opposition over the longer term.

Similar to legitimacy and nonmajoritarian models, insurance theories make an implicit connection between the public's electoral choices and the power of constitutional courts. Judicial efficacy in these accounts is a function of the relative distribution of support for political parties in the electorate as politically strong and judicially unfavored parties will promote judicial deference while politically weak and judicially favored parties will advocate for judicial independence. These accounts highlight two constraints on the power of judicial review. First, they suggest that if the judiciary is too demonstrably favorable to one party or the other, it will lose the support of both (Stephenson 2003). Second, they indicate that if a dominant party emerges in the electoral landscape, it may be more willing to take actions that weaken the judicial branch (Ramseyer 1994). In this way, judicial power is inexorably tied to partisan electoral politics and at heart is a question of electoral competition (Ferejohn 1998).

While each of these three theories motivate ebbs and flows in judicial efficacy through different mechanisms, key to all three of these accounts is the relationship between courts and the public. While some theories – especially the legitimacy-based theories – make this connection explicitly and others – the informational and insurance theories in particular – do so to a lesser extent, all three alternative accounts of judicial efficacy suggest that judicial power depends on the public, particularly as a nexus that conditions the judiciary's relationship to incumbents. As Clark and Vanberg (2022) write, "The most important factor that explains [the expansion of the judicial role] is the desire by powerful interests outside of the formal machinery of government – most obviously, citizens at large – to subject the political process to rules and constraints." And while we share a common focus for our interest in the public's involvement in state constraint, our theoretical account advances an alternative mechanism, under a more clearly defined scope condition, as to *why* courts might be effective participants in the business of state constraint.

These theories generally do not address the role of courts with respect to state constraint. The legitimacy-focused theories – taken to their extreme – suggest that a broadly supported judiciary may be able to create penalties for noncompliance but may pose a new threat to state constraint – juristocracy – by swaying the public toward the court's position on the salient issues it decides. And the nonmajoritarian and insurance theories focus more on the *benefits to incumbents* that come from the establishment of powerful and independent courts, rather than the consequences incumbents may face for defying the courts. By contrast, we look to courts and their associated power of judicial review as they exist in the world, with varying levels of judicial independence and constituents who vary in their reverence for the rule of law. In doing so, we ask whether judicial review is able to serve the role so often ascribed to it with the goal of assessing how – and under what conditions – courts can use judicial review to live up to their lofty function as an institutional guardrail to uphold state constraint.

As we elaborate in more detail in Chapter 2, we see both theoretical and empirical weaknesses to the legitimacy account. Theoretically, if courts are tools of state *constraint*, then they should impose penalties for violations of the constitutional order but not facilitate incumbents' rule of law violations. Our theory ascribes this more limited role to effective courts, one which allows judicial institutions to be critical mechanisms of state constraint, but whose institutional capacity does not include the ability to legitimate policy.

As to the nonmajoritarian accounts, our own theoretical model envisions a broader foundation of possible judicial influence. Courts may be influential not only on those controversial issues about which the public is divided or for which courts serve as convenient foils for incumbents to avoid electoral blame. Instead, courts should be able to create meaningful political penalties for rule of law violations, even in the face of popular incumbents who choose to take actions that violate legal dictates. For this reason, we devote a good deal of attention throughout this book to the potential for shared partisan ties to weaken (or completely hamper) judicial efficacy. Contra the nonmajoritarian account, we refocus the question of state constraint away from how it might benefit incumbents, and back to how it might contain them. And, much like the insurance models, we appreciate the context in which judicial review occurs and vary it accordingly in our research design. That said, we reorient the focus here from electoral competition to center more squarely on courts, the public and judicial review.

OUR ARGUMENT

Traditional accounts of judicial review emphasize its role in shaping legislation throughout the policymaking process, either with the idea that courts are veto players (Epstein and Knight 1998; Krehbiel 1998; Tsebelis 2011) or the idea that the threat of judicial review leads legislators to adjust legislation during the policymaking process (a concept called autolimitation) (e.g., Vanberg 2001). These accounts of judicial review focus on intraelite conflict, emphasizing courts' coequal role in the policymaking process and leaving aside the informational role that courts might play to the public.

But many accounts of judicial review view courts as fundamentally weak when it comes to fulfilling such roles. Focusing on the limited ability of courts to ensure the implementation of their decisions, political scientists have increasingly come to view the presence of judicial efficacy as the puzzle to be explained rather than the norm to be expected. This has led scholars to suggest that courts might need to behave strategically to avoid confrontation with executives (Clark 2010; Iaryczower, Spiller, and Tommasi 2002; Vanberg 2005). Other accounts have expanded on this logic by contending that courts strategically try to bolster their own public standing in order to make their judicial review more efficacious in the face of political constraints (e.g., Krehbiel 2016; Staton 2010). Throughout such accounts, scholars underscore the inherent weakness of judicial review that results from a lack of direct means of political enforcement for court decisions.

We emphasize its strengths. We take a step back, focusing on how the nature of constitutional review as an institutional tool can empower courts to affect public sentiment and constrain executives. We argue and demonstrate that, through the use of judicial review, courts help citizens solve a fundamental collective action and monitoring problems by removing ambiguity about the legality of an executive's action and giving the public a clear indication about the action's constitutional propriety. When independent courts tell citizens that an executive has transgressed the constitutional order, we expect citizens to withdraw acceptance from the executive's action. To test this argument, we draw on a series of original and harmonized survey experiments fielded in four countries (the United States, Germany, Hungary, and Poland), countries we selected for their diverging levels of judicial independence.[21]

We find that high levels of judicial independence are a prerequisite to judicial efficacy: courts with low levels of judicial independence lack the credibility necessary to shape public acceptance. Moreover, those citizens who profess a high level of support for the rule of law react more negatively to executive actions that contravene independent courts than their counterparts with weak commitments to the rule of law. Strikingly, we find that independent courts' ability to activate public opposition to controversial policies holds even in the face of partisanship. Citizens seem to care more that executives are playing by the rules than that their favored executive gets her way.

Independent judicial review can thus mobilize the public to act as a state constraint under the right conditions: courts must be independent and the public must be sufficiently supportive of the rule of law. Critically however, judicial decisions only affect public opinion when the court strikes down policies, meaning that the ability of courts to move public opinion *in favor of* an incumbent's policy (and thereby to weaken constraints on the state) is limited. Even where courts are independent and powerful, and even where the public is receptive to high courts' decisions, the efficacy of judicial review is asymmetric in that courts can only affect citizens' attitudes through decisions stating the executive has breached the rule of law.

The picture of judicial efficacy that emerges from our argument and analysis is both robust and limited. That judicial independence is a prerequisite to efficacy means that many constitutional courts – especially in contexts where judicial independence is precarious – may be limited in their ability to serve as a successful check on executive authority. Moreover, that the penalty for noncompliance is concentrated among citizens who attach a great deal of weight to the rule of law suggests that de jure independence, on its own, is not enough to guarantee that constitutional courts are effective tools of state constraint. Rather, courts must be independent *and* situated in political systems with citizens who have deeply held respect for the importance of the rule of law. Furthermore, even in polarized societies, partisanship seems to pose only a limited threat to the ability of independent courts to constrain the state. Finally, despite decades of scholarship yielding mixed and conflicting findings, we present a theoretical account – backed up by empirical evidence that is consistent across multiple experiments and countries – to

[21] We demonstrate in Chapter 3 that citizens in these countries have consistent and accurate assessments of their respective high courts' levels of judicial independence that map closely with expert and scholarly evaluations.

explain why courts are not effective agents of legitimation. This, we argue, is normatively good: incumbents that capture courts may remove a hurdle in the policymaking process, but they will not reap an additional reward, as courts cannot simply bend public opinion to their will.

OUTLINE OF THIS BOOK

Chapter 2 presents the theory we have just previewed in more detail. Even where public consensus exists regarding the appropriate bounds of constitutional action, the public's capacity to credibly punish executive overreach can be significantly hampered by citizens' lack of information about possible transgressions and the need for coordination to impose meaningful political penalties (Weingast 1997). Courts are key to overcoming these obstacles: under the right conditions, they are uniquely positioned to alert the public of governmental transgressions and to transform the public's support for the rule of law into a guardrail against executive overreach. Here, we explain why judicial review by independent courts, which the public regards as high credibility sources, can provide citizens with reliable and trustworthy information about their executive's behavior vis-à-vis constitutional norms. By contrast, courts with low levels of judicial independence are impotent: their decisions are not credible enough to matter. We further expect the rulings of independent courts to be most pursuasive to citizens who have a high level of support for the rule of law and to be effective even in the face of stark partisan polarization.

Chapter 3 presents our research design. After beginning the chapter with a brief discussion on the advantage of our comparative research design, we accomplish four tasks in the chapter. First, in recognition of our theory's emphasis on judicial independence, we select four cases – the United States, Germany, Hungary, and Poland – that give us vital variation in this respect but share important political, legal, and socio-economic characteristics. To further reinforce the appropriateness of our selected cases within the context of our theory, we use survey data to demonstrate that this variation in judicial independence is observed by citizens in these countries, just as it is by experts. Second, the chapter establishes the inferential role the COVID-19 pandemic plays in our analyses. In particular, we emphasize that the global pandemic presented a unique and fleeting opportunity to test citizens' reactions to rule-of-law violations as a result of the real governmental overreach it produced that were similar in every country around the world. Third, we discuss the benefits of using survey experiments for a study like ours, and conclude with a discussion of the strengths and weaknesses of our research design. Finally, we contextualize our quartet of cases by provide background information on their general political characteristics, the institutional characteristics of their constitutional courts, and their respective handling of the pandemic.

The public's support for the rule of law is a key democratic value and a cornerstone concept in our book. We therefore devote Chapter 4 to providing the most systematic analysis to date of its measurement, correlates, and stability. In the chapter, we draw on original survey data to validate an updated measure of the public's support for the rule of law. We demonstrate that support for the rule of law is highest among the most politically sophisticated and those with strong support for democratic values. Further, we illustrate the predictive validity of our measure through the analysis of a survey experiment. We then draw upon thousands of survey responses in the United States and an original six-wave survey panel in Germany to demonstrate the stability over time of the public's support for the rule of law – at both the aggregate and individual levels – even in the face of a myriad of potential challenges.

Chapters 5 and 6 present the core tests of our theory. In the former, we rely upon two experiments to demonstrate that the public withdraws acceptance of policies implemented through contravention – in other words, over the objection of a court – but only if that court has a high level of judicial independence. In so doing, we causally identify the effect of a court's decision against the government on public acceptance of the executive's rule of law violation. We show that contravention of an independent court causes the public to withhold its acceptance, relative to a situation where there was no judicial review. But, if executives contravene a low independence court, it is as if the court had not acted: there is no difference in the public's level of acceptance. Third, we find no evidence in any of our quartet of countries that judicial approval affects the public's acceptance of an executive's policy. Contrary to fears that citizens may blindly follow courts and adjust their opinions based on the court's verdict, even respondents in the United States and Germany accepted policies endorsed by their constitutional court as constitutional no differently than they would have if the policy was enacted without any action by the judicial branch.

In Chapter 6, we examine the effects of judicial review across citizens to demonstrate that the public's support for the rule of law lies at the heart of judicial efficacy. We find that, where courts enjoy high levels of judicial independence, their rulings' efficacy is amplified among citizens who have a strong regard for the rule of law. However, when citizens have low levels of support for the rule of law, the effect of a court's ruling is muted. For courts that lack judicial independence, even those citizens who hold the rule of law in the highest regard are unaffected by a court's determination that that an executive's behavior is unconstitutional. This implies that without credibility, these courts lack efficacy even for those citizens who are most predisposed to be favorable and responsive to them. And, regardless of the level of judicial independence, we find no evidence that even those most committed to the rule of law increase their level of acceptance after a court endorses a policy.

We also consider how the efficacy of judicial review varies based on the public's approval of the executive whose policy the court reviews. Here, we again find that only independent courts are able to make rulings that impact the public's response, although the variation in this effect is somewhat surprising. Echoing Reeves and Rogowski (2022a), we find that the public constraint on executives comes from their *supporters*, not their opponents. In other words, the penalty for implementing a policy by contravening a court is strongest among those citizens who hold the executive in high regard. Among those who dislike the executive, acceptance of the policy is unmoved by the manner in which the executive enacts it. These findings point to an important implication: political sympathy for the executive, here in the form of approval and copartisanship, may not necessarily be the Achilles heel of judicial efficacy it is often portrayed to be.

The second pair of empirical chapters, Chapters 7 and 8, build on these analyses by giving careful attention to a real and pernicious threat to judicial efficacy and the rule of law in modern societies: partisanship. In Chapter 7, we introduce what we term the Partisan Prioritization account: a rival explanation to our theory that suggests that citizens are affected more by whether a policy is championed by a copartisan than about whether or not a court says that the policy is compliant with the law. We test these rival perspectives in Germany and the United States, revealing through the use of a survey experiment that leverages the countries' federal structures that citizens of both countries are remarkably steadfast in their willingness to punish executives – including copartisan executives – for breaching constitutional limits and flouting court orders.

Then, in Chapter 8, we expand our consideration of the threat of partisanship in two ways. First, we take into account variation in levels of judicial independence, with our account again producing an expectation that judicial efficacy depends on strong judicial independence. Second, we shift the locus of partisanship from the executive to the litigant challenging a policy. Leveraging the presence of abstract review in three of our four cases, we demonstrate that judicial independence continues to be a powerful influence on judicial efficacy, even with the appearance of a discernible – but narrow – influence from partisanship.

The key takeaway from Chapters 7 and 8 is that judicial review holds the promise – at least where courts have high levels of judicial independence – to constrain executives even in contexts where partisanship is heightened. Contrary to fears that partisanship has become an overwhelmingly pernicious threat to the rule of law, our findings suggest that independent courts are remarkably resilient in their ability to cut through the binds of partisanship as they help citizens monitor executives and coordinate their actions to reign in incumbents' excesses.

Finally, in Chapter 9, we conclude. We discuss the implications of our findings for the broad set of research areas we engage throughout the book, ranging from theories of judicial independence to executive unilateral action to the relationship between the rule of law and democratic entrenchment. Where possible, we highlight what we see as strengths and weaknesses of our findings and research design, with a focus on opportunities for other scholars to advance the research we lay out here. We suggest that there is much left to study regarding when and how courts affect the public in the name of constraining the state. This book, we hope, is far from the last word on this important topic.

2

Theorizing Judicial Efficacy

Judicial review by independent courts has long been thought to be an effective tool of state constraint. Our task in this book is to present and test a theory about the conditions under which judicial review is effective. In this chapter, we lay out our theory. Incumbents around the world often push the boundaries of their legally authorized authority. As they work to constrain the state, citizens face substantial monitoring monitoring problems as they try to discern when elites have violated the law and coordination challenges as they try to work together to threaten collective retaliation. Courts can provide a solution to these problems: When they are independent, their decisions provide citizens with credible signals that the rule of law has been violated and that citizens should mobilize against the incumbent. In this way, the use of judicial review by independent constitutional courts can serve as an effective tool of state constraint; courts can ameliorate these collective action problems as they shape the responses of citizens to the actions of the elites.

Of course, not all courts are equally effective. Judicial institutions vary in their independence, both in reality and in the extent to which the public perceives them as independent. We argue that judicial independence is a prerequisite to judicial efficacy. Courts with low levels of judicial independence tend to be compromised both in their institutional capacity to communicate violations of the rule of law and in their perceived forthrightness in doing so – the two cornerstones of source credibility. As a result, their ability to rally citizens against an incumbent who has violated the rule of law is limited.

Judicial efficacy is further constrained by citizens' own attitudes. While citizens have a common interest in constraining the exercise of political power, they differ in the extent to which they prioritize the rule of law as a fundamental commitment. Even a credible decision that an executive has crossed the line may not be enough to convince some people to impose a meaningful penalty on the incumbent. Those citizens may not value the rule of law enough to care that it has been violated. Or, they may have such preexisting affinity for the executive that they are unwilling to impose political costs on a favored executive whose actions or policies are illegal.

We therefore pay particular attention to the extent to which the efficacy of judicial review varies across individuals. Regarding the public's commitment to the rule of law, we argue that, not only must courts be independent for them to be efficacious, but they must also be signaling to a citizenry that is sufficiently committed to the rule of law for their use of judicial review to spur political costs to incumbents.

Finally, we turn our attention to partisanship. Here, our expectations stand apart from a burgeoning line of scholarship that expects partisanship's pull to lead citizens to prioritize their party over their commitment to democratic norms, like the rule of law (e.g., Graham and Svolik 2020). We argue that judicial signals – specifically decisions by independent courts that are heard by citizens who support the rule of law – can cut through such partisan noise and retain their efficacy.

In short, the picture of judicial efficacy we provide is more limited than existing accounts suggest. Courts need both institutional independence and a committed citizenry to serve their proscribed role in democratic governance. At the same time, independent courts are able to overcome the partisan pressures that have characterized so much of contemporary politics and rally citizens without regard to partisan ties to hold incumbents to account.

WHY IS IT CHALLENGING FOR THE PUBLIC TO IMPOSE POLITICAL COSTS?

Citizens generally want incumbents to abide by the rule of law. But punishing violations of the rule of law is challenging. Citizens' ability to collectively impose meaningful political costs on incumbents is complicated by two fundamental problems. First, incumbents benefit from asymmetric information: citizens face considerable *monitoring* problems when it comes to surveilling state actions. Second, having detected that an incumbent has transgressed the rule of law, the public faces a significant *coordination* problem as citizens attempt to collectively punish said incumbent. We address both obstacles in turn. Then, we explain how judicial review by independent courts might attenuate these challenges.

Monitoring

The first fundamental obstacle a citizen faces is one of monitoring: people may be unaware or unable to fully appreciate that a transgression of the rule of law has occurred. The challenge of monitoring the executive's behavior is one endemic to hierarchical relationships, especially the sort observed in representative government. At the core of this problem is an information asymmetry: the person or institution taking actions (the agent) on behalf of another (the principal) has information about the process, their own effort, and/or their actions that may not be observable to the person on whose behalf they are acting. In an ideal world, a voter (a principal) could perfectly observe the intent, effort, and behavior of their elected officials (their agents), reward a faithful agent with their continued support, and withdraw support from those representatives whose behavior or effort did not comport with the voter's expectations.[1] Clearly, the reality of political representation diverges starkly from this ideal. Indeed, that a voter cannot perfectly observe and monitor an elected agent's behavior poses a *moral hazard* for the representative: she is incentivized to take actions and risks that do not align with the voter's preferences on the chance this behavior will go unobserved and unsanctioned.

In contemporary political systems, monitoring problems are ubiquitous. Monitoring requires attention, and the typical person doesn't pay much attention to politics (Lupia 2016). People are busy; their work, family, and leisure obligations take away from their ability to follow the ebb and flow of the electoral and policy processes. To compound the issue, most policy questions are complicated – even experts lack the inclination to decipher a federal budget – and laden with difficult questions about the "right" answer.[2] Both the public's general inattentiveness to the political system and the opaqueness of that process make it hard for citizens to monitor their elected officials (Sances 2017; Stiers 2021). Even under the best of circumstances citizens face ambiguity when it comes to discerning whether an executive's action violates the constitution. That the typical citizen lacks the ability or inclination to do so presents elected officials with many opportunities to take actions that benefit themselves rather than their constituents (e.g., Matějka and Tabellini 2021).

As this relates to the public monitoring of state transgressions of the rule of law, pronounced challenges emerge. Varol (2015) documents how autocratic governments often institute and consolidate their power through fully legal mechanisms, installing "stealth" autocratic manipulations under the formal guise of the rule of law. Only rarely is autocratic capture abrupt, obvious, and wholesale. Instead, constitutional regression often occurs incrementally, with ambitious politicos dismantling the checks and balances of democratic architecture through subtle changes that are imperceptible to the casual observer (Ginsburg and Huq 2018). Critically, incumbents are often incentivized to frame their efforts in terms that are

1 Principal–agency theory is a special class of game theoretic models that examines these dynamics. These models emphasize how the informational advantage of the agent (a relative expert) shapes the behaviors of both the agent charged with carrying out a task and the principal who tries to ensure that the agent is faithfully acting in line with the principal's preferences (Miller 2005).

2 People tend to focus their attention to politics on the issues that are most important to them personally, rather than those most important to democratic governance (Bolsen and Leeper 2013; Hutchings 2005).

popular or minimally palatable to the electoral audience to which they appeal (Levitsky and Ziblatt 2018; Nelson and Driscoll 2023). Thus, it might be difficult for members of the public to recognize constitutional transgressions as fundamental threats to the rule of law, making it impossible for them to punish incumbents for taking these actions (e.g., Carey et al. 2019; Svolik 2020).

Coordination

The second fundamental obstacle to public enforcement of the rule of law is the collective challenge of coordination. People disagree about what problems governments should address, what solutions are the optimal fix for societal problems, and whether the government is doing enough to advance the interests of citizens by providing policy solutions to the problems they face. Even in environments where a consensus on fundamentals or specifics exists among the public, citizens vary in the intensity of their preferences and their ability and willingness to act on those beliefs (Almond and Verba 1963; Dahl 1956). This is the sui generis of democratic governance.

Citizens may diverge in their preferences regarding their ideal level of state restraint, just as they may disagree about policy. Even if they are unanimous in their distaste for governmental tyranny – they may be united in a general preference for the freedom of expression and participation over the autocratic alternatives – citizens nevertheless vary in what they view to be an optimal approach to the rule of law. This lack of agreement about the appropriate bounds of state action poses a coordination problem: the public has a universal shared interest in preventing state tyranny but lacks a common equilibrium level of state restraint or shared understanding of what sorts of actions are clearly illegal or merely "on the line."

This latter challenge is amplified by the ambiguity of constitutional texts, a pronounced downstream consequence of the monitoring challenges we just explored. Constitutional and statutory texts are complex and often not easily interpreted, and the meaning of legal prescripts is genuinely contested even by well-meaning experts. For example, consider that the US Constitution provides Congress the ability to "regulate commerce with foreign nations, and among the several states, and with the Indian tribes." The US Supreme Court has decided, on average, at least one – and sometimes five or six – cases relating to Congress's power under this clause each year since the 1940s. The Court's bar for what sort of activity constitutes "regulating," "interstate," and "commerce" has changed over time, gradually expanding Congress's power throughout most of the 1900s before curtailing this authority during the Rehnquist era's "federalism revolution" of the late 1980's to the close of the century (Chemerinsky 2001). And, moving to more ambiguous constitutional guarantees, like freedom of speech or religion or the equality of citizens, the complexities of legal interpretation make it difficult to detect whether an incumbent's actions are, in fact, illegal. This ambiguity raises barriers to coordination and further hampers the public's ability to coalesce around a common interpretation on a matter of state restraint, let alone agree on an optimal level thereof.

But acquiring a shared understanding of whether a given action violates the rule of law is just part of the problem. Citizens must not only collectively recognize that an action violates the rule of law but also work together to impose a credible threat of punishment in response to the incumbent's action. The challenges to this sort of collective action are both obvious and numerous: it is difficult to coordinate on a particular type of punishment. And, even if one is selected, it is difficult to secure compliance across a broad enough swath of the population to make the threat credible. After all, many people are unwilling (or unable) to turn out to vote, much less attend a protest in response to executive overreach.

Instrumental and partisan concerns only compound these already hefty coordination problems. Although it may be true that the public in theory, dislikes blatant rule-of-law violations, these concerns may be small compared to pocket-book considerations closer to home or other substantive policy questions (Christenson and Kriner 2020a; Driscoll and Nelson 2023b; Graham and Svolik 2020). As a result, citizens may be willing to tolerate detected violations of the rule of law if they collect some instrumental benefit from the incumbent's decision to transgress the rule of law.

The organization of political systems into political parties further makes citizen coordination challenging. In the context of partisan competition, the public might prioritize advancement of partisan interests, rather than abstract commitments to state restraint (Carey et al. 2022; Graham and Svolik 2020). Especially in polarized political systems, choosing to divert one's vote away from a copartisan incumbent to punish them for a rule-of-law violation may mean supporting a candidate whose positions on other issues – perhaps equally or even more important – are noxious to the voter (Driscoll and Nelson 2023b). As such, reaching across partisan lines in divided societies to hold incumbents accountable for violating the rule of law is likely a tall order.

Solutions to coordination problems are often described as "focal": they are equilibria that independent agents can identify, even in the face of these challenges. When a focal solution to a coordination problem exists, individuals can unilaterally identify one possible course of action that may be collectively beneficial. In the best-case scenario, an equilibrium solution ensures the maximized payoff for individual actors so as to ensure a coordinated effort to constrain the state.[3] The challenge citizens face is identifying such a focal solution, that is the circumstance under which citizens agree that the state's actions have gone "too far" and warrant widespread public reproach (e.g., Schelling 1960; Vanberg 2011; Weingast 1997).

[3] Alternative equilibria are also possible where individuals coordinate on suboptimal outcomes. The existence of multiple (and sometimes many) equilibria is what makes the focal solution so powerful.

In sum, establishing a means of state constraint is critical to the perpetuation and consolidation of the rule of law. A credible threat of political consequences from the public is but one way to ensure this comes to fruition. Yet theory suggests – and abundant empirical examples substantiate – that the conditions required to bring about this public check on the state are difficult to achieve. We have identified two major obstacles that the public confronts in checking the state: citizens are disadvantaged in their monitoring of state action and the public as a collective faces considerable barriers to coordination and collective action. What is more, instrumental considerations such as partisanship can worsen these challenges. Taken together, existing accounts suggest the public is disadvantaged in the possible detection of incumbent transgressions, and it can be exceedingly difficult to both discern and collectively act upon a threat to the rule of law. In short, the challenges for effective state constraint are daunting.

HOW JUDICIAL REVIEW FACILITATES STATE CONSTRAINT

Having explained how the difficulties inherent in monitoring political elites and coordinating mass behavior make it difficult for citizens to impose credible political consequences on incumbents who violate the rule of law, we now explain how judicial review – under the right conditions – can help citizens overcome these challenges. The gist of our argument is this: judicial review can provide a credible signal to citizens that incumbents have overstepped their legitimate legal authority. Based on these decisions, citizens can coordinate to resolve ambiguity about the proper limits of legal action and take the necessary steps to hold incumbents to account. Judicial review by *independent* courts is uniquely suited to this task due to the credibility that judicial independence provides to courts (and that many other democratic institutions lack). In this way, judicial review provides a mechanism through which courts can be *effective*: they allow courts to create political costs for elites who violate the rule of law.

The Signaling Power of Judicial Review

Judicial review is “the ability of judges to supervise the constitution” (Ginsburg and Versteeg 2014, 587). Typically, courts exercise this authority when they adjudicate a claim that some government action is contrary to the constitution.[4] Judicial review is

[4] Beyond the mere procedural monitoring inherent in traditional judicial review mechanisms, recent work from Botero (2023) underscores how courts around the world have used and created new tools of monitoring, which can range from requiring reports and regular procedural check-ins, to establishing a more formalized and inclusive mechanisms of oversight. These tools can clarify the target of intended compliance, provide an accounting of the policy making process, and mandate future reports on implementation, thereby formalizing and publicizing the requirements for adherence (Driscoll and Gandur 2022).

an oversight power granted to courts to enable them to supervise (and check) decisions made by other parts of government, just as legislators can hold hearings or supervise the actions of administrative agencies (McCubbins, Noll, and Weingast 1987). As they investigate whether other political actors have exceeded their legal authority, constitutional courts monitor the actions of their peers and make written, publicly available, and (theoretically) binding decisions about the appropriateness of government action.[5] In this way, judicial review provides legislators, administrators, interest groups and the public important information about compliance with the rule of law.[6]

Judicial review presents a critical means to mitigate the monitoring and coordination problems that frustrate the public's ability to constrain the state. Information provided by constitutional courts through their use of judicial review can enhance the public's ability to *monitor* executive action and lessen the informational disadvantage at which the public is usually placed. When constitutional courts hold that some law or action is contrary to the constitution, they are essentially pulling a "fire alarm" that alerts citizens to a transgression of the rule of law. Just as McCubbins and Schwartz (1984) argued that Congress can achieve successful oversight of administrative agencies without laborious, resource-intensive, and regular "police patrol" oversight, judicial review can similarly provide otherwise-inattentive citizens with high-quality information about the appropriateness of government action.[7]

Of course, we are not the first to suggest that judicial review animates political actors or organizations – the public, media, interest groups, business elites – to hold incumbents into account (Botero 2023; Christenson and Kriner 2017c; Epp 1998; McCann 1994; Weingast 1997). Indeed, a great deal of scholarship concerned with theorizing the way in which judicial authorities are consequential for rights establishment and protections emphasizes how judicial review can activate and mobilize interest group constituencies and legal advocates. For example, Botero (2023) argues that when judicial review takes place in an environment with a receptive and mobilized reform constituency, courts enhance accountability by empowering third parties to monitor government actions. In this way, judicial review represents a

5 Although many facets of judicial procedure underscore how courts and judicial bodies are set apart from the rough and tumble of everyday politics (Gibson and Nelson 2017), a robust literature in political science and law documents the political foundations and impacts of judicial review (Friedman 2005; Shapiro 1988; Whittington 2005).

6 Judicial review also provides other informational benefits to elites and the public, such as monitoring downstream effects and unforeseen consequences of policy decisions that emerge over time (Rogers 2001; Sunstein 1989).

7 Although McCubbins and Schwartz originally coined the "fire alarm" analogy to describe congressional oversight of administrative agencies, the term has been extended to review dynamics in other administrative hierarchies (Beim, Hirsch, and Kastellec 2014; Turner 2017) and electoral contexts (Cameron and Gordon 2023; Gordon and Huber 2007).

potentially powerful inroad to groups who might be otherwise marginalized in other institutional fora of representative government (c.f., Landau 2012). Critically however, previous work has given less attention to the public's response to constitutional courts' use of judicial review, particularly how judicial–executive interactions affect citizens' decisions to impose costs on incumbents who violate the rule of law.

Second, constitutions, elite pacts, and judicial institutions have long been theorized as possible focal solutions to the public's *coordination* problem (Sutter 1997; Vanberg 2011, 2015). A constitutional court's decision after reviewing a law or action communicates to the public whether a coordinated public response is warranted. If the court endorses the constitutionality of the law or action it reviews (e.g., "clears" the action), the court tells the public that nothing is amiss; there is no need for collective action because there has been no breach of the rule of law. On the other hand, if the court rules that the law or action violates the constitution, it signals to its constituents that the rule of law has been transgressed, thereby cutting through the ambiguity everyday citizens might have about whether some action is "over" or simply "near" the line of legality. As such, a ruling that a legislature, executive, or bureaucrat has made a decision that is contrary to the constitution can serve as a strong signal to others in the political system that a coordinated response may be necessary.[8]

What Makes Signals Credible?

We have suggested that constitutional courts, through judicial review, are able to send credible signals to the public warning them of rule of law violations. The public can use these signals to coordinate an effective political response to constrain the executive. Of course, judicial review by constitutional courts is but one way that oversight is exercised in political systems. Other institutions common in modern democratic landscapes, such as the media, federalism, or the bureaucracy may serve a similar function (McAllister and Schakenberg 2022; Near and Miceli 1995; Över 2021; Potter and Baum 2014). Still, we expect that judicial review by constitutional courts is uniquely effective in its ability to help citizens constrain the state.

Our argument on this front is grounded in the large literature on source credibility. Researchers have demonstrated that the public's responses to information they receive about government and politics vary according to their assessment of the messenger (e.g., Hovland and Weiss 1953). Early research on this topic emphasized the importance of two particular source characteristics: "expertise, which is the amount of knowledge that a communicator is assumed to possess, and trustworthiness, which is the perceived intention of the communicator to deceive"

8 As we explain later in the chapter, courts' signals are not universally effective: courts differ in their levels of judicial independence, citizens vary in their concern for the rule of law, and the pull of partisan ties may lead citizens to put instrumental concerns above democratic ones.

(Franzoi 1996, 214). Later research has demonstrated that source credibility varies according to a myriad of potentially informative source attributes, such as ideology (Zaller 1992), trustworthiness or public support (Christenson and Kriner 2017c; Nelson and Gibson 2019; Popkin 1994; Mondak 1993; Page, Shapiro, and Dempsey 1987), and objectivity (Iyengar and Kinder 1987).[9] And, in some circumstances, even biased information may be helpful to receivers (e.g., Calvert 1985).

More recent research has integrated political psychology and rational choice theory, advancing a more unified framework that highlights two pillars of source credibility: (a) the messenger's knowledge or expertise and (b) the messenger's reputation for trustworthiness or forthrightness.[10] Lupia (2002, 56), for example, argues that "all cue-giver attributes – such as race, gender, ideology, partisanship, reputation, or likability – affect a cue's persuasiveness only if they are necessary to inform a cue-seeker's perceptions of a cue-giver's knowledge or interests." Or, as Druckman (2001) puts it, judgments of credibility require two things: "(1) the speaker's target audience must believe that the speaker possesses knowledge about which considerations are actually relevant to the decision at hand, and (2) the speaker's target audience must believe that the speaker can be trusted to reveal what he or she knows" (1045, see also Lupia and McCubbins 1998). These two cornerstones of source credibility readily apply to institutions as sources. And, compared to other types of oversight institutions, courts are advantaged in both arenas.

Institutional Expertise

First, consider institutional knowledge or expertise. While, in the individual sense, knowledge refers to a source's understanding of (or expertise about) the topic on which he or she is signaling, knowledge in an institutional sense is related to an institution's *capacity*.[11] Institutions vary greatly on this dimension: some have ample

9 For a review, see Druckman and Lupia (2000).

10 To combine the two terms for the second pillar of source credibility, forthrightness and trustworthiness, we use "reputation" to refer to the unified extent to which the public judges an institution as forthright and trusts it (Calvert 1985). This notion is similar, albeit narrower, than the definition provided by Garoupa and Ginsburg (2015): "the stock of judgments about an actor's past behavior (which may or may not be used to predict future behavior)" (4). Garoupa and Ginsburg also differentiate between judges' individual reputations and a court's collective reputation (see also Baum 2006; Hazelton, Hinkle, and Nelson 2023; Nelson, Hazelton, and Hinkle 2022). Our focus throughout this book is on a court's collective reputation and its effect on the efficacy of judicial review.

11 Our notion of capacity is similar to that put forward by Mooney (1995), relating to an institution's "expertise, seriousness, and effort" (48). We acknowledge that our use of the term "capacity" encompasses concepts like institutionalization (e.g., McGuire 2004; Polsby 1968) and professionalization (e.g., Miller 1992; Squire 1992, 2008). We view these characteristics as bringing about the sort of institutional independence from the government and the opposition that the models in both Carrubba (2005) and Staton, Reenock, and Holsinger (2022) require for

operating budgets with full-time staff and operational workforce, while others are limited in their financial resources and budgetary discretion. Some institutions have relatively low turnover, providing opportunities for members to accrue and wield expertise, whereas other institutions are not career destinations for members whose time in office is generally short (e.g., Kousser 2005). More broadly, Burns et al. (2008) identify two possible sources of capacity: *careerism*, "the expertise [built] up over multiple terms in office and the extent to which they identify with and prioritize their work" and *professionalism*, which relates to institutional features like staff support or session length "that enable it to play a stronger, more independent role" in government (230).

Judges on independent courts tend to be careerist and their courts professionalized. Judges on most constitutional courts have a claim to expertise that other actors in the political system do not. Membership requirements for appointments to many constitutional courts often require formal legal education that includes years of specialized training, previous experience as a litigator or judge, and/or a distinguished academic record (Brinks and Blass 2018; Elkins and Ginsburg 2022; Malleson and Russell 2006). Such requirements stand in stark contrast to those of elected politicians who come from more diverse occupational backgrounds (Carnes 2016; Carnes and Lupu 2015; Matthews 1954). Whereas a businesswoman, teacher, or farmer may arrive in the legislature and be immediately confronted with a need to legislate on complex policy issues on which they have no prior education or experience,[12] judges on constitutional courts usually arrive at their position having successfully undergone scrutiny on their ability to perform the legal reasoning their position requires them to do. Judicial decisions are (at least in theory) confined to the sorts of legal questions in which judges have received training, and the mastery of which was scrutinized in the process of their appointment.

This is not to say that judges may not have (or gain) expertise in particular policy areas over the course of their careers or that judges are necessarily experts in all areas of the law they will confront (much less the policy implications of the decisions they will make). The dockets of constitutional courts are diverse, and judges' behaviors on the bench can change as they acquire additional experience. Rather – inasmuch as our argument is about the ability of courts to signal to the public – we simply claim that judges are seen by many citizens as "applying the law" as they rule in cases and have a formal claim to expertise in their domain of work that many others involved in political oversight processes do not. This claim of expertise provides judges with an advantage over other potential oversight institutions in the credibility of the signals they send to the public.

review to be helpful in perpetuating peaceful and continued elite bargaining. Later in this chapter, we directly link these features of source credibility to the concept of judicial independence.

12 Although they may be aided by professional legislative and campaign staffers, or advice from interest groups, the extent to which this is true varies across contexts and legislators.

Additionally, judges on independent courts tend to have a bevy of institutional protections that professionalize their institutions.[13] While ministers or legislators must always be mindful of the next election, judges on constitutional courts do not face voters.[14] Further, legislative terms tend to be shorter than judicial terms, judicial salaries are often constitutionally protected, and constitutional court judges enjoy both de facto and de jure protections from political encroachment that give them a form of professionalized capacity that sets them apart from other branches of government (e.g., Linzer and Staton 2015; Ríos-Figueroa and Staton 2014).

A *Reputation for Trustworthiness*

Second, institutions are more credible sources when they have a reputation for forthrightness and trustworthiness. Citizens' expectations about institutions are crucial for their receptivity to the signals an institution sends: if the public believes that an institution's output is merely "the party line" or "what the government wants," institutional signals are likely to be met with skepticism regarding their credibility. But if the public believes that an institution can act forthrightly – and stand up to the executive when needed – its messages are more likely to be absorbed and acted upon.[15]

Key to forthrightness is an institution's procedures, norms, and approach to carrying out their day-to-day operations in a way that fosters trust (e.g., Krehbiel 2016; Staton 2010). Institutions that are more forthright make well-justified and well-reasoned decisions based on transparent and publicized procedures. Although the institutional outcomes might vary, forthright institutions make decisions in predicable ways, key personnel are professionalized, and institutional reliability is high. In such institutions, conflicts are resolved based on objective facts and impartial evaluations, and rationales for decisions are publicly stated. By contrast, when institutions are not forthright, their decisions are fickle and arbitrary, rooted more in politics than in principle. These sorts of institutions, perhaps out of a desire to save face and hide overt noncompliance from public view, may choose to issue vague or hard-to-understand decisions (Staton and Vanberg 2008).

Regarding institutional trust, the existing literature on public support for institutions has suggested that forthrightness is a key component of trustworthiness.

13 We discuss how professionalism – and level of capacity – varies *among* courts with levels of independence, and its consequences for courts' signaling capacity, later in this chapter.

14 Bolivia and Mexico excepted, see Driscoll and Nelson (2012).

15 As Garoupa and Ginsburg (2015) note, this reputation may be even more important than a court's actual capacity: "Many believe that a high-quality judiciary can improve the anticipated enforcement of property rights, security of contract, and investment, all of which should contribute to economic growth... The key factor may not be the actual quality of legal decision making as much as the reputation of the judiciary. A judiciary with real skill but a bad reputation will not produce the important developmental benefits that conventional theories expect" (21). By examining courts with varied levels of reputation (judicial independence), we are able to test the mechanism that underlies this sentiment directly.

Where institutional procedures are judged as transparent and fair, levels of public support for institutions are generally higher (e.g., Baird 2001; Tyler 2003). Other research has shown that institutional leaders care about institutional image and use procedures strategically to foster or maintain the public's support (Krehbiel 2016; Staton 2004).[16] By contrast, where decision-making processes are opaque or judged to be unfair, trust in institutions is lower (Benesh 2006; Hibbing and Theiss-Morse 1995; Lipset and Schneider 1987).

Compared to other types of oversight institutions, courts benefit from a reputational advantage. In contrast to the overtly political legislative process, courts are often viewed by citizens as neutral, politically disinterested arbiters of constitutional controversies (Hibbing and Theiss-Morse 1995). Due to constitutional courts' tendencies to follow staid, routine, and relatively transparent processes for resolving disputes and to usually justify their decisions in writing with direct reference to legal principles, citizens rightly expect their constitutional courts to be forthright.

As part of these procedures, courts publicly seek information and argumentation from both sides of a dispute at each stage of the judicial process. Compared to legislative hearings (whose guest lists are politically curated), interest group communications (which often only communicate the group's desired position), or the media (where an ability to attract viewers might matter more than hearing the best arguments on both sides of an issue), courts routinize the process of gathering information from all sides of a dispute through oral hearings and written briefs (Collins, Corley, and Hamner 2015; Hazelton and Hinkle 2022; Johnson, Wahlbeck, and Spriggs 2006; Nelson and Epstein 2022).

By routinizing the process of information gathering, courts can build upon a reputational advantage they possess compared to other types of oversight institutions. The symbols of judicial authority – gavels, robes, and temple-like courthouses – combined with a process of childhood socialization that often teaches children that courts are "different" than other political institutions and therefore more worthy of their trust and support, provide courts with an advantage of public support that begins early in life and persists throughout the lifecycle (Easton and Dennis 1969; Gibson and Nelson 2018).[17] Given that public support for institutions declines as the public perceives them to be "political" (Gibson and Caldeira 2009; Gibson and Nelson 2017; Nelson and Gibson 2019), courts have a structural trustworthiness advantage provided the public views them as separate from "normal politics." To this point, research documents that the public's trust and institutional

[16] This research highlights a key point about this concept: the issue is not whether the institution is *actually* forthright or trustworthy but rather the extent to which the public judges the institution as forthright and trusts it. We return to this point in our discussion of judicial independence later in this chapter.

[17] In comparison, legislatures and parliaments are often unpopular for being the locus of overt politicking and partisan conflict (Eurobarometer 2023; Hibbing and Theiss-Morse 1995, 2001).

commitment is fostered by exposure to institutional symbols and institutional lore (Gibson, Lodge, and Woodson 2014; Gibson and Nelson 2018).

The reputational advantage that courts enjoy comes with an additional benefit: by virtue of their reliance on legalistic procedures, judicial involvement in political questions can "turn down" the political temperature, moving a claim or controversy from the political realm to one of a legal character. Actions and determinations of legislatures or executives are clearly "political," whereas judicial decisions, with their basis in statutory and constitutional interpretation, are not (Field 1923; Grove 2015). Whereas the authority to resolve constitutional matters once and for all is reserved for the judiciary alone, the mere act of engaging in constitutional review reduces the political nature of a controversy – a strategy that lawmakers might strategically deploy to eschew responsibility or controversy (Graber 2004).[18] Empirical research has documented that the legalization of political questions can be beneficial for public acceptance and legitimacy (Braman 2016, 2023; Farganis 2012).

To summarize, constitutional documents enshrine and formalize the "rules of the game," spelling out formal limits of state power and legitimate governmental action. At the same time, constitutional courts are often granted the ability to serve as a watchdog on the limitatns on power enshrined in these documents. Through constitutional review, courts can "sound the alarm" of an executive's transgression, alerting citizens to constitutional violations and clarifying the ambiguity of the action's constitutionality. When an action is found to be unacceptable by the court, it becomes clearer to citizens that executive action is contrary to the norms set forth in the constitution. Critically, the process by which this is determined – the sui generis of judicial review – is rooted in constitutional and legal principles rather than explicitly political considerations.

We expect that the courts able to send the strongest signals are those with high levels of capacity and have a reputation for forthrightness and trustworthiness. The signals independent courts send about executive action are authoritative, rooted in transparent procedures and objectivity. By contrast, courts that lack either the means or will to make authoritative decisions about the executive overreach of constitutional bounds have a weaker signaling ability. If any institution is likely to fulfill the fire alarm function of effectively turning support for the rule of law into opposition to unconstitutional policies, independent constitutional courts are ideally situated to do so.

A TYPOLOGY OF EXECUTIVE–JUDICIAL INTERACTIONS

So far, we have suggested that judicial review can help solve citizens' monitoring and coordination problems by sending credible signals about rule of law violations.

[18] As Field (1923,499) describes: "Congress can divest a political question of its character by providing that it be settled by the courts."

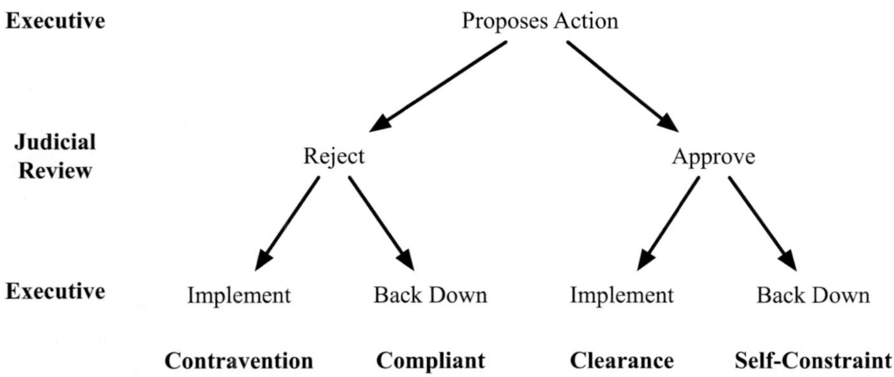

FIGURE 2.1 Typology of executive–judicial interactions. The figure illustrates the four possible conditions that follow from a constitutional court's use of judicial review and an executive's subsequent response to the court's decision.

Decisions by independent courts are likely to be particularly informative signals about the constitutional appropriateness of an executive's action, owing to their expertise and trustworthiness in the eyes of the public.

How might citizens respond to the decisions of constitutional courts? Before setting out some general hypotheses, it is helpful to first establish a vocabulary to discuss the relationship between a constitutional court's judicial review and an implementing authority's decision on whether to press forward with a policy. Our focus on state constraint leads us to focus on executive–judicial interactions, though we acknowledge that the general patterns of interactions we discuss can apply to a variety of policymakers.

We consider a simple sequence of actions, summarized in Figure 2.1.[19] When a constitutional court reviews an executive action, we assume that it faces a binary decision. The court can approve the executive action (such as a court upholding the law through judicial review), or it can reject it (striking down the executive action).[20] Following review, the executive must decide whether to press forward with the proposed executive action or to scrap the proposal altogether. As before, we construe the executive's decision as a binary choice. In the following sections, we discuss each potential outcome and the public's anticipated response.

[19] Although outside the scope of the theory we develop here, one might also consider the possibility that a court is precluded from reviewing an executive's action. This could come, for example, as a result of preemptive reforms designed to preempt potential legal challenges, what Pavone and Stiansen (2022) term the "shadow effect of courts."

[20] In practice, institutions sometimes chart a middle ground by approving policies on procedural grounds without discussing the substance of the policy. Such is the case when courts render a claim inadmissible by declining a case on the basis of its merits. We sidestep that possibility throughout this book, though we note when we get to our empirical exposition that our vignettes provide respondents with no information about the grounds under which the court (dis)approves of the executive's policy proposal.

Institutional Contravention and the Costs of Noncompliance

A first possibility outlined in Figure 2.1 occurs when the court strikes down the executive's action as unconstitutional and the executive defies the court by implementing the policy. We call this set of actions *contravention*. The court's decision in this instance signals to its constituents that the executive is trying to act in a way that violates the rule of law, and the executive presses forward in defiance. We expect a strong and negative response from citizens in response to this contravention of law.

Contravention provides the most obvious opportunity to assess the extent to which a court is efficacious. If a court is effective, incumbents who engage in contravention should face political costs for their decision to press forward in defiance of a court. If a court lacks efficacy, then incumbents will not face consequences for noncompliance.

High-profile examples of contravention abound. US President Andrew Jackson famously forced the displacement of tens of thousands of Native Americans in defiance of an 1832 Supreme Court ruling (Ford 2018). The government of Hungary led by Viktor Orbán reformed the constitution to drastically limit the institutional independence of the Hungarian Constitutional Court, despite repeated threats from the European Union that said reforms would not be tolerated (Than and Dunai 2013). The Polish Supreme Court ruled many new reforms unconstitutional in an effort to preserve its institutional independence, only to find the government pledged to ignore the rulings outright and summarily dismiss the justices from office (Pech and Kelemen 2020). Although overt executive noncompliance with the Supreme Court is less common in contemporary American politics, multiple recent administrations in the United States have openly flouted congressional subpoenas and efforts to investigate administrative actions with minimal public outcry.[21]

Contravention is quintessential noncompliance with a court's decision. The threat of incumbent noncompliance with a judicial decision is often suggested to be a fundamental challenge facing judicial institutions, whose lack of both the "purse and the sword" implies a limited recourse to compel or incentivize adherence to their decisions.[22] That the public will punish executive noncompliance is a common identifying assumption in many formal theories of interbranch relations (e.g., Carrubba 2009; Staton, Reenock, and Holsinger 2022; Stephenson 2004; Vanberg 2000, 2001).

[21] The nearest recent example of the presidential noncompliance with a Supreme Court ruling was President Nixon's refusal to surrender the Watergate tapes under the claim of executive privilege (Ford 2018). Of late, prominent political leaders have signaled their willingness to eschew high court decisions and have openly advocated for their followers to ignore the court (Denniston 2011; Ford 2018).

[22] The need to secure compliance with their decisions is often assumed to be a primary motivator of judicial behavior (e.g., Epstein and Knight 1998), although the recent work of Staton, Reenock, and Holsinger (2022) relaxes this assumption. For an excellent review of theories of comparative judicial behavior, see Epstein et al. (2024).

However, despite this intuitive and compelling logic, only recently have the effects of noncompliance on political behavior attracted sustained attention from empirical researchers (e.g., Carey et al. 2022; Carlin et al. 2022; Clayton et al. 2021; Driscoll et al. 2023; Driscoll, Çakir, and Schorpp 2024). Studies suggest that this accountability mechanism might be heavily conditioned by democratic context and elite adherence to the rule of law (Driscoll, Çakir, and Schorpp 2024). Krehbiel (2021c) considers 207 elections across 74 countries to find that that noncompliance with judicial orders decreases an incumbent government's vote share. This research further shows the conditional nature of citizens' willingness and ability to punish incumbents, as the relationship between noncompliance and electoral performance only manifests where a strong norm of compliance – and the rule of law – exists. In a similar vein, recent research documents that efforts to undermine the institutional independence of well-respected national high courts are met with some public hostility similar to the sort of public backlash that would presumably also follow incumbent noncompliance (Engst and Gschwend 2021). However, the extent of a public response – at least in terms of electoral choice – appears to be limited (c.f., Driscoll and Gandur 2022; Driscoll and Nelson 2023b).

Our expectations about the consequences of contravention are drawn from this rich literature on the costs of noncompliance. Scholars generally theorize that where public support for institutions is widespread, noncompliance should cost public support (Carrubba 2009; Clark 2010; Helmke 2010b; Stephenson 2004; Vanberg 2000, 2001). Therefore, we anticipate that executive contravention of an independent court will undermine the public's acceptance of the executive action, compared to a situation where no judicial review was exercised. It is when the constitutional court has told citizens that the executive's action violated the rule of law and she pressed forward to implement it that citizens' monitoring and coordination challenges of citizens are reduced thereby causing citizens to withdraw their acceptance of the action.

Institutional Clearance and the Power of Legitimation

We say an executive's action has been *cleared* by the constitutional court when the court upholds the action's constitutionality and the executive subsequently carries it out. Although this sort of review might enhance public awareness of the executive action (fulfilling the monitoring capacity of judicial review), judicial clearance should not have the same sort of coordinating force as a ruling against an executive. While legislators and executives may reap policy benefits from allied courts (e.g., Gibson and Nelson 2021; Hirschl 2004), we argue that the ability of courts to sway the public toward the incumbents' policy is fundamentally limited.

By declaring the executive's action as consistent with the rule of law, the court's decision provides citizens with little-to-no new information about the broader political controversy. The same political sides of the controversy or issue remain, leaving the debate about whether the policy *should* be implemented unchanged. In ruling that the executive's action conforms with the rule of law, the court's decision neither sounds an alarm nor generates a focal point around which the public can coordinate. We anticipate that governments are not given "extra credit" for their adherence to the law and constitutional boundaries; Citizens presume their executives will act within these bounds. As a result, our theoretical framework points to there being no noteworthy public reaction to judicial clearance.

This expectation admittedly runs contrary to prominent and well-established theories of judicial legitimation. For decades, scholars have suggested that respected courts may be able to persuade the public to increase its support for a policy (Christenson and Glick 2015a; Gibson, Caldeira, and Spence 2005; Tyler 1988). In perhaps the most well-known statement of this idea, Dahl (1957) argues that "[t]he main task of the [U.S. Supreme] Court is to confer legitimacy on the fundamental policies of the successful coalition" (294). In other words, by lending its seal of approval to controversial policies, courts can increase acceptance and public support for these controversial actions.[23]

The empirical support for this argument does not, however, match its intuitiveness. Some scholars have concluded that judicial approval can legitimize a controversial policy, often by changing citizens' attitudes toward the policies or increasing levels of acceptance or compliance for those policies (e.g., Gibson, Caldeira, and Spence 2005; Gibson and Nelson 2018; Johnson and Martin 1998). While most of this research has focused on the United States, scholars of comparative judicial politics have suggested that other constitutional courts may have a persuasive power as well (e.g., Baird and Javeline 2007; González-Ocantos and Dinas 2019; Sternberg, Brouard, and Hönnige 2021). However, the research on this subject has yielded conflicting or inconclusive results, with some (mainly experimental) designs suggesting that institutions have the ability to actually *change* public opinion (Christenson and Glick 2015a; Hoekstra 1995; Mondak 1994) and other (mainly observational) studies finding no evidence of any such effect (e.g., Marshall 1989). Further, even where studies have found that institutions *can* change public opinion, they differ on the nature of the effect. Franklin and Kosaki (1989), for example, demonstrated the ability of the US Supreme Court to change citizens' attitudes,

[23] Some scholars suggest procedural justice as a key mechanism underlying this effect: where institutions use principled and transparent procedures, the public is more willing to accept policy decisions that they dislike (e.g., Tyler 1988). Others contend that institutional legitimacy increases courts' persuasive power: Gibson, Caldeira, and Spence (2005) argue that more legitimate institutions can convert their reservoir of goodwill into public acceptance of decisions that may have otherwise inspired backlash. These various mechanisms are observationally equivalent for the purposes of our analyses here.

though their analysis of abortion-related attitudes in the wake of *Roe v. Wade* found that the Court polarizes, rather than leads, public opinion. This mixed empirical record, combined with only a tenuous theoretical rationale whereby a court's decision might legitimate a policy, leaves an unsettled debate over the legitimating power of courts. We are skeptical of any such effect as we anticipate that a court granting *clearance* to an executive's action will do little to impact the public's acceptance of a controversial policy.

Studying clearance provides an important opportunity to test the limits of judicial efficacy. We have focused our conceptualization of efficacy on the ability of courts to *impose* costs on incumbents for violating the rule of law. But, alternatively, courts may additionally be able to reduce or *remove* these costs if they have the power of legitimation so often ascribed to them. It might be the case that citizens trust courts so much that they update their views of executive action in response to a court.[24] If citizens' opinions simply reflect court rulings – which a legitimation perspective suggests – then smart elites may try to co-opt courts to secure judicial approval of legally questionable policies in order to skirt consequences for rule-of-law violations.

In the extreme, the ability of clearance to mute potential judicial fire alarms suggests why co-opting courts might be a useful strategy for authoritarians. With the seal of approval from an erstwhile respected and independent court, the executive might implement the chosen policy without fearing salient and harmful public backlash. Likewise, the scrutiny that comes through this sort of institutional oversight might lend procedural credibility to an otherwise questionable executive action, granting an executive's controversial policy an air of legitimacy (Moustafa 2007; Moustafa and Ginsburg 2008). By this logic, studying public responses to judicial clearance therefore helps us to not only understand the limits of judicial efficacy but also provides an opportunity to differentiate our account from an alternative perspective on how courts affect public opinion.

Self-Constraint and Compliance

Because we are most interested in how judicial review might constrain executives, our focus is on outcomes that involve the executive implementing their chosen policy either in defiance of or conformity with the constitutional court's decision. Yet two outcomes in Figure 2.1 remain. In the more theoretically interesting outcome, an executive is *compliant* when the executive obeys a judicial decision holding their action as unconstitutional. This condition is the mirror image of

[24] For more about the extent to which citizens' may base their attitudes on those of elites, see Lenz (2009, 2012).

contravention. Compliance represents "proper politics" with the role of judicial review within a system of checks and balances operating as intended.

We view this outcome to be the norm across systems with independent high courts, owing to a number of factors. For instance, public support for the rule of law in this scenario may serve as a "silent" guardrail that influences government behavior with the credible threat of a backlash (e.g., Christenson and Kriner 2017c, 2020a; Driscoll and Nelson 2023b; Vanberg 2015).[25] Alternatively, and consistent with studies documenting how judges behave strategically to cultivate public support and avoid interbranch disputes, courts may render decisions to hew closely to both public opinion and preferences of the dominant government authorities of the day (Caldeira 1987; Epstein and Knight 1998; Staton 2006). Given evidence that courts and judges behave strategically with an eye for maximizing compliance (Ford 2018), it should come as no surprise that general compliance is the norm in many contexts.

Indeed, compliance is so mundane it is easy to miss. It is perhaps most evident in the face of rulings that run counter to broad swaths of public opinion. The 2022 US Supreme Court ruling of *Dobbs vs. Jackson* reversed *Roe vs. Wade*, thus abruptly ending the federal protection of a women's right to abortion and turning over the issue over to the states. The decision set off a firestorm of public and legislative action, leading progressive-leaning states to constitutionalize abortion and conservative states to stringently limit women's access to the procedure (Williams 2023).[26] Yet, in spite of the social and political upheaval the *Dobbs* ruling caused, it is equally striking that the ruling did *not* spur widespread governmental noncompliance. Although the Biden administration deployed administrative instruments with the aim of protecting access,[27] the divergent and polarized response by the states is striking for its *adherence* rather than defiance to a broadly controversial judicial decision.

Despite the theoretical prominence of compliance and the fact that this situation – everyone playing by the rules – is the way modern government is supposed to work, it is of lower interest to us than clearance or contravention because it provides us with less theoretical leverage on the ability of courts to effectively constrain the state. When an executive complies with a court's order,

[25] This does not necessarily mean that citizens fail to react to a court's ruling or are blithe to the government's adherence to the court. Compliant executives may be rewarded for faithfully following the rules of the democratic game. Alternatively, citizens might nonetheless punish elected officials for simply attempting the policy even though the executive retreated in accordance with the court's decision.

[26] As of June of 2023, California, Michigan and Vermont had constitutionalized access to abortion with another seventeen states providing enhanced statutory and administrative protections. State governments in fourteen states had adopted complete abortion bans, with another six taking steps to abruptly curtail access (*New York Times* 2023; Smith and Sasani 2022).

[27] There is no information on public compliance with the abrupt criminalization of abortion in many states; for obvious reasons, this is information that will never be publicly known.

the public does not face a monitoring problem, and there is nothing on which they must coordinate. No punishment is necessary to enforce constitutional limits of executive power because governmental adherence is voluntary. In this sense, compliance functions in this study like a second baseline.[28]

Finally, we term the last outcome *self-constraint*. Here, the court rules that the executive's action is constitutional. Yet, the executive does not follow through with implementation.[29] This might occur when the review process straddles different governments, leaving a new executive in charge of responding to the review of a predecessor's policy. Because self-constraint is, by definition, an action taken by the executive – not the court or the public it is of limited theoretical interest to us. With this in mind, and because we expect it to occur only rarely in practice, we do not consider this situation in our research design and analyses moving forward.

VARIATION IN JUDICIAL EFFICACY

We have suggested that judicial review can provide citizens with signals that mitigate monitoring and coordination problems and thereby create credible political consequences for violations of the rule of law. The typology of judicial review and incumbent responses we just introduced establishes a framework for thinking about ways in which judicial actors interact with incumbent governments when exercising judicial review. We now turn to the main theoretical determinants of when signals sent by judicial review will affect citizens' acceptance of an executive's controversial action.

Judicial Independence

Earlier in this chapter, we argued that courts – compared to other types of oversight institutions – are generally more likely to send credible signals than other actors,

[28] Although we are primarily interested in estimating the effects of contravention or clearance against a situation in which the executive acts unilaterally, it is also interesting – though less central to our research aims – to understand how the public's responses to clearance and contravention relate to compliance, and how the public assesses adherence to institutional oversight differently than unilateral action. We address each of these issues empirically in subsequent chapters.

[29] Note that our concept of "self-constraint" is different than "autolimitation" in the constitutional politics literature (e.g., Stone 1992; Stone Sweet 1998; Vanberg 1998b). In Stone Sweet's (1998) words, autolimitation is "the exercise of self-restraint on the part of the government and the majority in anticipation of an eventual negative decision of the constitutional court" (329). When autolimitation happens, governments change their behavior *before* a court ruling. In situations of self-constraint, governmental behavior changes *after* the court rules: the judiciary allows the policy, but the executive nevertheless declines to carry it out. Governments might choose to self-constrain for any number of reasons: they decide that the policy is bad, they learn that the policy (though constitutional) is unpopular, or because (even despite the approval) they have concerns about the appropriateness of the policy.

such as ministers, legislators, or interest groups, who might raise arguments about a policy's constitutionality. Even so, however, not all constitutional courts are equal in their ability to send credible signals. We suspect that a court's ability to send credible signals is first and foremost a function of its judicial independence.

What is judicial independence? Judicial independence is associated with a variety of positive political and economic outcomes. Courts with greater levels of judicial independence are better able to protect property rights (North and Weingast 1989) in ways that can promote economic growth and development (e.g., Acemoglu, Johnson, and Robinson 2001; Ariotti, Dietrich, and Wright 2022; Barro 1997; Feld and Voigt 2003). Independent courts might likewise help to promote human rights (Keith 2002; Powell and Staton 2009) and regime stability (Gibler and Randazzo 2011; Staton, Reenock, and Holsinger 2022). For these reasons, international organizations like the World Bank and United Nations have pressed countries around the world to enhance the independence of their domestic courts.

Perhaps no concept in the study of comparative judicial politics and law has received more attention than judicial independence. There is an enormous literature on the "right" way to conceptualize and measure it.[30] Perhaps most notably, scholars have debated whether judicial independence is best understood by considering formal protections – de jure independence – or how the judicial system works in practice – de facto independence. The former refers to "formal rules designed to insulate judges from undue pressure, either from outside the judiciary or from within" (Ríos-Figueroa and Staton 2014, 106–7); whereas the latter is behavioral. Staton, Reenock, and Holsinger (2022) relate this second type of independence to judicial autonomy, describing it as "the ability of a judge to render a decision that reflects their sincere preferences." Notably, it is de facto independence that is captured by prominent measures such as that of the Varieties of Democracy (V-Dem) project. In this perspective of judicial independence, courts and governments might agree, but courts exhibit de facto judicial independence when they can and do make decisions that reflect their sincere views regardless of the government's position.

The upside of the vast literature on judicial independence is that researchers have taught us quite a bit about the characteristics of courts that are associated with high or low levels of judicial independence are well understood. With regard to measures of de jure judicial independence, Staton, Reenock, and Holsinger (2022) review prominent measures of the concept and note that the "correspondence between inputs [across measures] is quite high. Indices often include items related to the relative ease with which judicial institutions can be amended, judicial appointment and tenure, the political insulation of judicial salaries, the process of allocating cases, the existence of constitutional review, and the extent to which

30 It is perhaps for these reasons that Brinks and Blass (2022) characterize judicial independence as "empirically nonexistent and normatively suspect" (23).

the court publishes its decisions, including minority decisions" among other common indicators (37).[31] They follow Melton and Ginsburg (2014) and create an index of de jure judicial independence that includes six indicators, all of which relate to professionalism: "constitutional statements on judicial independence, judicial tenure, selection procedures, removal procedures, limited removal conditions, and salary insulation" (37–8).

Given the extent and depth of this extant work, our aim is not to develop a new conceptualization of judicial independence. Rather, we follow the conceptualization of judicial independence used by Staton, Reenock, and Holsinger (2022) and the V-Dem project, emphasizing judicial autonomy and judges' ability to make the decisions they think are right.

The importance of perceptions of judicial independence. It is one thing for a court to have a set of political characteristics – long-term lengths, salary protections, and the like – associated with high levels of judicial independence. It is another thing, however, for citizens to *perceive* their constitutional court as independent. Our argument is about how citizens respond to judicial decisions. What matters, then, is not necessarily how scholars categorize a court's level of independence but rather how the public *perceives* it. Critically for our argument, we show in Chapter 3 that the four countries in our study vary in their formal level of judicial independence and that this variation corresponds strongly to public perceptions of judicial independence. We further validate this claim by comparing expert and mass public evaluations of judicial independence in countries throughout Europe, finding a positive correlation between these two measures. Our analyses show that the public perceives judicial independence to be strong in the same countries where experts view the high courts as impartial and free from external influence. This demonstrated congruence between subjective evaluations and objective features of courts is particularly important because our theory centers on the ability of high courts to signal to the public and the power of such signals varies with a court's level of judicial independence. While not the focus of the book, it is worth noting that these analyses provide some of the first and only empirical evidence to demonstrate that the public's judgment of judicial independence coincides with that of experts.

We expect the public's perceptions of judicial independence to align with scholarly metrics for several reasons.[32] For one, although citizens may not closely follow judicial salaries or the details of most judicial decisions, attacks on judicial

[31] For more about the effects of judicial selection and retention on judicial behavior, see Pérez-Liñán and Castagnola (2024), Gibson and Nelson (2021), Nelson and Burnham (2024), Tiede (2022, 2024).

[32] To preview, in Chapter 3, we validate this assumption empirically for the cases that we have selected. And, as we explain in Chapter 9, testing our theory in contexts where lay and academic perceptions of judicial independence diverge is a fruitful path forward to understand the foundations of judicial efficacy.

independence often attract the attention of supranational organizations that can widely publicize rule-of-law violations. Consider two high-profile attacks on judicial independence in recent years. The Council of Europe's Commissioner for Human Rights criticized a suite of Polish judicial reforms in the late 2010s, noting that "Improving accountability or efficiency of the justice system may not be pursued at the expense of judicial independence" (Brzozowski 2019). The European Court of Human Rights ordered Poland to take "rapid remedial action" in response to concerns about judicial independence in that country in 2021 (Darmanin 2021). Institutions of the European Union similarly shined a spotlight on the reforms, with the European Court of Justice raising concerns about the independence of the Polish judiciary in a 2021 decision[33] and the Advocate General of the European Court of Justice holding that Polish reforms that granted the country's justice minister additional power over the composition of the courts were such that "the minimum guarantees necessary to ensure the indispensable separation of powers between the executive and the judiciary are no longer present" (Bayer 2021). Similarly, in response to a 2022–23 Israeli proposed judicial reform, the United Nations's High Commissioner for Human Rights issued a statement "urg[ing] those in power to heed the calls of the people in this movement – people who have put their trust in the enduring value of an independent judiciary to effectively hold the other branches of Government to fundamental legal standards and – ultimately – protect the rights of all people" (Türk 2023). The International Monetary Fund likewise highlighted the proposed judicial reforms and suggested they posed an economic risk for the country, observing that "as in any country, maintaining strength of the rule of law would be important for economic success" (International Monetary Fund 2023).

Closer to home, national politicians talk about judicial independence in ways that can inform citizens. Members of majority and opposition parties publicly debate proposals to reform courts with an eye toward judicial independence, thus providing additional opportunities for citizens to update their perceptions of judicial independence. These debates are communicated to citizens through the media, which regularly covers the judiciary with an eye toward informing the public about interference with judicial independence. Again, examples from Poland and Israel are instructive. Headlines, such as *Politico's* "On judicial independence, Poland slips furthest in global ranking" (Kotkamp 2021) and *The Guardian's* "Poland may be stripped of EU voting rights over judicial independence" (Boffey and Davies 2017) emphasize the consequences of the judicial reforms for judicial independence in Poland. Similar media coverage surrounded the contentious Israeli judicial reforms. The *Jerusalem Post* carried a headline arguing that "Israeli efforts to harm judicial independence hurt IDF," while two

[33] Judgment of 2 March 2021, *A.B. and others v the KRS*, C-824/18, C-824/18.

headlines from Reuters drew attention to the reform's potential economic consequences ("Israel's cenbank urges judicial independence, sees more rate hikes" [Scheer 2023]) and consequences for the country's foreign standing ("German foreign minister concerned about judicial independence in Israel" [Reuters Staff 2023]). While admittedly anecdotal, they provide some reason to suspect that citizens have access to information that gives them a sense of their judiciary's level of judicial independence.

Why Only Independent Courts are Credible Sources. We argue that only independent courts are able to issue rulings that send informative signals to the public. When courts that lack independence rule an executive action unconstitutional, the court's decision lacks the credibility necessary to compel citizens to update their judgment – and support – of the executive's behavior. To understand why we associate high levels of judicial independence with high levels of source credibility, we return to our discussion of this concept from earlier in the chapter. Recall that messengers with high levels of expertise and a reputation for trustworthiness are judged as more credible. Courts that lack judicial independence tend to suffer on both of these dimensions. As Garoupa and Ginsburg (2015) put it: "[a] judiciary with a poor reputation... will find itself starved of both resources and respect," exactly the two dimensions the source credibility literature emphasizes (5).[34]

First, recall that institutional expertise is associated with a higher level of capacity, and capacity is related to the careerism of an institution's membership and the professionalism of the institution. As Ríos-Figueroa and Staton (2014) note, higher levels of de jure judicial independence are associated with "[i]nstitutions like fixed tenure, multilateral appointment procedures, budgetary autonomy, and judicial councils" (107). These items each relate to either professionalism or careerism. Longer tenures with protections from purges or arbitrary removal and assurances that judicial salaries cannot be reduced are both associated with increased careerism, as they make it possible for judges to serve long tenures on the court. Similarly, selection procedures that require judicial councils or the approval of multiple actors limit the ability of executives or legislators to put unqualified or improper judges on

34 Our claim is simply that courts with lower levels of judicial independence tend to have lower source credibility and acknowledge that the process through which independence and credibility collectively decline is likely dynamic and endogenous. Garoupa and Ginsburg (2015) suggest implicitly that declines in reputation may precede attacks on judicial independence: "Collective reputation shapes the social and political influence of the judiciary as a whole and consequently has monetary and nonmonetary implications for the welfare of the judges. For example, collective reputation may impact the overall judicial budget, salaries, pensions, and other perks available to the judiciary" (23). An alternative perspective is that citizens learn – through the media, interest groups, NGOs, and others – about attacks on judicial independence and negatively update their sense of a court's signaling credibility. Resolving the causal ordering here is beyond the scope of our project; both accounts suggest the same prediction: lower independence corresponds to diminished signaling capacity.

the bench, enhancing the professionalism of the court. So too do statutory or constitutional protections for judicial budgets enhance judicial professionalism. By contrast, judicial careerism is undermined in places where weak salary protections may drive judges to leave their post soon after appointment or flimsy removal procedures make judicial purges and the resulting churn of judicial turnover possible. We expect that courts with such qualities, which form the basis for higher levels of judicial independence, tend to be viewed as having greater capacity and therefore are better able to send credible signals to the public.

Second, higher levels of source credibility are associated with a reputation for trustworthiness or forthrightness, whereas courts that lack judicial independence are likely to suffer in this regard. Perhaps the most obvious reason a court may not be judged as forthright is that it has been captured or co-opted by political forces. Exactly because independent judicial review represents a powerful mechanism for potential accountability, ambitious governments may seek to co-opt the institutions of oversight and thus limit obstacles to their political agenda. In doing so, governments can essentially dismantle an alarm system that might inform the public of its actions. This co-optation of oversight can take many forms, ranging from the mundane to unabashedly controversial. Governments have the power to gut institutional resources and to eliminate or reshape high courts altogether (e.g., Kosar and Sipulova 2020; Lewis 2003; Schwartz 2024). Executives might make membership of a court professionally inhospitable, incentivizing defection from seasoned experts and professionals, thus undermining institutional capacity to conduct an impartial process of judicial review (e.g., Driscoll and Nelson 2019; Helmke 2005; Peréz-Liñán and Castagnola 2009).[35] Other efforts to short circuit this oversight process are more baldfaced, including the appointment of unqualified political allies (Gandhi 2010; Svolik 2012), the manipulation of oversight-related rules and procedures (Corrales 2015; Ginsburg, Huq, and Versteeg 2018; Schepple 2018), or even outright bribery and corruption (Desposato 2008; Rose-Ackerman 2010). When this sort of co-optation and capture occur, public trust in the forthrightness of judicial decrees is undermined, and citizens become cynical about the independence of courts and judicial review.

Relatedly, courts with low levels of independence may be viewed by citizens as politicized and under the control of the government. Perceived politicization is the Achilles heel of public trust in political institutions, courts included (Gibson and Nelson 2017; Nelson and Gibson 2019). As the public perceives executive or legislative interference with judicial decision-making – by definition more common in less independent judiciaries – their level of trust in that court should decrease.

[35] Of course, not all institutional reforms or instances of membership turnover are malicious or inappropriate: new governments come into power and fill key posts with allies or redirect governmental resources in accordance with their electoral mandate. Such "normal politics" is not necessarily associated with an effect on an institution's perceived independence.

As noted earlier, fair and transparent procedures are associated with higher levels of public support (e.g., Baird 2001; Tyler 2003). Judicial review – especially in cases that directly implicate executive actions – by a low independence court is probably more likely to be seen as "political" than "legal," leaving these courts less likely to generate a rule-of-law motivated response to the executive's behavior. That is, because they are viewed as acting based on political motivations, low independence courts are poorly positioned to depoliticize controversial actions. If the court itself is seen as a political actor due to a lack of judicial independence, then its outputs will also be seen as political and citizens will essentially not update their beliefs about the policy. It is only independent courts that can be trusted by citizens to provide credible evaluations of an executive's action on constitutional or legal grounds and thereby move citizens to think about a policy in terms of its consistency with their support for the rule of law rather than their politics.

In short, a court's signaling capacity is inexorably tied to its level of judicial independence. Or, as Garoupa and Ginsburg (2015) explain, "[w]ithout a good reputation, judiciaries are doomed to irrelevance" (22) and "[a] better reputation will be correlated with an increased likelihood of compliance" (20). When the public sees their constitutional court's decisions as untrustworthy, politicized, and/or the result of an unfair process, they are unlikely to see the court's decision as one meriting a response. By examining the effects of judicial independence on signaling credibility, we identify and test this mechanism through which judicial efficacy should vary.

Judicial Review and Support for the Rule of Law

The discussion in the previous section suggested that courts vary in their ability to issue rulings that are seen as credible by the public. The efficacy of courts, however, likely does not vary only according to judicial independence but also based on the extent to which citizens are receptive to its signals. The effect of even the clearest judicial signal depends on whether citizens care about its content or if it falls upon the ears of citizens uninterested in the rule of law. In this way, judicial efficacy is inexorably linked with public attitudes. Not only must courts be able to issue decisions that are viewed as knowledgeable and trustworthy, but the signal sent by those rulings must be heard by citizens who care about rule of law violations.

What sort of citizens are likely to be more or less receptive to judicial signals? As we discussed in Chapter 1, a good deal of literature has suggested that judicial power is tied to the public standing of courts.[36] Throughout this chapter, we have suggested that courts viewed as more trustworthy send stronger signals and that trustworthiness and judicial legitimacy are closely – but not exactly – related

36 Later in this chapter we consider the alternative possibility that citizens' partisanship or support for the executive who is violating the rule of law muddles the efficacy of judicial review.

(Gibson, Caldeira, and Spence 2003). By this view, the more the public supports a court, the more effective that court's signals should be.

This is certainly a possibility. But, a court's use of judicial review provides citizens with information about a violation of the rule of law in the broader political system, and responses to that decision may be affected by system- rather than institutional-level attitudes. A citizen might love a court but simply not care that an executive is violating the rule of law. What assists with judicial efficacy, we expect, is less individual attachments to particular political institutions and instead one's broader sense that the rules of the game need to be followed. This argument is similar to that made by Reeves and Rogowski (2022a) who find that the American public's support for the rule of law conditions their negative response to unilateral action by the president. It is one's commitment to the broader political and constitutional system, not necessarily a particular political institution, that should shape the public's response to judicial review.

Thus, we posit that citizens' support for the rule of law can condition their receptiveness to judicial signals. Our expectations regarding the conditional effect of support for the rule of law is clearest in the face of an executive action that contravenes a constitutional court. When executives engage in noncompliance with judicial decisions, they are violating the rule of law. We would therefore expect such contravention to be particularly offensive to those citizens who hold the rule of law in high regard. Among citizens who do not value the rule of law, however, the penalty for contravention should be lower, if not absent entirely, since the executive's behavior is not a violation worth punishing to these citizens. Therefore, we expect that the effect of such defiance will increase across levels of support for the rule of law.

What, though, ought we expect when it comes to judicial clearance? In such instances, we contend that support for the rule of law will have little effect on the public's reaction. We suspect this for two reasons. First, support for the rule of law is a threshold judgment, one that we only fully observe in the case of contravention. Provided that an executive's behavior is legal, any number of other policy-relevant considerations may come into play to shape citizens' judgment of it. Second, judicial clearance may reinforce citizens' presumption of constitutionality – that is citizens' expectations prior to review that executives act within constitutional bounds – such that clearance does not provide citizens with new information with which to update their evaluations of the executive's action. Importantly, these dynamic should be just as true for strong supporters of the rule of law as it is for weak supporters, as citizens on either end of this spectrum may be expected to focus their evaluations on policy-relevant considerations rather than legal concerns like the rule of law.[37] In these ways, we do not expect that support for the rule of law will

[37] If anything, supporters of the rule of law might have a stronger prior expectation about the constitutionality of their chief executive's actions, which would make the signal sent by judicial clearance yet even less consequential.

make citizens more positively disposed toward executive actions that are cleared through judicial review.

Partisanship

Public support for the rule of law is not, however, the only individual-level dynamic that may plausibly shape the efficacy of judicial review. Given that political elites of all stripes around the world profess support for the rule of law – even as some of them work to undermine it – it might be the case that the public's support for the rule of law is similar puffery. That is, citizens' claim of support for the rule of law may simply reflect them giving "appropriate" answers on a survey that lack a connection to citizens' political behaviors. The public may simply not learn or otherwise know about a government's behavior, muting calls for coordination and thus neutering the threat of punishment for malfeasance. Or the public might be informed of an incumbent's behavior but be unable to discern whether it represents a breach of the government's constitutional obligations. This question is especially challenging since citizens sit at an informational disadvantage when monitoring the actions of an incumbent. And, when a particular incumbent is a personal favorite, instrumental considerations, such as support for the executive and partisanship, might lead citizens to prioritize the pull of partisan concerns over their commitment to democratic norms. These challenges suggest that, despite its importance as a core democratic norm, support for the rule of law may be fundamentally flawed as a democratic guardrail. If so, partisan ties have the distinct potential to stymie the efficacy of judicial review.

The organization of elites and mass publics into parties on the basis of shared interests and political priorities has long been regarded as inevitable and possibly even desirable for the stability and coherency it can bring to politics and political competition (Almond and Verba 1963; Lijphart 1999; Lipset 1963). Nevertheless, recent scholarship underscores the ways in which partisanship can pose a threat to public support for institutions, norms, and procedures and thereby accelerate democratic decay and backsliding (Aarslew 2023; Ahlquist et al. 2018; Carey et al. 2022; Gidengil, Stolle, and Bergeron-Boutin 2022; Mazepus and Toshkov 2022; McCoy and Somer 2021). This emergent concern for partisanship stems from modern trends in autocratization across the globe. Whereas democracies of the twentieth century fell to coups or military takeovers, modern democratic backsliding comes not with a bang but a whimper (Diamond 2018). Broadly popular incumbents ascend to elected office and then deploy the tools of majority rule to incrementally erode the norms and institutions that serve as the guardrails for the constitutional order. What is more, these autocratizing tactics are often met with minimal public outcry or alarm and are instead supported by masses of vociferous partisans who ostensibly support, or minimally do not actively penalize, incumbents for threatening democratic norms and institutions (Cohen et al. 2023; Gidengil,

Stolle, and Bergeron-Boutin 2022; Saikkonen and Christensen 2022; Simonovits, McCoy, and Littvay 2022). Critically, this vibrant body of scholarship challenges the conventional wisdom regarding partisanship's role in democratic accountability and the survival of democratic governance.

These studies have important potential implications for our argument, particularly the potential for the pull of partisanship to complicate citizens' ability to coordinate and impose political costs on incumbents who violate the rule of law.[38] This tension can manifest, for instance, with an overt preference for copartisans and a general mistrust for members of an outgroup party affiliation or tolerance for copartisan elites who transgress legal, institutional, or even constitutional norms and rules (Aarslew 2023; Simonovits, McCoy, and Littvay 2022). In this way, citizens may well understand that a copartisan incumbent's action contradicts the rule of law but nonetheless turn a blind eye to these transgressions or even justify it in the name of a partisan victory (Gidengil, Stolle, and Bergeron-Boutin 2022). While such dynamics may or may not correspond to a decline in public support for democracy itself, they do point to the potential for citizens to prioritize partisanship.[39] This in turn raises the possibility that one's desire for partisan victories supersedes commitment to democratic principles, providing justification for the old adage "for my friends, anything, for my enemies the law" (Graham and Svolik 2020; Krishnarajan 2023; Simonovits, McCoy, and Littvay 2022).[40] Similarly, partisanship can strongly condition support for anti-democratic reforms to undermine the efficacy of institutional constraints as those who do or expect to have their party in power favor expanding executive power even at the expense of democratic values (Albertus and Grossman 2021; Mazepus and Toshkov 2022; Şaşmaz, Yagci, and

[38] Scholars have identified the presence of partisanship undermining public reactions to democratic norms violations across widely divergent political, cultural, and social contexts. An important development in the literature has been the extension of the partisanship theoretical framework to countries that vary from the United States in important ways (Iyengar et al. 2019). This includes the structure of government (Becher and Brouard 2022), the extent of political polarization (Saikkonen and Christensen 2022), and the degree of democratic consolidation and development of party systems and identities (Fossati, Muhtadi, and Warburton 2022). In short, the power of partisan-motivated support for anti-democratic policies appears both substantial and widespread.

[39] Later in the book, we term this perspective the "Partisan Prioritization" account.

[40] Less blatantly egregious violations of democratic norms fare little better – and often worse – when it comes to withstanding the draw of partisanship. Legally questionable actions, such as limits on civil rights and liberties under public safety pretexts, are viewed as more acceptable by copartisans of the governing authority issuing the policies (Graham and Svolik 2020; Simonovits, McCoy, and Littvay 2022). Even breaches of critical democratic norms, like refusing to condemn (or even supporting) political violence may fail to elicit an electoral backlash against copartisan politicians (Saikkonen and Christensen 2022). Of particular concern for democratic vitality is the growing set of findings that citizens are unwilling to punish copartisan politicians when they violate the integrity of electoral systems for their own benefit (Aarslew 2023; Carey et al. 2022; Fossati, Muhtadi, and Warburton 2022).

Ziblatt 2022).[41] In sum, the powerful draw of partisanship poses challenges that are uniquely acute for the rule of law, insofar as it incentivizes the public to tolerate transgressions in the name of partisan victories or for the sake of inflicting losses on political opponents. Fortunately, as we detail in Chapters 7 and 8, we find limited evidence that the core claims advanced in our own theoretical account change in response to such partisan considerations.[42]

SUMMARY

A fundamental task of any political system is to aggregate and filter citizens' conflicting and contradictory beliefs into policies. Political regimes are helped in this process by the formal institutions of government, which Lipset (1963) famously praised for their ability to translate citizens' values into political stability. Insofar as they support consensus while mediating conflict, institutions help to mitigate the paradoxical tension that all political regimes must resolve.

While institutions may check and balance each other as they try to increase their authority at the expense of their peers, the *public* also has an important role to play in incentivizing elites to respect the rule of law. While there should be legal consequences for violating the law, legal consequences alone are not sufficient to reign in power-maximizing politicians. After all, it is difficult to jail or fine presidents or legislators while they are in power; provided they can win elections, their impunity is all but guaranteed. There must be some other, nonlegal, bounds on political power to maintain a stable rule of law tradition. Political consequences, such as a loss of public prestige and a corresponding fall from elected office, can provide those constraints (Tamanaha 2004).

Are there such political consequences for violating the rule of law? Citizens' checks on government are difficult to resolve in a decentralized manner owing to both monitoring and coordination problems. To effectively counteract and constrain the state, citizens must both share a consensus about the limits of legitimate state action and coordinate their political behaviors to demonstrate dissatisfaction in response to state overreach (Weingast 1997).

41 Not all aspects of democracy, however, are equally susceptible to being overwhelmed by the prioritization of partisan attachments. Rather, some studies suggest that citizens' willingness to abide anti-democratic policies is bounded, with violations of some democratic norms and values a bridge too far or only palatable under certain circumstances. Carey et al. (2022), for example, find that "both citizens and donors on either side of the partisan divide punish candidates who violate democratic norms of judicial deference, impartial investigations, and compromise" (232). Similarly, Broockman, Kalla, and Westwood (2023) find that shifts in affective polarization – a key mechanism by which partisanship is theorized to harm democracy – in fact has little effect on support for democratic norms.

42 As we show in those chapters, if anything, it appears that the public at times imposes especially harsh penalties on executive copartisans whose actions contravene the rule of law.

Warning signals sent from broadly respected institutions are one way of making the threat of public sanction credible. As we described above, courts are tasked with the authority to adjudicate state conflicts, and to review statutes and executive actions to ensure compliance with statutory and constitutional prescripts. Approval from an independent court may substantiate the government's claim to legitimate authority and foster broader public acceptance, or a negative signal from a well-respected judicial institution may serve as a fire alarm that alerts the public to contravention of the rule of law.

The efficacy of judicial review in this role is of utmost importance, but it is by no means guaranteed. When an executive transgresses the rule of law, courts can pull a fire alarm (McCubbins and Schwartz 1984), alerting the public to a contravention of constitutional norms or procedures and thereby empowering public enforcement of the rule of law (North and Weingast 1989; Weingast 1997). These institutional signals provide crucial information to citizens trying to monitor governmental actions, alerting them to a potential constitutional transgression and helping them to coordinate with others who might mobilize against executive overreach. The efficacy of these signals might vary based upon the institutional and political context, the type of institution, partisanship, and individual-level support for the rule of law. Throughout this book, we probe each of these factors as we attempt to understand how judicial review might help to uphold the rule of law.

3

How, When, and Where to Evaluate Judicial Efficacy

Having laid out our theoretical framework in Chapter 2, we now turn to the task of describing and justifying our research design. We assess our theory's expectations using survey data from four countries: the United States, Germany, Hungary, and Poland. While inferential challenges motivate us to adopt an experimental approach for many of our analyses, we also consider how these choices come with important limitations to the evidence we can bring to bear in support of our theory.

We begin the chapter with a discussion of comparative research design, focusing on the relative advantages and disadvantages of examining multiple countries rather than a single country or a large number of cases. Similarly, we consider the strengths and weaknesses of using survey experiments to understand citizens' attitudes in relation to the efficacy of judicial review. With these preliminaries out of the way, we introduce the four countries – the United States, Germany, Hungary, and Poland – that serve as the testing ground for our theory.

The theoretical argument that we outlined in Chapter 2 requires us to select countries that vary in their levels of judicial independence. We demonstrate that our selected pairs of countries – Germany alongside the United States and Hungary with Poland – have significant differences in the level of independence enjoyed by their respective constitutional courts. To reinforce this point, we use our survey data to demonstrate that these differences are recognized by citizens in these countries, just as they are by political scientists. We then demonstrate that citizens in the United States and Germany are more likely to expect that their constitutional court could stop an illegal executive action than those in Hungary and Poland, thus providing a sort of baseline test of our theory. In these ways, we also make novel empirical contribution in this chapter by illustrating that expert and lay judgments of judicial independence tend to track each other well.

Having discussed *where* to conduct our study, we turn next to the *when*. The COVID-19 pandemic serves as the backdrop of our research. We argue that the pandemic carried with it a set of desirable research design characteristics for a comparative study. In particular, it was a surprising event that began quickly, affected every country in the world, and presented major challenges for governance. It also created a situation where citizens' support for the rule of law was put to the test as pressing concerns about safety, security, and health came into tension with legal mandates. In placid times, there is often little conflict between respect for the rule of law and citizens' instrumental concerns. But, during the pandemic, these two often came into conflict. In this way, the pandemic presents a difficult test of our theory.

The chapter then turns its attention toward the *type* of data we should collect. In this regard, we highlight two aspects of our research design. First, we acknowledge that our focus on citizens' reactions to a constitutional court's signal necessitates the need for mass public opinion surveys in our selected cases. Second, we discuss the relative limitations of extant observational data and subsequently justify the book's reliance primarily on survey experimental evidence. In doing so, we argue that the unique timing and context of our study mitigates the potential disadvantages of such an approach.

We conclude the chapter by providing important contextual information about our cases. We detail each country's condition with respect to the political environment and national constitutional court, their response to the COVID-19 pandemic, and the political landscape in July 2021 when we collected the majority of our survey data. We also explain how our research design connects with the book's theoretical framework and sets up the ensuing chapters' analyses.

WHAT CASES SHOULD WE PICK?

Scholars of comparative politics vary widely in the number and sort of cases they bring to bear to evaluate their theories. On the one hand, single-case designs allow a researcher to effectively hold constant a myriad of potential confounding factors, such as historical context, culture, institutions, and even social and economic conditions, while also minimizing concerns about measurement "drift" that can occur when the same concept is measured in very different political contexts (Pepinsky 2019). Yet single or small-N research designs raise important generalizability concerns, particularly as it is difficult to know how the empirical patterns observed in a given case generalize across contexts. This is vital for critically evaluating our theory, which requires variation in constitutional court independence. While we could, in principle, test our theory within a single country over time as that country's level of judicial independence changes, we expect that a variety of external political factors would change alongside judicial independence and thus make it difficult to assess the specific impact of our theorized mechanism.

An alternative approach is to use a large, cross-national research design that enables researchers to identify generalizable statistical relationships that transcend context-specific factors while retaining external validity (Ariely and Davidov 2012; Jackman 1985). Yet these designs face their own set of challenges. For one, they raise questions about measurement equivalence across contexts. For another, ensuring that experimental designs are internally valid across contexts presents a formidable challenge of design. From a more practical perspective, deploying comparable surveys in a large number of cases can be prohibitively resource intensive.

Such challenges are made all the more acute by our focus on the rule of law. As we detail in Chapter 4, although the rule of law is a concept deployed in a wide variety of claims and contexts, systematic measurements of the public's support thereof have been few and far between. What reliable data exists has been, for the most part, concentrated in public opinion studies that center on the United States and undertaken by a small handful of authors (e.g., Gibson 2007a). Coupling this lack of well-vetted preexisting measures with the complex nature of support for the rule of law, we set our aims more modestly by measuring and carefully validating this concept in a handful of countries.

With these considerations in mind, we adopt an approach of selecting four cases with intention for our study. Doing so allows us to integrate positive aspects from both single country and large cross-national research designs while also ameliorating their respective limitations. For instance, the analysis of multiple cases allows us to observe variation in judicial independence and to draw comparisons about the efficacy of judicial review both in contexts where judicial institutions are poised to issue credible decisions and in contexts where the courts are broadly perceived to be compromised. Similarly, drawing from more than one case enhances the external validity and generalizability of our findings, particularly to the extent that we identify variation in institutional features or structures that might otherwise present a concern for potential confounding. Moreover, focusing on four cases gives us the opportunity to provide greater depth to our analyses, as we can more carefully consider how the key concepts in our theoretical account manifest in each country, thus enhancing the internal validity of our findings. Lastly, we note that this approach facilitates the collection of valid, comparable data across countries such that we are able to field identical surveys and experiments in each of the four countries we consider. This approach exploits the fact that our surveys were fielded as simultaneous crises occurred during the COVID-19 pandemic. In adopting this approach, our research design draws from a long tradition of research that has intentionally selected a set of cases to evaluate theoretical expectations (Almond and Verba 1963; Schmitter 2009).

Variation in Judicial Independence

Given the theory outlined in Chapter 2, we need to identify cases that are both theoretically relevant and at least unbiased toward, if not biased against, finding empirical evidence that supports our argument. Furthermore, we ought to intentionally leverage similarities and differences between cases to address potential challenges to making valid inferences. This means, for one, taking into account country-level confounding factors, which can be addressed by including cases that provide variation on such characteristics. It also directs us to consider the traits that we might want our cases to share in order to effectively hold these variables constant.

As our theory emphasizes the link between judicial review and citizens' attitudes, an implicit scope condition – and therefore critical consideration for case selection – is the presence of democratic institutions. Where judicial review does not exist, there are simply no signals from courts for citizens to interpret. For example, would-be oversight institutions in some nondemocratic regimes lack the legal or political power to render decisions related to the propriety of government actions. Even in authoritarian regimes with the ostensible trappings of democracy – an increasingly frequent occurrence – political participation is typically heavily regulated and curtailed such that citizens are preempted from providing a credible threat of political costs on elites who break the law. As such, we exclude autocratic regimes from our case selection criteria.[1]

From this point of departure, we turn to integrating three aspects of our theoretical framework – judicial independence, judicial review, and citizens' support for the rule of law – into our case selection. As we theorized in Chapter 2, a critical conditioning factor on the efficacy of judicial decisions as signals is the source credibility of courts, which we expect corresponds to judicial independence. With this in mind, we selected cases for our study with an eye for introducing country-level variation in the judicial independence of the country's constitutional court. Specifically, we sought to include countries with both high and low levels of judicial independence to evaluate the extent to which the public is more or less receptive to signals sent by courts with varying levels of credibility. We can also – considering individual-level variation in public support for the rule of law – observe how people with strong (or weak) support for the rule of law respond differently to the decisions of an independent court.

Having identified the forms of institutional variation we seek, we can further consider the facets of political culture and citizens' attitudes most relevant for our theory. Our focus on public support for the rule of law as a conditioning factor directs us to consider this aspect of countries' political environment. We do so in a few ways. First, countries with high levels of judicial independence and particularly strong norms surrounding public support for the rule of law may present difficult tests for our theory, as citizens in such contexts may be less likely to need judicial signals to identify executive malfeasance and coordinate their collective response. Second, in places where constitutional courts

[1] Although beyond the scope of what we do here, renewed recent scholarly attention to authoritarian institutions (Meng, Paine, and Powell 2023; Svolik 2012), including courts (Harvey 2022; Moustafa 2014), raises the question of judicial efficacy in such contexts as a potentially fruitful and interesting path for future research.

have low levels of judicial independence, citizens still ought to have a familiarity with the rule of law as a concept, even if they do not necessarily express substantial support for it. As we seek to conduct comparisons across countries, it is critical that citizens in each of our cases share this basic understanding of the rule of law. As such, we desire cases with a broadly shared tradition when it comes to democratic norms like the rule of law, even if those norms are not equally enforced or honored.

From these criteria, we identified four countries for our study: the United States, Germany, Hungary, and Poland. Each case was selected, in part, for the characteristics brought to our study. But we also selected these countries for the attributes they bring as a group. Our cases include two of the most established democracies (Germany and the United States), alongside two of the most prominent cases of democratic backsliding in recent history (Hungary and Poland).

As a group, the four countries share several important characteristics. First, the political structures of all four are based on the liberal democratic tradition, with the guarantee of citizens' rights enshrined in constitutions and – at least in theory – enforced by checks like constitutional review. Moreover, three of our cases – Germany, Poland, and Hungary – are members of the European Union and signatories to the European Convention on Human Rights, indicating at least a shared vocabulary of democratic norms and rights like the rule of law. Taken together with the United States – a country with a long tradition of veneration for such norms (Gibson 2007a) – our set of cases are well positioned for comparing the linkage between the efficacy of judicial review and support for the rule of law.

Second, we have selected four countries with broadly similar socioeconomic profiles. All four are Organisation for Economic Co-operation and Development (OECD) countries, with relatively high levels of wealth and economic development. While Germany and the United States rank ahead of both Poland and Hungary by most economic metrics, the latter two nonetheless are generally wealthy countries with per capita gross domestic products (GDPs) that rank similarly to other European Union (EU) countries like Spain and Estonia. This allows us to essentially account for the potential impact of such factors on the presence and strength of key features of our theory, such as the rule of law and judicial independence.

Third, the COVID-19 pandemic presented an unforeseen and universally experienced shock to the status quo, and the resulting threats to the rule of law we study were experienced simultaneously throughout the globe. This broadly shared experience presents a unique opportunity for us to conduct comparisons across all four cases using realistic hypothetical scenarios that are understood across national contexts. That is, the geopolitical, legal, and socioeconomic similarities of our four cases, coupled with facing the same fundamental challenge of confronting the pandemic, gives us a unique platform on which to build our research design.

Importantly, the cases also diverge on several important dimensions. As we noted earlier, a concern with limiting our analyses to a single country was the potential influence the political system's organization might have on the generalizability of our findings. Therefore, our cases span the three major forms of democratic systems. The United States represents the presidential form of democracy with its formal separation of powers between the legislative and executive branches. On the other end of the spectrum, Germany and Hungary's systems of parliamentary democracy provide cases of fused legislative and executive power. Poland, with its semi-presidential system, provides an useful comparison point to span institutional arrangements between the pure presidential and pure parliamentary poles. Notably, this variation in political system cuts across our classifications of low and high levels of judicial independence.

Having identified our four cases, we turn now to justifying their selection. To do so we begin by verifying the key distinction our theoretical framework demands: the level of judicial independence. In the following sections, we examine expert judgments of judicial independence, demonstrating both where our countries fall in the spectrum of independent courts worldwide and the stability of judicial independence in our four countries over time. Then, we turn to survey data to validate a key assumption of our theory: not only do experts see variation in judicial independence, but *citizens* recognize it too.

Expert Judgments of Judicial Independence

We first need to verify that the United States and Germany are countries with high levels of judicial independence and Hungary and Poland are countries with low levels of judicial independence. To do so, we turn to data from the Varieties of Democracy (V-Dem) project. While there are many competing measures of judicial independence (Ríos-Figueroa and Staton 2014; van Dijk 2024), the V-Dem measure combines expert judgements into a single numerical country-year score, which is a widely accepted measure of the concept.

We consider high court independence in 2021, the year of our study. The top panel of Figure 3.1 plots the V-Dem measure of high court independence for each country. To assess this concept, V-Dem asks experts: "When the high court in the judicial system is ruling in cases that are salient to the government, how often would you say that it makes decisions that merely reflect government wishes regardless of its sincere view of the legal record?" The figure shows the location of our four countries (dark gray bars) in comparison to the other high courts worldwide (light gray bar) to give a sense of where our four countries fall in the distribution of judicial independence and, relative to their global peers, and to each other. As shown in the top panel, Hungary and Poland both score on the negative end of the judicial independence scale, scoring −.74 and −.40, well below the global mean of .34. Both countries are in the second quartile of the distribution of global data, putting them on par with

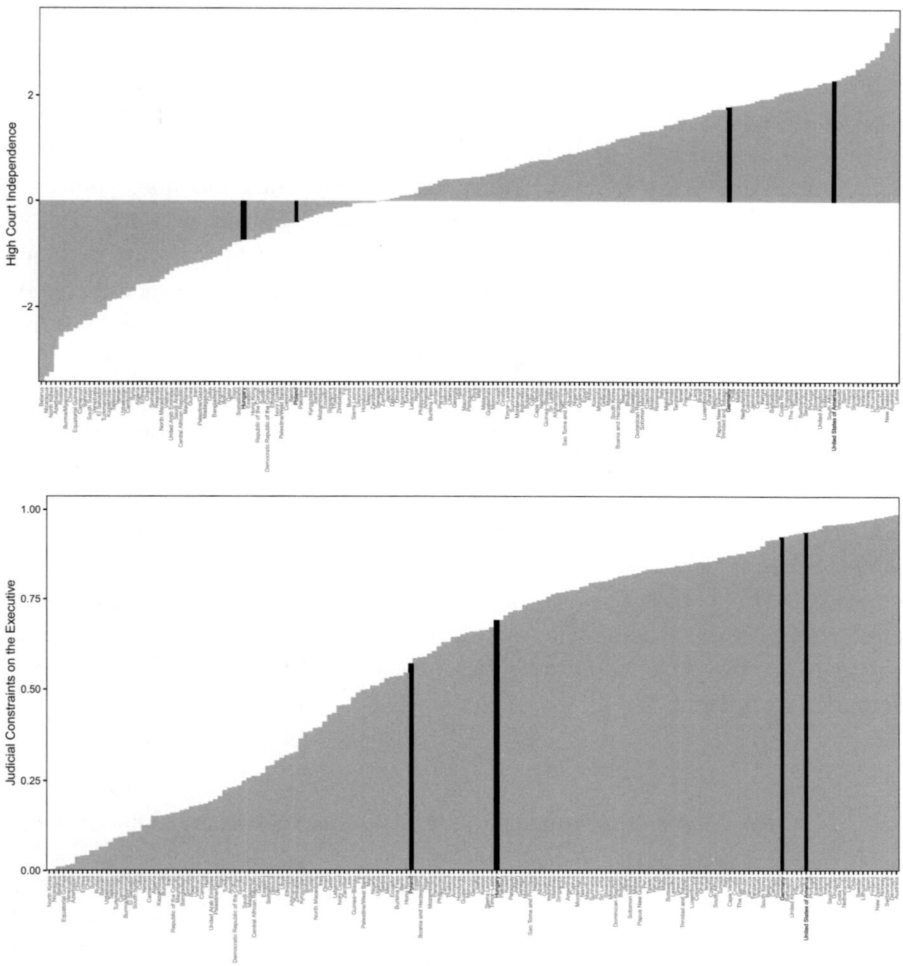

FIGURE 3.1 Global distribution of judicial independence and judicial constraints on the executive in 2021. The black bars in each panel illustrate the location of our four countries in the global distribution of V-Dem's measure of high court independence (top panel) and judicial constraints on the executive (bottom panel). The former is defined as "When the high court in the judicial system is ruling in cases that are salient to the government, how often would you say that it makes decisions that merely reflect government wishes regardless of its sincere view of the legal record?" The latter is defined as "To what extent does the executive respect the constitution and comply with court rulings, and to what extent is the judiciary able to act in an independent fashion?"

countries such as conflict-stricken Sudan, electoral democracies like Iraq and Bolivia where the rule of law and institutions are nevertheless precarious, and consolidated autocracies such as Qatar and Cuba. The United States and Germany, by contrast, are on the high end of the global scale of high court independence, scoring 2.31 and 1.80, respectively. This puts the United States at the 90th percentile of cases globally, and Germany above the 75th.

A related concept, shown in the lower panel of Figure 3.1, is V-Dem's measure of judicial constraints on the executive. Here, V-Dem asks expert coders "To what extent does the executive respect the constitution and comply with court rulings, and to what extent is the judiciary able to act in an independent fashion?" Here, we see our cases conform to a similar pattern: Poland and Hungary are ranked in the lower half of the worldwide data while both Germany and the United States are scored consistently at the high end of this scale. The V-Dem data suggest that both pairs of countries have relatively similar levels of judicial independence, but the pairs starkly diverge on that dimension as well.

What about the temporal stability of judicial independence in these four countries? Figure 3.2, plots the V-Dem scores for each country for high court independence (left-hand panel) and judicial constraints on the executive (right-hand panel) over time, from 2016 to 2022 (Coppedge et al. 2023). Evident in both panels is the extent to which judicial independence has remained robust in Germany and the United States, even in the face of challenges to democratic norms and institutions in recent years. In contrast, Poland – and even more so Hungary – have experienced prodigious declines on both indicators. Later in this chapter, we discuss the political environments that have led to these major declines in the independence of both countries' high courts.

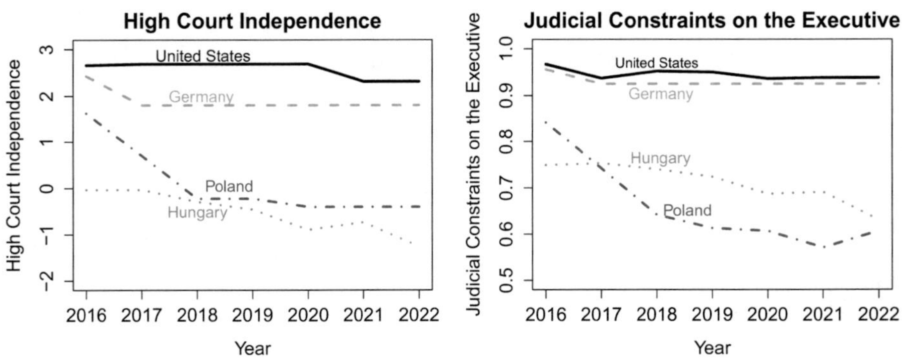

FIGURE 3.2 Temporal trends in judicial independence and judicial constraints on the executive in four countries. The left-hand panel plots the V-Dem measure of high court independence from 2016 to 2022; the right-hand panel plots V-Dem's measure of judicial constraints on the executive over the same time period. The former is defined as "When the high court in the judicial system is ruling in cases that are salient to the government, how often would you say that it makes decisions that merely reflect government wishes regardless of its sincere view of the legal record?" The latter is defined as "To what extent does the executive respect the constitution and comply with court rulings, and to what extent is the judiciary able to act in an independent fashion?"

Public Perceptions of Judicial Independence

Data on the level of judicial independence enjoyed by the four countries in our studies is informative about how academics and experts judge the level of influence other branches of government have over these countries' judicial systems. But the theory outlined in Chapter 2 has emphasized the *public's* judgments of judicial independence. Therefore, we need to understand how the independence of our four countries' high courts varies in the eyes of our survey respondents.

To this end, we asked respondents a series of questions related to the perceived independence of their constitutional court. Each question examines the public's perceptions of judicial independence from a slightly different perspective. Together, this series of questions helps us to ensure – as required by our case selection criteria – that Americans and Germans judge their constitutional court as independent, while Hungarians and Poles generally see their constitutional court as inexorably linked to the executive.

To begin, we posed a simple question to respondents in all four countries: "Thinking about the [Country] government, how much do you agree with the following statement: 'In practice, the [Constitutional Court] is actually independent from the [Executive] and [Legislature].'" We used the proper name of the constitutional court (e.g., US Supreme Court), executive (e.g., Chancellor), and legislature (e.g., Sjem) in each country. The question was fielded in the United States and Germany as part of our February 2021 surveys; we asked the question in Poland and Hungary in July 2021.

Figure 3.3 shows the distribution of responses across the four countries. Overall, we see a strong divergence between our pairs of countries. In the United States, a near majority – 47 percent of respondents – agreed with the statement that the US Supreme Court is independent with 31 percent of respondents disagreeing. The number was higher in Germany where 68 percent of respondents indicated that the Federal Constitutional Court is independent from the other branches of government, while only 15 percent of Germans disagreed with that statement. In Hungary and Poland, where we expected citizens' perceptions of judicial independence to be lower, this relationship is reversed: 32 percent of Hungarian respondents and 31 percent of Polish respondents agreed that their constitutional court is independent, while 54 percent of Hungarians and 57 percent of Poles disagreed with this characterization. Thus, the publics across these two country pairs diverge in their assessments of high court independence.

We acknowledge, though, that this question's wording has two major weaknesses. First, it asks about independence vis-à-vis both the executive and legislature while our main interest is in independence from the executive branch. It may be the case that including both other branches of government in the question stem clouds respondents' responses in a way where asking only about the executive would not. Second, this question wording uses "independent" directly, and respondents may be

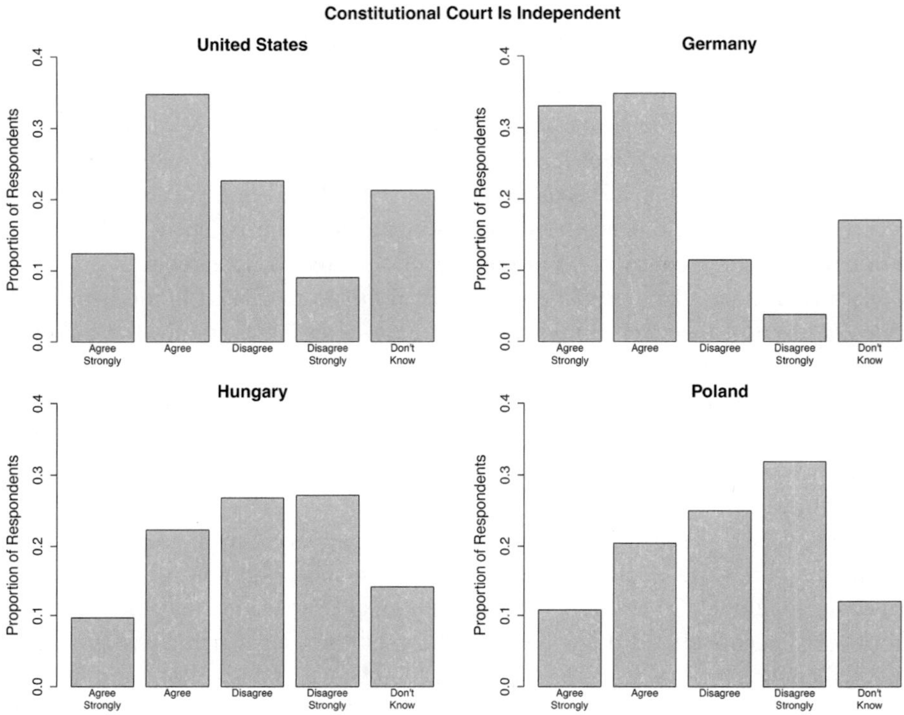

FIGURE 3.3 Perceptions of constitutional court independence from the executive and legislative branches. Each panel plots responses to the following item: "Thinking about the [Country] government, how much do you agree with the following statement: 'In practice, the [Constitutional Court] is actually independent from the [Executive] and [Legislature]?'"

unfamiliar with the concept of judicial independence (especially those respondents with lower levels of political sophistication) (Driscoll and Nelson 2024).

To this end, we asked respondents in all four countries to weigh in on a simpler question, modified from one used by Annenberg, in July 2021: "To what extent do you think the [Executive] influences the rulings that [Constitutional Court] makes?" This question asks about judicial independence in a way that does not use a term of art (referencing general "influence") and asks only about the executive. In each country, we used the title of the national executive and the constitutional court.

The responses in the country pairs, shown in Figure 3.4 are mirror images of one another. In the United States and Germany, a minority of respondents (38 percent and 35 percent, respectively) indicated that the executive influences the constitutional court to a "great" or "moderate" extent. In Hungary and Poland, by contrast, more than two-thirds of the respondents (70 percent and 67 percent, respectively) responded similarly. The responses to the most extreme category – those who

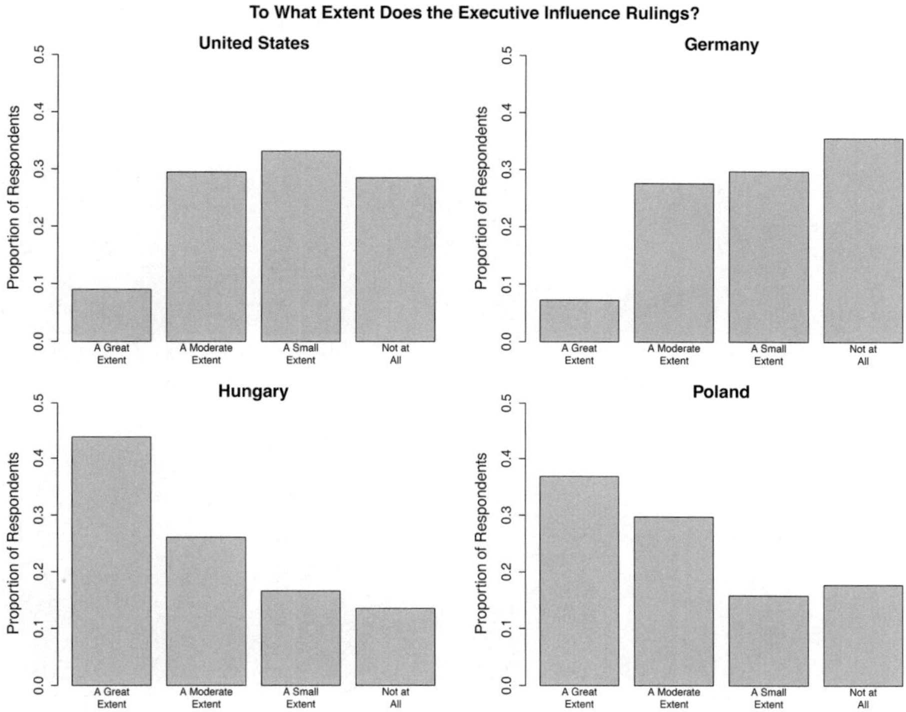

FIGURE 3.4 Perceived level of executive influence on constitutional court decisions. Each panel plots responses to the following item: "To what extent do you think the [Executive] influences the rulings that [Constitutional Court] makes?"

indicated that the executive influences the constitutional court's rulings to a great extent – is particularly instructive. Nine percent of Americans and 7 percent of Germans fall into this category, compared to 44 percent of Hungarians and 37 percent of Poles. Clearly, respondents in our country pairs judge the judicial independence of their constitutional court very differently.

As a third data point, we asked respondents about the level of influence the executive has over their constitutional court, again in July 2021. Specifically, we asked: "Do you think the [Executive] has too much, too little, or about the right amount of influence over the [Constitutional Court]?" The responses are shown in Figure 3.5. Again, we see a stark difference: 27 percent of Americans and 16 percent of Germans indicated that the executive had too much influence over the constitutional court while more than three-fifths of Hungarians and Poles gave the same response. By contrast, supermajorities of Americans and Germans (63 percent and 68 percent) responded that the executive's level of influence over the constitutional court was "about right," while only 30 percent of Hungarians and 25 percent of Poles responded in kind. Importantly, these divisions are not driven by large cross-country differences in respondents' beliefs that the executive needs *more* control over their

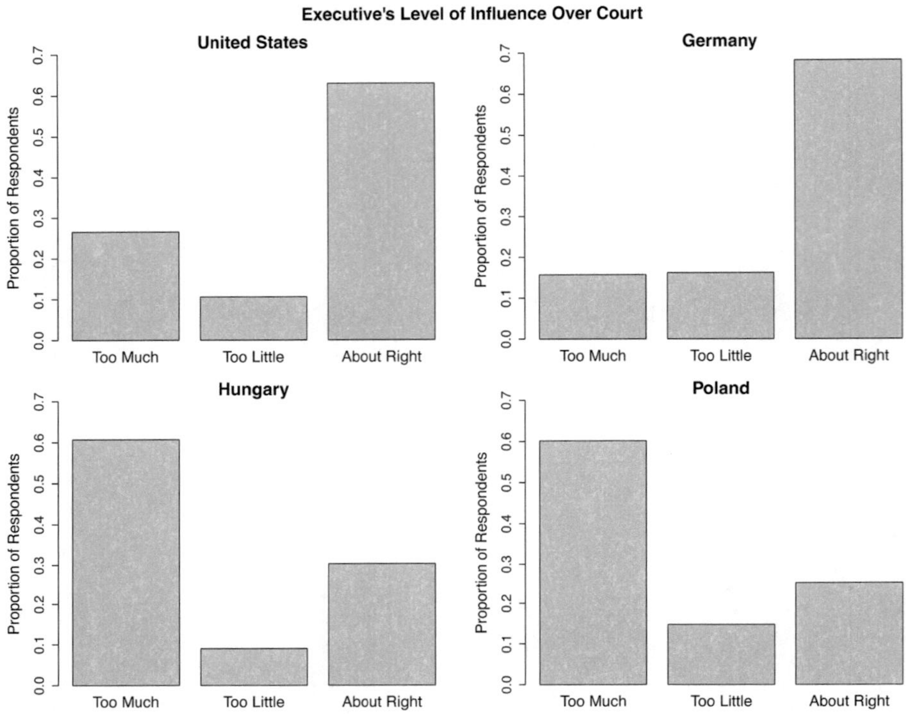

FIGURE 3.5 Perceived appropriateness of executive influence over the constitutional court. Each panel plots responses to the following item: "Do you think the [Executive] has too much, too little, or about the right amount of influence over the [Constitutional Court]?"

country's constitutional court; these responses range from 9 percent in Hungary to 16 percent in Germany.

Another way to understand judicial independence is to consider what the constitutional court would do if the executive oversteps their constitutional bounds. Here, To this end, we asked – using a question included on World Justice Project surveys – respondents to consider the following situation: "Imagine that one day in the future, the [Executive] decides to adopt a policy that is clearly against the [Country] constitution. How likely is it that the [Constitutional Court] would be able to stop the [Executive]'s illegal action?" The respondents selected a response on a four-point scale ranging from "Very Likely" to "Very Unlikely." To put responses in context, we asked respondents the same prompt asking also about the "the people." The ordering of these questions was randomized.

The percentage of respondents who answered that it is "very likely" or "likely" that the court or the public could stop the executive is plotted in Figure 3.6. We see a sharp distinction in beliefs that the constitutional court could stop the executive between our country pairs: 72 percent of Americans and 81 percent of Germans

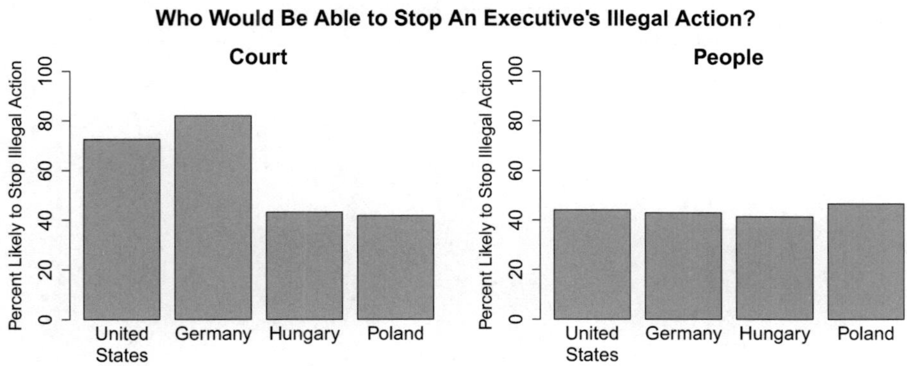

FIGURE 3.6 Perceptions of judicial and public efficacy in the face of executive overreach. Each panel plots responses to the following item: "Imagine that one day in the future, the [Executive] decides to adopt a policy that is clearly against the [Country] constitution. How likely is it that the [Constitutional Court/People] would be able to stop the [Executive]'s illegal action?"

indicated it was likely that their constitutional court could stop the executive; 43 percent of Hungarians and 41 percent of Poles responded similarly. Importantly, these distinctions disappear when we ask respondents about their belief in the efficacy of the public. The respondents across all four countries were relatively pessimistic about the ability of citizens to stop an executive who flouts the law. In no country did a majority of respondents give an affirmative answer to this item; the responses in all four countries hovered between 41 percent and 47 percent.[2]

Before concluding, we rule out an important alternative possibility: is it the case that citizens in our four countries have different preferences about the normatively desirable level of judicial independence? To assess this possibility, we asked respondents the following question: "Thinking about the [Country] government, how much do you agree with the following statement: 'In theory, the [Constitutional Court] should be independent from the [Executive] and [Legislature].'"

Figure 3.7 displays the distribution of responses across country. Across all four countries, a supermajority of respondents indicated that judicial independence is normatively desirable. The percentage of respondents who agreed with that statement ranges from 75 percent in the United States to 84 percent in Poland. The range of disagreement is even smaller across our four countries, ranging from 8 percent in Hungary to 11 percent in Poland. Ten percent of American and German respondents indicated that they disagreed with the sentiment that the constitutional court should be independent from the executive and legislative

[2] Forty-four percent of Americans, 43 percent of Germans, 41 percent of Hungarians, and 47 percent of Poles replied that it was "very likely" or "likely" that the public could stop an executive pursuing an unconstitutional action.

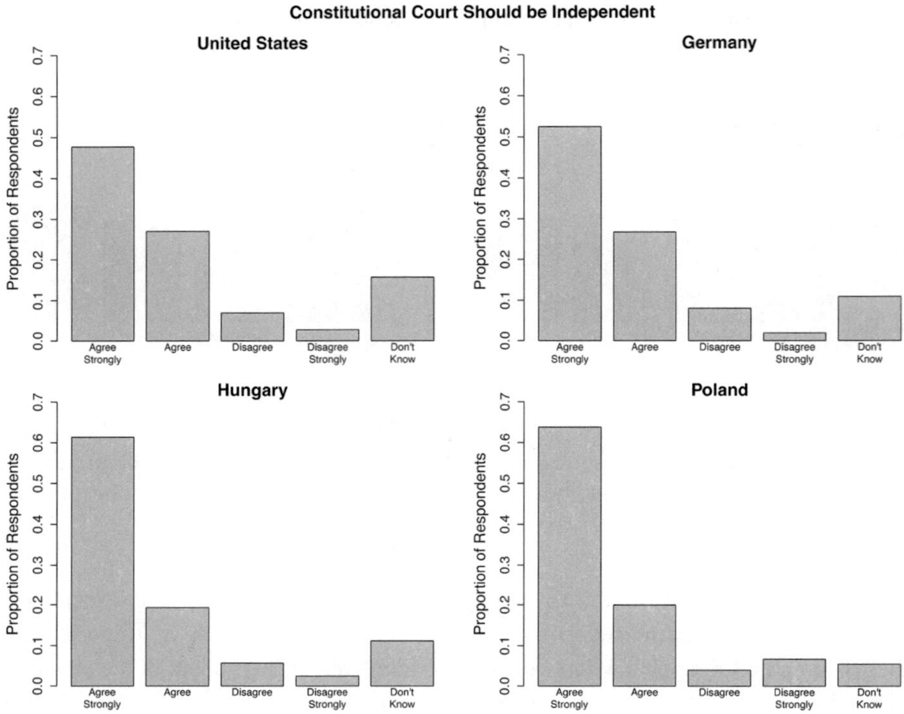

FIGURE 3.7 Public judgments of the normative desirability of judicial independence. Each panel plots responses to the following item: "In theory, the [Constitutional Court] should be independent from the [Executive] and [Legislature]," by country.

branches. Thus, though we observe marked differences in respondents' perceptions of judicial independence across our country pairs, all four countries are unified in their sentiment that judicial independence is desirable (Gandur, Chewning and Driscoll 2025).

Comparing Expert and Public Judgments of Independence

How do citizens' perceptions of judicial independence compare to those of scholars and academics? We return to the V-Dem data described earlier and compare those measures to a question that has been asked multiple times on Eurobarometer surveys over the past two decades: "From what you know, how would you rate the justice system in [Country] in terms of the independence of courts and judges? Would you say it is very good, fairly good, fairly bad, or very bad?" Because we fielded our surveys in 2021, we rely on V-Dem estimates from 2021 and estimates from Flash Eurobarometer 489, which was in the field in March–April 2021.[3]

[3] Importantly, the report accompanying this Eurobarometer notes that citizens' perceptions of judicial independence have "remained stable" since 2020 (3).

Overall, more than half of EU citizens positively rate judicial independence in their country: 9 percent of Europeans say judicial independence in their country is "very good" and 45 percent say it is "fairly good." Only 12 percent of EU citizens say that judicial independence in their country is "very bad." There is a large amount of heterogeneity across countries. For example, 83 percent of Austrians and Finns rate judicial independence in their country positively, while only 17 percent of Croatians and 28 percent of Slovakians do the same. Looking at our countries, 80 percent of Germans, 29 percent of Poles, and 40 percent of Hungarians gave a positive assessment of judicial independence in their country.

Some notes about the wording of this question are in order. First, as noted above, it is possible that citizens have different perceptions of what the "independence" of courts means. Second, this question asks about the independence of the "justice system." The V-Dem constraints on the executive measure assesses "To what extent does the executive respect the constitution and comply with court rulings, and to what extent is the judiciary able to act in an independent fashion?" – referring to the judiciary broadly – while the measure of the V-Dem measure of high court independence we employ assesses the independence of the constitutional court specifically. Recall that all the questions we have discussed previously in this section refer directly to the constitutional court, like the V-Dem independence measure. Still, that this question directly assesses citizens' perceptions of judicial independence and is available for all countries in the Eurobarometer makes it appropriate for our purposes.

Figure 3.8 plots the relationship between the two V-Dem measures and the Eurobarometer's perceived independence question, by country. It is clear in both figures that there is a positive relationship between expert measures and citizens' perceptions of judicial independence. The correlation between the Eurobarometer answers and the V-Dem measures of judicial constraints on the executive is $r = 0.50$, and the relationship between the public opinion survey and V-Dem's judicial independence measure is $r = 0.53$.[4] In other words, the measures are positively associated with one another, but not overwhelmingly so.

There are also several notable countries where citizens' and scholars' perceptions of judicial independence are out of sync. For both V-Dem measures, the four countries with the highest residuals from a simple linear model are Croatia, Italy, Slovakia, and Spain. In Slovakia, for example, the V-Dem measures of judicial independence are both above the mean (0.92 for the country's mean on the constraints measure compared to an EU mean of 0.88; 2.43 on the independence measure compared to an EU mean of 1.74) while only 28 percent of citizens responded favorably about the country's level of judicial independence on the

[4] In simple linear regressions, Eurobarometer $= -28.8 + 95.7\times$ Constraints and Eurobarometer $= 37.9 + 10.3 \times$ Independence. Both V-Dem measures are statistically significant at $p < 0.01$ in their respective regression models.

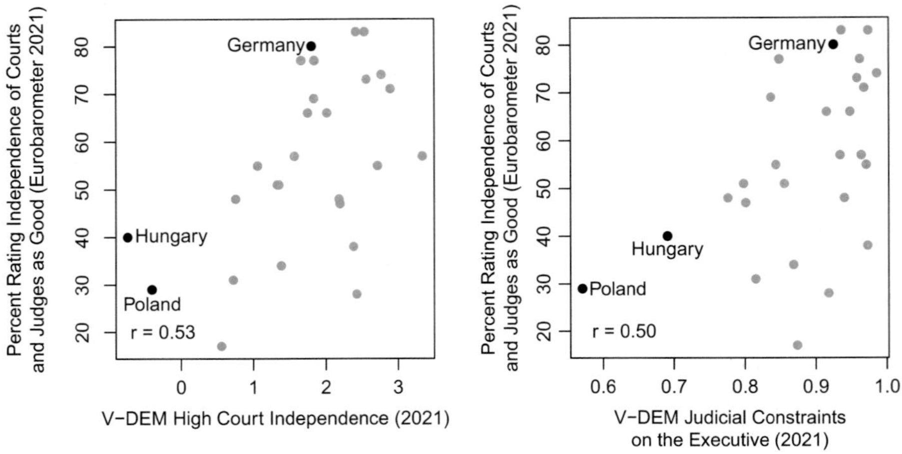

FIGURE 3.8 Comparing expert and public judgments of judicial independence. The panels plot the country-level relationship between 2021 Eurobarometer data on perceived judicial independence (the percent of respondents giving positive answers to the following question: "From what you know, how would you rate the justice system in [Country] in terms of the independence of courts and judges?") and V-Dem measures of high court independence (right-hand panel) and judicial constraints on the executive (right-hand panel).

Eurobarometer. Similarly, Spain also rates above the EU mean on both V-Dem measures (0.97 and 2.38 for constraints and independence, respectively), while only 38 percent of Spaniards provided a positive evaluation on the Eurobarometer. In short, perceived judicial independence is related to expert measures of judicial independence. But they are not the same thing.

From our analysis of V-Dem data and our survey responses, we make two major conclusions. First, expert judgments place the United States and Germany as countries with a high level of judicial independence, and Hungary and Poland are widely considered to have low levels of judicial independence. Second, across a range of survey questions, we find that the mass public in our four countries also perceive these distinctions, though these differences are not due to variation in the normative desirability of judicial independence across the four cases. While far from definitive, we count the data in this section as compelling initial validation of our case selection.

WHEN SHOULD WE CONDUCT OUR STUDY?

A critical global event set the stage that enabled our research: the COVID-19 pandemic. The first case of SARS-CoV-2 infection was reported in December of 2019 in Wuhan, China, when a patient reported to a hospital presenting with symptoms akin to pneumonia. The patient tested negative for influenza, adenoviruses, tuberculosis, and all other common respiratory ailments, and conventional medical interventions yielded no appreciable improvement (Wu et al. 2020). Medical practitioners quickly realized that the virus causing these symptoms was not well known to the medical community, and research scientists later confirmed that it was, in fact, a new strain of SARS-like coronavirus that had previously only been observed in bats (Zhou et al. 2020). Not only did this virus fail to respond to conventional treatments; it was lethal and highly contagious. As infections multiplied and overwhelmed hospitals, Chinese authorities imposed city lockdowns, closing first municipal, then state, and finally national borders in an attempt to contain the spread of the virus. Within weeks, outbreaks were seen in the Middle East, Europe, and North America. Soon, the COVID-19 virus became an omnipresent threat to mortality for billions of people across the planet.

No aspect of everyday life was left untouched. Beyond the hundreds of millions of infections and millions of deaths caused by the virus, the pandemic wrought unprecedented social and economic havoc. Millions of jobs disappeared overnight, and stock markets cratered. More mundane aspects of life were also thrown into upheaval to no less devastating effect. People were unable to see their family or loved ones or gather for social events. In many cases, trying to go to a restaurant or to a friend's home for dinner would risk legal or governmental repercussions. Most public spaces – schools, transport, libraries, community centers, union halls, recreation centers, and many private businesses – were precipitously shuttered as people were told to stay home and to maintain a regimen of strict "social distancing."

Governments' efforts to limit the human and economic impact of the COVID-19 pandemic were similarly unprecedented. Some of the first policy responses involved travel restrictions, particularly from China where the virus originated. On January 31, 2020, the Trump administration in the United States barred travelers from China. By mid-March, all travelers from the European Union were refused entry into the country. Many other countries pursued similar policies; New Zealand went so far as to completely close its borders to all foreigners in February 2020.[5] This was followed quickly by policies restricting the size of gatherings and ability of citizens to leave their homes in what became known as lockdowns. In March 2020, the German government announced a partial lockdown in which businesses like restaurants, daycares, and cinemas were closed and public gatherings heavily restricted (Bosen and Thurau 2021). Similarly, many governments closed or severely limited public infrastructure like schools and transportation.[6]

Our research leverages the pandemic's unique political and social conditions to our analytical benefit. First, the theory we have outlined in Chapter 2 demands cross-national testing. An issue with any cross-national research design is the extent

5 It was not until February 2022 – two years later – that New Zealand reopened its borders.

6 On the other end of the spectrum, in some instances executives appeared to "underreach" as they failed – or refused – to take meaningful action (Pozen and Scheppele 2020). While an important concern in its own right, we are more concerned here with the risk of overreach.

to which the policy and political stakes are comparable across countries. The global nature of the pandemic provides a near-universal contextualization of these stakes; every country in the world had to quickly develop a policy and public health response to the pandemic. As a result, threats to the rule of law were broadly felt around the world. For example, mask-wearing requirements (and problems with compliance) evoked similar controversies and backlash across borders (Al Jazeera 2020; El Español 2020; Terrel 2020; Wright 2020), and rumors of fast-tracked vaccines fueled vaccine skepticism in the United States, United Kingdom, and many other countries (Spring 2021). The shared experiences of citizens around the globe facilitate a similar understanding of survey questions across countries. And, because countries around the world were experimenting with similar policies (albeit in different ways), the pandemic conditions made it possible to construct internally and externally valid experimental vignettes that are similarly comparable across countries.

Second, our research is concerned with citizens' (and courts') ability to constrain the state. The threat to public health created by the pandemic brought the proper boundaries of state power into stark relief, creating potential opportunities for the expansion of state power.[7] The pandemic demanded swift action by governments to contain the virus and protect public health, and the laborious legislative process in most countries was outpaced by the ability of executives to act unilaterally. As a result, many of the most salient policies to contain the virus were put into practice by executives, rather than legislatures.

As Gibson (2007a) observed, if you merely ask people if they support the rule of law, they will almost always answer in the affirmative. Knowing whether, on a typical day when adherence to the rule of law is not under threat, people support the rule of law does not help us understand the conditions under which citizens will act to constrain the state. Instead, what is important is how citizens respond when they face real and important trade-offs between their own instrumental concerns and adherence to the rule of law. As the Council of Europe's Venice Commission – which focuses on the rule of law and human rights – explained, the pandemic created this tension in countries around the globe as it posed risks to democracy and the rule of law:

> Due to the pandemic, states are faced with the difficult task of having to find a balance between fundamental freedoms and principles of democratic decision-making on the one hand, and (prevention of the risk to) health policies and positive obligations that flow from the right to life as well as the necessity to effectively end this health crisis, on the other (Alivizatos et al. 2000, 4).

Governments were forced to determine how they would balance these potentially competing concerns during a rapidly evolving – and often deteriorating – political,

7 As an example of this sort of dynamic, Krehbiel and Cheruvu (2021) found that concern created by the pandemic corresponded with greater support for a more powerful European Union.

economic, and public health emergency. The scale and severity of the threat posed by the pandemic crystallized these potential costs for citizens as they directly confronted the risks associated with contracting COVID-19 and the pandemic policies enacted by their governments. That is, the material costs of balancing public health with democratic rules and norms like the rule of law were real and proximate for citizens. It is this tension that our research design leverages to evaluate the efficacy of judicial signals.

Third, we are most interested in the public's response to constitutional courts' use of judicial review. We therefore need a setting in which constitutional courts in various countries were passing judgment on similar policies. Fortunately for our research design, the pandemic put courts (and their power of judicial review) in an important position to constrain executive power. Pandemic policies often raised important legal and constitutional questions which found their way into the courts. Lockdown restrictions in many countries, for example, were challenged as exceeding government authority and unconstitutional. In the United States alone, courts issued more than 1,000 rulings on the legality of pandemic orders and regulations (Parmet and Khalik 2023). Similarly, the German Constitutional Court and Polish Constitutional Tribunal both received a considerable number of constitutional complaints from citizens against their countries' pandemic restrictions (Hestermeyer 2020; Tilles 2021).[8] At the international level, the European Court of Human Rights and the Court of Justice of the European Union rendered decisions on the conformity of pandemic restrictions with the European Convention on Human Rights and European Union treaties, respectively. In short, the judiciary became a critical venue for the oversight of executives' pandemic policies.

In these respects, the unfortunate presence of the global pandemic provides notable research design advantages. The COVID-19 pandemic provides a rare but near-universal event that created material and proximate threats to the rule of law in countries around the world. The pandemic required swift action, providing opportunities for executives to act unilaterally and for constitutional courts to review the legality of these new policies. These policies raised important tensions for everyday citizens, pitting their abstract support for the rule of law against their instrumental concerns for freedom of movement, good health, and personal economic situation. This tension was – importantly – common across boarders in ways that facilitate cross-national research.

At the same time, we are cognizant that – hopefully! – the COVID-19 pandemic was a once-in-a-generation event. A skeptic might suggest that, whatever the usefulness of the pandemic to facilitate cross-national comparisons, our focus on an

[8] Perhaps unsurprisingly given the state of judicial independence and access to constitutional review in the country, the Hungarian Constitutional Court was an exception to this trend of judicializing challenges to pandemic policies as the Court has primarily been a means of legitimizing government policies by upholding them when challenged (Kovács 2021).

admittedly rare event raises challenges to the generalizability of our findings. Are our analyses a reflection of this highly ideosyncratic event, or might they yield more general insights into our theoretical framework?

Our response to this critique is twofold. First, while the pandemic was indeed unique, the underlying tension between the scope of state power and the imperative to protect citizens – in this case from a virus – transcends the specific context of the COVID-19 pandemic. In this sense, we see the conditions created by the pandemic – at least as they are most relevant for our analyses – as exacerbating the monitoring and coordination challenges that citizens face as they try to constrain the state. With regard to monitoring, the quickly changing pandemic conditions made it difficult for even the most attentive citizens to monitor the actions of the state. Moreover, this considerable uncertainty also magnified the challenges to coordination. Citizens often had wildly different attitudes over the "right" actions for government to take, while physical restrictions on people's ability to congregate put real limitations on the public's literal ability to coordinate.

Second, the pandemic environment, if anything, represents a difficult test for our theory. In particular, the pandemic placed unusually great strain on the signaling capacity of courts and judicial authorities who were asked to adjudicate novel controversies between the state and the rule of law. If it is the case that courts are able to effectively convey signals to the public amidst the challenge of a pandemic, we might reasonably expect them to be able to do so in less turbulent times as well.

WHAT TYPE OF DATA?

Because our theory focuses on the efficacy of judicial review in affecting citizens' attitudes, we require data on mass public opinion. We acquire this data from surveys in each of the four countries we study. Existing survey datasets were ill-suited to engage our theoretical account. For one, they generally lack the consistent and valid measures we need for critical concepts like support for the rule of law. For another, such surveys are generally not designed to provide insights into the link between citizens' attitudes and courts' use of judicial review, the core relationship we want to understand. Accordingly, we partnered with YouGov (a leading survey firm) to conduct original, nearly identical, simultaneous, nationally representative surveys in each of the four countries in the summer of 2021. We supplement these core surveys with data from a six-wave panel survey conducted in Germany and several additional cross-sectional surveys fielded in the United States in 2020 and 2021.[9]

While the observational data from these surveys is useful to gather information about citizens' judgments of their constitutional courts (as we do later in this

[9] We leave our specific question and measurement choices to their respective chapters. We provide additional technical details about each survey in the chapter's Appendix.

chapter) and their support for the rule of law (the focus of Chapter 4), the bulk of our analyses rely on the use of survey experiments. This research focus is one that lends itself well to experimentation (Bartels and Mutz 2009; González-Ocantos and Dinas 2019; Madsen et al. 2022). Here, we can expose respondents to a carefully constructed set of facts designed to bring to subjects' minds exactly the considerations we are interested in studying. Further, our random assignment of respondents to different versions of experimental vignettes (bits of text that change only according to the theoretically informed factors that fuel our theory and hypotheses) means we can be confident that differences we observe across our respondents are due to the experimental factors we manipulate, rather than differences in respondents' demographic or political characteristics. This experimental approach – the so-called gold standard of research design – has the additional advantage of providing us with a stronger claim to estimating causal effects, a benefit to our study and something that is impossible to achieve with analysis of observational data (Gerber and Green 2012).

That we embed our experiments in nationally representative surveys also enables us to solve one of the greatest problems with traditional experiments: a lack of generalizability fueled by a subject pool full of college students (Sears 1986). Population-based survey experiments provide all the benefits of experimental research with the generalizability that comes from a diverse subject pool selected to match each country's population (Mutz 2011).

Of course, every research design comes with inferential limitations; survey experiments are no exception to this rule. One key concern with survey experiments is that they may overestimate treatment effects relative to real-world conditions (Barabas and Jerit 2010). In the real world, people vary in the attention that they pay to politics and government, meaning that some citizens are never "exposed" to a political decision or controversy, thereby denying the ability of that decision to change a citizen's attitudes. Similarly, the public might form impressions about politics and the political system based on their social networks and attitudes expressed by others, irrespective of an objective assessment of a situation at hand. In an experiment, on the other hand, every subject (provided they pay attention to the survey instrument) is exposed to the decision in a way that abstracts away the complex information environment that characterizes modern politics. In our case, we present this information as a hypothetical situation but one which is presented as objective fact, abstracting away the real-life nuance of transmission of political information. For our purposes, the sacrifice of this nuance is a trade-off worth making, as the careful comparisons the experiments enable us to make allow us to focus on specific aspects of policymaking in a way that other research designs are ill-equipped to do.

A related concern with survey experiments are so-called demand effects: respondents might guess what researchers are hoping to find and adjust their answers accordingly, rather than providing sincere responses that reflect their own opinions and beliefs. Recent research on demand effects, suggests that this concern has been overstated (e.g., Mummolo and Peterson 2019); as a result, we deploy our survey experiments with only minimal fears that respondents have collectively answered questions strategically in ways that might confound our analysis.

A final concern with any experimental study is the extent to which the researchers are entitled to make claims to external validity. We have a unique claim in this respect, as all our experiments were designed based on real-world political and legal controversies brought about by the global pandemic. As we have already explained, the Covid-19 pandemic universalized common threats to the rule of law in ways that implicated courts and publics similarly across the globe. The survey experiments we present in the following chapters were fielded in the midst of these unprecedented times, from October 2020 through September 2021. By leveraging the salient, real-world threats to the rule of law that citizens faced in all four countries, our experiments are uniquely placed to confront respondents with realistic choices whose consequences would at once be immediate and substantively meaningful. Still, we are upfront about the various limitations of our research design, and we move into our analyses knowing that the effects we estimate are subject to the various inferential caveats herein described.

CASE DETAILS

Having described the important features of our case selection, we provide a detailed discussion of the political context in each country with particular attention to its constitutional court and the political environment in the country during the summer of 2021 when we fielded our surveys. We also describe the responses of our four countries to the pandemic.

United States

Comparative politics research designs have long considered the United States a core case of a consolidated democracy. Schmitter (2009), for example, reflects that "I have yet to find a comparative study of 'stable Western liberal democracies' that does not include the United States – whatever the time frame," (55) and goes on to suggest that "comparativists should attempt to include the United States in their research designs when it seems apposite" (59).

Our inclusion of the United States, however, is for reasons beyond its substantive significance and to follow the example of past comparative research. Instead, key features of the United States link to our theoretical account and serve to further our research design in several important ways. First and foremost, the United States' separation of powers system makes it an ideal setting for evaluating the extent to which high-capacity judicial institutions are able to constrain executive power while also providing a key point of contrast to our other cases with respect to institutional design. A rich literature in American politics documents both Congress's ability to confront unilateral executive action (e.g., Christenson and Kriner 2017b, 2020a; Reeves and Rogowski 2018) and the Supreme Court's capacity to effectively exercise judicial review (e.g., Christenson and Kriner 2017c; Clark 2009; Whittington 2005). Moreover, Americans view the balance of power between three co-equal branches of government as a cornerstone of American democracy (Christenson and Kriner 2017a). In addition to the fundamental structuring of American democracy, the practical realities of the functioning of these interbranch relations ensures, to paraphrase Madison in Federalist 51, that ambition effectively counteracts ambition.

The United States Supreme Court. The US Supreme Court represents a (arguably the) canonical example of judicial constraint on executive power. Through the use of judicial review, the US Supreme Court has long been a central player in American politics (Dahl 1957). The Court is well-resourced, budgetarily independent from Congress and the President, its justices are credentialized from prestigious law schools and legal careers, and, once anointed with Senate confirmation, they are afforded the professional security of a lifetime appointment. While much of the American judicial politics literature has increasingly focused on the ways the Court acts strategically within the political system (e.g., Epstein and Knight 1998), underlying such discussions is the Court's fundamental role in American democracy as a key constitutional check on executive (and legislative) power. Although most judicial powers are not codified in the Constitution, the Court has developed a robust form of judicial review that encompasses the various forms of executive branch policymaking, reviewing the actions of both executive orders (Howell 2003) and administrative rules of bureaucratic agencies (Turner 2017). While the Court faces political limits on its capacity to effectively exercise its review powers (Bartels and Johnston 2020; Clark 2009; Rosenberg 2008), its strong foundation of public support (Gibson and Nelson 2015) and Americans' historic veneration for the rule of law (Gibson 2007a) have ensured that the Court largely fulfills its constitutional role without impediment.

The COVID-19 Pandemic in the United States. The United States's response was characterized by a pronounced decentralization and a generally narrow coordinated response from the federal government (Artiles, Gandur, and Driscoll 2021). President Trump publicly downplayed the severity of infections and possible outbreaks, and his administration's outspoken mistrust of the international community and the World Health Organization stymied early transnational coordination that might have better contained the viral spread throughout the month of February (Coleman 2020). President Trump would later recall his intentional downplaying of the seriousness of the threat, saying he did not want to incite widespread panic (Glasser 2020).

Although the first case of confirmed COVID-19 infection was recorded in January 2020, the federal government did not declare a state of emergency until March 13, 2020. By this point, 33 state governments had issued emergency declarations of their own. The federal government provided critical financial support to avoid an economic catastrophe, mobilized nationwide production of N-95 masks, and fast-tracked the development of rapid testing and vaccines. Nevertheless, most of the business of policy implementation, as well as measures to stop the spread of the virus, was devolved to the hands of state- and local-level executives and policymakers (Coleman 2020).

These state-led responses to the early viral outbreaks varied widely and would only diverge further as the pandemic marched on. With the exception of South Dakota, all states (as well as the District of Columbia and US territories) imposed some sort of "stay at home" or "shelter in place" policy that required closing of public schools, transport, public spaces, and nonessential businesses, while encouraging residents to stay in their home (Raifman et al. 2020). These measures were introduced by the end of March 2020, and lasted between 26 (Mississippi) and 87 (Oregon) days.[10] Still though, the character and implementation of these lockdown policies varied widely. Although many states imposed bans on groups larger than a handful of people, sixteen states provided an exemption for religious services. By mid-summer, thirty-five states and US territories had adopted mask-wearing mandates, with seventeen states and territories declining to do so. What is more, in many of the states where masking remained optional, states imposed strict regulations on private and public entities that prohibited requiring any citizen to wear a mask. This divergence in response to the pandemic was politicized along partisan lines: the vast majority of states led by Democratic governors adopted stricter pandemic policies, with Republican-led states opting for more lenient approaches to pandemic interventions (Artiles, Gandur, and Driscoll 2021).

July 2021 in the United States. The political conditions in the United States during summer 2021 reflected the tumultuous 2020 election and its fallout. For the first time since 2008, Democrats won unified control of the federal government, capturing a majority in the Senate, retaining their majority in the House of Representatives, and securing the election Joe Biden as president over incumbent president Donald Trump. Perhaps most politically significant were the events surrounding the January 6 insurrection and the subsequent impeachment of then-former president Donald Trump. At the same time, however, the successful appointment of Amy Coney Barrett to the Supreme Court the previous fall gave conservatives a 6–3 majority on the Court.[11]

The timing of our survey also has potential implications for the relative willingness of citizens to accept the kinds of stretching of executive power at the center of our theoretical argument. Democrats, including the president, appeared to be in a

[10] The average number of days of this first lockdown policy was 41, the median 46.

[11] Throughout our analyses, it is useful to take the partisan makeup of these institutions into account, as respondents' reactions to their decisions may reflect their composition at the time of our survey. We return more concretely to this concern later in the book when we evaluate the potential confounding effect of partisanship on judicial signals.

position of relative political strength in which their constituents appeared relatively more amenable to institutional reforms like eliminating the filibuster or expanding the Supreme Court. Moreover, our survey falls within the traditional "honeymoon" period for new presidents in which their approval tends to be strongest. Taken together with relatively weakened support for the Supreme Court, we might therefore expect that at this point that judicial signals regarding executive overreach would be most challenged, thus creating a difficult test case for our argument.

Germany

From its strong system of institutional oversight conducted by the country's constitutional court to the public's widespread regard for the rule of law, Germany represents a near-ideal setting for evaluating our hypotheses in a high-integrity institutional context. As one of the most powerful political and economic countries and an exemplar of a modern liberal democracy, the resilience of Germany's democracy represents an important case for scholars to study. Moreover, its widespread economic and cultural influence has made Germany a pivotal influencing force both within and beyond Europe's borders. Indeed, a number of democratizing countries, particularly in Eastern Europe, looked to Germany when designing their democratic institutions after the fall of the Soviet Union (Schwartz 2000). All told, the German case represents a setting of considerable substantive significance.

The Bundesverfassungsgericht. The German Federal Constitutional Court (*Bun desverfassungsgericht* or GFCC from here on) possesses and routinely wields considerable powers of oversight and has a high level of judicial independence. Established as part of Germany's post–Second World War political system, the GFCC serves as a critical check on state authority through its exercise of constitutional review. The GFCC is structured as a Kelsenian-style constitutional court, with the GFCC having exclusive jurisdiction over questions related to the German constitution (Basic Law – Grundgesetz). As such, the GFCC serves as the "supreme guardian of the constitution" and, despite not constitutionally part of the judiciary, is broadly regarded as the most influential and powerful court in the country (Kommers and Miller 2012).

The GFCC's primary form of oversight is the exercise of constitutional review, which allows the court to invalidate legislation and government actions for violating the constitution. Such constitutional challenges can reach the GFCC in a number of pathways, of which three dominate the court's docket. The first, and most common with more than 5,000 filings per year, is the constitutional complaint, which can be used to challenge a range of actions like legislation and the decisions of executive agencies. Since constitutional complaints can be brought directly to the court by citizens, they make the Court's oversight process effectively available to practically anyone (Kommers and Miller 2008). The second key form of constitutional oversight is concrete judicial review. Since the GFCC is the only institution empowered to interpret the constitution, if an interpretation is needed to resolve a case, then any court in the German judiciary must refer the matter to the GFCC. These cases are the second most common way the GFCC exercises constitutional review, with the court typically receiving between ten and twenty-five cases per year. Third, the GFCC can receive cases via abstract review, whereby privileged political institutions and actors like state governments and parliamentary party factions can challenge the constitutionality of a law.[12] While such proceedings are rare – typically fewer than five per year – they frequently deal with particularly contentious and salient issues (Vanberg 1998a).[13] The frequent – and impactful – use of these forms of constitutional review has allowed the GFCC to develop into one of the most powerful and influential constitutional courts in the world (Engst 2021; Kommers and Miller 2012; Schroeder 2022; Vanberg 2005). Even with this substantial power, however, scholars have noted that the GFCC is nonetheless responsive to political conditions, particularly as it relates to the public's role as a source of political costs for noncompliance (Krehbiel 2019, 2021b; Vanberg 2001).

The COVID-19 Pandemic in Germany. Germany's experience with the COVID pandemic resembled that of many other European nations, particularly at the pandemic's outset. Within months of the country's first confirmed case on January 27, 2020, the German government – both at the federal and state levels – had instituted strict stay-at-home orders and lockdowns in attempts to slow the spread of the virus. But with 100,000 cases recorded by the beginning of April that year, it quickly became clear that the virus was unlikely to be fully contained. Speaking to the country in March 2020, Chancellor Angela Merkel described the pandemic as Germany's greatest challenge since the Second World War (Morris, Beck, and Noack 2020).

A few characteristics defined the German government's response to the pandemic. The first was the use of nationwide lockdowns, particularly in the early months of the pandemic in 2020 and then again in early–mid 2021 (Beardsley and Schmitz 2021). These restrictions included limits on the number of people allowed to gather, quarantining requirements for travelers arriving into the country, and restrictions on the movement of individuals living in areas with particularly high levels of infection. In addition to the use of lockdowns, the federal government in late 2021 imposed restrictions on unvaccinated individuals along with a limited vaccine mandate for health care workers.[14]

A further defining feature of Germany's pandemic response was its collaborative nature between the federal and state governments. With Germany's federal structure

[12] Abstract review submissions can be brought by the federal government, state governments, or one quarter of the Bundestag's members.

[13] The GFCC has a number of other proceeding types, including election disputes, the constitutionality of political parties, and disputes between federal political institutions.

[14] This mandate was later upheld as constitutional by the GFCC. An attempt at passing a more extensive vaccine mandate failed in April 2022.

normally placing much public health authority in the hands of state governments, the capacity of the federal government to act was often constrained – legally, practically, or both – by the need to have the cooperation of state governments. As a result, much of the policymaking was done through a process of consultation between the federal and state governments. Moreover, state governments retained considerable latitude over many aspects of the COVID response, with some states taking stricter approaches than others. For example, Bremen – Germany's smallest state – was particularly effective at vaccinating its population (Schuetze 2022), while in the winter of 2021, both Bavaria and Saxony closed Christmas markets and imposed their own lockdowns focused on high-infection districts (Pancevski 2021). Later in the book, we leverage this aspect of Germany's federal political system in one of our experimental designs.

A final point on this topic is that Germany's pandemic response was seen as a case study in what states ought to do to effectively confront the crisis, especially early on in the crisis (Karnitschnig 2020). While the efficacy of the government's COVID policies appeared to flag over time (Eddy 2021), for much of the time period of our study, public support for the government's response was robust. For example, a fall 2020 Pew Research study found that 77 percent of German respondents rated the country as having done a "good job" dealing with the pandemic, a figure much higher than that in the United States (48 percent) (Devlin and Kent 2021), while an August 2020 poll by German news outlet Zweites Deutsches Fernsehen (ZDF) found that 77 percent of Germans favored stronger measures to combat the pandemic (Kafura et al. 2020). And, importantly, Germans tended to follow these restrictions, even at potential economic cost (Driscoll, Krehbiel, and Nelson 2020; Jaschke et al. 2023). The mixture of such broad support for doing what is necessary to confront the pandemic – although support for such policies began to wilt considerably over the course of our panel survey (Chewning, Driscoll, et al. 2020) – with German's robust support for the rule of law and limited state power makes Germany a particularly interesting context for our study.

July 2021 in Germany. The summer of 2021 in German politics was dominated by the impending national election scheduled for September of that year. With long-serving chancellor Angela Merkel not seeking reelection, her party, the Christian Democratic Union (CDU) and its Bavarian sister party the Christian Social Union (CSU) selected Armin Laschet, who was serving as CDU chair and minister-president of North Rhine-Westfalia, to be the party's candidate for chancellor. The CDU's erstwhile coalition partner, the Social Democratic Party (SPD), had meanwhile selected vice-chancellor and finance minister Olaf Scholz as their leader in the election. As the leaders of the traditionally two largest parties, both Laschet and Scholz figured prominently in the national political discourse at this time, as did the key smaller parties including the Greens, Free Democratic Party (FDP), the Left, and Alternative for Germany (AfD) (Angenendt and Kinski 2022). Interestingly, this wave of our panel survey came before the SPD's rapid rise in the polls that occurred in the six weeks or so immediately preceding the election and fueled the party's subsequent electoral victory. Rather, in May 2021 the Greens briefly challenged the CDU/CSU in the polls, though the latter pulled ahead by a sizable margin in June.

Although the electoral campaign was underway at the time of our survey, the federal government was still comprised of a grand coalition between the CDU and SPD with Merkel as chancellor.[15] Thus, when our respondents answered questions related to the actions of the executive, it was this Merkel-led government in power. With Merkel as something of a "lame duck" due to her already announced retirement from politics, we might expect respondents to have viewed the executive not solely as personified by Merkel but also as the institution soon to be run by one of the two major candidates. The timing of our survey thus came in the midst of a particularly competitive election that was widely seen as setting the path for the country's post-Merkel future.

Hungary

The story of Hungarian democracy is, in many ways, one of hopeful progress followed by steep decline. Since winning an unprecedented legislative supermajority in 2010 that enabled unilateral constitutional changes to both its electoral system and constitutional court, Prime Minister Viktor Orbán and his party, Fidesz, have systematically dismantled institutional barriers and guardrails to executive power (Scheppele, Bankuti, and Halmai 2012). Indeed, Hungary's democratic backsliding has been so substantial that some have challenged whether Hungary could still be considered a functioning democracy (European Parliament 2022; Freedom House 2023).

Since its precipitous ascension to power in 2010, Fidesz under the leadership of Prime Minister Orbán has pursued a plan of transforming Hungary into an "illiberal" democracy (Tóth 2014). To this end, the government has pursued a multi-pronged strategy of silencing critics and capturing or neutralizing potential barriers to its authority. Such actions have taken an array of forms, from weakening civil society organizations like NGOs (Laurent and Scheppele 2017) and universities (Enyedi 2018, 2022) to using the state's regulatory powers to inhibit independent media (Kornai 2015). Similarly, Fidesz has enacted laws targeting citizens' civil rights and freedoms, particularly those of the lesbian, gay, bisexual, transgender (LGBT+) community and refugees (Freedom House 2023). Indeed, the significant extent and depth of the erosion to democratic norms and institutions has made Hungary's status as a democracy contested even among its own citizens: only 42 percent of respondents in our survey answered affirmatively when asked if Hungary is a democracy.

15 The parliamentary opposition parties at the time were the left-leaning Greens, The Left, the fiscally conservative Free Democrats, and the right-wing Alternative for Germany.

The Hungarian Constitutional Court. The Hungarian Constitutional Court's powers of constitutional review have largely – with a few important exceptions – remained formally intact. The Court has the power to invalidate legislation, regulations, and executive decrees primarily through abstract review, concrete review, and constitutional complaints.[16] Ex ante abstract review can be brought to the Court by either the President or one-fourth of parliament, while ex post abstract review can additionally be brought by the Ombudsman, president of the Curia (supreme court), and general prosecutor. With a quarter of members of parliament (MPs) required to bring a case and all of the other offices controlled by Fidesz, abstract challenges of laws and executive actions are rare as they require the cooperation of parliamentary opposition forces (Epperly 2019).[17] Concrete review cases are brought by ordinary courts when they require a constitutional interpretation in order to resolve the case before them.[18] As such, in these proceedings, it is the ordinary court judge who acts as the gatekeeper, in that they may simply rely on existing Constitutional Court case law rather than submit a petition. Lastly, constitutional complaints allow individual citizens to challenge laws or government actions at the Court.[19] As is the case in Germany, these comprise the largest share of the Court's docket, although the number of complaints is far smaller with, for example, fewer than 600 filed in 2021.

While Fidesz's overwhelming legislative majorities have allowed it to stifle judicial oversight, their strategy for undermining the Hungarian Constitutional Court's independence has been a combination of wholesale personnel changes and significant constitutional revisions (Kovács and Scheppele 2018). That is, Fidesz's takeover of the court has been primarily through formal, legalized means rather than an informal, more explicitly political approach (Çakir 2023). To effectively take control of the Court, Fidesz began by altering the appointment process. Whereas the previous system had effectively balanced appointments between the main parliamentary blocs, Fidesz effectively took control of the committee in charge of nominations (Balogh 2010). Although appointments require a two-thirds majority, the party's legislative supermajority was sufficient to clear this hurdle. As a result, Fidesz had in effect total control over appointments to the Court, a power only enhanced by the government's expansion of the Court from eleven to fifteen judges (Epperly 2019). With both replacement and new judges selected by Fidesz without input from the opposition, the Court quickly became dominated – if not nearly exclusively composed of – Fidesz-backed judges.

16 The Court has other powers as well, including (among others): examination of conflicts with international treaties; Removal of the President of the Republic from office; opinion on the withdrawal of the acknowledgment of a Church operating contrary to the Fundamental Law; resolving conflicts of competence (between state organs); examination of local government decrees, public law regulatory instruments, and uniformity decisions.

17 For example, in 2021 the Court only received five ex post review cases.

18 Such cases are somewhat common, with twenty-seven submitted in 2021.

19 Citizens can also challenge judicial decisions.

Changes to the Court's jurisdiction and citizens' access to the Court furthered Fidesz's efforts to neutralize the country's primary constraint on potentially unbridled executive power. One such change was to effectively remove the Court's jurisdiction over matters related to the budget and taxation (Epperly 2019).[20] This constitutional revision, which was enacted in response to a 2011 decision striking down one of the new government's tax laws, essentially prevents the possibility of the Court conducting oversight over a massive set of highly consequential policies. A second major change restricted citizens' access to the Court. Under the previous constitutional arrangement, the *actio popularis* procedure at the Court granted ordinary citizens the right to challenge laws or government actions even if they themselves had not been harmed (Gárdos-Orosz 2012). This effectively amounted to granting any individual access to the Court through abstract review, which contributed considerably to the Court's earlier success as it ensured a steady stream of cases (Sólyom 2003). Seeing this, Fidesz abolished the procedure as part of its constitutional revisions. The removal of this form of access denied the Court a critical source of cases, one that was not sufficiently replaced by the creation of a constitutional complaint procedure that requires the applicant to have suffered a concrete harm (Gárdos-Orosz 2012).

The COVID-19 Pandemic in Hungary. The first national government response to COVID centered on the declaration of an emergency and the immediate shuttering of all institutions of higher education, banning international travel, and prohibiting gatherings of 500 persons or more.[21] A nationwide lockdown went into effect in March. During the lockdown, nonessential business were shuttered, public schools shifted to remote instruction, many public spaces were closed, and nonessential movement sharply curtailed. At this same time, the parliament conceded considerable lawmaking power to the executive branch: Prime Minster Orbán was officially sanctioned to rule by decree in the name of public health between March 30 and June 16, but this temporary validation also codified the government's ability to declare emergencies and impose unilateral rule with only limited parliamentary intervention in the future.

A second nationwide lockdown coincided with the second wave of COVID-19 throughout Eastern Europe, beginning in early November 2020 and extending into December. By then, mask-wearing was mandatory in most public spaces, as determined and enforced by local officials. A third and final nationwide lockdown and

[20] The Court can act if the complaint is solely based on a specific list of rights, including citizenship, life, dignity, the protection of personal data, and the freedom of thought, conscience, or religion (Epperly 2019). As Epperly (2019) notes, not included in this list are the rights most directly relevant to budgetary and taxation issues, such as the right to property.

[21] This early prioritization of university closures was an unusual tack for the national government, not only for the low concentration of vulnerable populations in universities, but also because of the long standing antagonism between the Fidesz government and institutions of higher education, which had previously been targeted by Orbán's administration (Bárd 2020; Krekó and Enyedi 2018).

curfew lasted from March until April 2021, which witnessed a return to remote learning for all public school students, a shuttering of all nonessential businesses, and a strict prohibition on movement and congregation. Public resistance to these measures swelled, leading to difficulties in enforcement and undermining governmental resolve to sustain restrictive measures; the curfews and mask mandates were officially suspended in late May 2021. Thus, by the time our Hungarian surveys were in the field, our respondents had endured three COVID-19-related nationwide lockdowns, but had also for the most part put the most restrictive policies in the rear-view mirror.

July 2021 in Hungary. Much like the United States and Germany, much of the political discourse in Hungary at this time was centered around an upcoming national election. Although Hungary's next election was scheduled for the spring of 2022, the country's political opposition to Viktor Orbán's Fidesz government had come to realize that coordinating on candidates would be crucial if they were to have any chance of being successful. To this end, nearly all of the country's opposition parties – from the social democratic (MSZP) to the right-wing (Jobbik) – set about organizing themselves into a singular electoral coalition that became known initially as the United Opposition and later as United for Hungary. By the time our survey went into the field, these efforts were well underway with each of the parties having selected their candidate for prime minister, with one of them to be selected in an October 2021 primary contest to run as the United Opposition's candidate. Thus, even though it was ten months away at the time of our survey, the national election was already looming large in the country's political conversation.

In terms of significant political issues in the summer of 2021, much continued to revolve around the efforts by Fidesz to extend its control over the country's institutions and continue its campaign against LGBTQ rights (Várnagy 2022). With respect to the former, the government pushed forward the privatization of public universities, with most universities coming under the auspices of government-backed – and controlled – quasi-public foundations. Regarding the latter, Fidesz passed a law implicitly linking homosexuality with pedophilia in a child sex abuse law by restricting portrayals of homosexuality and transgender people in material for children under eighteen. Both policy efforts were widely seen as part of Fidesz's longer term agenda to assert control over the country's politics, pursue its image as protector of Christian values, and set the narrative for the 2022 election. While none of our analyses deal directly with these issues, they speak to the broader political environment as one polarized by Fidesz's attacks on democratic norms and institutions, in these instances academic freedom and equal rights.

Poland

Much like Hungary, Poland's democracy has in many respects been defined in recent years by its decay, as the governing Law and Justice Party (PiS) has repeatedly sought to undermine the institutional infrastructure buttressing democratic governance. Once seen as a democratic success story in post–Cold War Eastern Europe, Poland's democratic backsliding since 2015 has brought the country into protracted legal conflict with the European Union and the Council of Europe over issues like the rule of law and the protection of human rights. From severely restricting the independence of the courts to degrading media freedoms, the PiS government centralized power within the executive branch while dismantling institutional powers that could otherwise be used to promote the rule of law.

Yet constitutionally speaking, Poland contains many of the standard, formal oversight features of a functioning liberal democracy. The country's constitution, passed in 1997, provides for a constitutional tribunal empowered with constitutional review and a legislative branch empowered to scrutinize government policy through tools such as committee proceedings, parliamentary questions, and no confidence motions. In particular, the lower house of the Polish legislature, the *Sejm*, was granted expansive oversight powers in the 1997 constitution.

The Polish Constitutional Tribunal. The Polish Constitutional Tribunal has a storied past as an important constraint on state power, although this reputation has been lost in the wake of the PiS government's judicial "reforms" in the 2010s. Initially established in the 1980s by the communist regime as part of its compromise with Solidarity, the Constitutional Tribunal came into its own after democratization and then the 1997 constitution (Schwartz 2000). Much like Hungary's constitutional court in its early years, the Constitutional Tribunal was consequently seen as a success story for its willingness to rule against the government's wishes (Sadurski 2019).

While the Tribunal's reputation has suffered from the attacks levied against it by PiS, its constitutional authority to exercise constitutional review has remained. The tribunal can conduct reviews through several pathways. Ex post abstract review can be brought by a broad set of political and social institutions, including government actors and institutions, minorities of either house of the bicameral legislature, leadership of any of the varied judicial bodies, or constitutional bodies including the Prosecutor-General or Ombudsman, local governments, and trade, educational, or religious interest groups, among others (Kantorowicz and Garoupa 2016).[22] With only privileged institutions granted access through abstract review, these cases tend – as they do in most countries – to be particularly contentious and politically sensitive (Bricker 2020). In addition, the Tribunal resolves disputes between state institutions (Article 189) and concrete review requests sent by ordinary courts (Article 193), as well as constitutional complaints brought by individual citizens claiming the state has infringed on their rights (Article 79). Taken together, the formal form and scope

[22] Based on Article 191 of the Polish Constitution. Also, only the President can request ex ante abstract review.

of review at the Constitutional Tribunal is largely consistent with the powers of courts in well-established democracies like Germany.

However, since the Law and Justice Party (PiS) came into power in 2015, the quality of liberal democracy in Poland declined to the point of being closer to countries such as Ukraine or El Salvador than consolidated democracies in the rest of the European Union (Alizada et al. 2021). This weakening of democratic institutions in the country is largely due to the PiS government's attempts to challenge democratic norms and standards. In particular, the government has, among other things, exerted political control over the judiciary, restricted civil rights and liberties, and amended electoral rules to its own benefit. With respect to the judiciary, the government has enacted several so-called reforms to stack the Constitutional Tribunal with loyalist judges and hamper the decision-making ability of the country's courts (Cienski 2016), actions that prompted the Council of Europe's Venice Commission – an expert body on the rule of law – to say of Poland that "not only is the rule of law in danger, but so is democracy and human rights" (Council of Europe 2016). This concern for Polish democracy remained as the PiS government continued to undermine the independence of Polish courts by, for example, establishing a disciplinary chamber with the ability to sanction judges for anti-PiS rulings and replacing the existing members of the independent body in charge of appointing judges with PiS loyalists (Pech and Kelemen 2020).

The PiS government has similarly challenged democratic norms regarding the country's elections, particularly the May 2020 presidential election. The government first attempted to pass last-minute changes to the election system by shifting to an entirely postal election administered by the postal service rather than by the national election commission, an attempt that an administrative court later found to be illegal (Freedom House 2021). The government then canceled the May election without any formal procedure and without fulfilling the government's constitutional obligations, opting instead to hold a rescheduled vote in June 2020. While considered free of significant irregularities and well organized, the election bore the hallmarks of a government engaging in democratic backsliding, particularly the attempt to manipulate electoral rules close to an election (which violated a 2006 Polish Constitutional Tribunal ruling prohibiting such changes within six months of an election) and the use of state media and resources to bolster the government's electoral prospects and undermine its opponents, with observers calling the public broadcaster "a campaign vehicle for the incumbent" (Organization for Security and Co-operation in Europe Office for Democratic Institutions and Human Rights 2020). PiS candidate Andrej Duda's close victory left observers concerned that future elections will feature such tactics (Tharoor 2020).

The PiS government also targeted civil rights and liberties, going after both institutions and groups in Polish society through the political system, proposing or passing laws aimed at weakening NGOs (Deutsche Welle 2017; Reuters 2020), attacking the LGBTI community (Picheta and Kottasová 2020), and stifling criticism of the government and the Polish state (Černušáková 2018; Kość 2021). The government's effective control of other Polish institutions exacerbated the deterioration of civil rights and liberties. For example, the Constitutional Tribunal ruled to remove the country's independent human rights watchdog (Wlodarczak-semczuk 2021) and instituted a near-total ban on abortions (BBC News 2021a). The Polish Helsinki Foundation for Human Rights (2019), thus, characterized the PiS government's actions as the country's "most significant regression in the field of human rights since 1989."

The COVID-19 Pandemic in Poland. By the time the first confirmed case of COVID arrived in Poland in early March 2020, the Sejm had passed an expansive COVID response law meant to preemptively absorb the shock from the pandemic and contain the virus's spread (Helsinki Foundation for Human Rights 2020). This sweeping statutory framework created both permanent and temporary legal instruments meant to impose new-found controls on many facets of life within the Polish borders. Among the new measures were new executive powers that could be quickly promulgated with the force of law in the name of public health and sanitation, a ban on "mass events," and the legalization of mandatory hospitalization of those infected that would be enforced by the police (Helsinki Foundation for Human Rights 2020). This first round of legal reforms paved the way for additional statutory and regulatory reforms that were passed on March 13, 20, and 31 that would shut down nearly all facets of public life (Rueters 2020). This included the shuttering of all nonessential businesses and public spaces, including public schools and transport, a near-total suspension of international flights and train services with mandatory quarantine for anyone entering the country, mandatory masking and bans on congregations or gathering larger than two people. The most limiting phase of COVID restrictions were imposed on March 31 and were scheduled to last just over a month. Movement restrictions began to ease starting on April 11, which allowed for the opening of public spaces and nonessential business, with most measures extending until early May 2020.

The summer of 2020 saw many pandemic restrictions loosened, in part to accommodate the mid-summer presidential elections (held on June 28, 2020, with a second round on July 12) that had been temporarily postponed in May (Reuters Staff 2020b). All of that came to a precipitous end in late October, when Poland was declare a "danger zone" and completely reinstated early pandemic lockdown measures, which were only eased in January 2021.[23] This cycle of easing and dramatic

[23] This total lockdown coincided with mass pro-choice protests in reaction to the Polish Constitutional Tribunal's near-total abortion ban (Walker 2020). The fallout from the decision, specifically regarding the lack of abortion rights in the country, became a major issue in the 2023 Polish national elections that saw PiS defeated by a pro-democracy coalition led by the Civic Platform (McMahon 2023). In December 2023, the European Court of Human Rights went on to declare the Constitutional Tribunal's ruling to be in contravention with the European Convention on Human Rights (Ngendakumana 2023).

reimposition of lockdown restrictions would repeat again in late March and early April, in response to the third wave, and would continue until the end of May (Notes from Poland 2021). Thus, by the time we entered the field with our surveys, the Polish public had experienced three full lockdowns during which movement and assembly were strictly limited, schools and nonessential businesses were closed or forced to operate remotely, masking and social distancing was widely expected and generally enforced.

July 2021 in Poland. Unlike our other cases, electoral politics were not a prominent topic in Polish politics at the time of the survey. With the next national election not set to occur for over another two years in the fall of 2023, "the year 2021 could have been one of a lull in Polish politics" (Jasiewicz and Jasiewicz-Betkiewicz 2022, 362). This was not the case, however, as important issues related to the rule of law and the country's relationship with the European Union kept politics front and center in the national dialogue. In June, the EU's high court, the Court of Justice, issued a stay on the activities of the Polish Supreme Court's controversial disciplinary chamber. This chamber had been at the center of the government's judicial reforms that were broadly criticized for undermining judicial independence and the rule of law. In response, the Polish Constitutional Tribunal declared that such measures taken by the European court are invalid under the Polish constitution, setting the stage for a direct confrontation between the two courts and contributing to the ongoing tension between Poland and the EU over the rule of law. With our survey out of the field on July 13, the resolution of these court cases were very much up in the air with the Court of Justice issuing its decision on July 15 (in which the Court questioned the legality of the Disciplinary Chamber) and a similar ruling from the European Court of Human Rights issued on July 22. Even with rule of law issues at the forefront of Polish politics since the Law and Justice Party came to power in 2015, our survey coincided with a particularly poignant time in the legal debate between Polish and EU institutions.

Two further domestic political topics were of significance at this time. The first was a law that would have limited non-European ownership of media outlets in the country. The law was widely seen as a move by the PiS government to strengthen its control over the media and specifically target one news outlet, TVN, for its criticism of the government. At the time of our survey, the proposed law was still under debate with considerable opposition coming from, among others, the American government due to American media company Discovery's majority ownership stake in TVN.[24] The second issue was a proposed tax reform, known as the "Polish Deal." The proposal, which the government revealed in May 2021, was intended to reduce taxes on middle and lower income citizens while stimulating investment (Jasiewicz

[24] Ultimately the bill passed, only to be rejected by the Polish Senate. When this veto was overridden by the lower house, the president in turn vetoed the law. The legislature was in turn unable to muster the votes necessary to override the president's veto.

and Jasiewicz-Betkiewicz 2022). The government invested considerable political capital into the reforms, with Law and Justice leader Jarosław Kaczyński claiming in July 2021 that the Polish Deal "was going to be an achievement to match the 1,050 years of Poland's history" and that "the devil himself wouldn't be able to stop us from completing this mission" (Jedrzejak 2022). Although the reforms were not passed until later in 2021, the timing of survey coincided with the rollout and promotion of the bill as one of the government's major legislative initiatives.[25]

DISCUSSION

This chapter serves as a bridge between the theoretical and empirical parts of the book. We want to understand the conditions under which courts can effectively create political costs for incumbents through the use of judicial review, and we have hypothesized that judicial efficacy varies according to a court's level of judicial independence and a citizen's own support for the rule of law. In this chapter, we explained how we designed our study to enable us to determine when and where judicial review serves as an effective tool of state constraint.

Our interest in levels of judicial independence led us to select two pairs of countries with variation in this respect. The United States and Germany represent countries with high courts widely recognized as independent while Hungary and Poland are cases with low levels of judicial independence. We selected these countries based upon expert judgments of judicial independence and validated, in this chapter, our assumption that lay and expert judgments of judicial independence generally align; the mass publics of these four countries perceive their courts to be of high or low institutional integrity in ways that correspond to their de facto independence. We demonstrated across a variety of different survey questions that our respondents in Germany and the United States generally espoused a much greater belief in their constitutional court's level of judicial independence than their counterparts in Hungary and Poland. And, in an important substantive contribution, we have shown that lay and expert judgments of judicial independence tend to track one another.

All this research was set against the backdrop of the COVID-19 pandemic, which despite its unfortunate disruption in the lives of nearly everyone on the planet, proved an inferential boon to the research question we aimed to interrogate here. Public support for the rule of law (as well as many other concepts) is difficult to study in a regular day-to-day setting, as it requires citizens to consider the values they hold in the abstract; it is only when the rule of law comes under threat that the costs and benefits of this given value are laid bare for all to consider in its concrete manifestations. The government policies and measures imposed during the

[25] Once passed, the implementation of the tax law became a "PR disaster" as the government struggled to effectively rollout the law's provisions (Makowski 2022).

COVID-19 pandemic were unprecedented tests of the rule of law that were felt in similar ways around the world.

While the overall quality of democracy was not the basis on which we selected our cases, it is also worth noting that our set of countries combines two stable, consolidated democracies – the United States and Germany – with two prominent modern instances of democratic backsliding – Hungary and Poland. That all of these countries are in the same study here presents a unique opportunity to keep in mind how the concept we seek to engage with here – judicial efficacy – fits into broader discussions regarding the survival and stability of liberal democracy more generally. That is to say, while each of these countries are important cases to better understand in their own rights, our ability here to draw direct and meaningful comparisons between them on such a fundamental feature of democratic governance represents a key contribution of the book.

In short, our discussion in this chapter explained some major pieces of our research design: which countries we study and the conditions in which we studied them. The next piece of our research design concerns individual-level variation in support for the rule of law among our survey respondents. Explaining how to measure this concept and validating our measure of it across countries is the goal of the Chapter 4.

Appendix

SURVEY TECHNICAL DETAILS

United States. YouGov interviewed 2,234 respondents from June 23, 2021 to July 6, 2021 who were then matched down to a sample of 2,000 to produce the final dataset. The respondents were matched to a sampling frame on gender, age, race, and education. The frame was constructed by stratified sampling from the full 2019 American Community Survey (ACS) one-year sample with selection within strata by weighted sampling with replacements (using the person weights on the public use file).

The matched cases were weighted to the sampling frame using propensity scores. The matched cases and the frame were combined and a logistic regression was estimated for inclusion in the frame. The propensity score function included age, gender, race/ethnicity, years of education, and region. The propensity scores were grouped into deciles of the estimated propensity score in the frame and post-stratified according to these deciles.

The weights were then post-stratified in 2016 and 2020 Presidential vote choice, and a four-way stratification of gender, age (four categories), race (four categories), and education (four categories), to produce the final weight.

Germany. YouGov interviewed 4,729 respondents in wave 1 who were then matched down to a sample of 4,400 to produce the final wave 1 dataset. The respondents were matched to a sampling frame on gender, age, and education. The frame was constructed by stratified sampling from the 2018 Eurobarometer with selection within strata by weighted sampling (using the person weights on the public use file).

The matched cases were weighted to the sampling frame using propensity scores. The matched cases and the frame were combined and a logistic regression was estimated for inclusion in the frame. The propensity score function included age, gender, years of education, and state. The propensity scores were grouped into deciles of the estimated propensity score in the frame and post-stratified according to these deciles.

The weights were then post-stratified on 2017 General Election vote choice, and a stratification of gender, state, age (four categories), and education (four categories), to produce the final weight.

In wave 2, YouGov re-contacted all 4,400 wave 1 respondents and achieved 3,697 completed wave 2 interviews. YouGov prepared a wave 2 weight following the same procedures as in wave 1.

In wave 3, YouGov re-contacted all 3,697 wave 2 respondents and achieved 3,189 completed wave 3 interviews. YouGov prepared a wave 3 weight following the same procedures as in wave 1.

In wave 4, YouGov re-contacted all 3,189 wave 3 respondents and achieved 2,633 completed wave 4 interviews. YouGov prepared a wave 4 weight following the same procedures as in wave 1.

In wave 5, YouGov re-contacted all 2,633 wave 4 respondents and achieved 1,334 completed wave 4 interviews. YouGov prepared a wave 4 weight following the same procedures as in wave 1.

Hungary. YouGov interviewed 2029 respondents who were then matched down to a sample of 2,000 to produce the final dataset. The respondents were matched to a sampling frame on gender, age, and education. The frame was constructed by stratified sampling from the 2019 Eurobarometer with selection within strata by weighted sampling with replacements (using the person weights on the public use file).

The matched cases were weighted to the sampling frame using propensity scores. The matched cases and the frame were combined and a logistic regression was estimated for inclusion in the frame. The propensity score function included age, gender, years of education, and region. The propensity scores were grouped into deciles of the estimated propensity score in the frame and post-stratified according to these deciles.

The weights were then post-stratified on ideology (ten categories), region, and a four-way stratification of gender, age (four categories), race (four categories), and education (four categories) to produce the final weight.

Poland. YouGov interviewed 2,000 respondents. The respondents were weighted to a sampling frame on gender, age, and education. The frame was constructed by stratified sampling from the 2019 Eurobarometer with selection within strata by weighted sampling with replacements (using the person weights on the public use file).

The matched cases were weighted to the sampling frame using propensity scores. The matched cases and the frame were combined and a logistic regression was estimated for inclusion in the frame. The propensity score function included age, gender, years of education, and region. The propensity scores were grouped into deciles of the estimated propensity score in the frame and post-stratified according to these deciles.

The weights were then post-stratified on ideology (ten categories), region, and a four-way stratification of gender, age (four categories), race (four categories), and education (four categories) to produce the final weight.

4

Measuring Public Support for the Rule of Law

The theory we articulated in Chapter 2 suggested that the efficacy of judicial review varies according to a court's level of judicial independence and the public's support for the rule of law. In Chapter 3, we articulated a research design that enables us to test our theory, relying upon survey experiments fielded in a quartet of countries with varying levels of judicial independence. Before we can move that test, we need to explain a second element our theoretical model requires: a measure of the public's support for the rule of law.

How do we know if the public is committed to the rule of law? For all of the ink that has been spilled on the importance of the rule of law (and the public's dedication to it), measurement of the public's support for it has been scattershot. The amount of scholarship examining support for the rule of law pales in comparison to the attention garnered by the public's support for democracy and for particular democratic institutions, including legislatures and high courts (e.g., Carlin and Singer 2011; Helmke 2010a; Walker 2009).

We begin the chapter by discussing how researchers have measured the public's support for the rule of law in a variety of settings, including major cross-national survey projects as well as multi-item (but often single-country) scales (e.g., Gibson 2007a; Gibson and Caldeira 1996). These previous approaches provide us with a firm foundation on which to understand the public's support for the rule of law, but also suggest a need for stronger theorizing about the indicators that comprise a valid measure of the concept. We then review conceptualizations of the rule of law proposed by legal scholars (e.g., Bingham 2011; Tamanaha 2004) and analyze more than twenty indicators previously used to measure this concept (e.g., Gibson 2007a; Gibson, Sonis, and Hean 2010; Vuković and Cvejić 2014). With these theoretical and empirical exercises complete, we propose a four-item measure of the public's support for the rule of law. In addition to describing the public's support for the rule of law, when our main surveys were fielded, we draw on on our multi-wave panel in Germany and repeated representative cross-sectional surveys in the United States to demonstrate the temporal stability of the public's support for this norm. We find an impressive level of stability in the public's attitudes in both cases, in line with previous research (Gibson 2007a; Reeves and Rogowski 2016).

We validate this measure extensively by drawing on the rich array of information about the political and demographic characteristics of our respondents in the United States, Germany, Hungary, and Poland. This analysis reveals the important role that legal sophistication and democratic values play in shaping citizens' support for the rule of law. Critically, we find stark differences in the structure of support for this norm between our country pairs. In Poland and Hungary, support for the rule of law is highest among those dissatisfied with democracy and is also inexorably tied to broader support for the executive. In the United States and Germany, by contrast, there is no such link between executive support and commitment to the rule of law. We conclude this chapter with a discussion of how we envision these commitments to affect citizens' ability to receive and act upon judicial signals that could sound the alarm regarding executive indiscretion.

PUBLIC SUPPORT FOR THE RULE OF LAW

Measures of a country's respect for the rule of law abound. So too do individual- (and country-) level measures of the public's commitment to this norm. We begin our investigation into the best way to measure the public's support for the rule of law by reviewing existing measures, most prominently the questions used on large cross-national surveys (e.g., the AmericasBarometer, Afrobarometer, and Asian Barometer) and the multi-item scales used in political science scholarship over the past three decades (e.g., Gibson 2007a; Gibson and Caldeira 1996; Gibson, Sonis, and Hean 2010; Vuković and Cvejić 2014).

The measures of the concept with the broadest geographic coverage come on large-scale collaborative survey projects. For example, the Afrobarometer measures commitment to the rule of law through a series of paired statements, asking respondents to select the statement that comes closest to their view. The respondents, in one illustrative item, must select between pairs like "Since the president was elected to lead the country, he should not be bound by laws or court decisions that he thinks are wrong" or "The president must always obey the laws and the courts, even if he thinks they are wrong" (Dumenu and Armah-Attoh 2018). The Afrobarometer also includes agree/disagree items to measure support for the rule of law as it applies to individual citizens, asking respondents how much they agree with statements like "The police always have the right to make people obey the law," "The tax authorities always have the right to make people pay taxes," and "The courts have the right to make decisions that people always have to abide by" (Little and Logan 2009).

As other examples, the AmericasBarometer measures commitment to the rule of law in Central and South America with a question that primes the necessity of law enforcement: "In order to apprehend criminals do you think that the authorities should always respect the law or that occasionally they can operate at the margin of the law?" Respondents then select whether (1) They should always respect the law; or (2) Can operate at the margin of the law occasionally" (Cruz 2009; Malone 2011). The Asian Barometer measures public support for the rule of law with agree/disagree items like "citizens should always obey the laws and regulations, even if they disagree with them," "in difficult situations for the country it would be ok for the government to disregard the law in order to deal with the situation," and "government leaders are like a head of family; we should all follow their decisions" (Dressel 2014). These large surveys also include items indirectly related to the application of the rule of law, especially as it relates to the appearance (or existence) of corruption.

These items are useful for scholars, especially those interested in making cross-national comparisons, as these large collaborative survey projects field the same items over time and across countries. Although this repetition enables researchers to gather some information about trends in the public's commitment to the rule of law across countries said repetition of these items can be sporadic, and the conceptualization that underpins these items is often left unstated. Further, the disadvantages of single-indicator measures of complicated concepts are well-known, and multi-item scales can enhance the reliability and validity of measures of unruly concepts like support for the rule of law (e.g., Allen, Iliescu, and Greiff 2022; Diamantopoulos et al. 2012).

For these reasons, recent research has tended to rely upon versions of a multi-item scale originally developed by Gibson and Caldeira (1996) in their study of European legal cultures. Gibson and Caldeira conceptualize support for the rule of law as one of three components of legal culture, alongside legal alienation and valuation of individual liberty. They view the public's support for the rule of law as existing on a dimension between universalism and particularism, describing it thusly:

> Willingness to tolerate exceptions to the law is an attitude of some importance in the operation of a legal system. At the extreme, of course, nearly everyone agrees that there are some circumstances under which law must be put aside in favor of justice or self-interest or the need to craft immediate solutions to pressing political and legal problems. At the opposite end of the continuum, nearly everyone also believes that, in general, laws just be followed, that citizens and rulers have a normative obligation to abide by the rule of law, and that under most circumstances the universal and equal application of the law should prevail. But between these two extremes, there is a great deal of latitude, and it is this variability that is most interest to use… The extent to which citizens believe that they ought to adhere rigidly to law is one aspect of legal values, and it is quite likely that nations differ significantly on this dimension (60).

In crafting their measure, Gibson and Caldeira are explicit that their conceptualization of support for the rule of law encompasses only part of the broader concept, arguing that the universalism-particularism dimension is "the essential element of this concept" (60).

Gibson and Caldeira further argue that people believe the government should be bound by law and should follow laws on the books, and that this is a general phenomenon across contexts. For this reason, survey items that simply ask respondents to rate their agreement with simplistic statements are unlikely to provide useful or valid indicators: people will uncritically rush to signal their dedication to the rule of law. Instead, they propose items that pit adherence to the rule of law against other considerations like fairness ("It is not necessary to obey a law you consider unjust"), efficiency ("Sometimes it might be better to ignore the law and solve problems immediately rather than wait for a legal solution") and ideology ("If you don't particularly agree with law, it is all right to break it if you are careful not to get caught"). These three items form Gibson and Caldeira's original measure of support for the rule of law.[1] From the measure, fielded across Europe, they conclude that support for the rule of law is high in Great Britain, West Germany, the Netherlands, and Denmark but low in Greece, Belgium, and Luxembourg. Further, they conclude that attitudes toward legal culture are shaped by education and social class, and are relatively stable over time.

Gibson and others have used this conceptualization – with varying combinations of items – in studies that explore the public's support for the rule of law across space and time.[2] Insofar that the public's support for the rule of law is difficult to measure in the abstract, and as most respondents will not openly refute their commitment to

[1] Vuković and Cvejić (2014) use these three items to study support for the rule of law in Serbia, as well.

[2] Studying South Africa, Gibson and Gouws (1997) use four items: the efficiency item, an ideological item ("It is not necessary to obey the laws of a government I did not vote for"), an emergency item ("In times of emergency, the government ought to be able to suspend the law in order to solve pressing social problems"), and an item that uses a technicality as the competing consideration ("It is alright to get around the law as long as you do not actually break it"). Gibson, Caldeira, and Spence (2003) assess commitment to the rule of law in Russia with the fairness item, a governmental "flexibility" item ("The government should have some ability to bend the law in order to solve pressing social and political problems"), an individual "flexibility" item ("The law should be flexible enough for the people to use it to achieve their own goals"), and a modified ideology item ("If you don't agree with a law, it is all right to break it"). Gibson's (2007a) four-item scale combines the expediency and fairness items from the 1996 scale, the ideology item from the South Africa scale, and the flexibility item to measure public support for the rule of law in the United States. Gibson, Sonis, and Hean (2010), studying support for the rule of law in Cambodia before the Khmer Rouge trials, uses a five-item scale, including the technicality, emergency, and efficiency items along with three other items: "Government officials who are guilty of crimes deserve the same punishment as anyone else" and "An individual is obligated to obey the law for the good of society as a whole, even if he/she finds it personally unjustifiable." More recently, Gibson and Nelson (2015) and Reeves and Rogowski (2016) measure support for the rule of law using a five-item scale: the fairness item, the efficiency item, the governmental flexibility item, the South African ideology item, and one new item "When it comes right down to it, law is not all that important; what's important is that our government solve society's problems and make us all better off."

this foundational principle, this multi-item approach to measurement has many benefits. Most importantly, it is grounded in a clearly identified conceptualization of the concept the items are seeking to measure: the universalism-particularism dimension. By articulating a key feature of the rule of law, it is clear what aspect of the rule of law this approach attempts to measure, making the assessment of validity less of a moving target given the diffuseness of "rule of law" as a concept. Second, several of the items have been asked repeatedly over time and across countries, providing some ability to assess stability over time and to compare cross-national differences (e.g., Gibson 2007a).

Of course, such an approach has drawbacks as well. The most obvious is the lack of consistency in the items asked across countries and time. While the general concept being measured remains the same, the set of items used to assess that concept varies without much discussion of why some items are added or excluded across countries and time. This is particularly important where items vary in their actor. Some items, like the emergency item ("In times of emergency, the government ought to be able to suspend the law in order to solve pressing social problems") ask respondents' attitudes toward the *government* obeying the law. Others, like the fairness item ("It is not necessary to obey a law you consider unjust") ask about whether *individuals* (presumably citizens) should follow the law. As we detail below, there is significant cross-national variation in government-actor items that is not present for individual-actor items. This raises the need to pay attention to the balance of those items in a battery used to measure this concept. With that in mind, we now turn to a discussion of how we conceptualize and measure the public's support for the rule of law.

MEASURING SUPPORT FOR THE RULE OF LAW

The foundation of any measure is a clear conceptualization of the underlying concept. With respect to the rule of law, "clear conceptualization" is a challenge. There are, as Taiwo (1999) quips, "almost as many conceptions of the rule of law as there are people defending it" (152). The universalism-particularism dimension used by Gibson provides a solid starting point for any measure of the public's support for the rule of law. But, before we adopt it uncritically, we review conceptualizations of the rule of law and explain why we too measure the public's support for the rule of law along the universalism-particularism dimension.

Conceptualizations of the rule of law tend to be either *formal* or *substantive*. Formal conceptualizations of this notion center on the institutionalization of law and subsequent compliance with legal edicts, while substantive theories "include requirements about the *content* of the law (usually that it must comport with justice or moral principle)" (Tamanaha 2004, 92 emphasis ours). For example, a government might follow the proper constitutional protocols to make laws authorizing slavery or mass torture of its citizens; such laws might be "legal" under a formal conception of the rule of law but would almost certainly fail muster under most substantive theories of the rule of law (Møller and Skaaning 2012; Shklar 1998). On the other hand, substantive theories induce more subjectivity into the concept, as what is moral or just is more difficult to determine than whether laws were made through the proper processes.

We focus on the formal conceptualizations of the rule of law for several reasons. First, we view proceduralism as fundamental to any conceptualization of the rule of law: laws set rules that govern the behavior of elites and the public, and a crucial element of any society governed by the rule of law is a recognition that laws must be followed. Indeed, any substantive conception of the rule of law rings hollow if this formalistic sense of the rule of law is not satisfied. In this way, a proceduralistic conception of the rule of law is a prerequisite to any more demanding, substantive conceptualization.

Second, a formalistic approach fits well with the three "themes" identified by Tamanaha (2004) in his review of the concept as used by political scientists, philosophers, and legal scholars. First, under the rule of law, governmental powers are limited. The government must abide by duly enacted laws, and – even when the government wishes to change the law – there are formal procedures to do so, and actions that are beyond their power. Second, the rule of law requires formal legality: the law must apply generally, equally, and with certainty. The government establishes, maintains, and enforces the rules by which citizens must abide, irrespective of their position or proximity to power. Finally, the rule of law implicates the age-old adage of "a government of laws, not men." As Tamanaha (2004) explains, "to live under the rule of law is not to be subject to the unpredictable vagaries of other individuals – whether monarchs, judges, government officials, or fellow citizens" (122). In other words, the rule of law affords insurance against capricious actions by the powerful, creating a set of rules that govern the behavior of the powerful and the powerless. In a succinct conceptualization, Bingham (2011) embraces all three of these themes: "all persons and authorities within the state, whether public or private, should be bound by and entitled to the benefit of laws publicly made, taking effect (generally) in the future and publicly administered in the courts" (8). In this way, a formalistic approach fits well.

Third, where others have sought to measure the public's support for the rule of law, they have relied upon a formalistic conceptualization.[3] The universalism–particularism dichotomy that Gibson and Caldeira use as the cornerstone of their measurement strategy is based on a formalistic conceptualization of the rule of law, and the various indicators used in the cross-national surveys discussed above also tend to emphasize a formalistic conceptualization of the concept. For this reason,

[3] For (advocates of) more substantive definitions, see Haggard, MacIntyre, and Tiede (2008), McCubbins, Rodriguez, and Weingast (2010), and Shklar (1998).

our decision keeps our measure in line with the general conceptualization used in other studies.

Finally, we are concerned that measures focused on a substantive conceptualization of the rule of law may suffer from validity concerns. Compared with formalistic notions of the rule of law, substantive theories require agreement on first principles about values and policy issues. These values might vary across space and time and might be attached to individuals' political commitments in ways that contaminate any measure of support for the rule of law.

With the formalistic conceptualization of the rule of law as our point of departure, we sought next to decide what sort of indicators are most likely to provide a balanced and valid measure of the concept. In our review of the extant measures, we noted differences in the actors about which information is solicited: some indicators ask respondents about whether *they* feel bound by law, while others ask respondents whether *elites or institutions* should be grounded in law. Thus, a key distinction we make in terms of the indicators in our measure relates to whether individuals or governmental institutions and representative actors should be bound by law.

Second, we noted Gibson's (2007a) point that successful attempts to measure the rule of law need to pit obedience to the law against some other consideration:

> Few people are likely to reject the rule of law in principle. Survey questions that ask people whether they agree that rulers should not act arbitrarily or capriciously, or that citizens should be free to ignore the law, are unlikely to be of much use in tapping popular commitments to the rule of law. Instead, the difficult test of support for the rule of law involves the juxtaposition of law and some other valued principle. This forces people to weigh the relative value of conflicting principles. Only when support for the rule of law comes at some cost can we begin to gauge how much citizens really value it (601).

Thus, when selecting items, we sought to select items that force citizens to weigh competing considerations in their mind in order to mitigate concerns about simplistic, abstract fealty to the rule of law.

How Do Respondents Describe the Rule of Law?

It is one thing for us to describe how legal scholars and political scientists have conceptualized this norm. But, given our interest in the *public's* support for the rule of law, we wanted to know how the typical citizen describes the concept. Ideally, our conceptualization of this concept would match the way our survey respondents understand the concept and describe it in their own words.

To this end, at the beginning of our Summer 2021 surveys, we asked our respondents directly about their understanding of the rule of law. We posed the following yes-or-no question: "Many people believe that it is important for a country to have a strong commitment to 'the rule of law.' Have you heard of this concept before?" Overall, respondents displayed awareness of the concept: 68 percent of Americans, 62 percent of Hungarians, and 57 percent of Poles said they had heard of the concept. Surprisingly, awareness of the rule of law was lower in Germany where only 36 percent of respondents indicated familiarity with the term.[4]

Then, we asked respondents who answered in the affirmative to describe how they would characterize a place with a strong commitment to the rule of law. To give a flavor of the responses we received, Table 4.1 displays five randomly selected responses from each of our four countries.

To provide a more systematic summary of the responses in our full sample of data, we code each response according to whether it espoused a formal or substantive conceptualization of the rule of law. In all four countries, the vast majority of responses discussed the rule of law in terms of formalistic ideas with many of the responses espousing ideas like "no one is above the law" or "the law must always be followed." In a minority of cases did respondents discuss particular substantive guarantees with statements like "protect human rights" or "a place that protects free speech." Overall, 79 percent of Americans, 64 percent of Germans, 65 percent of Hungarians, and 65 percent of Poles who were familiar with the rule of law and provided an answer that could be classified on this dimension responded in a way that suggested a formalistic, rather than substantive, conception of the rule of law.

Additionally, we coded whether each response invoked the universalism–particularism idea that is core to so much existing empirical research on the public's support for the rule of law. We code phrases like "no one is above the law," "people should be treated equally," or "everyone must follow the law" as invoking universalism. Overall, 86 percent of Americans, 91 percent of Germans, 88 percent of Hungarians, and 88 percent of Poles who gave a codable answer to this question articulated a response that maps onto the universalism–particularism dimension.

From this exercise, we make two conclusions. First, when asked to describe the rule of law, most respondents explained the concept in ways that invoked a formalistic, rather than substantive, conceptualization of the rule of law. Second, the universalism–particularism distinction that Gibson and others have relied upon in their research fits well with how survey respondents explain the rule of law. In short,

4 Our sense here is that "the rule of law" was a topic of conversation in the other three countries when these surveys went into the field with the aftermath of the 2020 American presidential election, and the EU's responses to governments in Poland and Hungary making headlines in those countries. The Google yearly time trend for the search terms "the rule of law" was at a localized nadir in all four of our countries during the timeframe of our studies, suggesting that our surveys did not coincide with a period of time where this concept was highly contested in public discourse.

TABLE 4.1 *Respondents' descriptions of countries with strong commitments to the rule of law. Respondents were provided an open text box to answer the following prompt: "In your own words, what comes to mind when you think of a country with a strong commitment to the rule of law?" Responses were selected at random.*

United States	Germany	Hungary	Poland
All persons no matter their station in life, they're race, religion, political affiliation, or position of power (or lack thereof) are all subject to the same exact laws and punishments	Fair negotiations, democracy	Free suffrage	Respecting the rights of citizens
The rule of law is what a country sticks to, so their society doesn't collapse and become a third world country	Reservation of the law	The exercise of rights, both for the state and for individuals	A government governed by, operating under, and within the limits of law
Laws that are passed and enforced	Criminals will be punished accordingly	I'm thinking more about independence, equality before the law	Compliance with the law applicable in a given country, fair punishment and rewards, lack of corruption, taking care of society, that is, health and social care
The supremacy of our laws	Compliance with laws and applicable regulations as well as the implementation of measures by offices and authorities in the event of repeated non-compliance by citizens	Common law system	No changes to the Constitution, independent courts, press, and television
All people, institutions, and businesses are accountable to a set of laws that ensure an orderly and supposedly just society where everyone is treated equally	Democratic behavior, basic law	Living according to the laws formulated precisely and clearly, in a way that is understandable for all citizens, observing and enforcing the laws for everyone without exception. Without discrimination. (here I mean that politicians can be punished in the same way as "little people")	Democracy, fair country

this exercise helps to validate our conceptualization of the rule of law as we move toward specific indicators of the public's support for this norm.

Item Selection

We began our item selection process with a pilot survey. We included more than two dozen items we found in our search of the literature on a survey fielded to a convenience sample of 1,000 adult respondents in the United States via Amazon's MTurk platform in the third week of March 2020.[5] When selecting our final set of items, we had several considerations, including strong content validity, variation in the respondent's level of agreement with the statement (to provide variation on the scaled measure), respondents' willingness to answer (had relatively low "Don't Know" percentages), and whether items loaded well on a single factor.[6]

We then took a subset of those items that had strong psychometric properties and captured the concepts we sought to include in the measure and fielded them on Wave 1 of our Germany panel survey as well as on YouGov's COVID-19 tracker in the United States, United Kingdom, and Spain. We did this both as a check on the replicability of our pilot data on a national sample in the United States, as well to evaluate the extent to which this measure had strong psychometric properties in multiple countries.[7] Armed with those data, we selected four items that form the measure of support for the rule of law that we use in the rest of this book:

- When the [Constitutional Court] hinders the work of our government, our government should ignore it.
- When the country is facing a difficult situation, it is ok for the government to disregard the law in order to deal with the situation.
- Sometimes it might be better to ignore the law and solve problems immediately rather than wait for a legal solution.
- If you don't particularly agree with a law, it is all right to break it if you are careful not to get caught.

5 The items, their sources, as well as descriptive statistics – the percentage of respondents who agreed with the statement (or picked the first option in a dichotomy), the percentage of Don't Know responses, the number of respondents who answered the question, and the factor loadings from a one- and two-factor solution – are provided in Table 4.A3 in the Appendix.

6 While many theoretical and empirical models of the rule of law are multidimensional (Carlin 2012; Haggard, MacIntyre, and Tiede 2008; Haggard and Tiede 2014; Ríos-Figueroa and Staton 2009; Shklar 1998), survey-based measures of the public's support for the rule of law are unidimensional (e.g., Gibson 2007a). We therefore also opt for a unidimensional measure of the concept while also acknowledging that our conceptualization of the rule of law is narrower than many others.

7 Tables 4.A1 and 4.A2 in the Appendix contain information on the distribution of the four items we chose as our measure of support for the rule of law in those countries (as well as additional information on the reliability and validity of the scale in those countries).

Two of these items query respondents about when *governments* should abide by laws; the other two items relate to beliefs about when average *citizens* must follow the law. Additionally, as suggested by Gibson (2007a), each of the chosen items provide some sort of cross-cutting considerations (e.g., policy concerns, expediency) that provide some reason why a person or government would choose to act in defiance of the law. Thus, our four items fulfill the two desired criteria we outlined above.

How well do the four items work as a scale? To answer this question, we assess the psychometric properties of the scale compared to scales used in other published research. In our original MTurk survey and the first wave of our Germany panel survey, we included the items in our scale alongside the Gibson and Caldeira (1996) and Gibson (2007a) items. Gibson and Caldeira (1996) used a three-item scale of support for the rule of law in their analysis of European legal cultures; Gibson (2007a) used a four-item scale of support for the rule of law in the United States. Our scale uses one item that appeared in the Gibson and Caldeira (1996) scale and another that is included in both the Gibson and Caldeira (1996) and Gibson (2007a) scales.

In the MTurk data, our measure of support for the rule of law is quite reliable: $\alpha = 0.71$. This reliability coefficient just inches out the reliability of the Gibson and Caldeira (1996) scale ($\alpha = 0.70$) and improves on the reliability of the Gibson (2007a) scale ($\alpha = 0.66$). In the Germany survey, our measure of support for the rule of law slightly improves on the Gibson (2007a) scale. The four-item scale we use is more reliable ($\alpha = 0.66$ compared to $\alpha = 0.59$) and has a slightly higher average factor loading (0.55 compared to 0.50). Additionally, one of the Gibson items loaded particularly poorly on the single factor, loading at only 0.31. The Gibson and Caldeira (1996) scale performed similarly to our scale, with a very slight decrease in reliability ($\alpha = 0.65$) and a slightly higher average factor loading (0.58).

Thus, our scale performs slightly better than the Gibson (2007a) scale in both the United States and Germany, and is on par with the Gibson and Caldeira (1996) scale. In terms of construct validity, the three measures of support for the rule of law correlate highly. In the MTurk data, our scale correlates with the Gibson and Caldeira (1996) and Gibson (2007a) scales at $r = 0.78$; those two scales correlate at $r = 0.88$ (which is not surprising considering two of the three Gibson and Caldeira (1996) items are in the Gibson (2007a) scale). In the Germany survey, our scale correlates with the Gibson and Caldeira (1996) scale at $r = 0.70$ and with the Gibson (2007a) scale at $r = 0.73$. The Gibson and Caldeira (1996) and Gibson (2007a) scales correlate at $r = 0.86$.[8]

8 Following our item selection, we were curious how our scale compares to the five-item scale used by Gibson and Nelson (2015), Reeves and Rogowski (2022a), and others. We fielded the items for our scale, as well as that scale, on the YouGov survey described in footnote 9. The two scales have almost very similar psychometric properties, with $\alpha = 0.80$ for both scales. Our measure has a slightly higher average factor loading (0.70 vs. 0.65). Our scale is balanced on government-individual items (whereas this scale is split 3–2); further, our scale contains one fewer item.

Why, then, should we not just use the Gibson and Caldeira (1996) scale? We do not make this choice lightly, but rather we return to the issue of content validity. As we have discussed, support for the rule of law involves beliefs about both individuals' obligations to follow the law *and* the duty of government to likewise adhere to existing laws. All three items in the Gibson and Caldeira (1996) scale, however, relate to individual – rather than governmental – compliance with legal mandates, at least under certain conditions. Our measure, by contrast, includes a balanced number of items relating to governments and institutions. This in turn makes us confident in the validity of our measure while also ensuring that it remains in conversation with existing metrics.

Comparing Support for the Rule of Law Across Countries

Having discussed the salutary psychometric properties of our measure, we now turn to substance. Do citizens support the rule of law in the four countries we study? Table 4.2 displays the distribution of responses across the four countries. In that table, higher agreement with the statement (a larger percentage) indicates *lower* commitment to the rule of law. Viewed in this light, we see that the first and fourth items elicited, on average, more pro-rule of law responses than did the second and third items. At the same time, it is perhaps surprising that more than one-in-seven Americans, Germans, Poles, and Hungarians indicated that it is acceptable to break laws so long as you will not get caught.[9]

On the two items that tap individual-level behavior (the third and fourth items in Table 4.1), we do not observe many differences across the four countries, with the possible exception of the American respondents being less willing than their European counterparts to respond that it is better to solve problems quickly rather than waiting for a legal solution. Especially on the fourth item, measuring an individual's belief that it is acceptable to break laws if one can skirt the consequences, we observe a fairly small range of responses across the four countries.

On the other hand, we observe stark differences across the pairs of countries on the two items that measure the government's behavior, illustrating the importance of including both individual and government actor items in a measure of this concept. While one-in-four Hungarian respondents and one-in-five Poles indicated that the government ought to ignore its Constitutional Court when its rulings place

9 To test the consequences of using a "Don't Know" response category instead of a "Neither agree nor disagree" option, we conducted a simple-question-wording experiment on a YouGov sample of 1,500 American adults in July 2023. A scale constructed with the don't know response option has $\alpha = 0.76$; with "neither agree nor disagree" the reliability is $\alpha = 0.79$. If we add the four indicators together to form a simple index, the averages are indistinguishable (15.8, sd =3.5 vs. 15.5, sd =3.4). Moreover, the correlations with respondents' demographic and political characteristics are similar (e.g., strong leader: −0.21 vs. −0.25; democratic support: 0.27 vs. 0.26). In short, both measures perform similarly.

TABLE 4.2 *Distribution of support for the rule-of-law indicators, by country, in July 2021. Data for all four countries come from July 2021. The percentages indicate the percentage of respondents who give an anti-rule of law response, somewhat or strongly agreeing with the statement.*

Question Wording	United States (%)	Germany (%)	Poland (%)	Hungary (%)
When the [Constitutional Court] hinders the work of our government, our government should ignore it	13	14	20	24
When the country is facing a difficult situation, it is ok for the government to disregard the law in order to deal with the situation	21	28	36	36
Sometimes it might be better to ignore the law and solve problems immediately rather than wait for a legal solution	29	39	39	36
If you don't particularly agree with a law, it is all right to break it if you are careful not to get caught	17	13	18	20

roadblocks in front of the government's priorities, those percentages are markedly smaller in the United States and Germany. And the percentage of respondents in Poland and Hungary who indicated that it is acceptable for the government to disregard the law in an emergency is much higher than the percentage of Germans and Americans who answered similarly.

We tested the fit of the four items with one-dimensional factor analysis. The four items fit onto a single factor, according to the eigenvalue for the second dimension. The factor loadings for the items are all quite good, with only one individual loading falling under 0.50, as shown in Table 4.3.

We use the scores from the factor analysis as our measure of the public's support for the rule of law. We rescaled the variable to range from 0 to 1; higher values indicate greater support for the rule of law. Figure 4.1 shows the distribution of this variable across the four countries. Overall, median support for the rule of law is higher in the United States (0.75) and Germany (0.73) than in Hungary (0.64) and Poland (0.64). The two countries with a greater level of judicial independence also show a slightly wider interquartile range: compare the United States (0.55–0.93) and Germany (0.54–0.88) with Hungary (0.50–0.81) and Poland (0.50–0.82).

Stability of Support for the Rule of Law

Scholars have long suggested that public support for the rule of law is stable over time, providing one explanation for key features of consolidated democracies like

TABLE 4.3 *Psychometric properties of support for the rule of law indicators. The cell entries are each item's loading on a unidimensional factor analysis. The last row in the table is the Cronbach's* α reliability coefficient for the four-item scale in each country.

Question Wording	United States	Germany	Hungary	Poland
When the [Constitutional Court] hinders the work of our government, our government should ignore it	0.63	0.61	0.63	0.66
When the country is facing a difficult situation, it is ok for the government to disregard the law in order to deal with the situation	0.62	0.65	0.57	0.61
Sometimes it might be better to ignore the law and solve problems immediately rather than wait for a legal solution	0.64	0.45	0.59	0.62
If you don't particularly agree with a law, it is all right to break it if you are careful not to get caught	0.64	0.63	0.52	0.62
α	0.83	0.70	0.69	0.75

regime stability and broad support for high courts even in the face of displeasing decisions (Gibson and Nelson 2015; Mondak and Smithey 1997; Nelson and Tucker 2021). In one example, Gibson (2007a) compares surveys of United States citizens in 1995, 2001, and 2005, finding that "public support for the rule of law has remained constant in the United States" during the decade under study (603). Reeves and Rogowski (2016) conduct a cursory check of stability using panel data of Americans, finding "strong correlations in our measure of the rule of law when comparing responses from the same individuals collected more than a year apart" (142). These two examples aside, we know little of the dynamics of the public's support, as neither panel data nor repeated cross-sectional studies are common in the field.

Thus, as another check of the validity of our measure, we draw upon our panel survey of Germans to examine the stability of the rule of law over time. Table 4.4 provides information about the panel including the field dates and the number of respondents per wave. We fielded Wave 1 of the survey at the beginning of the COVID-19 pandemic and finished the six-wave panel in the lead up to the federal German elections held in late September, 2021. No replenishment sample was needed; each of the 1,205 respondents who answered Wave 6 of the survey also completed Wave 1. Respondents were only eligible to participate in each successive wave of the survey if they had answered the previous wave.

We asked respondents about their support for the rule of law in each wave of the survey. The remaining columns of Table 4.4 provide information useful to assess the stability of our measure across the seventeen-month span of our panel. The fourth column in the table displays the average factor loading for a unidimensional factor analysis. Across the six waves, the average loading never falls below 0.55 nor

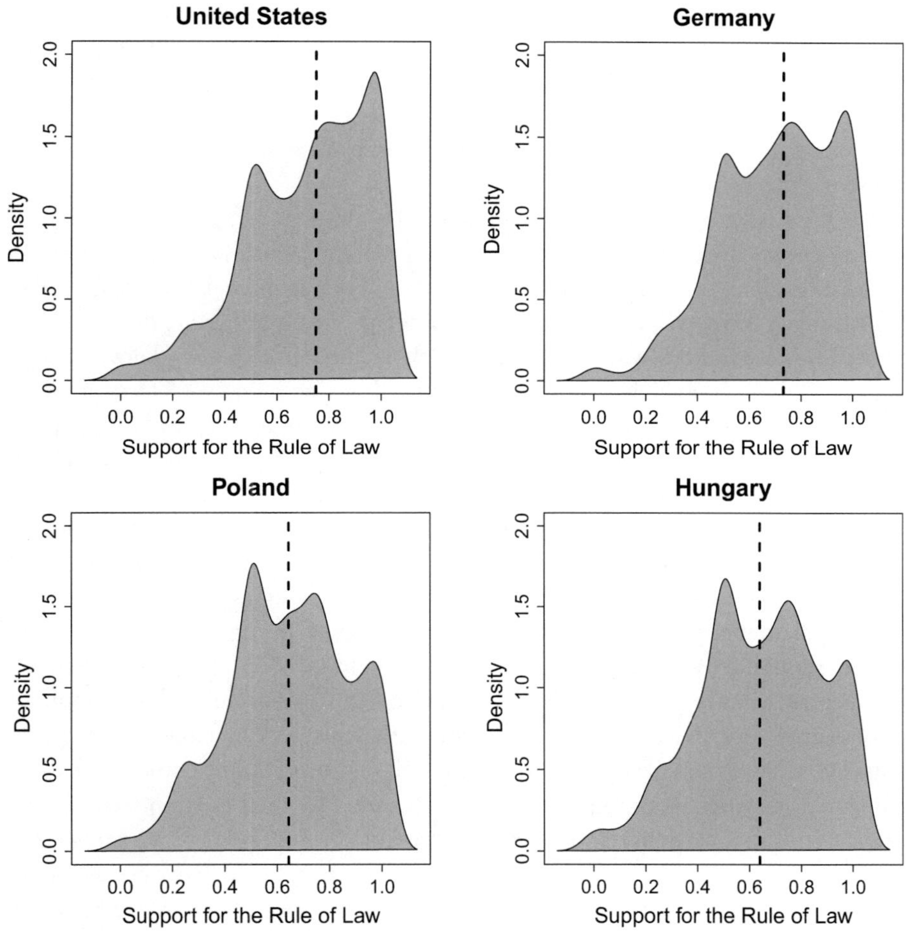

FIGURE 4.1 Distribution of support for the rule of law, by country. Higher values of the *x*-axis variable indicate more support for the rule of law. Dashed lines demarcate the median.

above 0.60, a very tight range of values. So too, looking at the next column, is the reliability of the scale stable across waves, ranging from $\alpha = 0.66$ in Wave 1 to $\alpha = 0.71$ in Waves 2–4.

To examine stability in the responses across waves, we summed respondents' answers to the four indicators, creating variables that range from four ("Strongly Agree" with all four items) to twenty ("Strongly Disagree" with all four items).[10] The

10 The summed scores are more useful than comparing the scores from the factor analysis across waves since the loadings do differ slightly across waves. The simple sum is a bit more comparable across waves and has an easy interpretation: a difference of 1 on this scale corresponds with a change of one response option on one item in the scale.

next two columns of Table 4.4 display the average summed score for all respondents (column 5) and only those respondents who answered all six waves (column 6), so as to ensure that our results are not driven by differential attrition. Regardless of which column one reviews, the average hovers between 15.01 and 15.41, a difference of less than one-half of one scale point on one indicator in the scale. This is a remarkable amount of aggregate-level stability.

Yet, the advantage of panel data is our ability to understand changes in individual-level responses over time. The final two columns of the table allow us to get a sense of the individual-level stability of these measures. The second-to-last column in the table displays the correlation between pairs of survey waves, restricting the sample to only those respondents who completed Wave 6. The correlations – between 0.56 and 0.61 – are moderately strong, illustrating stability across waves but with some movement from wave to wave. The Wave 1 to Wave 6 correlation is 0.54, only slightly smaller than the wave-to-wave correlations, providing some further evidence of stability across waves.

Is this individual-level variance consequential? There is a substantive difference in instability if it means respondents are moving from "Strongly Disagree" to "Disagree" on an item – some movement but not changing the thrust of their answer – than if respondents are moving from "Disagree" to "Agree" (changing their level of support for the rule of law, not just the magnitude). To answer this question, we created a variable that indicated the number of pro-rule of law responses respondents gave in each wave of the survey, a variable that ranges from 0 (all anti-rule of law or don't know responses) to 4 (all pro-rule of law responses). We then compared respondents on this metric across waves. The final column of the table displays the percentage of respondents who remained within one point on this scale across waves amongst those who answered in all six waves. Again, we see a very high level of stability: more than 80 percent of respondents gave stable answers on the scale from wave to wave. Comparing Wave 1 to Wave 6, the results are the same: 80 percent of respondents moved no more than one pro-rule of law response across the seventeen-month period of our survey.

Though we did not conduct a panel survey in the United States, we have collected more than 10,000 individual rule of law judgments since March 2020, providing us with another opportunity to assess the stability in public support for the rule of law. The summary statistics for our measure for these surveys are provided in Table 4.5. Across three years, we observe strong stability across these cross-sectional surveys. The average factor loading differs by no more than 0.09 across the nine samples, and the reliability coefficient remains within 0.08. For the summed score, which could range from 4 to 20, the difference in average support for the rule of law between the samples with the greatest and lowest support varies by only 2.13, a difference of 12 percent of the variable's range. Perhaps most interestingly, the highest support for the rule of law we observe is in the November 2020 survey – the period of time in our study when the rule of law was most under threat in that

TABLE 4.4 *The stability of support for the rule of law in Germany. Data from Germany panel survey fielded in 2020 and 2021.*

Survey Dates	N	Average Loading	Reliability (α)	Avg. Summed Score (All Respondents)	Avg. Summed Score (All Waves)	Correlation with Previous Wave	% with Three or Four Consistent Answers
April 28, 2020 to May 15, 2020	4,400	0.55	0.66	15.01	15.20		
June 30, 2020 to July 13, 2020	3,697	0.60	0.71	15.18	15.36	0.56	81.41
October 15, 2020 to October 29, 2020	3,189	0.60	0.71	15.07	15.19	0.60	81.99
February 18, 2021 to March 1, 2021	2,633	0.59	0.71	15.31	15.32	0.62	82.32
June 24, 2021 to July 6, 2021	1,334	0.58	0.70	15.34	15.41	0.58	82.89
September 3, 2021 to September 20, 2021	1,205	0.56	0.67	15.28	15.28	0.61	83.73

TABLE 4.5 *The stability of support for the rule of law in the United States. With the exception of the Fall 2020 surveys, each row summarizes a different cross-national sample of adult respondents in the United States.*

Survey Dates	N	Average Loading	Reliability (α)	Avg. Summed Score
April 9, 2020 to April 14, 2020	1,340	0.63	0.75	14.87
April 16, 2020 to April 21, 2020	1,125	0.61	0.72	15.30
April 23, 2020 to April 29, 2020	1,103	0.61	0.73	15.27
April 30, 2020 to May 7, 2020	1,111	0.63	0.75	14.95
September 29, 2020 to November 3, 2020	1,000	0.64	0.75	16.4
November 9, 2020 to December 7, 2020	822	0.58	0.70	17.00
February 18, 2021 to February 26, 2021	1,000	0.67	0.78	15.63
June 25, 2021 to July 1, 2021	2,000	0.62	0.74	15.40
July 11, 2023 to July 17, 2023	766	0.64	0.76	15.80

country due to Donald Trump's widely publicized campaign to overturn the results of the 2020 election.

In short, we find strong evidence that our measure is stable at both the aggregate and individual levels. Although we do observe some wave-to-wave movement among respondents, there is a remarkable amount of continuity across surveys. This stability is all the more important because the surveys were fielded during periods of time in both countries – the COVID-19 crisis and major national elections – where concerns about the rule of law were at the forefront of public discussion. That we observe so much stability is important evidence that our measure of support for the rule of law is reflects an enduring democratic value, not a fleeting instrumental attitude.

VALIDATING SUPPORT FOR THE RULE OF LAW

To this point, we have discussed our measure of support for the rule of law in terms of its content validity (whether the indicators reflect the conceptualization of the rule of law we seek to measure), the psychometric properties of the four items as a unidimensional scale, the overall cross-country differences in each item, and its stability over time. Our next task is to provide evidence of the scale's convergent, discriminant, and construct validity. To do so, we must assess the relationships between our measure and our respondents' demographic and political characteristics. In the process, we will begin to understand what sorts of people are more (or less) supportive of the rule of law.

Convergent and Discriminant Validity

Measures of public support for the rule of law have been available to scholars for decades, yet there has been surprisingly little systematic analysis of the correlates of the public's support for this norm. We are aware of no systematic, cross-national multivariate analysis of the relationship between citizens' demographic and political characteristics and their support for the rule of law. However, there is a large and well-developed literature on the correlates of other sorts of legal attitudes, such as judicial legitimacy and confidence in courts (e.g., Bartels and Johnston 2013; Christenson and Glick 2015a; Garoupa and Magalhães 2021; Gibson and Nelson 2014; Walker 2016), that – alongside these studies of the public's support for the rule of law – can help us form some expectations to test the convergent and discriminant validity of our measure.

Judicial Legitimacy

Support for the rule of law is a legal attitude. Thus, it makes sense to begin our investigation of our measure's validity by examining its relationship with the most studied legal attitude: judicial legitimacy. Whereas both concepts relate directly to legal considerations, we expect there to be a strong positive relationship between one's support for the rule of law and their ascribed level of constitutional court legitimacy. Importantly, we need to establish that these concepts are different than one another. As we discussed in Chapter 2, judicial legitimacy is an *institution-level* commitment: it measures the public's loyalty toward their constitutional court. Support for the rule of law, on the other hand, is a *system-level* commitment that encompasses people's opinions about how different parts of government should interact. For this reason, we do not expect the relationship between the two concepts to be perfect: for example, people can believe that significant reforms are needed to their constitutional court but believe, nonetheless, that their favored politicians need to play by the rules.

We measured respondents' judgments of the legitimacy of their country's constitutional court with five items that have been widely used in existing research (e.g., Gibson and Nelson 2014, 2015):

- If the [Constitutional Court] started making a lot of decisions that most people disagree with, it might be better to do away with the court altogether.
- The right of the [Constitutional Court] to decide certain types of controversial issues should be reduced.
- The [Constitutional Court] gets too mixed up in politics.
- Judges on the [Constitutional Court] who consistently make decisions at odds with what a majority of the people want should be removed from their position as judge.
- The [Constitutional Court] ought to be made less independent so that it listens a lot more to what the people want.

Consistent with previous research that utilizes these items (Gibson and Caldeira 1995, 2003; Gibson, Caldeira, and Baird 1998), we find that these five items form a reliable scale in all five countries ($\alpha = 0.81$ in the United States, 0.87 in Germany, 0.74 in Hungary, and 0.79 in Poland) with strong factor loadings in each country (average factor loadings are 0.67 in the United States, 0.76 in Germany, 0.59 in Hungary, and 0.64 in Poland) and very low second-dimension eigenvalues in each country. To give a sense of the cross-country variation on this measure, we summed respondents' replies to the five items (each answered on a 5-point scale) to create a variable that ranges from 5 to 25; higher values indicate greater levels of legitimacy. The average of this summed measure is higher in the United States (16.11) and Germany (18.18), than in Hungary (13.75) and Poland (13.38).[11] Thus, as one might expect, the constitutional courts in our two countries with high levels of judicial independence have deeper reservoirs of public goodwill than those enjoyed by the pair of courts with low levels of independence.

The relationship between the legitimacy battery and our support for the rule of law measure is as expected. In all four countries, there is a positive correlation between judicial legitimacy and public support for the rule of law. We observe the strongest correlation between these two concepts in the United States ($r = 0.48$) and in Germany ($r = 0.54$). In Poland and Hungary, by contrast, the magnitude of the correlation is still positive, but nevertheless considerably weaker, $r = 0.26$ in Hungary and $r = 0.28$ in Poland. Thus, although we observe the expected positive correlation, it is also evident that these two scales measure distinct concepts and not coterminous.

Political Knowledge and Sophistication

As with the case of judicial legitimacy, we anticipate a strong relationship positive relationship between individual-level political sophistication and support for the rule of law. Take, for example, the role of education. Gibson and Caldeira (1996) find a strong positive effect of education and their measure of legal values, acknowledging that the mechanism behind the relationship is difficult to parse. They write, "[e]-ducation is a variable that may characterize different processes. It can represent the acquisition of cognitive abilities, or it may stand for the amount of social learning (socialization) the individual has acquired" (73). This relationship is also found with other sorts of legal attitudes where those with higher levels of education and political knowledge express greater levels of support for the US Supreme Court and other national constitutional courts (see also Gibson, Caldeira, and Baird 1998; Gibson and Nelson 2014).[12]

[11] The spread is similar across countries; the standard deviations range from 4.5 (Hungary) to 5.2 (Germany).

[12] Among Black Americans, perhaps because of victimization from the legal system, this relationship does not hold. Scholars of comparative judicial politics have likewise observed an inverse relationship in a variety of other contexts (Çakir and Şekercioğlu 2016; Driscoll and Nelson 2018b).

We measure respondents' sophistication in four ways. First, we measure respondents' attention to politics with their answer (on a five-point scale) to "How often do you pay attention to what's going on in government and politics?" Second, we measure respondents' level of education. Because the educational systems (and measures of educational attainment) vary dramatically across our four countries, we measure education with a binary variable that indicates whether the respondent has finished a secondary school education. In the United States, we code respondents who completed high school as meeting this benchmark, while in Germany we do so for respondents who have completed Arbitur. In Hungary, respondents who have completed upper secondary school received a value of 1. In Poland, compulsory education ends at age eighteen, and so we coded respondents who indicated they completed their formal education at eighteen years or older as 'educated'.

These first two items measure general political sophistication; we also include two items that assess respondents' legal sophistication. Our third item measures respondents' awareness of their constitutional court (e.g., Gibson, Caldeira, and Baird 1998) on a four-point scale ("Would you say that you are very aware, somewhat aware, not very aware, or have you never heard of the [Constitutional Court Name], that is, one of the [Country] courts?"). Our final measure of sophistication is respondents' knowledge of their constitutional court.[13] In the United States, Poland, and Hungary, we asked respondents the number of justices on their constitutional court, whether the justices of that court serve for life or a set term of office, and whether decisions by the constitutional court are final. In Germany, we asked the latter two questions; the third item in the battery queried respondents about the method of selection for the German FCC.

To help us assess convergent and discriminant validity, Figure 4.2 displays the bivariate correlation between our measure of support for the rule of law and a variety of respondents' demographic and political characteristics. Positive values on the plot indicate a positive relationship between that respondent characteristic (e.g., age or court awareness) and support for the rule of law.

Beginning at the top of the figure, the first four groups of points show our measures of respondents' political sophistication. For all four indicators and across all four countries, higher levels of political and legal sophistication are associated with greater support for the rule of law, as expected.

[13] We prefaced the knowledge questions with an admonishment for respondents to not look up the answers to their knowledge questions. We instructed: "We'd like to ask you a few questions about the courts in Poland to learn what people know about the judiciary. It is important to us that you do not use outside sources like the Internet to search for the correct answers. We are trying to understand what people know about politics, not what they can look up."

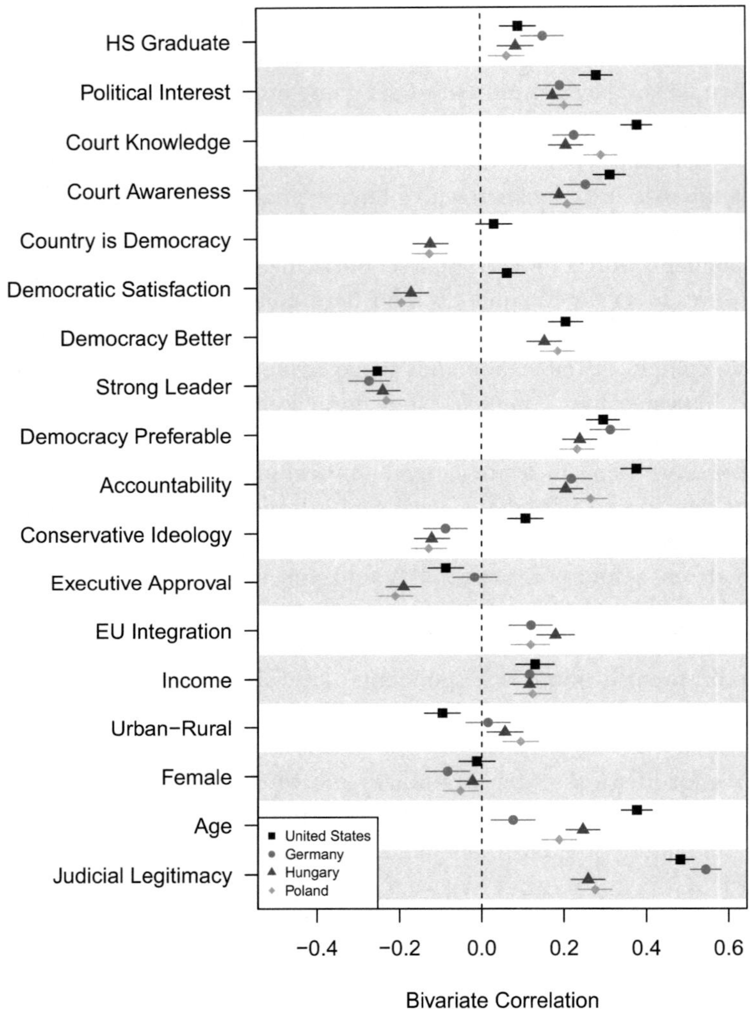

FIGURE 4.2 Bivariate correlations between Support for the Rule of Law and respondents' demographic and political characteristics. The horizontal lines provide 95% confidence intervals around the estimated Pearson correlation.

Democratic Values

A second category of covariates of interest concern individuals' other democratic values. Studies of support for legal institutions have long suggested that support for democracy and other democratic norms serve a fundamental role in structuring citizens' support for the law (e.g., Gibson and Caldeira 1992; Gibson and Nelson 2014, 2015). Support for the rule of law is part of a broader constellation of democratic values; it therefore stands to reason that those who support other sorts of democratic principles, like electoral accountability and the necessity of the popular vote, will value the rule of law at higher levels than those who embrace authoritarian principles, such as supporting a strongman leader over the will of the people.

In all four countries, we asked three questions that posed differing views of democracy and asked respondents to select the statement that came closest to their view (or indicate they didn't know). First, respondents selected between "Democracy is preferable, even if it is sometimes unstable" and "Ordered society is preferable, even if that means limiting democracy." Second, to measure authoritarian preferences, respondents selected between "We need a strong leader who does not have to be elected by the vote of the people" and "Although things may not always work, electoral democracy, or the popular vote, is always best." Finally, respondents selected between "It is more important to have a government that can get things done, even if we have no influence over what it does" and "It is more important for citizens to be able to hold government accountable, even if that means it makes decisions more slowly," to gauge respondents' preferences about democratic accountability. We recode these items into binary variables with a preference for democracy, the popular vote, and accountability taking a value of 1 and ordered society, a strong leader, and a government that can get things done (or "don't know") as 0.

We asked three additional questions about democracy in the United States, Poland, and Hungary; space constraints prohibited us from asking these questions in Germany. First, we asked respondents to indicate on a seven-point sliding scale their agreement with "Democracy may have problems, but it is better than any other form of government." Second, we measured satisfaction with democracy ("In general, how satisfied are you with the way that democracy works in [country]?") on a four-point scale. Finally, we asked respondents to answer a binary question: "In your opinion, is [country] a democracy?"

Looking at the next two rows of Figure 4.2, we see stark differences between Poland and Hungary, on the one hand, and the United States, on the other. Respondents in the United States who are more satisfied with the way democracy works in the United States are, on average, more supportive of the rule of law than those dissatisfied with democracy in the country. The inverse is true in Poland and Hungary: those dissatisfied with the way democracy is working in those two countries are *more* supportive of the rule of law than respondents satisfied with the quality of democracy in that country. Similarly, while there is no relationship between support for the rule of law according to whether one says the United States is a democracy,[14] Hungarians and Poles who say their country is not a democracy tend to be more supportive of the rule of law than respondents in

[14] After fielding the survey, we came to realize some measurement error in the United States on this question with (mainly conservative) respondents who believe the United States is a "republic" rather than a "democracy" answering no to this question.

those countries who said they live in a democracy. Although these analyses leave us to speculate for now, a likely explanation for this finding in Hungary and Poland is that supporters of the political opposition parties in these countries – many of which have built their platform around issues related to the rule of law and democratic decay – are at the same time dissatisfied with the state of democracy in their country and steadfast in their desire to see the rule of law restored (Gandur, Chewning, and Driscoll 2025).

We see more similarity across the four countries in terms of the other three democratic values. Respondents who support a strong leader over electoral democracy are, on average, less supportive of the rule of law. Those who believe democracy is preferable over "ordered society" are more supportive of the rule of law than are those respondents who prioritize electoral accountability over a government who can "get things done." With the exception of the very large difference in the United States on that latter question, the average differences across the four countries are relatively small: the three items have similar effects in all four countries.

Political Orientations

Third, beyond sophistication and values, respondents' political orientations might structure commitments to the rule of law. We are less sure. Ideally, one's support for the rule of law should be disconnected from instrumental concerns: valuing the rule of law requires prioritizing consistency, even when your political allies have behaved badly. In this way, we expect that support for the executive in power and one's political ideology would have only a minimal role in explaining cross-individual variation in support for the rule of law.

Our measure of respondents' ideology is their standard 10-point left-right self-placement in Germany, Poland, and Hungary. In the United States, we use YouGov's standard five-point ideological self-placement question. In the European countries, we asked respondents for their opinions on EU integration, asking them to select whether they believe integration hasn't gone far enough, has gone as far as it should go, or whether it has gone too far. In all four countries, we asked respondents for their views of the performance of the executive on a four-point scale. Support for the executive was higher in our pair of countries with higher levels of judicial independence; 65 percent of German respondents and 58 percent of American respondents gave a favorable response to this item while only 34 percent of Hungarian respondents and 28 percent of Polish respondents responded positively toward their executive.

Figure 4.2 shows that conservatives in the United States are, on average, more supportive of the rule of law while liberals in the European countries displayed more support for the rule of law. And, in all three European countries, respondents who support additional European integration are more likely to support the rule of law than those who oppose any further integration. Finally, in the United States, Poland, and Hungary, those who have greater satisfaction with the executive are less supportive of the rule of law than those who believe the executive is doing a poor job governing the country.[15]

Demographic Characteristics

Existing studies of support for the rule of law have found minimal correlations between individuals' demographic characteristics and their support for the rule of law. Gibson, Sonis, and Hean (2010) find no relationship between age and support for the rule of law in Cambodia. Similarly, Gibson and Caldeira (1996) report "[n]either age, gender, nor religion has much substantial or consistent impact on legal values" while suggesting that social class plays an important role in some countries to structure citizens' support for this norm. Studying South Africa, Gibson and Gouws (1997) report no differences in support for the rule of law according to citizens' race, a particularly striking finding given the importance of that cleavage in that country. Using AmericasBarometer data, Malone (2011) finds only sporadic correlations between age and urban residence and support for the rule of law.

Thus it is difficult to have any strong expectations about the relationship between citizens' demographic characteristics and their support for the rule of law. The broader literature on legal attitudes offers similarly scattershot findings, with some studies suggesting that demographic characteristics like gender (Krewson and Schroedel 2023), race (Caldeira and Gibson 1992; Clawson and Waltenburg 2009; Gibson and Nelson 2018), or other group-based considerations (Zilis 2021) affect Americans' willingness to ascribe legitimacy to the US Supreme Court. We therefore expect to observe only negligible correlations between respondents' demographic characteristics and support for the rule of law.

Our measure of the respondent's gender is binary, indicating whether the respondent identifies as female. To measure age, we rely on a question asking about the respondent's year of birth in Germany, Poland, and Hungary; in the United States, YouGov provided us with a direct measure of respondents' age. We measure the respondent's geographic context with a four-point measure. Respondents selected whether they lived in a "big city" or urban area, a suburb (or "outskirts of a big city"), a "small city, town, or country village," or a rural area ("farm or home in the country").

We used YouGov's standard measure of household income in each country. The question is worded differently across countries, asking about average monthly household income in Germany and Poland and yearly household income in the United States and Hungary. The measures also differ in their precision; the question in the United States contains sixteen scale points while only six points in Poland.

[15] In Germany, we also asked respondents on a four-point scale about their support for the Querdenker movement. The respondents who oppose the movement have higher levels of support for the rule of law (0.72) than those who support it (0.67), though the difference is not statistically significant ($p = 0.07$).

TABLE 4.6 *Correlates of support for the rule of law. Cell entries are linear regression coefficients and their associated standard errors. The outcome variable and all independent variables are scaled from 0 to 1 with higher values indicating greater levels of the concept.*

	United States	Germany	Hungary	Poland
Secondary school graduate	−0.02	0.05*	0.01	0.02
	(0.02)	(0.01)	(0.01)	(0.02)
Political interest	0.04*	0.02	0.01	0.04
	(0.02)	(0.03)	(0.02)	(0.02)
Court awareness	0.05*	0.11*	0.06*	0.04
	(0.02)	(0.03)	(0.03)	(0.03)
Court knowledge	0.09*	0.07*	0.06*	0.12*
	(0.02)	(0.02)	(0.02)	(0.02)
Accountability	0.11*	0.05*	0.03*	0.05*
	(0.01)	(0.01)	(0.01)	(0.01)
Democracy preferable	0.04*	0.10*	0.06*	0.06*
	(0.01)	(0.02)	(0.01)	(0.01)
Strong leader	−0.13*	−0.15*	−0.10*	−0.09*
	(0.02)	(0.02)	(0.01)	(0.01)
Age	0.19*	0.09*	0.19*	0.16*
	(0.02)	(0.03)	(0.03)	(0.03)
Female	0.03*	−0.01	0.01	−0.01
	(0.01)	(0.01)	(0.01)	(0.01)
Urban–Rural	−0.03*	−0.02	0.02	0.01
	(0.01)	(0.02)	(0.02)	(0.01)
Income	0.01	0.04	0.13*	0.06*
	(0.02)	(0.03)	(0.04)	(0.02)
Conservative ideology	0.08*	−0.04	0.004	−0.01
	(0.02)	(0.03)	(0.02)	(0.02)
Executive approval	0.01	−0.03	−0.09*	−0.10*
	(0.02)	(0.02)	(0.02)	(0.02)
Constant	0.36*	0.47*	0.45*	0.38*
	(0.03)	(0.04)	(0.03)	(0.03)
Observations	1,684	1,102	1,708	1,794
R^2	0.29	0.23	0.19	0.23

Note: * $p < 0.05$.

As is always a concern when asking about income, there is substantial nonresponse to this question; 14 percent of American respondents, 17 percent of German respondents, 15 percent of Hungarian respondents, and 10 percent of Polish respondents either indicated they did not know their income or declined to answer the question.[16]

[16] We have reestimated the multivariate regression model in Table 4.6 without the income measure to ensure that the large decrease in *N* does not materially alter the conclusions we draw. It does not.

Figure 4.2 shows that, across all four countries, older and wealthier respondents are more highly committed to the rule of law. In the United States, rural respondents are more supportive of the rule of law than urban respondents; in Poland and Hungary, urban respondents support the rule of law at higher levels than rural respondents.[17] And, finally, in Germany and Poland, women tend to be less supportive of the rule of law than men.[18]

Multivariate Analysis

Table 4.6 displays the results of four linear regressions, one for each country. For this analysis, we focus on items that are available across all four countries to maximize comparability. The outcome variable in each regression is support for the rule of law, measured on the 0–1 scale such that higher values indicate more support for the rule of law. Recall that all of the independent variables are also scaled from 0 to 1 with higher values indicating greater levels of the concept.

The first four rows of the table display the results for respondents' political sophistication. Having a high school education and general political interest are only related to support for the rule of law in Germany and the United States, respectively. Our two measures of legal sophistication perform more strongly, with greater knowledge and awareness of the constitutional court strongly associated with greater support for the rule of law. Combining these two influences, movement from no knowledge or awareness to maximum values on these two variables accounts of nearly 20 percent of the theoretical range of the rule of law variable.

We thus conclude that political sophistication is associated with greater support for the rule of law. But, importantly, not all sophistication is equal. Rather, it is legal sophistication – knowledge and awareness of constitutional courts – that plays the most important role in fostering greater support for the rule of law.

The next three rows of the table display the relationship between our measures of citizens' democratic values and their support for the rule of law. The relationship between each of the three variables and support for the rule of law is statistically significant in all four countries. People who support electoral accountability, believe that democracy is preferable (even if it can be messy), and reject strong leaders over electoral democracy all tend to support the rule of law at higher levels. The effects of

[17] German respondents who reported living in the former German Democratic Republic before 1989 had, on average, lower levels of support for the rule of law (0.67) than respondents who did not (0.71) ($p = 0.01$).

[18] We examined the effect of race in the United States: average support for the rule of law is higher among white respondents (0.75) than nonwhite respondents (0.65) ($p < 0.01$), among white respondents than Black respondents (0.63) ($p < 0.01$), and among nonhispanic (0.73) than Hispanic (0.65) respondents ($p < 0.01$).

these indicators are all meaningful in magnitude. The association effect of the strong leader variable is particularly noteworthy: in all four countries, rejecting a strong leader is associated with an increase in support for the rule of law equal to 10 percent of the range of the outcome.

Finally, we turn to the correlates of demographic characteristics. Our results on this front are more consistent than those presented in existing studies. We find that gender and urban–rural location have a statistically significant relationship in the United States, though not in any of the other three countries. These associations are rather small, however. Perhaps most surprisingly we find a robust and strong correlation between of age across all four countries. The oldest survey respondents score markedly higher on support for the rule of law than the youngest respondents in our survey. The difference is between 10 and 20 percent of the range of the outcome variable, an association rivaling the combined effect of the democratic values or legal sophistication variables.

Recall that Gibson and Caldeira (1996) found a positive relationship between social class and legal culture; although we do not have a direct measure of social class, our surveys did include income. While, all else being equal, there was no effect of income in the United States and Germany, we see that wealthier respondents in Hungary and Poland are more supportive of the rule of law. One possible explanation for this is the tendency of professionals and those with higher levels of education – who are consequently likelier to have higher incomes – to support the opposition in those countries and its emphasis on democracy-related issues like the rule of law.

Finally, we find an association between ideology in the United States, Poland, and Hungary. But the direction of the effect is not the same. In the United States, more conservative respondents are more supportive of the rule of law; in the European countries, we observe no independent effect of ideology. But, in Poland and Hungary – but not the pair of countries with higher levels of judicial independence – we see a link between executive approval and support for the rule of law: those who believe the executive is doing a good job governing the country are, on average, less supportive of the rule of law.

Predictive Validity

Turning now to predictive validity, we fielded a simple question-wording experiment. If our measure of support for the rule of law is valid, then individuals with a greater commitment to the norm should be less likely to allow governments to take actions that are not legal. We test this with a simple experiment that asked respondents whether or not they believed it could be justifiable for the national executive to postpone elections. Respondents in the control condition read the following text: "Do you believe that it could ever be justifiable for the [Executive] to postpone elections?" In two other conditions, one related to the coronavirus pandemic and another related to the threat of violence, respondents read a slightly different beginning to the question: "Do you believe that when there is a public health emergency like the coronavirus..." or "Do you believe that when there is a lot of violence..." In all three conditions, respondents gave a binary response, either "Yes, it could be justified" or "No, it could not be justified." Overall, 26 percent of Americans, 57 percent of Germans, 32 percent of Hungarians, and 65 percent of Poles responded in the affirmative, illustrating a diversity of responses across countries.

We begin by addressing the relationship between support for the rule of law and respondents' belief that election postponement could be justified. These results are shown in the first four columns of Table 4.7. We test this relationship in a logistic regression model since the outcome variable is binary, and we include indicator variables for the two alternative treatments. In the United States, a respondent with an average value of support for the rule of law has a 0.20 probability of indicating that postponement could be justified. For the COVID-19 and violence justifications – in which respondents are learning about more exigent considerations – the probability jumps to 0.29 and 0.24, respectively. In Germany, such a respondent would support election denial with a 0.54 probability, and the COVID-19 and violence justifications would raise the probability to 0.58 and 0.60. The analogous probabilities (control, COVID-19, and violence) are 0.22, 0.33, and 0.38 in Hungary and 0.64, 0.80, and 0.52 in Poland, respectively.

Our real interest is in the variation in responses according to respondents' commitment to the rule of law. In all four models, the coefficient for support for the rule of law is negative and statistically significant, indicating that respondents are less likely to countenance election postponement as justifiable as support for the rule of law increases. In the United States, the difference in predicted probabilities is 0.56 for the control condition as this variable increases from its minimum to its maximum. In Germany, that difference is 0.36; in Hungary, it is 0.39; and in Poland, the predicted probability of believing election postponement could be justified drops 0.16 as support for the rule of law changes from its minimum to its maximum. Thus, there is some difference in the strength of this effect across our four countries, but the effect is both statistically significant and substantively meaningful in all of them.

Finally, while our main interest is the direct effect of support for the rule of law, we would also expect that support for the rule of law operates similarly across the three experimental conditions. That is, the effect of support for the rule of law should not vary according to the exigent circumstances cited in the question. The final four columns of Table 4.7 enable us to assess that possibility. With one exception – the effect of support for the rule of law is magnified in the presence of violence in Poland – we observe no evidence that the effect of support for the rule of law varies across circumstances. Our interest is less in the direct effects of the treatments and more the ability of support for the rule of law to predict which respondents believe election postponement could be justified.

TABLE 4.7 *Logistic regression results, 2021 question wording experiment. The dependent variable indicates that the respondent believes that postponing elections could be justified.*

	Direct Effects				Conditional Effects			
	United States	Germany	Hungary	Poland	United States	Germany	Hungary	Poland
Support for the rule of law	−2.88*	−1.60*	−2.04*	−0.74*	−2.33*	−1.50*	−2.13*	−0.18
	(0.23)	(0.26)	(0.22)	(0.21)	(0.39)	(0.45)	(0.41)	(0.33)
COVID justification	0.54*	0.16	0.54*	0.83*	1.15*	0.46	0.46	0.60
	(0.13)	(0.14)	(0.13)	(0.13)	(0.40)	(0.48)	(0.36)	(0.36)
Violence justification	0.24	0.27*	0.78*	−0.48*	0.69	0.17	0.70*	0.68*
	(0.14)	(0.14)	(0.12)	(0.11)	(0.39)	(0.49)	(0.35)	(0.34)
COVID justification × Support for the rule of law					−0.93	−0.43	0.14	0.35
					(0.56)	(0.64)	(0.57)	(0.53)
Violence justification × Support for the rule of law					−0.69	0.15	0.13	−1.78*
					(0.56)	(0.65)	(0.54)	(0.49)
Constant	0.64*	1.28*	0.04	1.05*	0.29	1.21*	0.10	0.69*
	(0.18)	(0.21)	(0.16)	(0.16)	(0.27)	(0.34)	(0.26)	(0.23)
Observations	1,999	1,334	2,000	2,000	1,999	1,334	2,000	2,000
Log likelihood	−1,052.72	−890.24	−1,182.28	−1,223.01	−1,051.24	−889.80	−1,182.24	−1,212.96
Akaike inf. crit.	2,113.44	1,788.47	2,372.55	2,454.01	2,114.47	1,791.60	2,376.47	2,437.91

Note: * $p < 0.05$.

In short, this exercise provides some additional support for the validity of our measure: not only does it correlate as expected with respondents' demographic and political characteristics, but it also is able to predict respondents' answers in an unrelated survey experiment.

CONCLUSION

In this chapter, we set out to conceptualize, validate, and analyze our measure of public support for the rule of law. Building on extant work that conceptualizes public support for the rule of law in formalistic terms, we distinguish the orientation of citizens' support for this democratic norm insofar as these expectations are held to refer to individuals or government institutions. The items we selected to measure these two features were drawn from a broad cross-section of questions that have appeared in cross-national survey research, which we pretested on pilots in the United States as well as the United Kingdom, Spain, and Germany. Shifting our analyses to the four country cases that are the focus of our study, this index shows desirable psychometric properties across both time and space, and that our measure of the public's support for the rule of law varies in ways we would reasonably anticipate, given our theory and research design.

Having explained and validated our measure of public support for the rule of law, we have all of the necessary building blocks to test the theory we outlined in Chapter 2. Moving forward, we will use this measure not as an outcome but rather as an explanation. Recall that we have theorized individual-level variation in the extent to which citizens will respond to the signals of independent courts. In subsequent chapters, this measure of public support for the rule of law will help us assess this receptivity. Having now explained our argument, research design, and measurement strategy, we can now turn to tests of our theory.

Appendix

ADDITIONAL COUNTRY DATA

In addition to the Wave 1 Germany data described in the body of this chapter, we also fielded our items as part of YouGov's COVID-19 tracker, a series of weekly nationally representative surveys conducted for eight weeks beginning in mid-March 2020, in the United States, United Kingdom, and Spain. We purchased space in each of the three countries for the final four waves of the survey. Fieldwork in all three countries began on March 9, 2020. Sampling was done using a three-wave rolling exclusion procedure. Each survey was nationally representative with 1,000 respondents in each United States and Spain wave and 2,000 respondents in every United Kingdom wave.

TABLE 4.A1 *Distribution of support for the rule of law indicators, alternative country selection. The cell entries indicate the percent of respondents who give an anti-rule of law response, "somewhat" or "strongly" agreeing with the statement.*

Question Wording	United States (%)	UK (%)	Spain (%)	Germany (%)
When the [Constitutional Court] hinders the work of our government, our government should ignore it.	13	25	19	13
When the country is facing a difficult situation, it is ok for the government to disregard the law in order to deal with the situation.	19	32	35	30
Sometimes it might be better to ignore the law and solve problems immediately rather than wait for a legal solution.	29	26	32	38
If you don't particularly agree with a law, it is all right to break it if you are careful not to get caught.	14	6	12	13

Table 4.A1 shows the distribution of these items on these surveys alongside the results from Wave 1 of the Germany survey. Importantly, higher agreement with the statement (a larger percentage) indicates *lower* commitment to the rule of law. So, when the table suggests that only 6 percent of UK citizens agree with the fourth item in the battery, it means that 94 percent of respondents in that country gave a pro-rule of law response to the survey item. Viewed in this light, we see that the first and fourth items elicited, on average, more pro-rule of law responses than did the second and third items. At the same time, it is perhaps surprising that more than 10 percent of Americans, Spaniards, and Germans suggested that it is acceptable to break laws so long as you will not get caught. Similarly, one-in-four UK citizens indicated that the government ought to ignore its Supreme Court when its rulings place roadblocks in front of the government's priorities.

As we did in the body of the chapter, we reverse-coded each item so that higher values of the items indicate greater support for the rule of law and summed the items to create a variable with a range of 4 to 20. In the United States, this variable had a mean of 15.1, a median of 16, and a standard deviation of 3.5. In the United Kingdom, the variable had a mean of 14.5, a median of 14, and a standard deviation of 3.2. In Spain, the variable had a mean of 15.1, a median of 16, and a standard deviation of 3.8. In Germany, the variable has a mean of 15.0, a median of 15, and a standard deviation of 3.5.

TABLE 4.A2 *Psychometric properties of support for the rule-of-law indicators, alternative country selection. The cell entries are each item's loading on a unidimensional factor analysis. The last row in the table is the Cronbach's α reliability coefficient for the four-item scale in each country.*

Question Wording	United States	UK	Spain	Germany
When the [Constitutional Court] hinders the work of our government, our government should ignore it. (Government compliance)	0.60	0.67	0.65	0.59
When the country is facing a difficult situation, it is ok for the government to disregard the law in order to deal with the situation. (Government conditions)	0.67	0.71	0.62	0.57
Sometimes it might be better to ignore the law and solve problems immediately rather than wait for a legal solution. (Individual compliance)	0.64	0.55	0.60	0.57
If you don't particularly agree with a law, it is all right to break it if you are careful not to get caught. (Individual conditions)	0.61	0.36	0.53	0.46
α	0.75	0.67	0.71	0.65

TABLE 4.A3 *Item selection table: March 2020 MTurk Survey. The items are sorted by the factor loading on the first dimension. The columns provide the percentage of respondents who agreed with the statement, the percentage of respondents who gave a don't know response, and the factor loadings (λ) and uniqueness (U) for one- and two-dimension solutions.*

Item	Wording	% Agree	% DK	λ_1	U_1	$\lambda_{2,1}$	$\lambda_{2,2}$	U_2
Asian Barometer Wave 4	When the country is facing a difficult situation, it is ok for the government to disregard the law in order to deal with the situation	19.34	7.75	0.70	0.51	0.70	0.17	0.48
AmericasBarometer 2008	When the Congress hinders the work of our government, our president should govern without the Congress	14.47	8.54	0.69	0.53	0.69	0.29	0.45
AmericasBarometer 2010	When the Supreme Court hinders the work of our government, our president should ignore it	9.95	6.93	0.68	0.53	0.68	0.14	0.51
AmericasBarometer 2012	Do you believe that when the country is facing very difficult times it is justifiable for the president to dissolve the United States Supreme Court and govern without it?	15.38	9.05	0.65	0.58	0.65	0.21	0.54
Gibson, Sonis, and Hean (2010)	In times of emergency, the government ought to be able to suspend law in order to solve pressing social problems	24.1	12.35	0.63	0.60	0.63	0.24	0.54
Gibson and Caldeira (1996)	If you don't particularly agree with a law, it is all right to break it if you are careful not to get caught	13.18	4.53	0.59	0.65	0.59	-0.42	0.47
AmericasBarometer 2008	Do you believe that there could be a sufficient reason for the president to dissolve the Supreme Court and govern without it, or do you think a sufficient reason could never exist	20.16	11.39	0.59	0.66	0.59	0.21	0.61
Gibson (2007a)	The government should have some ability to bend the law in order to solve pressing social and political problems	28.27	9.15	0.57	0.68	0.57	0.13	0.66
Afrobarometer Round 3	Which of the following statements is closest to your view? Choose Statement 1 or Statement 2. Statement 1: Since the President was elected to lead the country, he should not be bound by laws or court decisions that he thinks are wrong. Statement 2: The Pres- ident must always obey the laws and the courts, even if he thinks they are wrong	11.95	4.12	0.56	0.68	0.56	0.07	0.68

Gibson (2007a)	It is not necessary to obey the laws of a government that I did not vote for	10.55	4.02	0.55	0.69	0.55	-0.25	0.63
Gibson and Caldeira (1996)	Sometimes it might be better to ignore the law and solve problems immediately rather than wait for a legal solution	26.03	10.15	0.54	0.70	0.54	-0.18	0.67
Gibson, Sonis, and Hean (2010)	It's all right to get around the law as long as you don't actually break it	26.10	9.34	0.53	0.72	0.53	-0.20	0.68
AmericasBarometer (2006)	There are people who say that we need a strong leader who does not have to be elected by the vote of the people. Others say that although things may not work, electoral democracy, or the popular vote, is always best. What do you think?	12.03	7.25	0.52	0.73	0.52	0.10	0.72
Gibson and Caldeira (1996)	It is not necessary to obey a law you consider unjust	17.69	9.15	0.45	0.80	0.45	-0.45	0.59
Driscoll and Nelson (2018a)	When the Supreme Court blocks the work of the government, the justices of the Supreme Court ought to be personally held accountable via impeachment trials	26.00	5.93	0.42	0.82	0.42	0.19	0.79
Smithey and Malone (2013)	The police always have the right to make people obey the law	46.93	5.33	0.08	0.99	0.08	0.52	0.72
Gibson (2007b)	Even if laws are not always fair, it is more important that government actions follow the law than that they be fair	47.99	10.74	-0.11	0.99	-0.11	0.41	0.82
Smithey and Malone (2013)	The courts have the right to make decisions that people have to abide by	62.01	5.33	-0.21	0.95	-0.21	0.35	0.83
Gibson, Sonis, and Hean (2010)	An individual is obligated to obey the law for the good of society as a whole, even if he/she finds it personally unjustifiable	53.97	5.93	-0.23	0.95	-0.23	0.55	0.64
Cruz (2009)	In order to apprehend criminals do you think that the authorities should always respect the law or that occasionally they can skate close to the limits of the law?	77.39	6.13	-0.29	0.92	-0.29	0.09	0.91
Gibson, Sonis, and Hean (2010)	Government officials who are guilty of crimes deserve the same punishment as anyone else	19.40	1.51	-0.46	0.79	-0.46	0.08	0.78

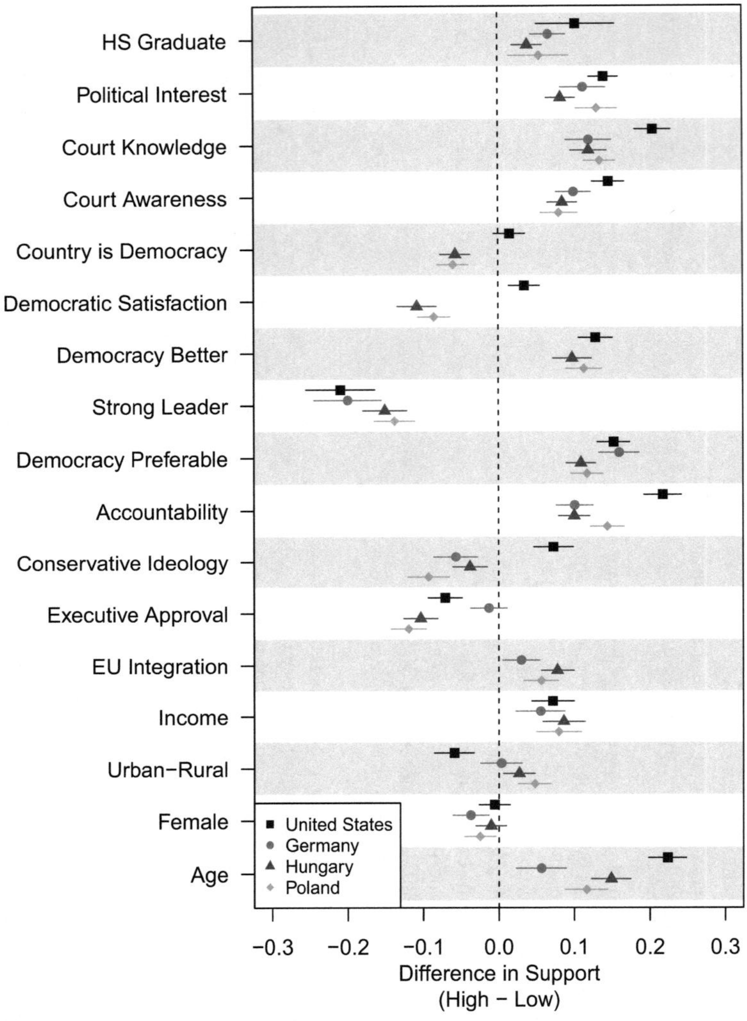

FIGURE 4.A1 Difference in average support for the rule of law, by demographic and political characteristics. For dichotomous variables, the value is the difference between the two categories; for interval-level variables, the value is the difference between respondents who scored at or above the 75th percentile and those who scored at or below the 25th percentile. The horizontal lines provide 95% confidence intervals. Positive values on the plot indicate that respondents with higher values of the independent variable have, on average, greater support for the rule of law than those with lower values of the independent variable.

RELIABILITY AND VALIDITY

We tested the fit of the four items with one-dimensional factor analysis. Table 4.A2 provides information on the factor analyses we conducted to create our outcome variable. In all four countries, the four items fit onto a single factor, according to the eigenvalue for the second dimension. The factor loadings for the items are all quite good, with only two individual loadings falling under 0.50, as shown in Table 4.A2.

Table 4.A3 displays the results of the item selection exercise we conducted on MTurk in March 2020.

DIFFERENCES IN MEANS

To help us assess convergent and discriminant validity, Figure 4.A1 displays differences in the average value of support for the rule of law across a variety of respondents' demographic and political characteristics. For dichotomous variables, the figure plots the difference between the two categories. For interval-level variables, the dots are the average difference between respondents who scored at or above the 75th percentile and those who scored at or below the 25th percentile. Positive values on the plot indicate that respondents with higher values of the independent variable have, on average, greater support for the rule of law than those with lower values of the independent variable.

5

How Judicial Independence Facilitates State Constraint

We have argued that judicial review conducted by independent courts mobilizes public opposition to unconstitutional executive behaviors. We test this argument in this chapter by focusing on the foundational expectation of our theoretical argument: the public withdraws support from executives that contravene the decisions of independent courts.[1]

We also consider the potential consequences of a court upholding a challenged policy for public support. Not every exercise of judicial review strikes down a policy; constitutional courts often clear the policies they review, thus endorsing a given policy's constitutionality. In contrast to the vast literature on the legitimizing power of constitutional courts (e.g., Dahl 1957), we are pessimistic about the power of constitutional courts to change public opinion by confirming the constitutionality of the policies they review. Instead, we expect that the endorsement of an independent constitutional court will not, on average, yield a change in the public's acceptance of an executive action.

We first test this argument in a survey experiment that randomizes a hypothetical German Constitutional Court ruling on a proposal by the German government to fast-track the approval of a COVID-19 vaccine. We find support for our expectations about the efficacy of judicial review: the public withdraws support from the action when it contravenes the Constitutional Court, while clearance by the German Court provides no boost in approval of the German government's hypothetical action.

Next, we address how the efficacy of courts varies according to their level of judicial independence. We argue that, when courts lack independence, their efficacy is fundamentally compromised: they are powerless to affect the public's acceptance of a constitutionally suspect policy regardless of whether they deem it is constitutional or not. To gain the necessary variation in judicial independence to

[1] We defer to Chapter 6 our discussion of factors, such as public support for the rule of law, that we argue have conditional effects on the efficacy of judicial review.

adequately test this expectation, we analyze a second survey experiment fielded in all four of the countries in our study. As predicted by our theory, we observe that the efficacy of courts varies according to their level of judicial independence: contravention of the US and German high courts convinces citizens to withdraw acceptance. Noncompliance with the high courts of Hungary and Poland, however, yields no change in public acceptance. Instead, Hungarians and Poles react no differently to a policy implemented over the objection of the constitutional court as they do to a policy that was not reviewed by the court at all. Further, as hypothesized, in no case do we observe judicial approval increasing citizens' acceptance of the executive's policy.

We conclude the chapter by assessing how the public responds to executives who play by the rules. We outline two possible responses to an executive who backs down and declines to implement her chosen policy after a court strikes it down. We first consider that the public might still punish the executive for pursuing an illegal policy. We then account for the possibility that citizens might reward the executive for complying with the rule of law. Our results indicate that – regardless of the court's level of judicial independence – executives who comply with court orders enjoy higher levels of acceptance than those who do not.

By evaluating citizens' responses to executive policies implemented following judicial review, our analyses reveal support for our book's central contention: so long as judicial review is exercised by an independent court, it may act as an effective tool of state constraint. In these contexts, independent judicial review helps the public to recognize an executive's action as a violation of the rule of law and a focal point around which they can coordinate their response. On the other hand, when courts lack independence, the public does not punish executives for defying court orders, and judicial opposition to the executive is not an informative signal that the executive is pushing the bounds of constitutional impropriety. It has long been posited that courts might serve as a focal point around which the public might coordinate to constrain political elites and uphold the rule of law (Sutter 1997; Vanberg 2015; Weingast 1997). We are among the first to directly test this proposition and are the first to do so experimentally with nationally representative samples in multiple countries.

We further highlight that our findings regarding the scant positive effects of judicial clearance speak to the value of judicial co-optation. Scholars of autocratic politics have long observed that institutional co-optation is a common strategy of autocrats (Gandhi 2010; Gandhi and Przworski 2006; Levitsky and Ziblatt 2018; Svolik 2020), as is the use of formally legal processes to fortify an autocrat's grip on power and to suppress democratic contestation (Varol 2015). In its worst manifestation, courts might even legitimize an autocrat's rule, lending a glean of judicial impartiality to executive actions that overstep the bounds of the social contract embodied in the constitution. Throughout this chapter (as well as the next), we provide direct empirical evidence into the relative value of neutralizing judicial institutions, particularly as it relates to how constitutional review might facilitate public resistance to executive encroachment. Although co-opting a high court might silence an alarm that would otherwise animate public opposition to an autocrat, we find no evidence that judicial review serves to legitimate an executive's controversial policies. Thus, while independent courts are a critical component of efficacious state constraint, their power is not absolute. Public acceptance does not blindly follow a court's assertion of constitutionality; the ability of courts to legitimize controversial policy is limited, if not nil.

THE EFFICACY OF JUDICIAL REVIEW

Courts famously lack the powers of both the purse and the sword. Individuals or governments come to courts for dispute resolution, courts decide litigants' cases, and judges depend on executive branch officials to accept and implement their decisions. Courts are fundamentally reactive institutions: they rely on legislatures to craft the laws they interpret and on others to enforce their decisions. For these reasons, public acceptance translates into political capital for courts, helping them to achieve implementation of their decisions (e.g., Nelson and Uribe-McGuire 2017).

As we discussed in Chapter 2, courts are not helpless in their dependence on public sentiment. Through judicial review, some courts can also *shape* citizens' attitudes. Specifically, we have argued that, through their use of judicial review, constitutional courts can activate the public and affect citizens' acceptance of the policies brought before the court. When a constitutional court exercises the power of judicial review, it sends a signal to the public about whether a policy put forward by others in government complies with the rule of law. Given general public inattentiveness to the nuances of politics and their constitutional implications, information provided by trustworthy courts through judicial review can mobilize citizens' opposition to unconstitutional policymaking. When striking down a government's action, the court provides a focal solution to the public's coordination and monitoring problems with independent judicial authorities uniquely poised to assist the public in their efforts to constrain the state due to their high level of source credibility.

There are two important caveats to courts' capacity monitor executives and coordinate public responses to executive actions. First, the public is likely to respond differently to a constitutional court's use of judicial review according to the court's decision: whether the court rules a policy as unconstitutional or it endorses the policy's constitutionality (it "clears" the policy). Whereas we contend that courts can mobilize public opposition to unconstitutional policies, we do not anticipate a comparable *boost* to public acceptance for policies upheld by a court. In this sense, our theory predicts an asymmetric effect of judicial review, with its efficacy found only when courts determine that a policy violates the constitution.

The second caveat relates to judicial credibility. Court rulings on the constitutionality of policies are only effective if citizens can rely on the court's expertise and view it as forthright. Independent courts are able to send credible signals about the constitutionality of policies to the public because citizens know that the rulings these courts make, and, by extension, the signals they send, are not controlled by the executive or the legislature. Instead, these courts' decisions are, in a word, independent. On the other hand, where courts lack independence, perhaps because they have been co-opted or are heavily reliant on the executive or legislative branches, they lack credible signaling authority. Citizens in these contexts cannot trust that a judicial review decision is informative about the congruence between the executive's policy and rule of law. For instance, the court may say that a policy is constitutional, but citizens cannot trust the court to reliably tell them whether the policy is actually congruent with the rule of law or whether the policy is instead an unconstitutional extension of the executive's goals. In short, we expect that courts with low levels of judicial independence have compromised signaling authority and therefore their rulings are less effective at persuading citizens to update their levels of acceptance for a policy.

These considerations help motivate our hypotheses about how the public's acceptance of an executive action changes according to a constitutional court's ruling. But, before discussing those hypotheses, we need to resolve one other preliminary matter. When we say we are interested in how the public's acceptance *changes* according to an executive action, we need to have a clear baseline: *compared to what circumstance* is the public's level of acceptance lower (or higher) because of a judicial ruling. Our interest throughout this book is the causal effect of judicial review: when courts rule a policy unconstitutional or endorse it as compliant with the constitution, how do public attitudes change? Accordingly, we are interested in comparing the public's reaction to executive actions that were taken after judicial review to those in which the executive implements a policy without judicial review. This approach enables us to identify the effect of the judicial review signal, holding constant the policy consequences of the executive's decision.

To begin, we anticipate that an executive implementing a policy in defiance of a judicial order – a circumstance we term "contravention" – will result in lower acceptance of the executive's action. More formally:

- H_1: Judicial contravention decreases acceptance of an executive's action.

With regard to instances in which a court clears an executive's policy, we expect such judicial approval to have little effect on the level of public acceptance. Thus:

- H_2: Judicial clearance neither increases nor decreases acceptance of an executive's action.

Third, we expect that the efficacy of judicial review, as evidenced by a contravention penalty, is limited to courts with high judicial independence:

- H_3: The penalty for contravention is limited to courts with a high level of judicial independence.

STUDY 1: VACCINE APPROVAL EXPERIMENT

We begin by testing our first two hypotheses with an experiment regarding the fast-tracking of vaccine approvals fielded in Germany. The Vaccine Approval Experiment presented respondents in Germany with information about a potential COVID-19 vaccine rollout. The dubiously constitutional executive action in this experiment was one that many nations faced during the pandemic: how soon is "too soon" to deploy a vaccine for public inoculation? Must a vaccine pass all of the "normal" legal and regulatory hurdles, or does the emergency situation give the executive leeway to bypass statutory authority in the name of public health?

This experiment was fielded from October 15–29, 2020, before a vaccine for COVID-19 was available to the general public in Germany or anywhere else. The COVID-19 vaccine that was furthest along in its clinical development at the time of survey administration was the BioNTech/Pfizer vaccine, which had entered Phase 3 trials but had not been cleared for distribution by either the Standing Committee on Vaccination (STIKO), or by European (EU) authorities (German Ministry of Health 2020). The first German vaccinations were administered on December 27, prioritizing healthcare and nursing home workers as well as the elderly (Ellyat 2021b; Martin 2020). Vaccines would not be widely available until the second quarter of 2021 (Eddy 2021), a fact which a frustrated public blamed on both German and EU authorities (Gehrke 2021a).

All respondents began the experiment by reading some brief background information about the hypothetical executive action:

> Imagine that the government announced that a vaccine for coronavirus would be available to the general public next week. The vaccine has passed initial safety trials, but the final safety tests required by law will not be complete. The government contends that the benefits of distributing the vaccine as quickly as possible outweigh the legal safety requirements.

The remainder of the text varied by experimental condition. Respondents in the Control condition saw no additional text. Treated respondents learned that the Bundesverfassungsgericht either (a) prohibited the federal government from distributing the vaccine, which the government would later *contravene*, or (b) authorized the government action, meaning the court *cleared* the executive's action. Regardless

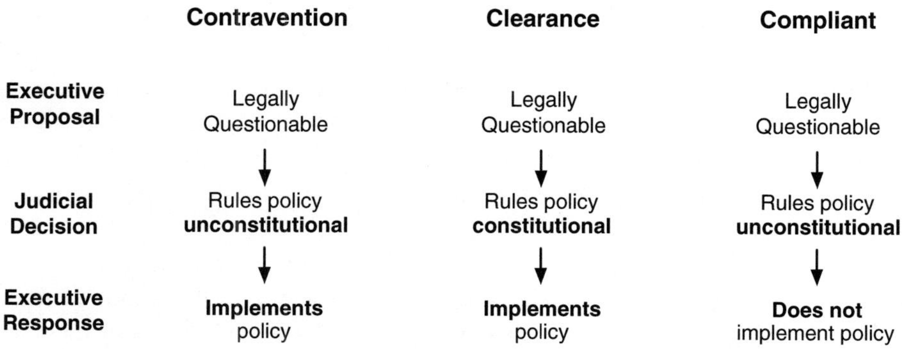

FIGURE 5.1 Illustration of executive–judicial interactions in the treatment conditions in the Vaccine Approval and Lockdown Experiments.

of whether the action was endorsed or overruled by the constitutional court, respondents learned that the government would press on with its plan, distributing the vaccine without waiting for legally required safety trials.[2] The first two columns in Figure 5.1 illustrate the executive–judicial interactions underlying the Contravention and Clearance conditions in the Vaccine Approval Experiment.[3] The Contravention treatment read:

> In response, the Bundesverfassungsgericht issued an emergency ruling prohibiting the government from distributing the vaccine due to the existing legal requirements. The government announced it would distribute the vaccine in defiance of the Bundesverfassungsgericht's decision.

The Clearance treatment read:

> In response, the Bundesverfassungsgericht issued an emergency ruling authorizing the government to distribute the vaccine despite the existing legal requirements. The government announced it would distribute the vaccine in accordance with the Bundesverfassungsgericht's decision.

We pause to emphasize three features of our research design. First, all respondents were exposed to a fictitious situation in which the executive pushed the bounds of objective legal authority: all respondents read that safety tests "required by law" were not yet complete. This was also an unprecedented scenario in public life. Never before had so many people and their government been asked to weigh this sort of

[2] There were two analogous treatment conditions where the Bundestag (the national legislature) either cleared the action or was contravened by the government. Throughout this chapter, the summary statistics we provide are for all respondents, including those in both the Court and Legislature treatments. We report the results from the legislative treatments in the appendix to Chapter 6, which serves as a test of our claim that courts are well-positioned to animate public opposition to executive recalcitrance.

[3] The Compliant condition was only included in the chapter's second experiment (the Lockdown Experiment), and is discussed later in this chapter.

calculus; the constitutional ambiguity was both pressing and concrete. Second, all the treated respondents learned about a judicial ruling made *after* the federal government announced its plan to disregard the law and distribute the vaccine. In the Contravention treatment, the constitutional court formally prohibited the federal government's plan; in the Clearance treatment, the court made post hoc rulings to declare the government's actions consistent with constitutional and statutory procedures.

Third, our dependent variable is respondents' acceptance of the executive's action. Most existing studies of the public's support for unilateral executive action focus on the public's approval of a particular action, measured with a single survey question. For example, Christenson and Kriner (2019) vary justifications for executive actions and ask respondents the following question: "Presidents have the power in some cases to bypass Congress and take action by executive order to accomplish their administration's goals. Do you support or oppose this approach?" (4). Respondents answered the question on a four-point Likert scale which the authors collapsed into a dichotomous outcome (see also Christenson and Kriner 2017c, 2020b).[4] Similarly, Reeves and Rogowski (2018) use respondents' attitudes toward the president's handling of the issue, collapsed into a dichotomy, as their outcome variable (see also Reeves and Rogowski 2016, 2022a).[5,6] Reeves and Rogowski supplement their analyses of action approval with other outcome variables, including evaluations of executive traits, like being a "strong leader" or a president's ability to "get things done" (Reeves and Rogowski 2018, 2022a, see also). More importantly for our purposes, they also evaluate the effects of unilateral action on candidate support (Reeves and Rogowski 2018) or job performance evaluation (Reeves and Rogowski 2022b). These outcomes, together, assess a more general concept related to the public's acceptance of the executive action than the more specific items that focus on the approval of the executive. As we explained in Chapter 1, this more general approval concept is a useful way to understand the public's responses to executive action, and is therefore the concept we seek to measure across all of the experiments in this book.

To measure this concept, our respondents were asked immediately following the vignette to answer three questions about the federal government's actions regarding the vaccine distribution plan. Our conceptualization on this front is similar to Gibson, Caldeira, and Spence (2005): requiring "citizens to respect [the court's decision], to cease opposition and get on with politics" (194). Our operationalization

4 In another experiment in that paper, respondents were asked whether the believed the Obama administration "has gone too far, has been about right, or has not gone far enough – in expanding the power of the presidency and executive branch to combat terrorism?" The authors collapse that variable into a dichotomy indicating whether respondents suggested the president has gone "too far."

5 For example, "Do you approve or disapprove of Candidate [name]'s handling of [issue]?" asked on a five-point scale (Reeves and Rogowski 2018).

6 Reeves and Rogowski use hypothetical candidates; Christenson and Kriner reference actual presidential incumbents.

of this concept takes a slightly different track due to the nature of our study. Many previous studies of institutional acquiescence expose all respondents to a disappointing decision and measure acquiescence as respondents' willingness to support efforts to overturn the decision, perhaps by removing justices or packing the Court (Gibson, Lodge, and Woodson 2014; Gibson and Nelson 2018). Our respondents, by contrast, were treated without regard for their level of policy support. We therefore include a basic measure of support for the executive's action as the first item in our battery.[7] Specifically, we asked respondents to rate their approval of the federal government's action (again on a 4-point scale). A near majority – 49 percent – of respondents said they "strongly" or "somewhat" supported the government's action.

Our second and third items relate directly to the two major facets of Gibson, Caldeira, and Spence's conceptualization of acceptance: respecting the decision and ceasing opposition. To measure the former, we ask about respondents' beliefs about whether the executive's action was "a legitimate exercise of power."[8] Conceptually, this is a different concept than support: one can support an executive's action but believe it is an abuse of power (just as someone can oppose an executive's action but believe the executive had the authority to take that action). To assess the latter, we include a measure of compliance, asking respondents (on a four-point scale) how likely they were to get this vaccine. By asking respondents about their willingness to take an action in line with the executive's policy, this item taps respondents' level of acceptance in a way that goes beyond measuring approval alone.[9] The three items correlate highly, but not overwhelmingly, with one another; the compliance item correlates at $r = 0.61$ with the support item and at $r = 0.57$ with the legitimate action item.

Overall, these three items form a reliable scale, with $\alpha = 0.86$. The items all load on a single dimension, with the eigenvalue for the second factor a mere –0.04. The three items load on this first factor at 0.65, 0.90, and 0.88, respectively. We use as our outcome variable the scores from this factor analysis, scaled from 0 to 1. Higher values of the outcome variable indicate more positive affect toward the federal government's action.

Study 1: *Vaccine Experiment Results*

Our first hypothesis suggests that acceptance of an executive action that contravenes a court will be lower than acceptance of the same action, implemented without

7 It is for this reason that our measure of acceptance does not include the "would you work to overturn the decision" item common in other measures of acceptance. Because we do not assign all respondents to a decision they should disagree with, this item would require us to make an unfounded assumption that all respondents would want to overturn the decision.

8 Eleven percent of the respondents strongly believed the government's action was legitimate while 21 percent of respondents somewhat believed the government's action was lacking in this regard.

9 Thirty-eight percent of respondents said they would "probably" or "definitely" get vaccinated.

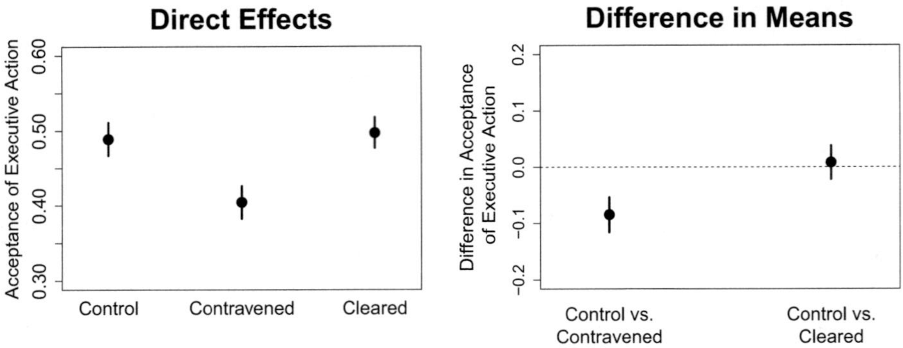

FIGURE 5.2 Direct effects of the Vaccine Approval Experiment. The left-hand panel plots the average value of acceptance of the executive's action, by condition. This variable has a range of 0–1; higher values of this variable indicate a greater level of acceptance. The right-hand panel illustrates the difference in means between experimental conditions. Positive values of the *y*-axis in this panel indicate an increase in acceptance, relative to the Control condition. The vertical lines in both panels provide 95% confidence intervals.

judicial oversight. The left-hand panel of Figure 5.2 shows the average value of the outcome variable for the Control, Contravention, and Clearance treatments, and the right-hand panel shows the difference between the Control condition and the two treatment conditions.[10] To test this hypothesis, we look to the first point estimate in the right-hand panel, which displays the difference in means between the Control and Contravened conditions. This hypothesis is supported by the data: we see a statistically significant decrease in acceptance ($p < 0.01$). This difference – 0.08 – is substantively significant: when the executive acts in explicit noncompliance with the constitutional court, we witness a decline of roughly one-third of a standard deviation in acceptance.

Our second hypothesis suggested that judicial clearance would not be associated with an increase in acceptance, relative to the Control condition. The point estimate to test this hypothesis is the second point estimate in the right-hand panel of Figure 5.2. This hypothesis is supported by the data: the average levels of acceptance in the two conditions are nearly identical (0.50 for the Cleared condition and 0.49 for the Control condition), and the difference between the treatments is not statistically significant ($p = 0.59$). In line with our expectations, there is no evidence that judicial clearance bolsters support for executives who push constitutional boundaries. Instead, citizens' responses to the executive action are no different than if the court had not weighed in at all.

[10] Linear regression results underlying the results of this experiment, as well as a discussion of the robustness of our results to models including respondents' political and demographic characteristics, are provided in the appendix to Chapter 6.

From the two panels in Figure 5.2, we draw two important conclusions about judicial review in the context of high judicial independence. First, and in line with our theoretical expectations regarding the efficacy of judicial review, judicial contravention yielded a decline in public acceptance. This penalty is present compared to an executive who announces a plan without oversight and when compared to the Clearance condition.[11] Second, as our argument regarding the efficacy of review suggested, we find no evidence that an institution providing clearance to an executive's action increases the public's acceptance of it. However, while institutional clearance does not *boost* acceptance, it does appear to *blunt* disapproval, rendering the public's response to the executive's illegal action essentially the same as if the court had not ruled.

STUDY 2: LOCKDOWN EXPERIMENT

Having found clear evidence in support of two of our central theoretical expectations, we now turn to testing for differences in judicial efficacy according to levels of judicial independence. Recall we expect that, where courts are lacking in independence, their decisions will fail to alter citizens' support or opposition for a constitutionally suspect policy. That is, constitutional courts such as those in Poland and Hungary should be unable to generate a contravention penalty. This proposition, which we characterized above as our third hypothesis, thus requires us to conduct an analysis that allows us to leverage variation in judicial independence.

To do so, we turn to a survey experiment fielded in July 2021 in the United States, Germany, Poland, and Hungary. As we established in Chapter 3, the constitutional courts in the United States and Germany are both exemplary constitutional courts with high levels of judicial independence. They are capable and transparent and are well regarded as forthright by a broad cross-section of the German and American public. We, therefore, expect them to have high levels of source credibility such that executives who cross them will face a loss of public support.

In Poland and Hungary, by contrast, we have a pair of countries where the constitutional courts lack independence. They pose flimsy constraints on the political executive because they are generally unable or unwilling to challenge the government. As we saw in Chapter 3, the public recognizes that these courts have been captured by the ruling right-wing governments, leaving them regarded as institutions that fail to command the public's trust or deeper institutional fealty.[12] Taken together, these four cases thus provide critical variation in judicial independence such that we can probe the relative efficacy of the independent US and German courts vis-à-vis their non-independent counterparts in Hungary and Poland.

[11] The difference between the Cleared and Contravene treatments is 0.09 ($p < 0.01$).

[12] We focus on the Constitutional Court and Tribunal in Hungary and Poland, respectively, rather than the Supreme Courts in these countries. Both constitutional authorities became dominated by the ruling parties at the time of our study.

The experiment is similar to the Vaccine Approval Experiment in its form, though it differs in the policy issue it addresses. The vignette describes a hypothetical increase in the severity of the coronavirus pandemic and a proposed response by the executive involving an especially strict nationwide lockdown. All respondents read a short paragraph describing the increase in COVID-19 cases and the national executive's proposed response to the crisis. By way of example, the text seen by respondents in the United States read as follows:

> Imagine that coronavirus cases increase throughout the country next month to rates higher than at any point since the pandemic began. This surge is due to the spread of a variant of the coronavirus that is resistant to existing vaccines, meaning that even vaccinated people are at risk of contracting the disease. To limit the severity of the surge, the President announced a nation-wide lockdown, restricting gatherings of more than five people, closing all but the most essential businesses, and imposing a curfew from 8 p.m. to 5 a.m. The lockdown will last for one month, and individuals who break the lockdown will face a substantial fine. The President contends that these measures are necessary to contain the virus' spread.

Respondents were then randomized into one of four conditions, a Control condition in which no further information was provided to respondents and three conditions in which respondents learned about the intervention of the country's constitutional court in response to a challenge to the policy:[13]

- *Control*: [No further text provided]
- *Contravened*: In response, the US Supreme Court issued a decision stopping the government from implementing the lockdown plan. The President announced that he will move forward with the lockdown, in defiance of the Supreme Court's decision.
- *Cleared*: In response, the US Supreme Court issued a decision allowing the government to implement the lockdown plan. The President announced that he will move forward with the lockdown, as allowed by the Supreme Court's decision.
- *Compliant*: In response, the US Supreme Court issued a decision stopping the government from implementing the lockdown plan. The President announced that he will not move forward with the lockdown, in response to the US Supreme Court's decision.

Figure 5.1, shown earlier in this chapter, illustrates the three treatment conditions included in the Lockdown Experiment. Note that the Lockdown Experiment

[13] One design difference between the Lockdown and Vaccine Approval Experiments deserves note. In the Vaccine Approval Experiment, all respondents were exposed to a fictitious situation in which the executive was pushing the bounds of objective legal authority; in the Lockdown Experiment, whether the executive action broke existing law was a fact not included explicitly in the vignette.

includes an additional experimental treatment in which the government "follows" the law by acquiescing to the constitutional court's decision and not moving forward with the lockdown policy. To mirror our discussion of the Vaccine Approval Experiment and test the hypotheses we outlined earlier in the chapter, we set this treatment aside for the moment and return to it at the end of the chapter.

As with the Vaccine Approval Experiment, our outcome variable is the respondent's acceptance of the executive's action, again measured with a three-item battery incorporating support, appropriateness, and compliance. First, we asked respondents, "To what extent do you support or oppose the President's decision [to move forward with the lockdown/to not move forward with the lockdown]?" (US wording). In the United States, 61 percent of respondents supported the President's decision; the analogous percentage was 65 percent in Germany, 55 percent in Hungary, and 50 percent in Poland.

Our second item, which probes support for the executive's behavior as a legitimate action, asks respondents, "Do you believe the President's decision [to move forward with the lockdown/to not move forward with the lockdown] is an appropriate exercise of power?" The decision was viewed as at least "somewhat appropriate" by 64 percent of American respondents, 66 percent of German respondents, 51 percent of Hungarian respondents, and 53 percent of Polish respondents.

Our final item measured respondents' likely compliance with the executive action, asking respondents (on a four-point scale) how likely they were to comply with the lockdown. The percentage of respondents who gave a pro-compliance answer to this item was 71 percent in the United States, 80 percent in Germany, 80 percent in Hungary, and 69 percent in Poland.

We combine the three items in each country using factor analysis. In all four countries, the items formed a reliable scale, with α values of 0.92 in the United States, 0.90 in Germany, 0.84 in Hungary, and 0.90 in Poland. The items also loaded strongly on a single factor in each country, with average factor loadings of 0.88 in the United States, 0.87 in Germany, 0.79 in Hungary, and 0.87 in Poland. We rescaled the resulting factor scores to range from 0 to 1 with higher values indicating higher levels of acceptance. The average values of the outcome are 0.57 in the United States, 0.63 in Germany, 0.54 in Hungary, and 0.47 in Poland.

The Lockdown Experiment has a strong claim to external validity because our design was unfortunately prescient. A surge in COVID-19 cases due to the Delta variant challenged all four countries shortly after our surveys were out of the field.[14]

[14] For example, the US survey ended on July 6, 2021 and the US Centers for Disease Control and Prevention (CDC) updated its recommendations on July 27, 2021 to encourage masking even among vaccinated individuals in response to the Delta variant. As the CDC described it: "In late June, the 7-day moving average of reported cases was around 12,000. On July 27, the 7-day moving average of cases reached over 60,000. This case rate looked more like the rate of cases we had seen before the vaccine was widely available" (Centers for Disease Control and Prevention 2021).

While none of the countries in our sample issued a lockdown while our surveys were in the field, lockdowns were common in both countries earlier in the COVID-19 pandemic. Although the US federal government never issued a nationwide lockdown, Adolph et al. (2022) report that all 50 US states adopted some form of movement restriction in March and April 2020, the early months of the pandemic.[15] Germany took a more nationalized response to the pandemic, instituting a lockdown policy on March 22, 2020 that banned more than two people (other than families) from meeting, closed restaurants for dining, and also shuttered many other businesses (Bennhold and Eddy 2020). Poland enacted a lockdown policy in March and April 2020 restricting minors from leaving their homes, closing public spaces, and limiting the number of people allowed in businesses at a time (Polish Government 2020). Hungary also had a lockdown early in the pandemic, even instituting an overnight curfew (Kovács 2021). As a result, the inconveniences of pandemic-driven lockdowns were a lived experience of many (if not all) of our respondents.

The external validity of our experimental design is further strengthened by the presence of high-profile legal challenges to governments' pandemic-related policies. In Germany, the Federal Constitutional Court received a number of cases calling for the invalidation of federal and state government policies involving the closure of businesses, schools and other restrictions (e.g., Gehrke 2021b; Nienaber 2021; Reuters Staff 2020a). Similar challenges were filed in state and federal courts in the United States (Couloumbis et al. 2020; Feldman 2020; Liptak 2020; Mok and Posner 2022; Vigdor 2020), as well as in countries around the world (BBC News 2020, 2021b; Cerulus and Bouzi 2021; Corder 2021; Karp 2020). With the courts clearly seen as an appropriate venue for adjudicating the constitutionality of restrictions like lockdowns, vaccine mandates and other policies, our vignette's focus on a court challenge would not have been far-fetched in the minds of respondents.

Study 2: *Lockdown Experiment Results*

Figure 5.3 displays the direct effects of the experiment.[16] The left-hand panels show the average values of acceptance of the executive's action, by condition. The right-hand panels illustrate the difference in means between the control group and the two treatment groups. Positive values in this panel indicate that, relative to the Control condition, the treatment increases acceptance; negative values indicate that, compared to the Control condition, the treatment reduces acceptance.

[15] Also by this time, the Biden administration was firmly ensconced in the federal government, which had signaled a willingness to lead a more concerted federal effort to constrain the virus, in contrast with the preceding government led by President Trump.

[16] Linear regression results underlying the results of this experiment, as well as a discussion of the robustness of our results to models including respondents' political and demographic characteristics, are provided in the appendix to Chapter 6.

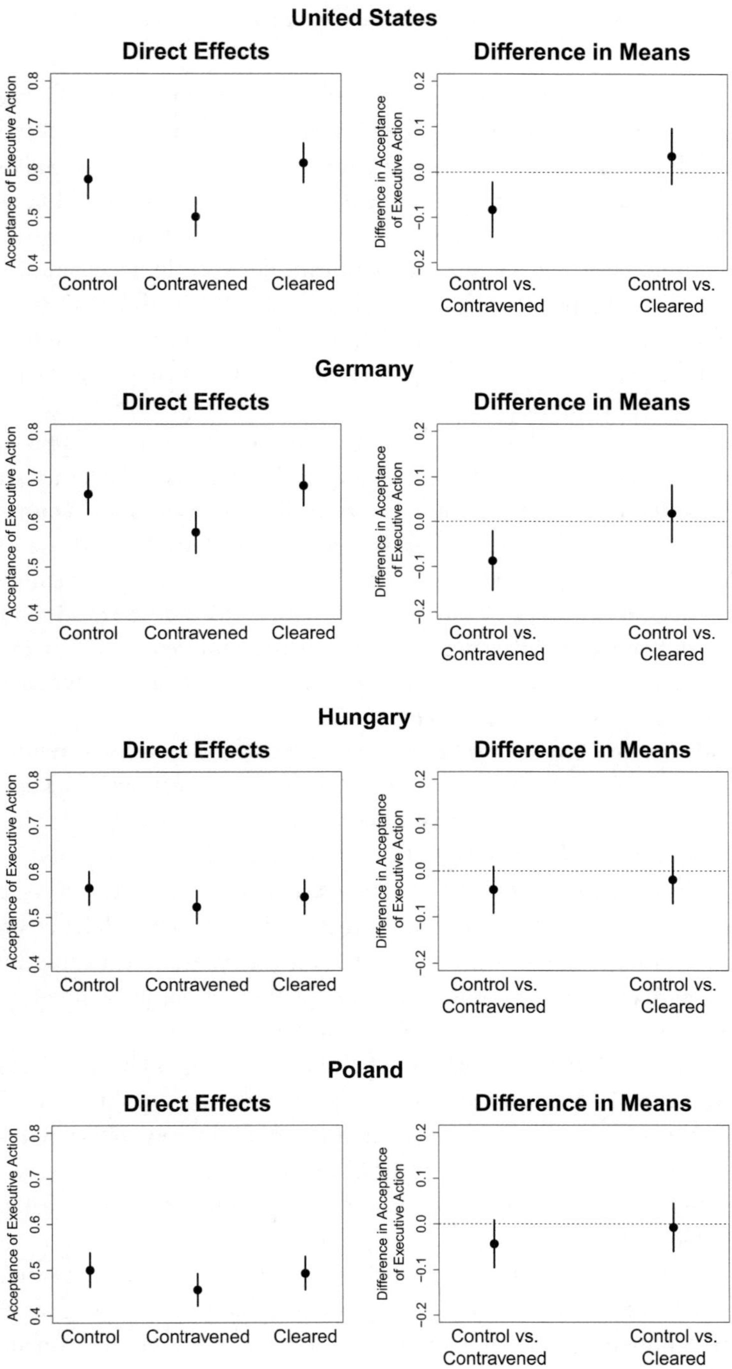

FIGURE 5.3 Direct effects of the Lockdown Experiment. The left-hand panels plot the average value of acceptance of the executive's action, by condition. This variable has a range of 0–1; higher values of this variable indicate a greater level of acceptance. The right-hand panels illustrate the difference in means between experimental conditions. Positive values of the *y*-axis in these panels indicate an increase in acceptance, relative to the Control condition. The vertical lines in both panels provide 95% confidence intervals.

Our first hypothesis related to the difference between the Contravention and Control conditions, so we begin by focusing on the first point estimates in the right-hand panels of Figure 5.3. For countries with high levels of judicial independence (the United States and Germany), we expected contravention would be associated with a decrease in acceptance relative to the Control condition. As expected, we see a substantively large and statistically significant decrease in acceptance associated with contravention of the constitutional court (−0.08 in the United States and −0.09 in Germany, $p < 0.01$ in both countries). This difference is also substantively considerable: a decline of roughly one-quarter of a standard deviation of the outcome in both countries.[17]

In contrast to the findings of a contravention penalty in the United States and Germany, in Hungary and Poland, we anticipated there would be no deleterious effect for an executive action that contravenes these constitutional courts with low levels of judicial independence. This is exactly the pattern we observe in the right-hand panels of Figure 5.3. The estimated difference in means between the contravention and control groups is close to zero in both cases, indicating no substantive or statistical difference: a difference of 0.04 in both countries ($p = 0.11$ in Hungary and $p = 0.10$ in Poland). As we anticipated, courts lacking in independence do not inspire public reaction to their rulings.

Considering our second hypothesis, we expected that courts in neither pair of countries would be able to increase acceptance of the executive's lockdown policy by endorsing it. As Figure 5.3 shows, these expectations are borne out in the data. In high judicial independence contexts, a court's endorsement of the executive's proposal does not boost the public's acceptance (United States: 0.04, $p = 0.26$; Germany: 0.02; $p = 0.58$). The same is true in the low independence contexts of Poland and Hungary. Here, the difference in means between the treated and control group are both close to zero, indicating no substantive or statistical difference (−0.02, $p = 0.46$ in Hungary and −0.01, $p = 0.77$ in Poland).

To summarize, Figure 5.3 enables us to draw several important conclusions. First, executives who disregard an independent court's order pay a political price: the loss of public acceptance. This sort of blatant disregard for the rule of law is not routine, and it is not well-tolerated in the court of public opinion. In this way, we observe direct, causally identified evidence regarding the conditions under which courts are efficacious.

Second, and in line with our expectations, we find that this contravention penalty is limited to *independent* constitutional courts. Judicial independence exerts a powerful influence on the ability of courts to mobilize opposition to

[17] Our theory also implies that there should be a statistically significant difference between the Contravention and Cleared treatments in Germany and the United States. This is the case: the difference is statistically significant: a 0.12 decrease in the United States and a 0.11 decrease in Germany, accounting for a decline in acceptance of about one-third of a standard deviation in both countries ($p < 0.01$ in both the United States and Germany).

unconstitutional executive actions. In the two countries where judicial independence is compromised, we see no effect of contravening the court: there is no difference in acceptance when a constitutional court is contravened by the executive and when the court is not involved. Without independence, it seems, courts are impotent.

Third, we find no evidence that constitutional courts exhibit an ability to boost support for policies by clearing them. In no case do we observe clearance by a court legitimating the actions of an executive by boosting the public's acceptance of a constitutionally questionable action. Though this result mirrors the results of the Vaccine Approval Experiment, it runs counter to many studies of the legitimizing capacity of courts (e.g., Christenson and Glick 2015b; Dahl 1957).

WHAT IF THE EXECUTIVE COMPLIES?

Our theoretical and empirical focus has been on citizens' reactions to governments pursuing constitutionally dubious policies, yet it leaves open the question of how citizens respond when their government complies with a court's decision to invalidate its policy. This is, after all, how constitutional review is supposed to function as a safeguard in liberal democracies. Although a public backlash is unnecessary when an executive plays by the rules and obeys a court order, the court's decision nonetheless signals to the public that the executive had championed an unconstitutional policy. This information need not mobilize the public, yet it may still shape citizens' acceptance of the executive's now-abandoned policy.

This effect could take one of two forms. First, citizens might reward – or at least not punish – government officials in recognition that they are following the "rules of the game" by complying. People may recognize the government's acquiescence as the proper action to take and thus reward the executive for backing down. For governments in this scenario, the cost of compliance borne from the invalidation of its preferred policy may be offset, at least to some degree, by the plaudits won from some citizens and the willingness of others to consider the government's attempt as harmless. This emphasis on the rules of the game over the questionableness of the initial policy suggests that compliance might be associated with an increase in acceptance.

Alternatively, compliance may be associated with a decrease in acceptance. Citizens may be disappointed that the executive would pursue an illegal action, even though it was successfully stymied by the courts, because they expect the government to willingly and faithfully pursue only actions that are clearly constitutional. Rather than see the government's attempt as harmless, the public might view the proposed policy as sufficient on its own to warrant punishment. By this logic, the court's signal is still powerful, as it warns the citizenry that the executive had tried to act in violation of the rule of law.

Both accounts have important potential implications for the functioning of judicial review and the relationship between citizens, executives, and courts. Scholars have posited that the presence of judicial review facilitates pandering, as executives can pass unwise – and legally-suspect – policies to appease their constituents in the knowledge that the courts will strike it down and rescue them from the law's worst consequences (Fox and Stephenson 2011; Ward and Gabel 2019). Similarly, informational accounts of judicial review depict courts as improving the quality of legislation by, if needed, striking down laws (Rogers 2001). If, however, citizens punish their government for having its policies struck down by a court, then such strategies may be costlier than previously considered. Alternatively, a public that rewards compliance may make tactics like pandering and passing riskier policies all the more attractive, as executives can reap the benefits of doing so and then also profit from the public's appreciation for adhering to the "normal" constitutional process. With the potentially damaging effects of such strategies, how citizens respond to governments when they comply may have significant consequences for the quality and content of policymaking.

The nature of citizens' reactions to a compliant government also speaks to the potential value of co-opting the courts. If the public is concerned more with whether the government's reaction is in line with the court's decision than whether the policy was constitutionally unacceptable in the first place, then complying is almost as good as having judicial clearance, at least in terms of public reaction. The government can advance a constitutionally questionable policy with relatively little risk; the government wins if the court upholds the policy, and, if it strikes it down, the government can still save face or even possibly gain acceptance by complying. In such contexts, the value of co-opting or neutralizing the courts may be less attractive to public opinion-focused executives.

In contrast, co-opting the judiciary may be of significantly more use to an executive facing a public that will punish it if its policy is declared unconstitutional, regardless of the executive's response. If this is the case, then a court's decision still represents a powerful signal to citizens and places the government in a difficult position. Once it proposes a constitutionally suspect policy is proposed, the only outcome that can save the executive from losing public support is the backing of a court. Here, the incentive is strong for the executive to bring the court to its side whether through political pressure, co-optation, court curbing, or some other measure. In this way, the strength of a court's ability to direct punishment for attempting unconstitutional policies may correlate directly with the incentive for a government to silence it.

We return to our Lockdown Experiment to examine if either dynamic is at work. Our "Compliant" treatment informed respondents that the executive would not move forward with the lockdown policy in response to the court's decision requiring a stop to its implementation. We can compare this Compliant treatment with the

Control treatment to estimate the effect of abiding by a judicial order, relative to no judicial intervention. Additionally, we can compare the two treatments in which the court tells the executive their proposed action is inappropriate, the Compliant and Contravene treatments, to quantify directly the effect of ignoring, rather than obeying, a judicial declaration of unconstitutionality.[18]

Figure 5.4 illustrates these comparisons.[19] The first column plots the average value of the Control, Contravene, and Compliant treatments. The second column plots the difference between the Compliant condition relative to those baselines. Positive values on this panel indicate that compliance increases acceptance of the executive's action relative to the Control or Contravene treatments.

In the United States, respondents reacted no differently to an executive who backed down after the Supreme Court nullified the lockdown policy than they did to the Control condition ($0.05, p = 0.09$). However, as one would expect, there is a statistically and substantively distinct difference between the Contravened condition (in which the executive does not comply with the Court's decision striking down the policy) and the Compliant condition (in which the executive does comply), with a clear acceptance benefit to compliance relative to outright defiance. The difference of 0.14 is nearly 40 percent of a standard deviation of the outcome variable ($p < 0.01$). Thus, the results from the United States verify the oft-hypothesized notion that there is a cost to noncompliance (e.g., Driscoll, Çakir, and Schorpp 2024; Krehbiel 2021c).

We see different results in Germany. Here, we observe no average differences in acceptance of the executive's action between the Compliant and Control conditions ($-0.06, p = 0.09$) nor do we observe a statistically significant benefit to compliance with the constitutional court relative to contravention ($0.04, p = 0.24$).

We can only speculate here as to the source of the divergence in response to the Compliance treatment between respondents across countries. One possibility is different conceptions of what constitutes "normal" politics, with American respondents seeing the president's compliance as making up for the constitutional questionableness of the policy while Germans viewed the policy itself as a violation of the rule of law. Alternatively, it may be that our German respondents cue more strongly off of the constitutional court than our other respondents who relied more so on the constitutional rules of the game to inform their reaction. As it is beyond the scope of our present focus, though, we are left to hope that future research may be able to more fully untangle this puzzle.

[18] The Clearance and Control treatments are very similar, we thus, we omit discussion of the Clearance treatment in this section in the interest of simplicity.

[19] Because the government does not move forward with the lockdown policy in the Compliant condition, respondents in that condition did not answer the compliance question (there was no lockdown with which they could indicate their level of compliance). Therefore, the outcome variable in this section is the mean of the remaining two items in the scale. The two- and three-item outcome variables are correlated at $r > 0.90$ in all four countries.

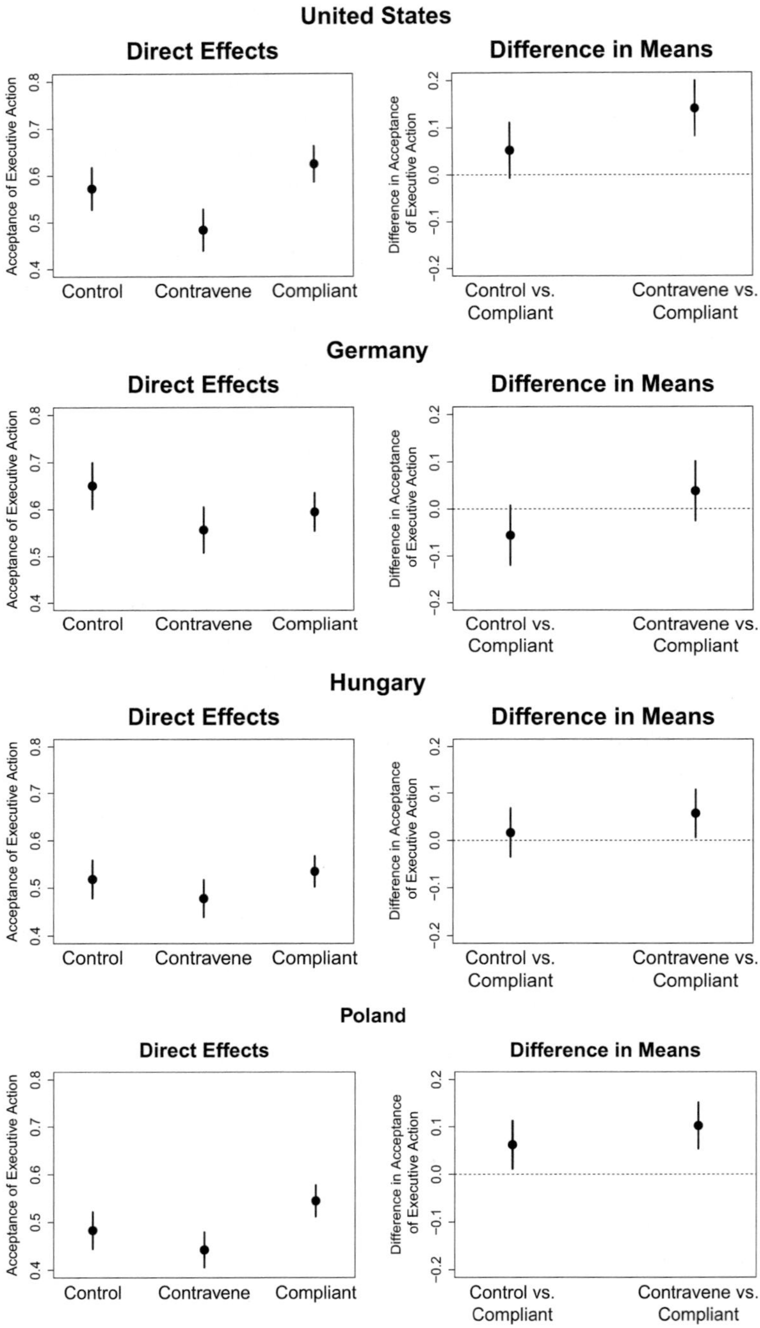

FIGURE 5.4 Direct effects of the Lockdown Experiment (with Compliant condition). The left-hand panels plot the average value of acceptance of the executive's action, by condition. This variable has a range of 0–1; higher values of this variable indicate a greater level of acceptance. The right-hand panels illustrate the difference in means between experimental conditions. Positive values of the *y*-axis in these panels indicate an increase in acceptance, relative to the Control condition. The vertical lines in both panels provide 95% confidence intervals.

In Poland and Hungary, we see the same pattern as the United States. We observe a statistically significant benefit for executives who comply with judicial orders compared to acceptance of a policy enacted in defiance of the judiciary.[20] In Hungary, the difference in acceptance is 0.06, or about one-fifth of a standard deviation ($p = 0.03$). In Poland, the difference in acceptance is 0.10 and about one-third of a standard deviation ($p < 0.01$). The effect in these two countries is particularly noteworthy given the null results for these countries earlier in the chapter: it is not that the experiment "failed" and there is no discernible pattern to respondents' responses in these two cases. Instead, respondents across all contexts in our study are more accepting of executive actions that "follow the rules" than those that defy the rule of law.

DISCUSSION

The separation of authority across institutions pits ambitions against ambitions. This limits, in theory, the extent to which power is concentrated in a single arm of representative government. Armed with the power of judicial review, constitutional courts are thought to provide one line of defense for limiting executive overreach. In democracies, the ultimate mechanism by which these guarantees are enforced rests in the hands of the people: citizens have the power to withhold their acceptance and their support, and may even remove incumbents from office, provided they are willing and able to punish officeholders for transgressions.

This chapter offers a novel look into situations when courts, through judicial review, can serve as effective institutional guardrails by alerting the public of executive overreach. Our experimental vignettes presented respondents with examples of executive transgressions of the rule of law. We compared the public's willingness to accept instances of executive overreach according to whether the constitutional court endorsed or prohibited those policies. Across two experiments, we show that the public is more likely to take issue with a government skirting the law when independent courts signal that an executive's policy is unconstitutional. At the same time, clearance by a court in places like the United States and Germany has no discernible impact on citizens' evaluation of an executive's action. But, in Poland and Hungary – where the constitutional courts are widely viewed to be under the thumb of the political executive – the public is no less willing to accept an action that contravenes a constitutional court than a policy that court has endorsed. Executives, it seems, are penalized for overtly defying independent courts, although the magnitude of that threat may or may not be sufficient to deter noncompliance.

[20] Interestingly, in Poland (but not any of the other three countries), there is a benefit to compliance with the constitutional court relative to the Control condition.

Our results also provide direct empirical evidence for the value of executive co-optation of courts, a common strategy of would-be autocrats (Gandhi 2010; Gandhi and Przworski 2006; Svolik 2020).[21] Democratic backsliding often occurs with an authoritarian's actions gaining a glean of legality and even formal approval from legal institutions that fortifies autocratic governance and suppresses democratic contestation (Helmke, Kroeger, and Paine 2022; Varol 2015). Critically, such backsliding can occur even where citizens support democracy and oppose authoritarianism. This means that democratic norms and values – like the rule of law – may on their own be insufficient to effectively ensure the maintenance of democratic governance (Chiopri, Nalepa, and Vanberg 2023; Grillo and Prato 2023), with independent courts left to potentially stall backsliding in some cases (Gibler and Randazzo 2011; Staton, Reenock, and Holsinger 2022).

Our research demonstrates why this *stealth authoritarianism* might be an attractive plan, but we also identify its limits. Successfully co-opting a well-regarded court may stifle a constraint or install an ally in governance – a veto player who might pose an obstacle or facilitate policy implementation. But the results show here that this institutional co-optation does not provide a basis for public legitimation that might in turn yield public acquiescence to autocratic rule. Courts' power is limited in this critical respect, such that a court once co-opted, does not inspire confidence that would legitimate executive excesses.

Our results raise important implications for further research. First, our vignette is relatively sparse, abstracting away important features of modern politics. Especially given the important role of parties and the powerful influence of partisan polarization in many countries, partisan congruence between citizens and executives might condition the effects we uncover here. Citizens might be more willing to withhold support from outpartisan executives who contravene institutions just as they may be more willing to look the other way when a copartisan engages in a similar action. We return to this inquiry in Chapters 7 and 8.

Second, further research is necessary to probe the generalizability of our findings. Here, our results suggest fruitful pathways forward. What threshold level of de jure judicial independence is necessary for a court to be an effective fire alarm? Under what conditions will the public recognize "rubber stamp" oversight as feeble and punish executives for co-opting other institutions? What level of political knowledge is necessary for individuals to recognize that an institution has been contravened (or co-opted)? That our results are consistent across two experiments and within our

[21] Co-optation of oversight can take many forms from the appointment of allies to courts, legislatures, and agencies (Gandhi 2010; Svolik 2012) to the manipulation of oversight-related rules and procedures (Corrales 2015; Ginsburg, Huq, and Versteeg 2018; Schepple 2018) to outright bribery and corruption (Rose-Ackerman 2010).

country pairs provides some reassurance about the strength of our findings, but nonetheless leaves such questions for future research.

Lastly, the analyses we have presented in this chapter have focused on establishing empirical evidence in support of our theory's central contention and its relationship with judicial independence. In doing so, we have left unexamined the effect of factors we discussed in Chapter 2, like public support for the rule of law. It is to these conditional effects that we now turn.

6

Citizens' Convictions and Judicial Review

In Chapter 5, we presented empirical evidence in support of our primary contention that independent courts are capable, through the use of judicial review, of creating political costs for executives who exceed their constitutional authority. We showed that constitutional courts with high levels of judicial independence have this capacity: if an executive implements a policy over an independent court's objection, the public's acceptance of that policy decreases. We further showed that when courts lack independence, their signaling credibility is constrained, and as a consequence the public does not change its views of an executive's policy on the basis of such a court's decision. Lastly, we found no evidence that courts – regardless of their level of judicial independence – exhibit an ability to increase acceptance of an executive action through judicial endorsement.

While these results provide a strong empirical foundation, they do not address differences in responses to judicial decisions across citizens. We theorized that not all citizens will be equally responsive to the information conveyed by judicial review. For some, the signal may resonate strongly and consequently have a powerful effect on their evaluation of an executive's constitutionally dubious behavior. Yet for others, a court's decision may leave little to no impression.

Our theory suggests that this variation should correspond with citizens' support the rule of law. We contend that those with strong support for the rule of law should be most receptive to judicial signals regarding executive overreach, and therefore more prone to withhold their acceptance from an executive who implements a policy in contravention of an independent court's order. In contrast, those citizens with weak attachments to the rule of law are unlikely to be swayed by a court's ruling, such that their acceptance calculus is unmoved when an executive ignores the ruling of even an independent court. In this way, judicial efficacy may depend both on institutional independence and a citizenry committed to the rule of law.

We test these expectations by returning to the Vaccine Approval and Lockdown Experiments discussed in Chapter 5 and incorporating the measure of support for the rule of law we presented in Chapter 4. We present heterogeneous treatment effects across respondents' support for the rule of law and their support for the incumbent executive to show how the efficacy of judicial review varies depending on citizens' normative and political commitments. We show that the efficacy of judicial review, as evidenced by a contravention penalty, is not only conditioned by judicial independence, as we demonstrated in Chapter 5, but it is also constrained by the receptivity of citizens to the information conveyed by review: the contravention penalty is magnified as citizens' commitment to the rule of law grows.

Yet, as was the case with our earlier analyses, we find that even high levels of support for the rule of law are unable to overcome the deficiency created by a lack of judicial independence. The end result, then, is that judicial efficacy appears limited to settings in which *both* courts are independent *and* citizens are supportive of the rule of law. Our research serves as a rejoinder to a long and well-established literature that underscores the effects of institutions, individuals' attitudes, and the interplay between them (Almond and Verba 1963; Putnam 1993).

In the second half of the chapter, we turn our attention to a second factor that might condition the public's response to judicial review: their affinity for the executive who is championing the policy. This analysis begins our examination – continued in Chapters 7 and 8 – of how partisan attitudes might weaken or even drown out the impact of support for the rule of law. Partisanship organizes the political world on the basis of shared values and political priorities, often dividing elites and the mass public along ideological lines. The pull of partisanship poses a potential complication for the public's ability to coordinate to constrain the state, as allegiances to copartisan incumbents may undermine citizens' willingness to impose penalties for violations to the rule of law. We outline two possible ways that the penalty for contravening an independent court might covary with support for the executive. On the one hand, we might expect the contravention penalty to be largest among an executive's opponents. On the other hand, due to floor effects, it may be that an executive's supporters are those most likely to withdraw their acceptance in the face of judicial contravention.

Assessing the conditional effects of executive approval, we observe a surprising result. Whereas those who hold the executive in low regard are unlikely to support an executive's policy regardless of its content, citizens who support the executive are more likely to impose a contravention penalty. These findings are consistent with the findings of Reeves and Rogowski (2022a), who demonstrate that checks on executive power come primarily from the same supporters who vote for them at the ballot box.

We conclude the chapter by discussing the implications of our findings and highlighting the book's path moving forward. Our results emphasize the continued importance of democratic norms for the effective functioning of institutional guard-rails. To the extent that the threat of political costs is key for disincentivizing executives from flouting constitutional rules and judicial rulings, citizens' continued attachment to the rule of law plays a vital role in countering potential democratic backsliding. While recent research casts doubt on the extent to which support for democratic norms actually can translate into an effective political constraint (Carey et al. 2022; Graham and Svolik 2020), our results suggest that support for the rule of law continues to exert an important influence on the efficacy of judicial review.

JUDICIAL EFFICACY AND SUPPORT FOR THE RULE OF LAW

Judicial efficacy is not wholly determined by institutional characteristics. It is *citizens* – not institutions – that actually impose political costs for rule of law violations by withholding their approval or acceptance of an executive's actions (or, eventually, by voting the executive out of office in response to their bad behavior). For this reason, the efficacy of a court should be conditioned not only by its own institutional characteristics but also the characteristics of those citizens it is seeking to mobilize in opposition to an executive's overreach. That is, judicial efficacy may also depend on having a receptive audience.

We identify support for the rule of law as the vital linkage between citizens and the efficacy of judicial review. A commitment to the rule of law is support for an expectation that even the most powerful political executives stay within the bounds of their constitutional power. In this sense, the rule of law is an essential feature of state constraint in that the public comes to demand that politicians abide by these limits. This direct linkage between the rule of law and state constraint thus implicates the importance of support for this core democratic norm for our account of judicial efficacy. Lacking this vital democratic value, courts may well be vulnerable to being undermined by an executive's defiance, noncompliance, and political attack (e.g., Christenson and Kriner 2017c; Driscoll and Nelson 2023b; Krehbiel 2021c; Vanberg 2015).

Support for the rule of law relates to expectations about the constitutional order, rather than a particular individual or institution. It is tightly tied to the existing "rules of the game" – that is a country's constitutional order. Those citizens with little support for upholding the constitutional order should be more tolerant of actions that exceed or otherwise contravene constitutional norms and obligations, even in the face of judicial review. Conversely, citizens who support the rule of law should more forcefully compel officials, irrespective of position or party, to act within the scope and limits of their legal authority.

Importantly, enforcement of the rule of law – and by extension the interpretation and monitoring of constitutional boundaries of executive authority – is a central and expressly stated function of courts. With courts carrying out this role through the exercise of judicial review, there is a direct connection between review and citizens' commitment to the rule of law that makes the efficacy of the former a reflection, at least in part, of the latter. Such a tight interlacing of judicial institutions and the rule of law thus makes public support for this norm a key consideration to the efficacy of judicial review.

This discussion also helps us distinguish support for the rule of law from other attitudinal explanations for judicial efficacy. For instance, scholars have long noted the significance of judicial legitimacy for empowering courts (Caldeira and Gibson 1992; Gibson, Caldeira, and Baird 1998; Gibson and Nelson 2015; Vanberg 2008). These arguments suggest that judicial power stems from citizens' evaluations of a court. By implication, these theories suggest that widely supported courts should be efficacious regardless of whether they are ruling that an executive action is compliant with the rule of law. Our emphasis on the rule of law brings into focus citizens' support for the underlying norm that forms the basis for judicial review. This more foundational focus reveals an asymmetric nature to judicial efficacy: courts are able to mobilize citizens to confront overreaching executives, but they do not affect attitudes when executives are deemed to be acting in conformity with constitutional norms. In this way, the rule of law can contribute to institutional guardrails against unconstitutional excesses, but executives cannot count on these institutions to sway a skeptical public to their side by legitimizing constitutionally dubious policies.

THE CONDITIONAL EFFECTS OF SUPPORT FOR THE RULE OF LAW

We now turn to the central question of this chapter: how should support for the rule of law affect the efficacy of judicial review? As we saw conceptually in Chapter 2 and empirically in Chapter 4, just as people differ in their opinions about policies, they also vary in the extent to which they value the fundamental pillars of the rule of law. For one, individuals balance competing considerations of strict adherence to the law and expediency differently, especially in emergency situations (Gibson 2007a). For another, and as we saw in Chapter 4, individual-level factors such as political sophistication and attachment to broader democratic values influence citizens' respective levels of support for the rule of law. With country-level characteristics like judicial independence providing insight into cross-national variation in judicial efficacy, tapping into cross-citizen variation in support for the rule of law will allow us to evaluate individual differences in receptivity to judicial signals.

Contravention and Support for the Rule of Law

We begin with a focus on instances in which state constraint is most in question: when executives overstep their constitutional authority and contravene judicial review. In such scenarios, consider first the reaction of citizens who highly value the sanctity of the rule of law. These citizens place a premium on adhering to the established legal and constitutional order, and as such have an expectation that their elected officials will do so as well. When officials fail to act in this way, however, support for the rule of law compels them to withdraw their acceptance of the executive's behavior. As a consequence, we expect courts' use of judicial review to constrain the executive to be most effective among this set of citizens.

As we established in the preceding chapters, an independent judiciary remains a necessary condition for judicial efficacy. This continues to be the case even when considering the reaction of those citizens who support the rule of law. Following our argument from earlier chapters, only independent courts can produce credible signals regarding the constitutional propriety of an executive's behavior; where courts lack independence, the information conveyed through judicial review is compromised and thus ineffective at coordinating citizens' reactions. Put differently, for support for the rule of law to amplify the contravention penalty, first the court exercising review must have the credibility conveyed by judicial independence.

Now, consider individuals with low levels of support for the rule of law. For these citizens, the rule of law (and by extension its emphasis on the bounds on executive power) is a low priority. As such, their views of an executive's behavior are unlikely to be moved by judicial decisions indicating that the government's behavior contravenes constitutional norms. Thus, citizens who have little commitment to the rule of law are likely to dismiss or otherwise discount the information sent through judicial review. The efficacy of judicial review is likely to be weakest among this segment of the public.

This inhospitability to the rule of law affects these citizens' responses (or lack thereof) to judicial decisions irrespective of a court's level of judicial independence. Where courts are independent, the accompanying credibility of judicial review is inconsequential to citizens lacking support for the rule of law. That is, even the most well-regarded and independent court will be incapable of mobilizing those who are uninterested in its signals. And, in environments where judicial independence is compromised, the efficacy of review is already hamstrung before considering one's support for the rule of law. In short, weak supporters of the rule of law are unlikely to be swayed by even the most compelling of judicial signals.

Taken together, we are left with a picture of judicial efficacy that is a function of these two conditions: judicial independence and support for the rule of law. Where both are present, courts are able to effectively mobilize public sentiment against executives for breaching the constitutional limits of their authority. But where one or the other of these conditions is absent, judicial review is likely to be limited in its capacity to do so.

Clearance and Support for the Rule of Law

We turn now to how support for the rule of law might condition citizens' reactions to a court endorsing a potentially unconstitutional policy. As we have demonstrated, courts are generally unable to legitimize policies by approving them. We expect this is the case regardless of a citizen's support for the rule of law. Consider first those who have strong support for the rule of law. For these citizens, a court approving the executive's suspect policy might assuage concerns of executive overreach, severing the relationship between support for the rule of law and acceptance of the executive's questionable action. Put differently, judicial endorsement of a policy effectively concludes constitution-based evaluations of the policy, and makes the rule of law a less relevant dimension on which citizens assess the executive and their action. Rather, with a court's endorsement, evaluation of the policy is more likely to take place upon politicized or instrumental lines. As a result, individuals who value the rule of law at high levels should be no more or less likely to approve of the executive's action when it is approved by a court.

Likewise, our expectation for citizens with weak support for the rule of law is that judicial clearance has little to no effect on their evaluation of an executive's behavior. As these individuals were less likely to be concerned about potential executive overreach in the first place, learning that a court has endorsed the action leaves them to evaluate the policy on the same terms as they would have had the court not acted at all. The indifference of these citizens to judicial decisions, irrespective of their content, makes them unlikely to react when a court signs off on a constitutionally dubious policy.

With this discussion in mind, we can specify three empirical expectations. First, our theoretical account points to a positive relationship between judicial efficacy and support for the rule of law. When executives exceed their constitutional limits, courts should be more effective at generating political costs – a contravention penalty – among citizens who espouse a strong commitment to the rule of law. Second, judicial independence is needed for judicial efficacy. Given that the presence of a contravention penalty is evidence of judicial efficacy, the relationship between support for the rule of law and a contravention penalty should be limited to courts with high judicial independence. Our third hypothesis captures our expectation that when a court clears an executive's behavior, support for the rule of law will fail to exert an influence on approval irrespective of judicial independence. We define these hypotheses more formally below:

- H_1: The penalty for contravening a court increases with support for the rule of law.
- H_2: Support for the rule of law only increases the penalty for contravening courts with a high level of judicial independence.
- H_3: Regardless of a court's level of judicial independence, acceptance of an executive's action that is cleared by judicial review neither increases nor decreases with support for the rule of law.

Evaluating Support for the Rule of Law's Influence

To test these hypotheses, we return to the Vaccine Approval Experiment and the Lockdown Experiment described in the Chapter 5. Recall first that in both experiments, we present respondents with a hypothetical action taken by the country's executive (either the disbursement of a vaccine without the necessary approvals or a mandatory lockdown) that is in turn reviewed by the country's high court. With the executive moving forward with the policy irrespective of the court's decision, both experiments provide an opportunity to assess citizens' responses to judicial decisions regarding the constitutional propriety of the executive's behavior.

Second, the outcome variable for both experiments is, as it was in Chapter 5, based on a series of questions tapping into citizens' approval of the executive's behavior. This approach, as we have noted earlier, allows us to assess the attitudinal response that serves as the foundation for the kinds of political action (e.g., voting, protesting, etc.) that we and others theorize enters into executives' decision-making calculus.

Third, we note that the use of both experiments provides a robustness check to our findings, as we can assess whether the predicted conditional relationship between support for the rule of law and a contravention penalty is present across different vignettes. Moreover, while the Vaccine Approval Experiment focuses on Germany, the Lockdown Experiment provides us with the cross-national variation we need to assess the interactive role of judicial independence with support for the rule of law.

The key addition we make here to our analyses of the Vaccine Approval Experiment and the Lockdown Experiment is our measure of public support for the rule of law, which we introduced and validated in Chapter 4. This variable, which is comprised of responses to four questions, is scaled from 0 to 1 with higher values indicating more support for the rule of law. Armed with this measure, we estimated a linear regression with dichotomous indicators for each treatment (using the Control condition as the baseline), and multiplicative interaction terms between each treatment and our measure of support for the rule of law.

Vaccine Approval Experiment

We begin with the analysis of the Vaccine Approval Experiment. Figure 6.1 plots the marginal effects of each treatment (compared to the Control condition) across support for the rule of law.[1] We anticipated that acceptance of the executive's action would decline with individual-level support for the rule of law in cases where the executive contravened an independent court's ruling (the first panel of Figure 6.1). Here, we observe support for our first hypothesis: as citizens' support for the rule of law increases, the effect of contravention (compared to a Control condition without judicial review) becomes increasingly negative. This effect is significant for respondents at (or above) a value of 0.45 (the 15th percentile) in their support for the rule of law. Looking at the binned estimator, the effect of the Contravention treatment is statistically significant for those respondents in the highest tercile of support for the

[1] Linear regression results underlying the analyses presented in this chapter, as well as a discussion of the robustness of our results to models including respondents' political and demographic characteristics, are provided in the Appendix.

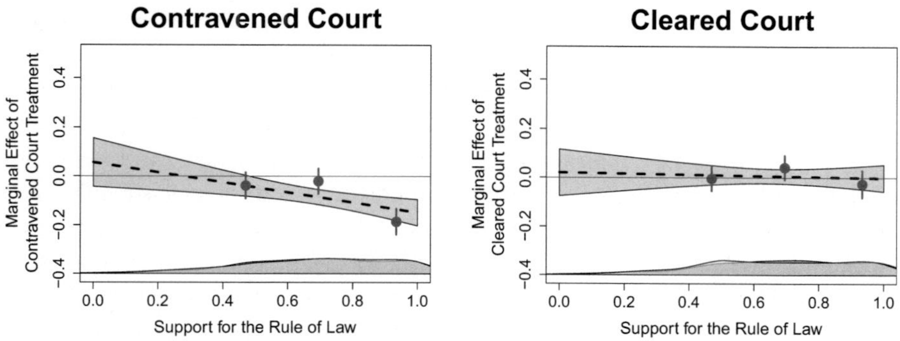

FIGURE 6.1 Conditional effects from the Vaccine Approval Experiment (Support for the Rule of Law). Support for the Rule of Law increases with the *x*-axis. The shaded areas are 95% confidence intervals. The point estimates and associated confidence intervals are the Hainmueller, Mummolo, and Xu (2019) estimates of the marginal effect for each tercile of Support for the Rule of Law. The density plot shows the distribution for support for the rule of law by treatment; the darker density is the baseline group. Full regression results are provided in Model 2 of Table 6.A1 in the Appendix.

rule of law. In short, it is those Germans with strong support for the rule of law who withdraw their approval of the executive's policy when it is conducted in contravention of the constitutional court's order.

We turn next to our second hypothesis, which predicts a flat line in the second panel of Figure 6.1. This is exactly the pattern we observe. Compared to a Control condition with no review, there is no effect of a court decision in favor of executive action on acceptance of that executive action. This null effect is noteworthy because even those respondents with the *highest* levels of support for the rule of law are no more or less likely to accept the legally dubious executive action.

This finding speaks to two important points. First, it highlights the special place of courts and, for enterprising executives, the value of "capturing" the courts. So long as a court will credibly approve of an executive's action, it can blunt public disapproval of executive malfeasance. Second, it is further evidence of the asymmetric nature of judicial efficacy, with support for the rule of law contributing to a contravention penalty only when a court actively seeks to constrain the state by declaring a policy or action unconstitutional. When a court endorses a policy as constitutional, it appears to essentially sever support for the rule of law from citizens' evaluations. In these senses, our findings here represent further support for our theoretical expectation regarding reactions to judicial clearance.

Lockdown Experiment

Of course, the major weakness of the Vaccine Approval Experiment is its inability to test our expectations about cross-country variation in judicial independence.

To this end, we return to the Lockdown Experiment, which we fielded in all four countries. Following our discussion of these cases in previous chapters, we expect to observe the conditional relationship between approval of the executive's policy and support for the rule of law in the two cases – the United States and Germany – where the courts have high levels of independence. Conversely, in the two low judicial independence cases – Hungary and Poland – we anticipate support for the rule of law to have no bearing on citizens' evaluations of the executive's lockdown policy.

Figure 6.2 plots the marginal effects of each treatment (compared to the Control condition) across support for the rule of law. Our first hypothesis predicts a negative-sloping line for the United States and Germany in the first panel of this figure, indicating that the cost of contravention increases with individual-level support for the rule of law. In both cases, we observe support for the hypothesis: as citizens' support for the rule of law increases, they tend to become less accepting of the executive's lockdown policy (compared to the Control condition). Indeed, the findings – both in their direction and magnitude – closely mirror those of the Lockdown Experiment we discussed Chapter 5. Yet this analysis underscores that the average treatment effect described in Chapter 5 is fueled in large part by the responses of the members of the public with robust support for the rule of law.

Turning to Poland and Hungary in the bottom two rows of Figure 6.2, we can see how these patterns manifest in two cases where judicial independence is low. Recall from our discussion in Chapter 5 that neither of the two average treatment effects were statistically significant: judicial decisions of either form failed to generate a response from citizens. What these panels make clear is that this null result is not contingent upon respondents' support for the rule of law whereby these courts are efficacious among the most fervent rule of law supporters. Even for the highest tercile of rule of law support in both countries, the effect of defying a court is not statistically different from zero. Again, the conclusion from this pair of countries – which supports our expectations for a lack of efficacy in low judicial independence environments – is that judicial intervention in these contexts does little to signal to the public that the executive is pushing legal boundaries and, by extension, to lower acceptance of the executive's action. The credibility of these courts is so compromised that even those people who would otherwise be most receptive to judicial decisions do not react to the court's decision to declare a policy unconstitutional.

Although we find a conditional effect between citizens' support for the rule of law and their reaction to an independent court declaring a policy unconstitutional, the results for the clearance condition again demonstrate how judicial clearance has a limited impact. Consistent with our hypothesis, we observe a flat line in the right-hand panel for each of the four countries. Approval of a cleared executive's behavior is unrelated to one's support for the rule of law. Even those respondents with the *highest* levels of support for the rule of law are no more likely to accept the executive

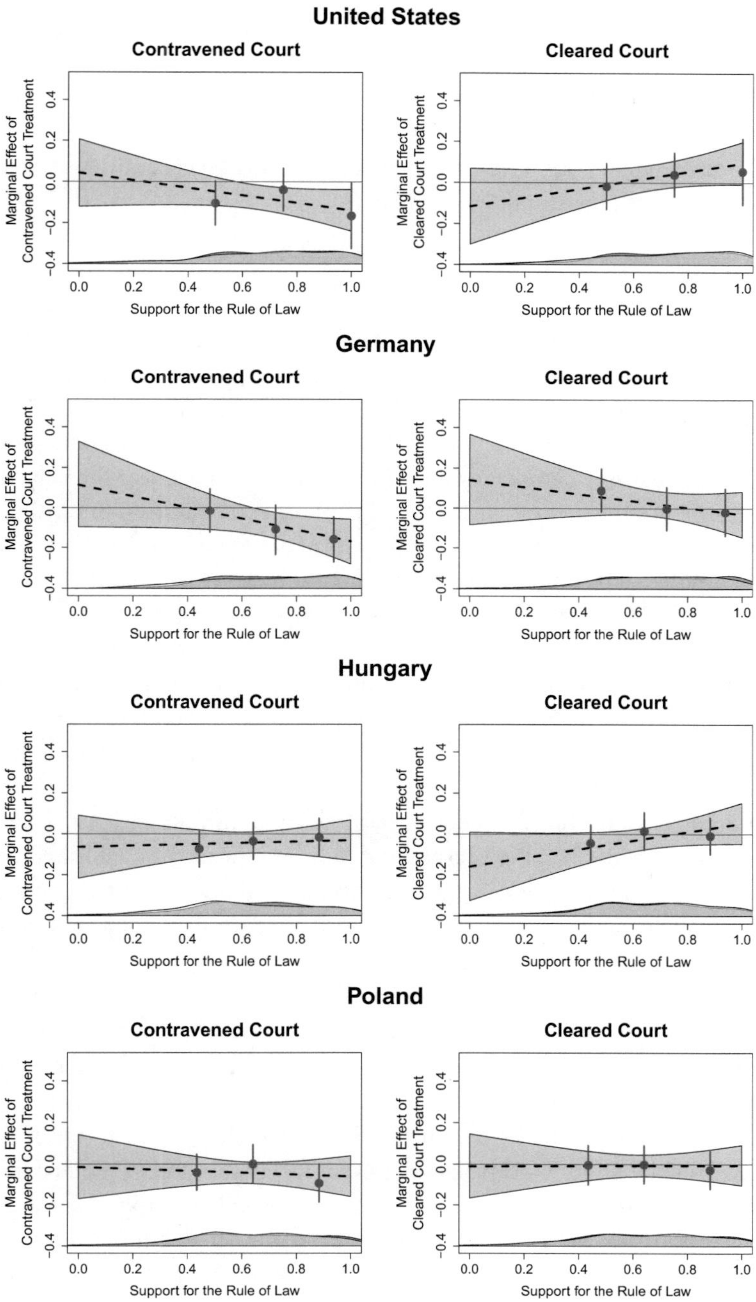

FIGURE 6.2 Conditional effects from the Lockdown Experiment (Support for the Rule of Law). Support for the Rule of Law increases with the *x*-axis. The shaded areas are 95% confidence intervals. The point estimates and associated confidence intervals are the Hainmueller, Mummolo, and Xu (2019) estimates of the marginal effect for each tercile of Support for the Rule of Law. The density plot shows the distribution for support for the rule of law by treatment; the darker density is the baseline group. Full regression results are provided in Models 2 and 5 of Tables 6.A2 and 6.A3 in the Appendix.

action. Importantly, that we see this across all four cases highlights the limited ability of even independent, powerful courts such as the high courts of the United States and Germany to alter public sentiment when deeming an executive's behavior to be in conformity with constitutional norms.

Discussion

These findings have several important implications both for our theoretical argument and more generally for the efficacy of judicial review as a credible guardrail against executive overreach. In a broad sense, our results reveal how political institutions and political attitudes interact to constrain – or not constrain – executive behavior. Scholars of democracy have long posited that each of these matter: that democracy will struggle to survive without a robust democratic culture (Almond and Verba 1963), or that the longevity and success of democratic polities is a function of how their political institutions are arranged (Linz 1990). That we find the efficacy of judicial review to be conditioned by citizens' support for the rule of law *and* judicial independence underscores that these two influences are complementary. While our focus here is on judicial review, our findings suggest that other institutional constraints, such as legislative oversight, might similarly be contingent not only on institutional capacity and reputation but also public values that justify those constraints in the first place.

This interactive relationship between attitudes and institutions itself yields important lessons. Consider first the prospects of judicial efficacy in established democracies where judicial independence is well entrenched and respected. Even in such contexts, the efficacy of judicial review is not assured. Its dependence on support for the rule of law means that continued support for that norm is vital for courts to constrain the executive. It is not enough to simply enshrine institutional protections for the courts from political interference; even the most independent of courts can have its decisions take little effect if the public is not committed to the rule of law. This raises, among other things, the possibility that judicial efficacy can wane even when judicial independence is assured. If citizens' attachment to the rule of law weakens, judicial efficacy likely declines even if a court's level of judicial independence is held constant. In this respect, maintaining robust support for democratic values like the rule of law may be just as critical as maintaining the integrity of institutions such as courts when it comes to buttressing democracy against the threat of backsliding and autocratization.

Conversely, our results depict a rather bleak picture for judicial efficacy's prospects in contexts with low judicial independence. When courts are captured or otherwise rendered incapable of credibly constraining executives, the best hope for reversing democratic backsliding often lies with citizens' continued support for democratic norms. Indeed, efforts in several countries – including Poland and Hungary – to redress attacks against democratic institutions often focus on trying to coordinate supporters of opposition parties around their shared support for checks and balances and related democratic values. Our results suggest that such coordination attempts are deprived of courts' ability to contribute to these efforts (to the extent that courts in such contexts might wish to), as their decisions fail to elicit a response even from those with the strongest support for the rule of law. Moreover, this disconnect between support for the rule of law and judicial review points again to the value of co-opting or capturing courts, as a lack of judicial independence appears to weaken support for the rule of law as a democratic guardrail.

There are limitations to the conclusions we can draw. None is probably more significant than the absence of citizens' *political*, rather than legal, considerations from our story (and analyses). As we saw in Chapter 4, support for the rule of law is far from "randomly assigned" to individuals; it is a correlate of a myriad of factors, including one's demographics, political sophistication and – of particular potential importance in the context of judicial efficacy – political preferences. While we have sought to engage with the potential confounding effect of political considerations in our robustness analyses,[2] these efforts can only go so far given that the experiments we have examined to this point do not randomize the partisanship or political position in our designs. As such, to put our theoretical account more fully to the test, we look in the remainder of the book to confront head-on the threat of political preferences and partisanship to judicial efficacy. To this end, we conclude this chapter with one final set of analyses using the Lockdown Experiment to explore the role of citizens' approval of the executive.[3]

CONSIDERING EXECUTIVE APPROVAL

There is good reason to think that citizens' (dis)approval of the sitting executive might influence their response to judicial review. For one, citizens' evaluations of elected officials probably color how they react to their actions. In this sense, one's level of approval for the executive might inform a sort of "baseline" of support that may, in turn, be shifted by the signals communicated by judicial review. For another, extant research has emphasized the connection between public approval for the executive and support for executive unilateral actions (e.g., Reeves and Rogowski 2018, 2022a; Braman 2021). We thus see an exploratory analysis here as both providing a starting point for considering how political considerations affect the presence and magnitude of contravention penalties and

[2] See the Appendix.

[3] Given the limitations of these experiments when it comes to fully engaging with the question of partisanship's potential impact, we dedicate the final two empirical chapters of the book to this topic with survey experiments explicitly designed for this purpose.

as a useful extension of our experimental design into a salient issue in the study of executive politics.

We refrain here from explicit theorizing (this is a task we carry out in Chapters 7 and 8). Broadly, we see two potential means by which executive approval might shape citizens' reaction to judicial review. On the one hand, higher levels of executive approval might correspond with a desire to see the executive's policies carried out irrespective of their legality (Braman 2021). If so, those with greater approval for the executive may be more likely to ignore judicial signals and, in so doing, give the executive a "pass" for contravening a court's order. Supporters' positive affinity toward the executive may cause them to give the executive the benefit of the doubt when confronted with behavior that flouts the rule of law.

On the other hand, it could be the case that higher levels of executive approval actually make citizens *more* responsive to judicial signals (e.g., Reeves and Rogowski 2018, 2022a). The rationale for this flows from the observation that an executive's opponents are not likely, a priori, to accept the executive's policy, creating a "floor effect" for executive actions that contravene judicial authority: opponents of the executive have a preexisting distaste for the executive that leaves them with no room to further disapprove of the executive's behavior. In contrast, supporters' higher baseline level of support provides more opportunity for their approval to decline in response to negative news such as judicial contravention. By this logic, public constraints on the executive may be more likely to come from an executive's supporters than opponents.

We return to the Lockdown Experiment to explore how Executive Approval might aggravate or ameliorate the size of contravention penalties.[4] Our measure Executive Approval is based on responses to a single item querying respondents about their support for the executive on a four-point scale. Fifty-eight percent of Americans, 65 percent of Germans, 34 percent of Hungarians, and 28 percent of Poles reported a favorable impression of their national executive. To test our hypotheses, we estimated a linear regression model that included this measure of executive approval, indicators for the Contravention and Clearance treatments, and the multiplicative interactions between Approval and the treatments.

Figure 6.3 plots the marginal effect of the treatments (vs. control) across Executive Approval for each of our four countries. We begin by considering whether the effect of contravention on acceptance increases or decreases with executive approval. In the United States and Germany, contravening the court, as compared to no court involvement at all, has the effect of weakening approval for the challenged policy most among those who otherwise approve of the executive. In the United States, this effect is significant for those in the highest tercile of Executive Approval;

[4] The survey containing the Vaccine Approval Experiment did not contain a direct measure of support for the executive.

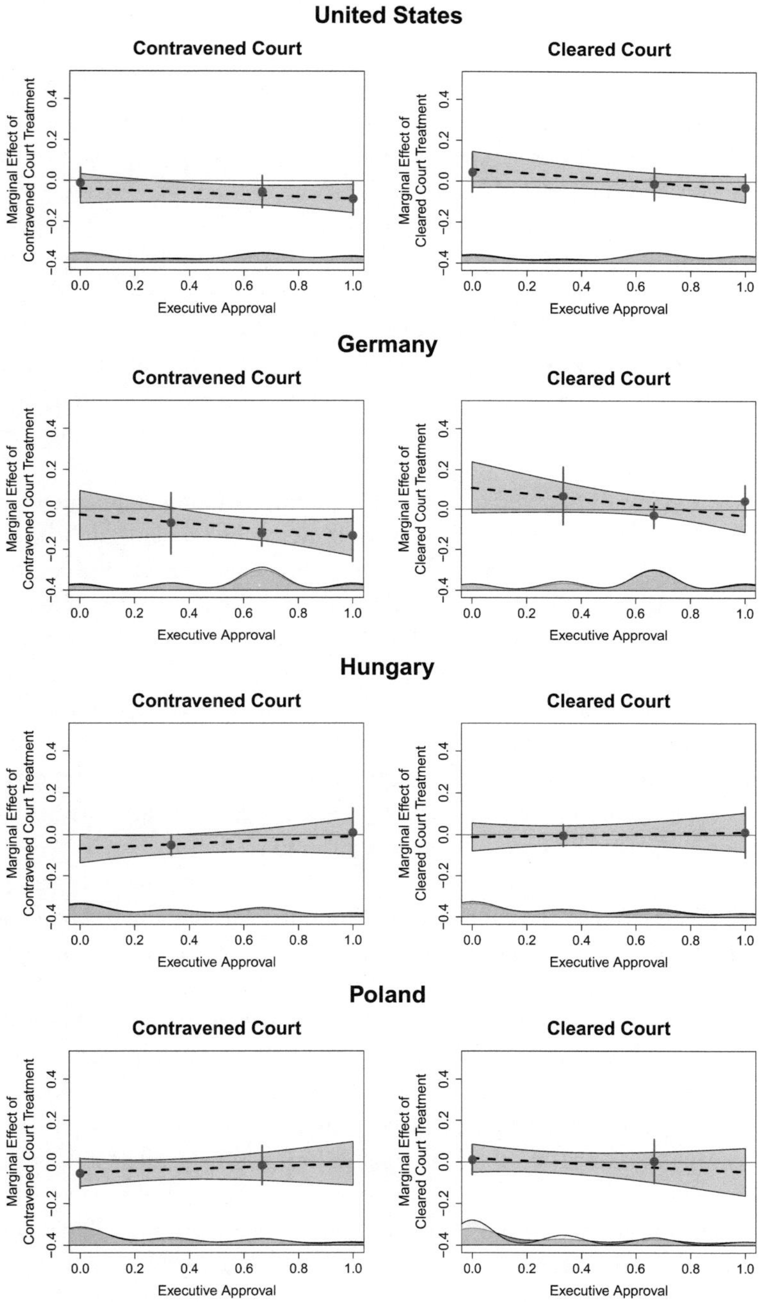

FIGURE 6.3 Conditional effects from the Lockdown Experiment (Executive Approval). Executive Approval increases with the *x*-axis. The shaded areas are 95% confidence intervals. The point estimates and associated confidence intervals are the Hainmueller, Mummolo, and Xu (2019) estimates of the marginal effect for each tercile of Executive Approval (note that some terciles are identical). The density plot shows the distribution for support for the rule of law by treatment; the darker density is the baseline group. Full regression results are provided in Models 3 and 6 of Tables 6.A2 and 6.A3 in theAppendix.

in Germany, this effect is statistically significant for those in the highest two-thirds of Executive Approval. These results are consistent with the second theoretical logic outlined above: it is the executive's supporters, not their opponents, that are most likely to withhold support.

We want to take care not to overemphasize these findings. For respondents in the highest tercile of Executive Approval, the effects of contravention are smaller for the Executive Approval interaction than the Support for the Rule of Law interaction.[5] The slope of the marginal effect is not very steep, particularly when compared to our findings with respect to support for the rule of law. Nonetheless, it appears that at least in these two cases there is a political cost for executives who contravene a court, and that cost may be most pronounced among the executive's own erstwhile supporters.

We also observe distinct differences between our high judicial independence and low judicial independence cases. This is made clear when looking at the bottom two panels of Figure 6.3.[6] In the bottom left two panels, which present the contravention results for Hungary and Poland, neither the linear estimator nor the binned estimator provide any evidence that contravention is associated with a decrease in Acceptance for any level of Executive Approval. Specifically, we see no evidence for a contravention penalty in Hungary or Poland at any level of Executive Approval. Indeed, befitting our argument that judicial independence is a prerequisite for judicial efficacy, it is only in the high judicial independence contexts of the United States and Germany that we see a relationship emerge between Acceptance, Executive Approval, and contravention.

Lastly, we can see how executive approval might moderate acceptance of an action that is cleared by the courts as constitutional. Throughout the book, we have argued that judicial clearance has no discernible effect on citizens' acceptance of executive actions. Yet we recognize that it could be the case that those who strongly approve of the executive behave differently than those who do not. For instance, a legitimization effect could be at play in which the erstwhile opponents of the executive are particularly convinced to accept a policy as a result of judicial clearance. Or, alternatively, it may be those who already approve of the executive who become bolstered in their acceptance of a policy after it is cleared by judicial review.

The results presented in the right-hand panels of Figure 6.3 again suggest that judicial clearance is not associated with an increase in acceptance of the executive's policy. In no country do we see any evidence – from either the linear estimator or

5 In the United States, the effect of contravention for respondents in the highest tercile of Support for the Rule of Law was −0.12; for those in the highest third of Executive Approval, it is only −0.08. In Germany, the analogous values are −0.16 and −0.08.

6 Because the Executive Approval variable only takes four categories, some of the terciles are the same (e.g., the 33rd and 66th percentiles of Executive Approval in Poland are both "strongly disapprove"). In these cases, there are only two binned estimators in the figure.

the binned estimator – that clearance is associated with an increase in acceptance, *even among supporters of the executive*. This analysis is yet even more evidence that the efficacy of judicial clearance is nil, regardless of a court's level of judicial independence.

Discussion

That we find the efficacy of judicial review is heightened among supporters of the executive is a finding with important implications. With past research emphasizing the role of the public when it comes to holding executives accountable for engaging in unilateral policymaking (e.g., Reeves and Rogowski 2018), it is encouraging that our evidence similarly depicts a public – one who otherwise approves of the executive – that is willing to withdraw their support from an executive who violates the rule of law. Whereas opposition supporters might have limited leverage, electorally or otherwise, over an executive, one might expect that the potential loss of one's own backers would give an electorally motivated executive reason to take pause before pushing their authority beyond its constitutional scope. That is to say, insofar that we are concerned about effectively constraining executive behavior, an executive's supporters are the segment of citizens best equipped to do so. In this sense, this dynamic suggests that the interaction between executive approval and judicial efficacy is actually one that strengthens, rather than weakens, judicial efforts at constraining the state.

That only independent courts can marshal the sentiment of those who approve of an executive against that same executive's unconstitutional policy highlights the crucial role judicial independence plays in facilitating judicial efficacy. While Previous research has found that legal challenges and criticisms can weaken public support for executive behavior (Christenson and Kriner 2017b), our findings suggest a key condition to this dynamic is judicial independence. With limited scholarly confidence in the willingness and capacity of the public to exercise a constraint on executive power, the addition of this further condition – judicial independence – reinforces the potential fragility of the public as a democratic guardrail.

A more concerning potential implication of these findings comes when we turn our attention to contexts with courts that lack judicial independence. With the inability of such courts to convey credible signals and thereby mobilize public sentiment against executive overreach, executives may have an incentive to stifle judicial independence. That is, those who approve of an executive may view their basis for that support as more reliable or credible than the information provided by a non-independent judiciary. As we saw in Hungary and Poland, our results suggest that executives in contexts like these may be able to pursue constitutionally dubious policies contra court orders and nonetheless retain citizens' approval. Just as our analyses regarding support for the rule of law highlighted the value of a compromised court to an executive, so too do these analyses suggest that eroding judicial independence can, under the right circumstances, help an executive retain support for unconstitutional policies.

We underscore here again the lack of a legitimizing effect for judicial clearance. In Chapter 5, we saw no evidence, on average, that courts can increase the public's acceptance of policies. The results in this analysis extend that finding to demonstrate that even supporters of the executive – those people most predisposed to support the executive's policy – do not further increase their acceptance of policies when it garners judicial support. In this respect, these analyses provide a "best case scenario" for legitimation accounts; if there is *any* analysis in which we should expect to see courts legitimate policy, it would be this one. That we do not find any such effect is a strong indicator of the profound limitation to courts' – even powerful independent courts' – abilities to shift public sentiment.

Importantly, we emphasize that this analysis was merely exploratory in nature. As a result, we remain cautious about the conclusions we can draw from it. The Lockdown Experiment was not designed explicitly to address the role of citizens' political preferences, including partisanship. It did not randomize the partisanship of the executive carrying out a constitutionally dubious policy, nor did it remind respondents of the partisanship of the executive. Although executive approval is probably closely associated with partisanship, we acknowledge that the two are not synonymous. A proper examination of partisanship's potential effects would explicitly bring respondents' partisan preferences to the fore.[7] These are issues we address in the coming chapters.

CONCLUSION

In this chapter, we tested how the efficacy of judicial review varies with citizens' attitudes. We began by emphasizing the importance of citizens' support for the rule of law as a vital condition for judicial efficacy. Whereas in Chapter 5 we established judicial independence as a necessary condition for judicial efficacy, we argued here that judicial independence on its own is not sufficient. Rather, even independent courts require a receptive audience – a citizenry that supports the rule of law – to allow judicial review to translate into meaningful political penalties. Further probing the Vaccine Approval and Lockdown Experiments we introduced in Chapter 5, we demonstrate that such penalties are only present (1) when a court uses judicial review to declare an executive's action unconstitutional; (2) the court has a high level of judicial independence; and (3) when citizens exhibit a strong support for the rule of law.

[7] As we detail in the next two chapters, the multiparty nature of our European cases requires important experimental design choices that were beyond the feasible scope of the Lockdown and Vaccine experiments.

We then turned to an exploratory analysis of how citizens' approval for the executive – a political rather than legal attitude – influences evaluations of executive behavior in the aftermath of judicial review. Somewhat surprisingly, that the contravention penalty is greatest among an executive's supporters. This result, coupled with our remarkably consistent findings of judicial independence as a precondition for efficacy and the lack of any legitimizing effect from judicial clearance, hints that perhaps political attitudes might not overwhelm values like the rule of law to the extent that scholars have increasingly warned. Indeed, if anything, our findings in this respect would suggest the opposite, as an executive's erstwhile supporters are more likely to withdraw acceptance from actions that contravene a court's ruling.

The last set of analyses started our consideration of how citizens' political considerations might impact judicial efficacy. Partisanship represents perhaps the most powerful political force raising theoretical and empirical questions that penetrate to the core of our argument. Are citizens' responses to judicial review simply a reflection of their partisan interests? Can judicial decisions effectively reverberate through the proverbial noise created by partisan polarization? Or is judicial review only efficacious in theory such that it falls apart when citizens are beckoned to consider their partisanship interests? These concerns underscore the extent to which partisanship represents a compelling alternative to our rule of law-focused theoretical account, and so we endeavor in the remaining two chapters to engage more forcefully and intentionally with the challenge posed by partisanship.

Appendix

REGRESSION RESULTS AND ROBUSTNESS ANALYSIS

This appendix reports linear regression results that underlie the analyses in Chapters 5 and 6. Table 6.A1 provides the results of the Vaccine Approval Experiment; Tables 6.A2 and 6.A3 provide results from the Lockdown Experiment. The tables each report, in linear regression form, estimates of the

TABLE 6.A1 *Linear regression results: Vaccine Approval Experiment. Model 1 presents the direct effects of the experimental manipulations. Model 2 provides the model estimates underlying Figure 6.1. The reference category for the experimental manipulation is the Control condition. The dependent variable in the models is Acceptance of the Executive's Action; higher values indicate more acceptance. All variables are scaled to range from 0 to 1.*

	Model 1	Model 2
Contravention	−0.08*	0.06
	(0.02)	(0.05)
Clearance	0.01	0.02
	(0.02)	(0.05)
Support for the Rule of Law		−0.16*
		(0.05)
Contravention × Support for the Rule of Law		−0.21*
		(0.07)
Clearance × Support for the Rule of Law		−0.02
		(0.07)
Constant	0.49*	0.60*
	(0.01)	(0.03)
Observations	1,900	1,896
R^2	0.02	0.07

Note: * $p < 0.05$.

TABLE 6.A2 *Linear regression results: Lockdown Experiment (United States and Germany). Models 1 and 4 present the direct effects of the experimental manipulations. Models 2 and 5 provide the model estimates underlying Figure 6.2; Models 3 and 6 provide the results underlying Figure 6.3. The reference category for the experimental manipulation is the Control condition. The dependent variable in the models is Acceptance of the Executive's Action; higher values indicate more acceptance. All variables are scaled to range from 0 to 1.*

	United States			Germany		
	Model 1	Model 2	Model 3	Model 4	Model 5	Model 6
Contravention	−0.08*	0.04	−0.04	−0.09*	0.12	−0.03
	(0.03)	(0.10)	(0.04)	(0.03)	(0.11)	(0.06)
Clearance	0.04	−0.12	0.06	0.02	0.14	0.11
	(0.03)	(0.10)	(0.04)	(0.03)	(0.11)	(0.06)
Support for the Rule of Law		−0.15			0.15	
		(0.10)			(0.11)	
Contravention × Support for the Rule of Law		−0.18			−0.28	
		(0.13)			(0.15)	
Clearance × Support for the Rule of Law		0.21			−0.17	
		(0.14)			(0.15)	
Executive Approval			0.69*			0.69*
			(0.04)			(0.06)
Contravention × Executive Approval			−0.05			−0.11
			(0.06)			(0.09)
Clearance × Executive Approval			−0.09			−0.14
			(0.06)			(0.09)
Constant	0.58*	0.69*	0.24*	0.66*	0.56*	0.28*
	(0.02)	(0.07)	(0.03)	(0.02)	(0.08)	(0.04)
Observations	865	864	865	576	576	576
R^2	0.02	0.04	0.44	0.02	0.03	0.34

Note: * $p < 0.05$.

direct effects of the experimental manipulations discussed in Chapter 5, as well as the conditional effects of the treatments discussed in Chapter 6.

In the online appendix, we replicate and extend these models by adding respondents' political and demographic characteristics as control variables to these regression models. These covariates include respondents' level of political interest, court knowledge, democratic values (belief that a strong leader is preferable), gender, age, and left–right ideology, all as described in Chapter 4. Additionally, we controlled for respondents' partisanship. In Germany, we used a standard question that asked respondents what party they would vote for were federal elections to be held soon. In the United States, we used a seven-point measure of Republican–Democratic

TABLE 6.A3 *Linear regression results: Lockdown Experiment (Hungary and Poland). Models 1 and 4 present the direct effects of the experimental manipulations. Models 2 and 5 provide the model estimates underlying Figure 6.2; Models 3 and 6 provide the results underlying Figure 6.3. The reference category for the experimental manipulation is the Control condition. The dependent variable in the models is Acceptance of the Executive's Action; higher values indicate more acceptance. All variables are scaled to range from 0 to 1.*

	Hungary			Poland		
	Model 1	Model 2	Model 3	Model 4	Model 5	Model 6
Contravention	−0.04	−0.06	−0.07*	−0.04	−0.01	−0.05
	(0.03)	(0.08)	(0.03)	(0.03)	(0.08)	(0.03)
Clearance	−0.02	−0.16*	−0.01	−0.01	−0.01	0.02
	(0.03)	(0.08)	(0.03)	(0.03)	(0.08)	(0.03)
Support for the Rule of Law		−0.07			0.02	
		(0.08)			(0.08)	
Contravention × Support for the Rule of Law		0.03			−0.05	
		(0.11)			(0.11)	
Clearance × Support for the Rule of Law		0.21			0.004	
		(0.12)			(0.11)	
Executive Approval			0.35*			0.30*
			(0.05)			(0.05)
Contravention × Executive Approval			0.06			0.04
			(0.07)			(0.07)
Clearance × Executive Approval			0.02			−0.07
			(0.07)			(0.07)
Constant	0.56*	0.61*	0.44*	0.50*	0.49*	0.41*
	(0.02)	(0.06)	(0.02)	(0.02)	(0.06)	(0.02)
Observations	854	854	852	863	863	863
R^2	0.003	0.01	0.18	0.004	0.004	0.10

Note: * $p < 0.05$.

identification. In Poland and Hungary, we used respondents' answers to a question that asked them which major party they felt closest to.[8]

Overall, the results we discuss in Chapters 5 and 6 are remarkably robust to the inclusion of control variables. In both experiments, the contravention penalty we estimate is robust to the inclusion of control variables, as are the direct effects of

8 We used the question about federal elections in Germany, rather than the closeness question, because we did not ask the closeness question on the Germany panel survey until two waves after the Vaccine Approval Experiment was fielded. The German results for the Lockdown Experiment we discuss here are invariant to the measure of partisan affiliation we use.

Clearance and Compliance discussed in Chapter 5. Turning to conditional effects, the multiplicative interaction term Support for the Rule of Law×Contravention actually *gains* statistical significance in the United States once the model includes control variables. The estimates of the marginal effects remain basically unchanged when control variables are included. The effect of contravention is still significant for the highest tercile of Support for the Rule of Law in the United States and Germany and is never significant in Poland or Hungary. Looking at the executive approval interaction, the confidence interval for the effect of contravention for the highest tercile of approval in the United States crosses the zero line just slightly, though the estimated effect is identical (Estimate: –0.08; CI: –0.16, 0.004). In short, the conclusions we draw in Chapters 5 and 6 remain robust when we account for respondents' demographic and political characteristics.

THE WEAKER SIGNALING POWER OF LEGISLATURES

We have argued that – compared to other sorts of institutions that provide oversight, like legislators or bureaucracies – courts are uniquely positioned to provide credible signals of executive overreach to the public. In this appendix, we draw on an additional arm of the Lockdown Experiment to bring some data to bear on the unique authority of constitutional courts and judicial review. In all four countries, a different subset of respondents read about legislative responses to an executive action, rather than the constitutional court's use of judicial review. For example, in the United States, respondents who read about legislative contravention read the following text at the end of the vignette: "In response, Congress passed a resolution stopping the government from implementing the lockdown plan. The President announced that he will move forward with the lockdown, in defiance of Congress' resolution." The analogous clearance text read as follows: "In response, Congress passed a resolution allowing the government to implement the lockdown plan. The President announced that he will move forward with the lockdown, as allowed by Congress' resolution."

Direct Effects

Figure 6.A1 displays the direct effects of legislative treatments. The left-hand panels contain the direct effects of the Cleared and Contravened treatments relative to the Control condition, the right-hand panels contain the difference in means between the Control condition and the two main treatment groups. Positive values reflect an increase in average support relative to the Control condition; negative values represent an average decline in support relative to the control.

These results support our expectation that the signaling power of legislatures is muted. In Germany, legislative contravention is associated with a decrease in acceptance of –0.07 ($p = 0.03$). However, there is no statistically discernible penalty

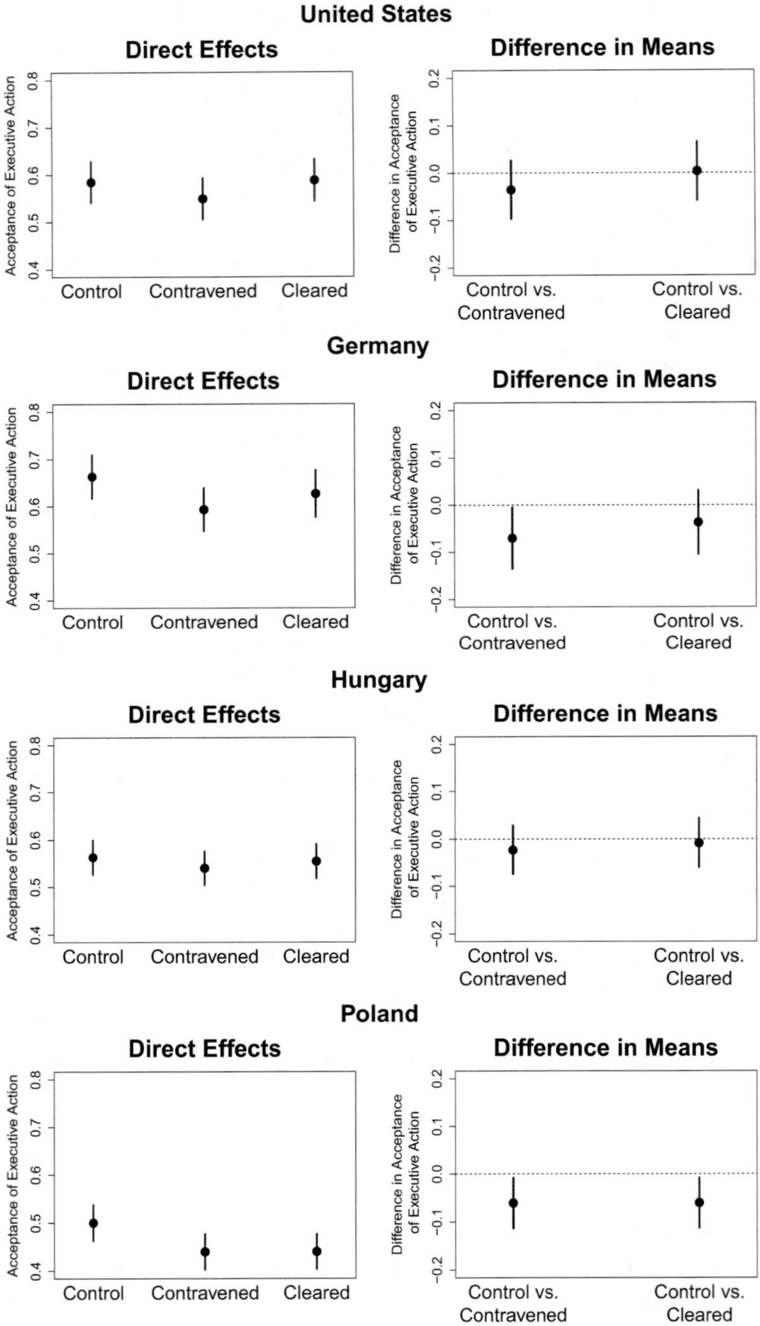

FIGURE 6.A1 Direct effects of the Lockdown Experiment (Legislature Treatments). The left-hand panels plot the average value of acceptance of the executive's action, by condition. This variable has a range of 0–1; higher values of this variable indicate a greater level of acceptance. The right-hand panels illustrate the difference in means between experimental conditions. Positive values of the *y*-axis in these panels indicate an increase in acceptance, relative to the Control condition. The vertical lines in both panels provide 95% confidence intervals.

for defying the legislature in the United States (–0.04; $p = 0.26$). That is, a Congressional objection to the President's lockdown policy failed to generate public opposition to the policy relative to a scenario where respondents did not read about congressional or judicial action. In Hungary, an executive action that contravened the legislature is not associated with a decrease in acceptance (–0.02; $p = 0.38$). In Poland, however, we observe a result contrary to our expectations and contrary to all previous results: a statistically significant decrease (–0.06; $p = 0.02$) in acceptance of the executive's decision to move forward with a lockdown policy when it contravenes legislative oversight (compared to unilateral action). This interesting and unexpected result indicates that Polish respondents withdrew their support for the prime minister's policy when carried out in defiance of the Sejm.

Second, we turn to the effects of clearance by a legislature. We anticipated that legislative approval cannot boost approval of an executive's policy. Only in the United States do we observe the expected greater level of acceptance for actions that were cleared by the legislature than those that received no oversight. Yet, this difference is minuscule and not statistically significant. In fact, in the United States, Germany, and Hungary, legislative clearance does not change average levels of acceptance. In Poland, however, we observe a curious result: respondents who read that the prime minister moved forward with a lockdown policy that had been approved by the legislature have, on average, *lower* levels of acceptance than those who read that the policy was implemented without any oversight (-0.06; $p = 0.02$).

Taken together, the analyses of the direct effects of clearance and contravention suggest – as we have expected – that the signaling capacity of legislatures is generally muted. While our results from Germany and Poland indicate that defying a legislature may weaken support for executive policy, the findings from Hungary and United States reveal no such dynamic.

Conditional Effects: Support for the Rule of Law

To assess our conditional expectations regarding support for the rule of law, we estimated a linear regression with dichotomous indicators for each treatment (using the Control condition as the baseline), and multiplicative interaction terms between each treatment and our measure of support for the rule of law.

Figure 6.A2 plots the marginal effects of each treatment (compared to the Control condition) across support for the rule of law. We generally expected null results. In Germany, we find some evidence of legislative efficacy: greater support for the rule of law is associated with an increased penalty for contravention of a legislative resolution. However, there is no analogous effect in the United States: just as we found no overall direct effect for contravening the US Congress, the second panel of the top row of Figure 6.A2 illustrates that this finding holds regardless of one's support for the rule of law. Again, we suspect this may be a reflection of broad

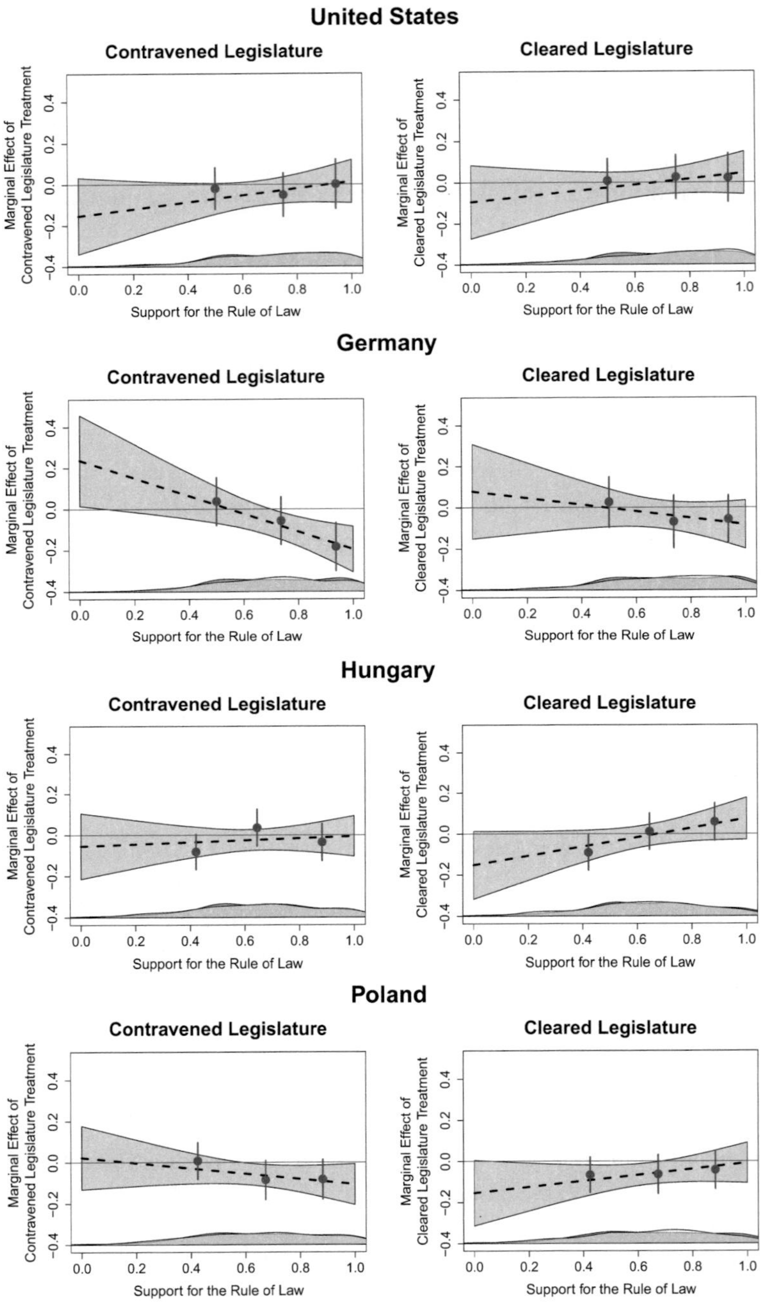

FIGURE 6.A2 Conditional effects from the Lockdown Experiment (Legislature Treatments). Support for the Rule of Law increases with the *x*-axis. The shaded areas are 95% confidence intervals. The point estimates and associated confidence intervals are the Hainmueller, Mummolo, and Xu (2019) estimates of the marginal effect for each tercile of Support for the Rule of Law. The density plot shows the distribution for support for the rule of law by treatment; the darker density is the baseline group. Full regression results are provided in Table 6.A4.

TABLE 6.A4 *Linear regression results: Lockdown Experiment (Legislature Treatments). The odd-numbered models present the direct effects of the experimental manipulations. The even-numbered models provide the model estimates underlying Figure 6.A2. The reference category for the experimental manipulation is the Control condition. The dependent variable in the models is Acceptance of the Executive's Action; higher values indicate more acceptance. All variables are scaled to range from 0 to 1.*

	United States		Germany		Hungary		Poland	
	Model 1	Model 2	Model 3	Model 4	Model 5	Model 6	Model 7	Model 8
Contravention	−0.04	−0.15	−0.07*	0.24*	−0.02	−0.05	−0.06*	0.02
	(0.03)	(0.10)	(0.03)	(0.12)	(0.03)	(0.08)	(0.03)	(0.08)
Clearance	0.004	−0.10	−0.04	0.08	−0.01	−0.15	−0.06*	−0.15
	(0.03)	(0.10)	(0.03)	(0.12)	(0.03)	(0.08)	(0.03)	(0.08)
Support for the Rule of Law		−0.15		0.15		−0.07		0.02
		(0.10)		(0.11)		(0.08)		(0.08)
Contravention × Support for the Rule of Law		0.17		−0.43*		0.05		−0.13
		(0.14)		(0.16)		(0.11)		(0.11)
Clearance × Support for the Rule of Law		0.14		−0.16		0.23		0.15
		(0.14)		(0.16)		(0.12)		(0.11)
Constant	0.58*	0.69*	0.66*	0.56*	0.56*	0.61*	0.50*	0.49*
	(0.02)	(0.07)	(0.02)	(0.08)	(0.02)	(0.06)	(0.02)	(0.06)
Observations	857	857	567	567	865	865	846	846
R^2	0.002	0.005	0.01	0.02	0.001	0.01	0.01	0.01

Note: * $p < 0.05$.

negative public sentiment toward Congress that negates the influence of citizens' support for the rule of law.

Turning to Poland and Hungary in the bottom two rows of Figure 6.A2, none of the Hainmueller, Mummolo, and Xu (2019) binned estimators reach statistical significance.[9] Even for the highest tercile of rule of law support in both countries, the effect of defying a legislature, compared to no oversight, is not statistically significant. Again, the conclusion from this pair of countries is that legislative intervention does little to signal to the public that the executive is pushing legal boundaries and, by extension, to lower acceptance of the executive's action.

Turning to our expectations regarding clearance, we expected a flat line in the right-hand panels of each row. This is essentially the pattern we see in all four countries. Compared to the Control condition in which there is no oversight, there is no effect of a legislative decision in favor of executive action on acceptance. Notably, we find this to consistently be the case across all four countries. This finding is consistent with our earlier observation that legislative approval of an executive action – particularly when carried out by a legislative majority of the same partisan makeup as the executive – may be a particularly weak signal as even citizens with a strong attachment to the rule of law view such an action as "normal" politics.

9 In Poland, we find an effect among those with high levels of support for the rule of law when we consider the variable in its continuous form. This is consistent with the account of opposition supporters potentially driving punishment for contravening the legislature.

7

Judicial Review Amid Partisan Publics

In Chapters 5 and 6, we demonstrated that independent courts can ensure that executives who contravene constitutional limits pay a political cost. In this way, the use of judicial review by independent courts holds the promise of state constraint. However, when courts lack independence, their ability to send credible signals about executive overreach is compromised; executives who transgress low-independence courts face no loss of support. That is, judicial independence is a prerequisite to judicial efficacy.

Further, we have demonstrated that the efficacy of independent courts varies with the public's attitudes and values. As we saw in Chapter 6, the price executives pay for contravening independent courts increases with the public's commitment to the rule of law. Among citizens who have low support for the rule of law, the effect of contravening an independent court is nil. It is among those who are committed to the rule of law that the effect of judicial review is both statistically and substantively meaningful. Collectively, from here on we refer to our argument and these supporting findings as the "Rule of Law account."

As we alluded to in Chapter 2, citizens' affinity for the executive shapes the magnitude of the penalty the executive faces from contravening an independent court. We saw at the end of Chapter 6 that executive approval can matter, but perhaps not in the way one would expect: the negative consequences of contravening a court are greatest among those who hold the executive in the highest regard. With this in mind, we turn our attention to one of the most powerful forces in modern politics, partisanship. An influential and growing literature identifies partisanship, and its frequent companion polarization, as posing a potent threat to liberal democracy and the rule of law (Aarslew 2023; Ahlquist et al. 2018; Carey et al. 2022; Simonovits, McCoy, and Littvay 2022). Although the particulars of such accounts vary, they generally suggest that partisan attachments and polarization can alter, overwhelm, or otherwise negate citizen's commitment to ostensibly apolitical democratic norms and values (e.g., Arbatli and Rosenberg 2020; Driscoll and Nelson 2023b; Fossati, Muhtadi, and Warburton 2022; Gidengil, Stolle, and Bergeron-Boutin 2022; Graham and Svolik 2020; Nelson and Driscoll 2023). By making the rule of law a second-order priority behind partisan policy goals, partisanship might erode the shared consensus around what constitutes a constitutionally legitimate state action and in so doing potentially undermine citizens' ability to act collectively to impede executive overreach.

Addressing this challenge head on is a critical task: what good is judicial independence, or for that matter support for the rule of law, if judicial efficacy falters in the face of political cleavages? The ability of a court to overcome this challenge and hold executives to account for unconstitutional behavior presents, in some respects, the ultimate test of judicial efficacy. And, with polarization a potent accelerant of democratic backsliding (Grillo and Prato 2023; Orhan 2022; Svolik 2019), a court's failure to meet this challenge has important implications for the capacity of judicial institutions to serve as guardrails against such democratic retrocession. If courts – at least independent ones – are able to generate political costs for constitutional transgressions even when doing so is contrary to citizens' partisan interests, we can be more confident in the potential for courts to successfully constrain the state.

Our task in Chapters 7 and 8 is to assess the extent to which partisanship can override rule of law considerations. We do so by developing a competing logic to our own theory – what we refer to as the Partisan Prioritization account account – which suggests that people prioritize partisanship over the rule of law. By this account, what matters to judgments of acceptance is partisan congruence with the executive, not the information conveyed by judicial review or fealty to the rule of law. Citizens may allow copartisans to flout legal norms but punish outpartisans; or, as we saw in the last chapter, citizens might hold their copartisans to a higher standard than outpartisans. In these scenerios, the rule of law becomes more like rule *by* law because its application is contingent on the alignment of a citizens' partisanship with that of the executive.

We limit our focus in this chapter to contexts in which judicial independence is high. Then, in the next chapter, we expand our theorizing and analysis across levels of judicial independence. There are compelling research design reasons for this preliminary focus on high-independence contexts. First, high judicial independence contexts provide a "hard" test of partisanship accounts. As we have seen, we expect rule of law considerations to "work" in these settings: the public withdraws their acceptance from executives who ignore rulings of independent courts. As such, these are the settings where we are most confident that the empirical evidence will support our Rule of Law account over the Partisan Prioritization account. If our Rule of Law account does not bear out in these most conducive of environments, then there is little reason to expect it to do so where judicial independence is weak.

Second, our focus on Germany and the United States reflects that of much of the related literature, which takes as a particular concern the threat partisanship poses to more established democracies (e.g., Graham and Svolik 2020). Whereas scholars have long been concerned about the survival and stability of more fragile democracies (Booth and Seligson 2009), the established wisdom had been that consolidated democracies had little to fear, thanks to citizens' deep commitment to democratic norms and the entrenchment of strong democratic institutions (Claassen 2020). With recent scholarship casting doubt on the ability of established democracies to rely on citizens' support for democratic values to stymie democratic backsliding (Ahmed 2023), increasing attention is being paid to reassessing democracy's prospects in its erstwhile most fertile grounds. Our initial emphasis on two such cases is consistent with this mounting scholarly concern.

Third, in both countries, we are able to convincingly randomize the partisanship of an executive in a way that is difficult to do with a high degree of external validity in other contexts. It is difficult to manipulate the partisanship of executives, especially national executives, in experimental designs. They are singular, salient individuals whose partisanship is widely known. Leveraging the federal nature of the United States and Germany, we are able to resolve these concerns. We manipulate the executive's partisanship in our experimental design by having respondents confront constitutionally dubious behavior by subnational executives.

Our results suggest that judicial review by independent courts remains efficacious in the face of pernicious partisanship. Critically, we find no consistent evidence that the public is more lenient on copartisans, or more willing to exact punishment on an outpartisan executive who contravenes the rule of law. Rather, and consistent with the findings reported in Chapters 5 and 6, we observe a contravention penalty for executives, regardless of party, that disregard the directions of an independent court. These results are reflective of judicial review's resilience to partisan contamination, giving us further confidence in our Rule of Law account.

These findings stand in stark contrast to accounts suggesting that intense partisanship threatens the health of democracy by encouraging citizens to look the other way when a copartisan violates democratic norms (e.g., Gadarian, Goodman, and Pepinsky 2022; Kalmoe and Mason 2022). Our results should thus provide some comfort to those who are concerned about the deleterious effects of partisanship for the rule of law. Moreover, the chapter's results speak to the unique place that independent judicial institutions may occupy in modern democratic societies, particularly in comparison to other aspects of democratic governance that past research has found to be susceptible to partisanship's damaging effects.

PARTISAN PRIORITIZATION

While partisanship has long been recognized as an inevitable – and at times beneficial (McCoy and Somer 2021) – aspect of democratic competition, the seemingly rapid retrocession of democracy around the world has led scholars to reconsider both the nature and extent of partisanship's ability to undermine citizens' support for democratic norms and ultimately democracy itself (Aarslew 2023; Ahlquist et al. 2018; Carey et al. 2022; Gidengil, Stolle, and Bergeron-Boutin 2022; Mazepus and Toshkov 2022). This concern stems, in part, from a recognition that democratic decay increasingly comes not from would-be dictators conducting an overt autocratic takeovers but rather by from democratically elected politicians enacting incremental autocratizing reforms incrementally through legal and constitutional processes. Rather than consistently punishing officials at the ballot box for such behavior, however, there is ample evidence of voters rewarding, or at least not penalizing, these actions (Gidengil, Stolle, and Bergeron-Boutin 2022; Saikkonen and Christensen 2022; Simonovits, McCoy, and Littvay 2022). That citizens are *electing* officials who engage in anti-rule of law behavior has thus turned the received wisdom of democratic accountability on its head (Cohen et al. 2023). By integrating the influence of partisanship into extant accounts of the importance of democratic-supporting norms for regime vitality (Almond and Verba 1963; Putnam 1993), this growing body of research has yielded a number of significant theoretical and empirical answers to this puzzle of great consequence for democracy.

Another large literature on partisanship only amplifies this concern. The rapid expansion of affective polarization – the active dislike and distrust of political opponents (Iyengar et al. 2019) – has raised concerns that democratic norms may be undermined not only by a prejudice in favor of copartisans, but also a desire to see political rivals "lose" (Simonovits, McCoy, and Littvay 2022). A result of this phenomenon is that citizens can come to view their political rivals so negatively that they almost reflexively oppose actions or policies – including those they would otherwise support – perceived as benefiting the disliked political party. In the context of institutional signals and the rule of law, we might expect citizens to be less receptive simply because their reactions are driven effectively entirely by partisanship.

This partisanship account stands in stark contrast to the one we have advanced in this book. Our argument is that judicial review provides a signal that allows citizens to learn about rule of law violations, and to coordinate their attitudes and behaviors to constrain the state. A high court decision striking down an incumbent's action informs citizens that the incumbent's proposed action falls outside the bounds of constitutional appropriateness, and should be opposed on legal grounds *even if doing so runs contrary to one's partisan interests*. In a world devoid of partisanship, citizens' coordination poses a difficult challenge to state constraint: although they may have a shared interest in constraining the state – citizens are better off in a state where power is not willfully abused – they are also not homogeneous in their preferences regarding the content and scope of the rules. Partisanship exacerbates these divisions, casting controversies – those with legal implications as well as those without – into the realm of political contestation, where feuding sides of political stances are settled via electoral processes and by majority rule.

It is therefore critical for us to evaluate the extent to which our theoretical account stands up in the face of this partisan pull. More emphatically, if there is any environment where an independent court might be needed to rise above the fray, and inform citizens about a claim of higher authority, it is in the face of partisanship and affective polarization. Indeed, at the foundation of the idea of the rule of law is the notion that – regardless of who is making policy – there are enforcable limits to political power. If citizens are willing to look the other way when their favored politicians bypass legal dictates, then the rule of law is compromised. For this reason, it is essential to probe the extent to which judicial review can help to enforce the rule of law in the face of such potentially compelling and powerful partisan considerations.

In our theoretical account (which we refer to as the Rule of Law account), independent courts send signals to citizens about potential executive rule of law transgressions. We have shown in Chapters 5 and 6 that acceptance of an executive's action hinges primarily on the content of the signal: citizens' acceptance decreases when the executive contravenes a judicial decision, provided the court is sufficiently independent and the public is sufficiently supportive of the rule of law. By our theory, *who* – that is, the partisan congruence of the policymaker and the citizen – is trying to implement the policy matters less than *how* the policy is made – that is, whether the executive carries out the policy in defiance of judicial review.

By contrast, consider an alternative – Partisan Prioritization – logic of the public's evaluation of executive actions. This account is straightforward: citizens like it when their party wins, and they dislike it when the outparty wins. Put into our framework, partisan-motivated citizens' acceptance of a constitutionally dubious action will hinge not on whether it is consistent with a court's ruling, but rather on whether the outcome of that review can be seen as a success for their copartisans. In contrast to the Rule of Law account, this partisan-centric account anticipates that the public will prioritize *who* is seeking to carry out a particular policy, irrespective of *how* that policy is accomplished.

Combining Institutional Signals and Copartisanship

Armed with these dueling theoretical accounts, we return to our typology of judicial–executive interactions in Figure 7.1. Two factors loom large: (a) whether the policy was implemented through judicial clearance or contravention and (b) the partisanship of the executive carrying out the policy.[1]

The first condition is Copartisan Contravention. Here, a copartisan executive makes a constitutionally suspect proposal. The constitutional court then rules that the policy is unconstitutional, and the executive contravenes the court by implementing the policy despite the judicial directive. This scenario creates potent cross-

1 We acknowledge an important assumption we make: respondents' personal policy preferences are always the same as their political party's. While this may not always be the case, we think, on average, respondents tend to favor policies their party champions.

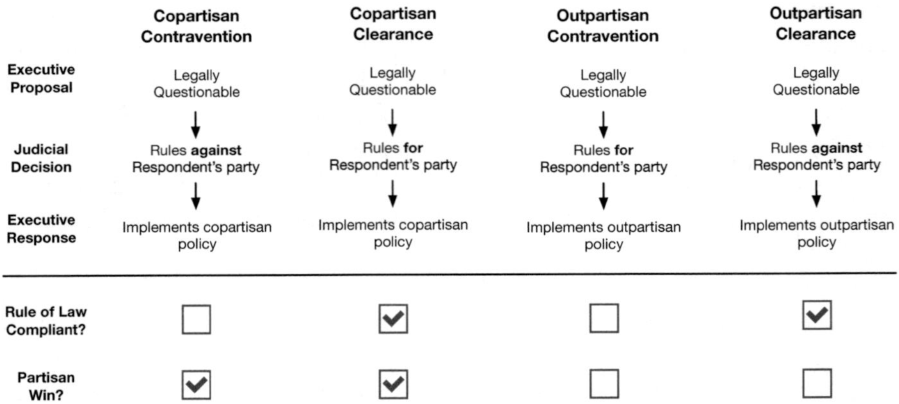

FIGURE 7.1 Typology of responses to contravention and clearance by a copartisan and outpartisan executive. Thus, "copartisan" and "outpartisan" refer to the respondent's congruence with the executive championing the policy.

cutting considerations. On the one hand, the policy has been implemented in violation of the rule of law. On the other hand, the policy was championed by a copartisan.

The second condition in Figure 7.1, Copartisan Clearance, happens when a copartisan executive makes a constitutionally dubious proposal, that policy is cleared by the constitutional court, and the copartisan's policy is implemented. Judicial clearance allows citizens to base their evaluation of the policy on their shared partisanship with the executive since the court has endorsed the policy's constitutionality. Our Rule of Law account suggests that the court's decision will neither raise nor lower citizens' support for the action, leaving them, to evaluate the policy based on other considerations – including partisanship. For its part, the Partisan Prioritization account predicts high acceptance for the policy since it is championed by a copartisan executive. Put differently, both of our theoretical accounts expect relatively high levels of acceptance in this condition.

Third, we turn to Outpartisan Contravention. In this sequence of events, an outpartisan executive makes a constitutionally dubious proposal and the constitutional court strikes it down. The outparty executive ignores the court and implements the policy. This situation is characterized by a win for the outparty and a violation of the rule of law. Accordingly, both theoretical accounts expect that respondents' level of acceptance will be particularly low in this condition.

Finally, consider Outpartisan Clearance. Here, an outparty executive proposes a questionable policy, and that policy is endorsed by the constitutional court. From the Partisan Prioritization viewpoint, this scenario is a loss for the respondent and thus should result in lower levels of acceptance. However, from our theoretical perspective, the proposal was implemented by following constitutional norms, suggesting no loss of acceptance.

In short, both theoretical accounts expect relatively high levels of acceptance in situations of Copartisan Clearance and low levels of acceptance under Outpartisan Contravention. The other two conditions provide opportunities to distinguish between the theoretical accounts. Our Rule of Law account suggests that acceptance should be higher under Outpartisan Clearance than Copartisan Contravention while the Partisan Prioritization account suggests that acceptance will be higher under Copartisan Contravention than Outpartisan Clearance.

Hypotheses

The preceding discussion presented two theoretical frameworks and described how citizens' acceptance of executive behavior might vary according to the party of the executive making the policy proposal and the constitutional court's oversight signal. We therefore have a theoretical foundation to formulate a set of concrete hypotheses. Given our consistent findings in Chapters 5 and 6 that Acceptance is no different when a court clears a policy than when it does not act, we construct our hypotheses with clearance, rather than no oversight, as the baseline condition.

We begin by considering the difference in respondents' acceptance of an executive action under contravention. Recall that our Rule of Law account suggests that the public will punish rule of law violations irrespective of the executive's partisanship, but that there is no benefit to adhering to the rule of law under the clearance condition. Therefore, we expect that the penalty for Contravention, as compared to Clearance, should be negative and statistically significant. This is simply another way of restating the first hypothesis from Chapters 5 and 6:

- H_{1ROL}: Judicial contravention decreases acceptance of an executive's action.

In contrast, the Partisan Prioritization account emphasizes citizens' partisanship and that of the executive. As such, this account suggests that the signal sent by a court is inconsequential to citizens' attitudes toward the challenged policy. Therefore:

- $H_{1Partisan}$: Judicial contravention neither increases nor decreases acceptance of an executive's action.

The second comparison of theoretical interest is the difference in acceptance between a copartisan executive's policy compared to an outpartisan executive's policy, holding the court's signal constant. If the Rule of Law account is correct, acceptance of a constitutionally suspect policy should be the same regardless of whether the executive is a copartisan or outpartisan.

In the Partisan Prioritization account, by contrast, it is not a concern for the rules that governs the public's acceptance of policy, but instead prioritization of their own partisan affiliation. This account would instead predict that acceptance of a copartisan executive's policy will be greater than that of an outpartisan executive. Consequentially, these two empirical expectations lead to the following hypotheses:

- H_{2ROL}: Acceptance of an action taken by a copartisan executive is neither higher nor lower than an action taken by an outpartisan executive.
- $H_{2Partisan}$: Acceptance of an action taken by a copartisan executive is higher than an action taken by an outpartisan executive.

Lastly, we consider the conditional effect of support for the rule of law under each of these accounts. Recall that we showed in Chapter 6 that the size of the contravention penalty varied as a function of the public's commitment to the rule of law. Those citizens who profess a more profound commitment to the rule of law exact larger penalties on the executive for their contravention of the court's direct orders. Our theoretical expectations for this conditional effect follows directly from these previous findings. As support for the rule of law increases, so too should the contravention penalty. Thus:

- H_{3ROL}: The penalty for contravening a court increases with support for the rule of law.

On the other hand, central to the Partisan Prioritization account is the contention that citizens prioritize partisan considerations over their support for democratic norms like the rule of law. Therefore, even those who have high levels of support for the rule of law will be less likely to support sanctioning a copartisan for rule of law violations. Indeed, a wealth of previous research documents these partisan dynamics across a wide variety of institutional considerations (Gidengil, Stolle, and Bergeron-Boutin 2022; Graham and Svolik 2020; Simonovits, McCoy, and Littvay 2022). This suggests that the efficacy of judicial review should not be conditioned by one's commitment to the rule of law, but rather driven by partisanship. Therefore:

- $H_{3Partisan}$: The penalty for contravening a court neither increases nor decreases with support for the rule of law.

EVALUATING THE EFFECTS OF PARTISANSHIP AND INSTITUTIONAL SIGNALS

To test the theoretical expectations, we need an experiment that manipulates both the partisanship of the policymaker and the constitutional court's signal regarding the constitutionality of the policy. Our Mandatory Vaccine Experiment does precisely this. This experiment, fielded in the United States and Germany, is a 2×2

fully-crossed experimental design fielded four months before the Lockdown Experiment analyzed in Chapters 5 and 6.

The experiment asked respondents to read about a hypothetical action taken by a state-level executive (a governor in the United States or a minister-president in Germany) that would require all adults in that state to receive the COVID-19 vaccine. The first pair of treatment conditions in the experiment randomized whether the state executive was a member of one of the two largest national parties in each country: the Democrats or the Republicans in the United States, and the Christian Democratic Union (CDU) or the Social Democratic Party (SPD) in Germany. Importantly, at the time of our study there was balance in the partisan control of state governments in both countries. In the United States, 27 states had Republican governors compared to 23 Democratic state executives. In Germany, of the sixteen Länder, six had a CDU executive (and one a CSU executive) and seven a SPD executive. By way of example, the treatments for German respondents read as follows:

> Imagine that the [CDU/SPD] minister-president of a nearby state issued an order this spring requiring all state residents above the age of 18 to receive a coronavirus vaccine. The minister-president contends that it is important to vaccinate all state residents in order to improve the economy.

The second pair of conditions randomized whether the state-level executive implemented the policy through contravention or clearance. In Germany, respondents were exposed to one of the following conditions:

- *Contravened*: In response, the Bundesverfassungsgericht issued a decision stopping the state government from requiring all adult residents to receive a coronavirus vaccine. The [CDU/SPD] minister-president announced that all adult state residents will be required to get the vaccine, in defiance of the Bundesverfassungsgericht's decision.
- *Cleared*: In response, the Bundesverfassungsgericht issued a decision allowing the state government to require all adult residents to receive a coronavirus vaccine. The [CDU/SPD] minister-president announced that all adult state residents will be required to get the vaccine, as allowed by the Bundesverfassungsgericht's decision.

In order to test our hypotheses, we needed to match respondents' partisanship with that of the state-level executive in the vignette. In the United States, this was straightforward. We coded respondents as copartisans if the governor shared their partisanship (including leaners), and we coded respondents as outpartisans if they indicated an affiliation with the other party.[2]

[2] Because "pure" independents – those who do not lean toward either party – can not be coded as copartisans to either the Democrats or the Republicans, we exclude those 19 percent of respondents from the analyses that follow.

Germany's multiparty system makes this determination more complicated. But, the panel design of our survey assisted our attempts to determine whether each German respondent preferred the CDU or the SPD. Because this experiment was fielded on the fourth wave of a panel survey, we had access to a wealth of information about respondents' attitudes toward Germany's political parties. In each wave of the survey, we asked respondents both (a) which German party they liked the most and (b) their level of confidence in the ability of each major German party to handle the COVID-19 pandemic. We categorized respondents as preferring the CDU (or the SPD) if they listed that party as their favored party in the current (fourth) wave of the survey.[3] For respondents who neither favored the CDU or the SPD, we next looked to see if they indicated more confidence in one of those parties to handle the pandemic; if they indicated differential confidence, we used that determination to code their copartisanship with the state-level executive in the experiment. For those respondents we could not classify (typically because they gave both parties the same confidence ranking), we returned to the previous wave of the survey and repeated the same procedure. We repeated this procedure, as needed, for prior waves of the survey to maximize the number of respondents whose copartisanship with the experimental conditions we could determine. We are able to classify 71 percent of respondents as preferring either the CDU or the SPD. Of those respondents, 58 percent supported the CDU and 42 percent preferred SPD. Our decision to exclude the remaining respondents from the analysis mirrors our decision to exclude pure independents in the United States from the analysis that follows.

We use as our outcome variable respondents' scaled responses to three questions they answered after reading the vignette. First, we asked, "To what extent would you support or oppose the [state executive]'s action to require all state residents above the age of 18 to receive a coronavirus vaccine?" To this question, 48 percent of American respondents and 44 percent of German respondents were at least "somewhat" supportive of the executive's proposed requirement (on a four-point scale). Second, we asked, "Do you believe this action by the [state executive] would be legitimate exercise of power?" Compared to our first item, the central tendency of responses to this question is lower in both countries: 43 percent of respondents in the United States and 40 percent in Germany expressed support. Finally, we asked respondents, "If you had the opportunity to vote for this [state executive] in the next election, what would you do?" with answers on a four-point scale ranging from "I would definitely vote for this [state executive]" to "I would definitely not vote for this [state executive]."[4] Forty-two percent of American respondents and 38 percent of

3 For Bavarian respondents who selected the Christian Social Union (CSU), which is the CDU's sister party in Bavaria, we coded them as preferring the CDU.

4 Concerned about the ethical implications of asking respondents to confess to hypothetical illegal activity, we opted to include vote choice rather than a measure of compliance. In Chapter 8 (which also uses an experiment about a mandatory vaccine policy), we resolve

German respondents gave a supportive response to this item. The scales in both countries are reliable ($\alpha = 0.89$ in the United States and $\alpha = 0.91$ in Germany) and load strongly on a single factor. In the United States, the average factor loading is 0.83 with a second-dimension eigenvalue of –0.09; in Germany, the average factor loading is 0.86 and the second dimension eigenvalue is –0.09.

A few points about the experimental design are necessary. First, the proposer in this experiment is a state-level executive. In the previous experiments, the proposer was the national executive. We were concerned about external validity concerns that would arise from asking respondents to imagine a hypothetical national-level executive. Given variation in both countries regarding the partisanship of state-level executives, using these policymakers as the proposers enabled us to study the decisions of executives with meaningful policymaking authority but who realistically come from different political parties. Further, by abstracting away from actual executives, we sidestep issues that may have arisen in our previous experiments as respondents use their real-world judgments of executives to evaluate our vignettes: the likelihood that Joe Biden or Angela Merkel would ignore their national constitutional court is, we acknowledge, slim. Thus, to mitigate differences created by respondents' reaction to the variation according to their political knowledge or sophistication, and to avoid deception, we do not name the subnational government. Instead, following others (e.g., Butler and Powell 2014; Nelson and Driscoll 2023), we phrased the vignette in hypothetical language, asking respondents to "Imagine that the [partisan] [executive] from a nearby state…" While this approach does come at the cost of some realism (since some respondents are more "nearby" subnational governments controlled by copartisans or outpartisans than others), it has the benefit of not passing misinformation to respondents about mandatory vaccine policies they may have strong reactions to (and would need to be debriefed about following the survey).

Second, because we rely on subnational executives as the proposers in our experiment, we could only field our experiment in countries with federal systems. Of our four countries, this means we only fielded the experiment in Germany and the United States. For this reason, we confine our discussion in this chapter to the consequences of partisanship in countries with high levels of judicial independence. In Chapter 8, we theorize and test the implications of our dueling theoretical accounts as levels of high court independence vary.

Third, though neither the United States nor Germany enacted a nationwide mandatory vaccine policy, such proposals were hotly debated in both countries. In many states in both countries, citizens' ability to travel and to work was governed by vaccine availability and adherence. At least twenty-four state governments in the United States issued vaccine mandates for some workers (Howard-Williams et al.

this issue differently, asking respondents to give advice to a hypothetical friend about whether to comply.

2022), and these policies were sometimes challenged in court. Similar policies were enacted in Germany in late 2021 for health workers (Ellyat 2021a). This requirement was subsequently upheld as constitutional by the German Federal Constitutional Court (Jordans 2022).[5] These events speak to the external validity of our vignette.

Finally, as previewed above, the Mandatory Vaccine Experiment does not contain a pure control condition. We made this design decision out of a concern to statistical power. In the United States, we had only 1,000 respondents, and we knew that we would face different (but also important) power concerns in Germany because that country's multiparty system would require us to eliminate many respondents who were agnostic between the CDU and the SPD. Thus, while the experimental designs in Chapters 5 and 6 enabled us to compare directly situations where policies were implemented with no judicial review to those that were implemented after the constitutional court acted, all subjects in this experiment read about a policy implemented after judicial review. We are heartened by the fact that we have found no evidence in Chapters 5 and 6 that the average level of acceptance differs between that control condition and one involving judicial clearance, suggesting that the comparison in this chapter is similar to the one we made in Chapters 5 and 6.

RESULTS

We begin our analysis of the experiment by looking at the average level of Acceptance in each of the four treatment conditions. These averages are shown in the left-hand panels of Figure 7.2.[6] Both theoretical accounts suggest high levels of Acceptance in the Copartisan Clearance condition. By contrast, both theoretical perspectives suggested that Acceptance should be low in the Outpartisan Contravention condition. We find this pattern in both countries. The average value of Acceptance for the Copartisan Clearance condition is 0.53 in the United States and 0.48 in Germany; the average level of Acceptance in the Outpartisan Contravention condition, by contrast, is 0.41 in the United States and 0.36 in Germany. This difference is statistically significant ($p < 0.01$) in both countries.

The empirical implications of the two accounts diverge in their expectations about the average level of Acceptance in the Copartisan Contravention and Outpartisan Clearance conditions. In the former condition, the Partisan Prioritization account suggests a high level of Acceptance: while the policy was implemented by contravening the constitutional court, the policy was supported by

5 The German government proposed a national COVID vaccine mandate in 2022 but withdrew the proposal when it became clear it would not pass the legislature (Schuetze 2022; Thurau 2022).

6 Linear regression results underlying the analyses presented in this chapter, as well as a discussion of the robustness of our results to models including respondents' political and demographic characteristics, are provided in the Appendix.

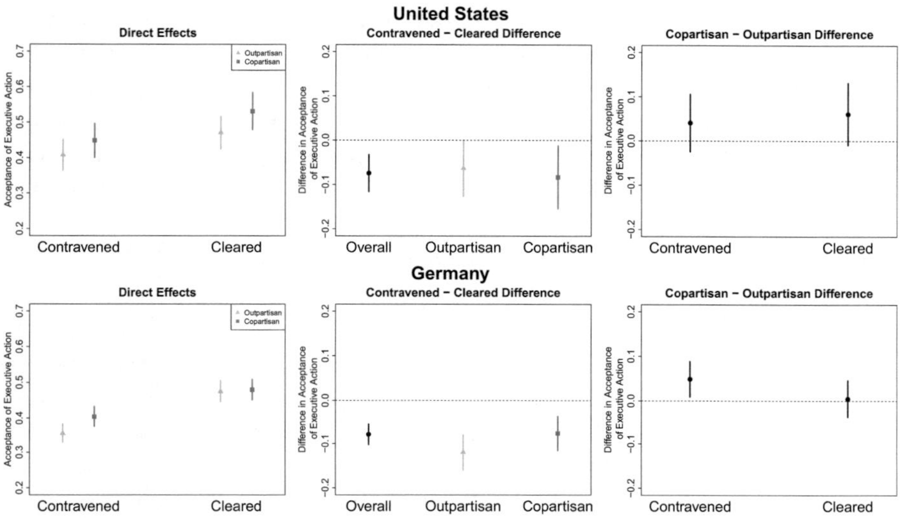

FIGURE 7.2 Direct effects of the Mandatory Vaccine Experiment. The left-hand panels plot the average value of Acceptance of the executive's action, by condition. This variable has a range of 0–1; higher values of this variable indicate a greater level of Acceptance. The middle- and right-hand panels illustrate the difference in means between experimental conditions. Positive values of the *y*-axis in these panels indicate an increase in Acceptance, relative to the Cleared condition (middle panel) or the Outpartisan condition (right-hand panel). The vertical lines in all three panels provide 95% confidence intervals.

a copartisan. The situation is reversed in the Outpartisan Clearance condition. Here, the policy was championed by an outpartisan who followed the rule of law.

In the United States, the average value of Acceptance in the Outpartisan Clearance condition is 0.47; in the Copartisan Contravention condition, the average is 0.45 ($p = 0.51$). In Germany, the means are 0.48 and 0.40, respectively ($p < 0.01$). Thus, the average values of acceptance fall in the ordering predicted by our account – and not the Partisan Prioritization account. However, only in Germany is there a statistically distinguishable difference between these two averages.

Before turning to our hypotheses, we have one additional point. In Chapter 5, we observed a contravention penalty: acceptance of policies implemented by ignoring the court was lower than acceptance of policies implemented through a rule-of-law compliant process. We can examine the robustness of this finding in a different experimental vignette by looking at the leftmost point estimate in the middle panels of Figure 7.2. This point estimate displays the difference between the Contravened and Cleared conditions for the entire sample. The Rule of Law account and related hypotheses anticipate that respondents will be less supportive of executive actions that are contravened by the Court than those that are cleared by judicial review.

Across both countries, we see lower values of Acceptance for respondents in the Contravened condition than the Cleared condition ($p < 0.01$). The difference in both countries is about 0.08 and accounts for between 22 percent and 25 percent of a standard deviation in the outcome variable. That this effect size is very similar to those seen in Chapters 5 and 6 – even in an experiment that explicitly incorporates a partisan cue – suggests that the fundamental dynamic of our our Rule of Law account holds steadfast.

Testing Hypothesis 1

Our first set of hypotheses refers to the difference in Acceptance between policies implemented through clearance and contravention. Our rule of law-centric account suggests a contravention penalty that should remain stable regardless of the partisanship of the proposer. Applied to the middle panel of Figure 7.2, our theoretical account would predict a negative and statistically significant difference in means. The Partisan Prioritization account, by contrast, suggests that the Contravention–Clearance difference should be minimal and perhaps not statistically distinguishable from zero, owing to the fact that people prioritize partisanship over rule of law compliance.

Turning to the second and third point estimates in the middle panel of Figure 7.2, we find evidence that supports the Rule of Law account, and is inconsistent with the Partisan Prioritization account. Both differences are negative and statistically significant, just as our theory suggests. In Germany, the results are similar: a –0.12 ($p < 0.01$) decline for respondents who read of an outpartisan's proposal and a –0.08 decline for respondents who read of a copartisan's proposal ($p < 0.01$). The former penalty accounts for nearly 40 percent of a standard deviation in the outcome variable. In the United States, the contravention penalty is –0.06 ($p = 0.05$) for respondents who read about an outpartisan proposer and –0.08 ($p = 0.02$) for respondents who read that a copartisan governor made the proposal. Both differences account for about a quarter of a standard deviation of Acceptance. In short, our respondents withdrew their acceptance of the executive's policy when it was carried out in defiance a high court ruling, *regardless of the executive's partisanship.*

Testing Hypothesis 2

The second hypothesis concerned the difference in Acceptance according to respondents' shared copartisanship with the proposer. This difference is plotted in the right-hand panels of Figure 7.2. The positive values in these panels indicate greater levels of Acceptance for policies proposed by copartisans rather than outpartisans.

The empirical implications of the theoretical perspectives are reversed from those suggested by Hypothesis 1. Our Rule of Law account leads us to expect a negligible difference in Acceptance according to the partisanship of the executive proposer. In the right-hand panel of Figure 7.2, we expect to observe a small – and likely indistinguishable from zero – difference. The Partisan Prioritization account, by contrast, implies a positive and statistically significant difference in means: regardless of how a policy is implemented, citizens accept copartisans' policies at much higher levels than they accept outpartisans' policies.

In the figure, the results from the United States align with the predictions of our Rule of Law account: neither difference is statistically distinguishable from zero. This suggests that, on average, respondents are no more accepting of copartisan governors' mandatory vaccine policies than outpartisan governors' proposals. That the effect is similar for both clearance (0.06; $p = 0.09$) and contravention (0.04; $p = 0.22$) is further evidence for our theoretical perspective; there is no difference in Acceptance according to the partisanship of the executive.

In Germany, however, we do see some evidence of a partisan divide. Consistent with our Rule of Law account, we observe no difference in the average level of Acceptance by copartisanship when the minister-president's policy is implemented after a blessing by the German Constitutional Court (0.01; $p = 0.82$). However, German respondents accepted policies implemented through contravention at higher levels when the executive who ignored the court was a copartisan rather than an outpartisan. Germans thus appear marginally more supportive of copartisans whose action is challenged by the constitutional court compared to an outpartisan governor (0.05; $p = 0.02$).[7] Importantly though, as we see in the middle panel of the figure, German respondents nonetheless still punish both copartisan and outpartisan minister-presidents by withdrawing acceptance when they implement policies through contravention. Further, the difference in means in the right-hand figure is relatively small. In this sense, the partisan differential found in our results is about the extent of the punishment meted out, rather than a total reprieve from punishment for copartisans. In other words, although we have some limited evidence that the public grants some leeway to copartisans who implement controversial policies against the ruling of a constitutional court (relative to outpartisans), it does not appear the case that the effects of partisanship are so strong so as to undermine the coordinating effect of judicial review.[8]

To summarize, the direct effects of the Mandatory Vaccine Experiment provide considerable support for our theoretical account and no strong evidence for the Partisan Prioritization account. In the US, respondents seem to be no more willing to tolerate copartisans' contravention (relative to judicial approval) than they are to

7 Although we note this divergence across contexts is surprising given that polarization is generally seen as higher in the United States.

8 One way to think of this finding is that it reflects a partisan "double standard" whereby partisans hold outpartisans to account for breaching the rule of law but do not do so for their copartisans. This is, in a sense, a middle ground of sorts between our Rule of Law account and the Partisan Prioritization account.

accept the same behavior by an outpartisan. And while Germans may punish outpartisans slightly more than copartisans for contravention, they nevertheless still punish executives of both parties for such behavior. Overall, this evidence is consistent with our Rule of Law theory.

Testing Hypothesis 3

We turn now to the conditional effects of respondents' support for the rule of law. Recall in Chapter 6 we hypothesized and demonstrated that, in places with high levels of judicial independence, the size of the contravention penalty increases with respondent's support for the rule of law. Therefore, before turning to Hypothesis 3, we first verify that this pattern continues to hold in the Mandatory Vaccine Experiment.

The left-hand panels of Figure 7.3 display the marginal effect of contravention (compared to clearance) across Support for the Rule of Law. We expect negative values in the figure, which would indicate respondents are less accepting of a policy enacted in contravention of a court decision than one that has been cleared. This is precisely what we see. In Germany, the estimated effect for respondents in the highest tercile of Support for the Rule of Law is –0.13, a decline of more than 40 percent of a standard deviation; the decline of –0.10 in the United States is about one-third of a standard deviation. Both of these effects are sizable and are virtually identical to those shown in Chapter 6.

How does this effect differ according to the partisanship of the subnational executive? Hypothesis 3 provides the dueling expectations from the two theoretical accounts. Our Rule of Law–focused account suggested that the pattern we observed in the left-hand panel would be mirrored in the other two panels: regardless of whether the proposer is a copartisan or an outpartisan, the effect of contravention should be negative and strongest among those with the greatest commitment to the rule of law. The Partisan Prioritization account, on the other hand, suggests Acceptance should be driven more by partisan success than rule of law compliance. Accordingly, this logic would expect no variation in Acceptance – a flat line – in either the second or third panels of Figure 7.3.

The results in the United States suggest a limited partisan effect. The size of the contravention penalty does not increase according to support for the rule of law among those respondents who read about an outpartisan's policy proposal. But, when a *copartisan's* policy is on the agenda, those most supportive of the rule of law exact the greatest punishment; for those in the highest tercile of support for the rule of law, the estimated contravention penalty is –0.15, an effect size nearly equal to half of a standard deviation in the outcome variable. In other words, Americans with greater commitments to the rule of law punish copartisans who implement policies through contravention at higher levels than do Americans with weaker commitments to the rule of law. The direction of this

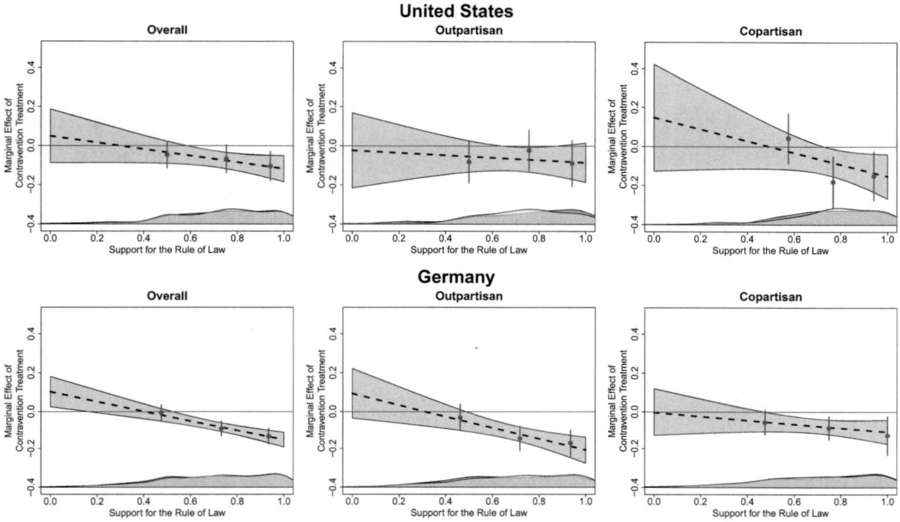

FIGURE 7.3 Conditional effects from the Mandatory Vaccine Experiment. Support for the Rule of Law increases with the *x*-axis. The shaded areas are 95% confidence intervals. The point estimates and associated confidence intervals are the Hainmueller, Mummolo, and Xu (2019) estimates of the marginal effect for each tercile of Support for the Rule of Law. The density plot shows the distribution for support for the rule of law by treatment; the darker density is the baseline group. Full regression results are provided in the even numbered models of Tables 7.A1 and 7.A2 of the Appendix. The baseline in all panels is Clearance.

partisan effect – that elites face greater constraints from copartisans than outpartisans – is akin to our findings regarding the conditional effect of executive approval in Chapter 6, where we found that a contravention penalty was most pronounced among those who approved of the executive. Notably, our finding here is also consistent with the results of Reeves and Rogowski (2022a), who demonstrate that copartisans are punished more than outpartisans for unilateral action. In short, to the extent that our results reveal a partisan effect in the United States, it is one that connects partisanship with *stronger*, rather than weaker judicial efficacy.

In Germany, on the other hand, the results are entirely in line with our Rule of Law account. Regardless of the partisan affiliation of the proposer, the contravention penalty becomes increasingly negative in magnitude as support for the rule of law increases. Among respondents who read of a proposal made by an outpartisan, the estimated contravention penalty for those in the highest tercile of support for the rule of law is –0.17. For those respondents who read about a copartisan's proposal, the effect for those with high commitment to the rule of law is –0.13, differences of 54 percent and 41 percent of a standard deviation of Acceptance. Moreover, while the slope for outpartisans is slightly steeper than that for copartisans, the difference in slopes is not statistically significant. Taken together, these results from Germany depict an efficacy of judicial review that, while critically dependent on citizens' support for the rule of law, is remarkably robust to partisan interference.

In short, the theoretical argument that best explains these results is our Rule of Law account. Across all respondents and in an experiment that explicitly primes partisan considerations, the magnitude of the contravention penalty increases with respondents' support for the rule of law. So too does this pattern hold in Germany across respondents who read about either a proposal by a copartisan executive and those that read of an outpartisan's proposal. And, though the United States results suggest a sort of partisan "double standard," this dynamic goes in the opposite direction of the Partisan Prioritization account as copartisans face a stronger – not weaker – backlash.

DISCUSSION

In this chapter, we considered the potential challenge partisanship poses to our theoretical account. To do so, we pitted our argument and its predictions against those from an alternative account we referred to as Partisan Prioritization. The results of our survey experiment, which randomized the partisanship of a state-level executive carrying out a constitutionally suspect policy, reveal consistent support for our argument and, at best, limited evidence of partisan-based public responses. In our two high judicial independence cases, Germany and the United States, we find that citizens do not systematically give a pass to copartisans but rather are indeed responsive to the signals conveyed by judicial review. Importantly, this means that respondents withdrew acceptance of policies implemented through contravention rather than clearance irrespective of the partisanship of the executive doing so. While we found some evidence in Germany of a lower contravention penalty for copartisan executives, we emphasize that Germans nonetheless still punish both parties for defying the constitutional court. And, we find some evidence that respondents in the United States with a strong commitment to the rule of law actually punish their copartisans *more* than outpartisans. Taken together, these findings are indicative of the strength of our rule of law-based argument even in the face of a political force as powerful as partisanship.

Even so, this chapter leaves two critical questions unanswered. First, we have not engaged here with the potential interaction between partisanship and judicial independence. As we demonstrated in Chapters 5 and 6, not all institutions are equally well-suited for conveying credible signals to citizens about rule-of-law violations. If it is the case that partisanship similarly may weaken or otherwise impede these signals, then it may be that partisanship is particularly likely to do so where institutions are already incapable of sending effective signals. While our analyses in this chapter represented a "hard" test for partisan accounts, insofar that the high judicial independence of the United States and German courts buttresses the strength of their signals, a similar examination in low judicial independence cases might provide an "easier" test. Second, our experiment's focus on the partisanship of the enacting executive leaves unaddressed the potential partisan identity of the actor who brought the case in the first place. If partisanship's effects are in part a result of citizens adopting a zero-sum game mentality whereby victories for political opponents are perceived as defeats for copartisans, it may be the case that simply observing an opponent benefit from oversight undermines the efficacy of the institutional signal. As a result, we might expect, for example, the identity of *who* is instigating institutional oversight to matter. It is to these questions that we turn to in Chapter 8.

Appendix

REGRESSION RESULTS AND ROBUSTNESS ANALYSIS

This appendix provides linear regression results that underlie our analyses of the Mandatory Vaccine Experiment described in this chapter. Tables 7.A1 and 7.A2 present linear regression results from the United States and Germany, respectively.

TABLE 7.A1 *Linear regression results: Mandatory Vaccine Experiment (United States). The odd-numbered models estimate the contravention penalty for all respondents (Model 1), among those who read of an outpartisan proposer (Model 3), and among those who read of a copartisan proposer (Model 5), akin to the results shown in Figure 7.2. The even-numbered models provide the results underlying Figure 7.3. The reference category for the experimental manipulation is the Cleared condition. The dependent variable in the models is Acceptance of the Executive's Action; higher values indicate more acceptance. All variables are scaled to range from 0 to 1.*

	Overall		Outpartisan		Copartisan	
	Model 1	Model 2	Model 3	Model 4	Model 5	Model 6
Contravention	−0.07*	0.05	−0.06	−0.02	−0.08*	0.15
	(0.02)	(0.07)	(0.03)	(0.11)	(0.04)	(0.14)
Support for the Rule of Law		−0.15*		−0.28*		−0.09
		(0.07)		(0.10)		(0.13)
Contravention × Support for the Rule of Law		−0.17		−0.06		−0.30
		(0.10)		(0.14)		(0.18)
Constant	0.47*	0.57*	0.47*	0.67*	0.53*	0.60*
	(0.01)	(0.05)	(0.02)	(0.07)	(0.03)	(0.10)
Observations	999	999	403	403	369	369
R^2	0.01	0.04	0.01	0.05	0.01	0.04

Note: * $p < 0.05$.

TABLE 7.A2 *Linear regression results: Mandatory Vaccine Experiment (Germany). The odd-numbered models estimate the contravention penalty for all respondents (Model 1), among those who read of an outpartisan proposer (Model 3), and among those who read of a copartisan proposer (Model 5), akin to the results shown in Figure 7.2. The even-numbered models provide the results underlying Figure 7.3. The reference category for the experimental manipulation is the Cleared condition. The dependent variable in the models is Acceptance of the Executive's Action; higher values indicate more acceptance. All variables are scaled to range from 0 to 1.*

	Overall		Outpartisan		Copartisan	
	Model 1	Model 2	Model 3	Model 4	Model 5	Model 6
Contravention	−0.08*	0.10*	−0.12*	0.09	−0.08*	−0.004
	(0.01)	(0.04)	(0.02)	(0.06)	(0.02)	(0.06)
Support for the Rule of Law		−0.13*		−0.08		−0.25*
		(0.04)		(0.06)		(0.06)
Contravention × Support for the Rule of Law		−0.25*		−0.30*		−0.11
		(0.05)		(0.09)		(0.08)
Constant	0.44*	0.53*	0.48*	0.53*	0.48*	0.66*
	(0.01)	(0.03)	(0.01)	(0.04)	(0.01)	(0.04)
Observations	2,625	2,624	952	951	912	912
R^2	0.02	0.06	0.03	0.07	0.01	0.07

Note: * $p < 0.05$.

The even-numbered models in these tables provide the estimates that underlie Figure 7.2.

The online appendix presents additional results that control for respondents' political and demographic characteristics, both for the contravention penalty that formed the basis for Hypotheses 1 and 3 and the Copartisan–Outpartisan difference that related to our second hypothesis. These additional models include the same control variables we used in our robustness analyses for the Lockdown and Vaccine Approval Experiments with two exceptions. First, because the US survey that contained the Mandatory Vaccine Experiment did not include a measure of court knowledge, our measure of knowledge is the dichotomous indicator of education (whether the respondent has completed secondary school) described in Chapter 4. Second, because partisanship is randomized in the experiment, we should not additionally control for respondents' partisan identity. We therefore do not do so.

Our results are generally robust to the inclusion of these control variables. Regarding our first hypothesis, the contravention penalty is significant at $p < 0.05$ in the United States and Germany for all respondents as well as both partisan subgroups. Notably, the p-value on the United States-Outpartisan subgroup declines from $p = 0.05$ in the bivariate difference-in-means to $p < 0.01$ in the linear regression model that accounts for respondent characteristics. The results for our second hypothesis remain the same regardless of whether we rely on models that include control variables: there is a statistically significant Copartisan–Outpartisan difference in Germany among respondents who read about contravention; none of the other Copartisan–Outpartisan differences are statistically significant, even in models that account for additional respondent-level characteristics. Finally, turning to the estimated marginal effects of contravention across support for the rule of law, the substantive results for all respondents and those who read of an outpartisan proposer remain the same as those shown here. However, though the linear marginal effect remains statistically significant among high rule of law respondents in the United States who read of a copartisan governor's proposer, the Hainmueller, Mummolo, and Xu (2019) estimates have confidence intervals that slightly cross the zero line: (–0.24, 0.005) for respondents in the middle tercile and (–0.22, 0.01) for respondents in the highest tercile.

8

Do Partisan Litigants Weaken Judicial Efficacy?

In Chapter 7, we acknowledged the potential challenge that partisanship presents for our Rule of Law account. In doing so, we laid out a competing logic – the Partisan Prioritization account – that might threaten the ability of judicial review to constrain executives in the face of partisan considerations. To test this possibility, we analyzed a survey experiment in which we randomized the partisan identity of a state-level executive in Germany and the United States who pursues a constitutionally questionable policy. Encouragingly, we found very little evidence that partisanship fundamentally undermines the ability of independent courts to create public costs for executives who flout the rule of law.

Nonetheless, two key issues remain. First, we did not address how the level of judicial independence enjoyed by a constitutional court affects the prospects for judicial efficacy in the face of partisan considerations. As a result, it remains unclear whether the limited effect of partisanship is constrained to environments where the signals sent by judicial decisions are credible, or if signals from low-independence courts may be more susceptible to partisanship's effects. Second, we left unaddressed the possibility that the partisanship of who *instigates* judicial review might affect people's responses to judicial decisions.

We engage with these unresolved questions in this chapter by considering how the partisan identity of those challenging an executive's policy might influence citizens' responses to a judicial ruling. In doing so, we shift our focus to the possibility that citizens might preferentially accept judicial rulings if the court's decision is a "win" for their copartisans. Were it the case that the partisanship of those bringing a challenge colors citizens' responses, then the efficacy of decisions by even independent and powerful courts may well be muted if they conflict with an individual's partisan alignment.

To examine this possibility, we leverage the practice of abstract review in three of our cases – Germany, Hungary, and Poland – which allows political parties and members of parliament to directly challenge the constitutionality of an executive's proposal or legal statute (Landfried 1992; Smithey and Ishiyama 2000; Vanberg

1998a).[1] Specifically, we take advantage of the fact that abstract review makes the partisanship of a policy's challenger unambiguous. We return to the two competing theoretical perspectives – our own Rule of Law account and the Partisan Prioritization account – to understand how partisanship and the use of judicial review might affect citizens' acceptance of constitutionally dubious executive actions in the context of partisan-charged abstract review, and in contexts with varying degrees of judicial independence.

Summarizing our results, we again find only limited evidence of a partisan effect on citizens' acceptance of a constitutionally dubious policy. In Germany, we observe that respondents may be slightly more likely to withdraw acceptance for policies depending on the partisanship of the challenger. This aside, we find baseline evidence in support of our Rule of Law account, particularly insofar that Germans overall punish contravention. Where judicial independence is low – in Hungary and in Poland – we observe that constitutional courts are unable to shape citizens' responses, irrespective of the partisanship of the litigant challenging the policy. Taken together, the chapter's findings point to partisanship having – at most – a limited influence on citizens' evaluations, regardless of whether the decision is issued by a low- or high-independence apex court.

ABSTRACT REVIEW

To this point in the book, we have relied on a broad usage of the term judicial (or constitutional) review. To be sure, such an approach is logical given that it allows us to capture the key elements of interest to us – the capacity of courts to use judicial review to signal to the public – without muddying the waters with specific details about judicial procedures. In considering how the partisanship of litigants might impact the efficacy of constitutional courts, we are presented with an opportunity to leverage such details. Specifically, we take advantage of the oft-present form of judicial review known as abstract review.

Abstract review is the exercise of judicial review in cases brought by a litigant who has not been directly harmed by the challenged policy or statute. This stands in contrast to concrete review, which involves challenges based on specific harm and therefore is litigated by the party who has experienced direct and concrete harm.[2] Abstract review is conducted either before a law takes effect (a priori) or after it has done so (a posteriori), although the latter tends to be more frequently available than

[1] We did not field the experiment in the United States because the US Supreme Court lacks abstract review powers.

[2] We can also consider this distinction to apply when differentiating abstract review from constitutional complaints, which are applications submitted by individuals to a court that their rights have been violated.

the former. Notably, either (or both) forms of abstract review have become commonplace, particularly in centralized systems of constitutional review based on the Kelsenian model of review such as those of Germany and most of Eastern Europe, including Hungary and Poland.

The distinctive nature of abstract review introduces the potential for the constitutionality of laws to be challenged irrespective of whether the litigant bringing the case has been harmed. In most settings in which abstract review is permitted, the identity of which parties are qualified to bring challenges is specified in statutory or constitutional texts. Such privileged parties typically include specific political actors, such as presidents and prime ministers, ombudspeople or attorneys general, as well as a specified number of members of parliament.[3] While prime ministers are unlikely to proactively bring their own laws up for judicial review, the ability of legislators to do so has turned abstract review into a critical tool for parliamentary opposition parties to challenge government policies on constitutional grounds. Because filing an abstract review challenge typically requires less than a majority of members of parliament (MPs), opposition parties can, in effect, challenge the constitutionality of any legislative or governmental proposal. Moreover, constitutional courts generally lack docket control when it comes to abstract review cases, meaning the courts must decide even long-shot cases or those brought for political rather than sincere constitutional reasons.[4]

This dynamic has several important consequences. For one, it creates an incentive for governments to moderate policy proposals to mitigate the risk (or desire) of opposition parties to bring abstract review challenges (Vanberg 1998a). Relatedly, the presence of abstract review – and the relative ease with which it can be activated – can lead governments to tailor legislation to survive potential judicial review, a concept referred to as "autolimitation" (Stone 1992). Such preemptive moves, however, do not always prevent the use of abstract review. Abstract review cases are widely seen as being among the most politically salient and contentious parts of constitutional courts' dockets (Ginsburg 2003). Indeed, studies of judicial independence or other questions regarding the intersection of constitutional review and politics often limit their analyses exclusively to abstract review precisely because of its almost inherent political nature and the ease with which one can identify the respective political positions of the litigants (e.g., Castro-Montero and Van Dijck 2017; Garoupa, Gomez-Pomar, and Grembi 2013; Vanberg 1998a).

3 Other common actors granted the authority to initiate abstract review include subnational governments (particularly in federal systems), human rights officials, and individual leaders of legislative bodies (e.g., president of the senate or assembly).

4 The frequency of its use varies from country to country. The German Constitutional Court decides only a handful of abstract review cases each year. By contrast, Bricker (2020) reports anywhere from twelve to over thirty abstract review cases in Poland per year.

For our purposes, this final characteristic of abstract review – that the partisan identity of those challenging an executive's policy is unambiguous and highly publicized – represents a unique opportunity to investigate the potential influence of partisan cues on the efficacy of judicial decisions. There are frequently clear partisan winners and losers in abstract review decisions, precisely because they always involve the government on one side and usually a parliamentary party (or political institution controlled by a party) on the other. As such, we can conceive of abstract review cases as pitting partisan camps against each other in a manner that provides clear information to citizens about the partisan positions in a case. Thus we use the partisan nature of abstract review to our advantage by randomizing the partisanship of those challenging an executive's proposal.

Our use of abstract review in this chapter not only represents a means of analyzing the influence of partisanship on the signals sent by judicial review but also contributes to the broader literature on public support for courts. Although previous research has explored the ways in which shared partisanship might influence the public's support for policies or the incumbents themselves using a broad range of empirical designs (e.g., Armaly 2017; Clark and Kastellec 2015; Driscoll and Nelson 2023b), we believe this to be the first experiment of its kind to explore how litigant partisanship might influence the public's attitudes toward public acceptance of decisions rendered through abstract review.

JUDICIAL REVIEW AND LITIGANT PARTISANSHIP

Abstract review, at least procedurally speaking, enables those with constitutional standing to activate the judiciary's role of evaluating whether an executive's behavior exceeds constitutional bounds. Yet this mechanism for democratic accountability might be compromised if partisanship colors the public's evaluation of the claims brought to court or their evaluation of the subsequent judicial ruling. Rather than take a court's decision on its face as a clear, credible signal about how an executive's action should be evaluated, citizens might instead assess the decision's credibility based on the partisanship of the side who won the case. If this latter dynamic is at play, then judicial efficacy may be dependent on which party is seen as "winning" in court. As such, in the terms of our argument, the rule of law is imperiled if citizens only accept judicial wins for their "team" and losses for their political opponents. Moreover, were it the case that the partisanship of those bringing a challenge shades citizens' responses to the outcome of the challenge, then not only would the efficacy of judicial review be constrained, but so too would the ability of political minorities to hold majorities into account.

To examine this possibility, we return to the two competing theoretical perspectives we introduced in Chapter 7. Our theory – which we term the Rule of Law

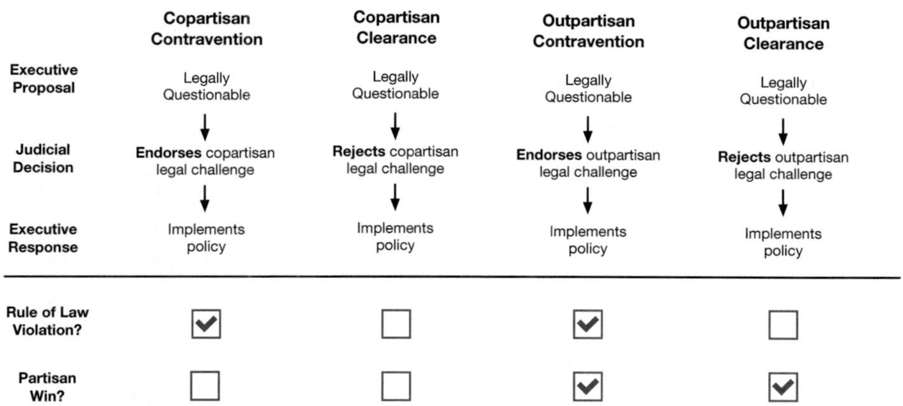

FIGURE 8.1 Typology of responses to contravention and clearance according to the partisanship of an abstract review challenger. Thus, "copartisan" and "outpartisan" refer to the affiliation of the litigant challenging the policy before the constitutional court, not to the respondent's congruence with the executive championing the policy.

account – suggests that citizens are concerned about the means through which policies are implemented. Following this logic, they should be more accepting of policies implemented through procedures that follow the rule of law than those that do not. The second perspective, which we term Partisan Prioritization, suggests that people care more about their party winning the day than how a policy is implemented. By this account, citizens' evaluations of executives overstepping the constitutional bounds of their authority is informed by the partisanship of those involved in the policy making process.

We apply these perspectives in the context of abstract review by constitutional courts, where litigants of varying parties can challenge policies before a constitutional court.[5] Figure 8.1 lays out the sequence of events for clearance and contravention in the face of a copartisan and outpartisan challenge to the law. Critically, a key difference between the process outlined in Figure 8.1 and those considered in the last chapter is the meaning of "copartisan" and "outpartisan." In our discussion in Chapter 7, partisanship referred to the affiliation of the executive who proposed and implemented the policy. By contrast, when examining the effects of partisanship in the context of abstract review, citizens' partisanship is linked to the affiliation of the litigant *challenging* the party. In practice, this generally means that the challenge is to a policy proposed by a different party than that of the litigant.[6] As such, we consider it a "Partisan Win" when the ultimate

[5] Since we are initially most concerned with partisanship's potential impacts on the efficacy of independent courts, for now we presume a court has judicial independence as we work through the potential interactions. We explicitly discuss variation in judicial independence in the following section.

[6] As we explain below, we did not expressly state this in the vignette.

policy outcome – that is what the executive carries out after judicial review – conforms with the policy goal of the respondent's preferred party.

The first condition in Figure 8.1, Copartisan Contravention, happens when a citizen's copartisan is successful in their challenge at the constitutional court. But the executive ignores the court and the policy – which was objectionable to the copartisan – is implemented over the court's objection. Both theoretical perspectives suggest low levels of acceptance under this condition: the outcome is a violation of the rule of law and does not represent a copartisan's preferred policy outcome.

Under Copartisan Clearance, the second type of executive–judicial interaction we examine, a citizen's copartisan challenges the executive's policy. The policy is endorsed by the constitutional court (over the copartisan's objection) and is implemented by the executive. In this situation, respondents have cross-cutting considerations. On the one hand, the outcome is rule-of-law compliant: the court judged the policy to be consistent with the law, and the executive has implemented it. On the other hand, the final policy was so disliked by the citizen's copartisan that they raised a constitutional challenge to stop its implementation. As a result, the implemented policy is a "loss" for the citizen's partisan team. Thus, in this condition, the Partisan Prioritization account predicts a lower level of acceptance of the policy as compared to our theoretical account.

Outpartisan Contravention, the third type of interaction, reverses this scenario. The policy is challenged by an outpartisan, and the constitutional court rules in favor of the challenge. When the executive implements the policy, she does so in noncompliance with the judicial decision. The resulting outcome is a "win" from the Partisan Prioritization perspective, suggesting a high level of acceptance: the policy challenged by the outpartisan litigant (presumably a policy endorsed by a copartisan), was implemented. Our theory, by contrast, expects low levels of acceptance in this condition because the government has carried out the policy while ignoring a constitutional court.

The final condition we consider is that of Outpartisan Clearance. In this condition, the executive's policy is challenged by an outpartisan litigant. The constitutional court rejects the outpartisan challenge, and the policy is implemented with the constitutional court's approval. Both perspectives predict a high level of acceptance under this condition: the policy is implemented in compliance with the rule of law, and is one that outpartisans disliked enough to challenge, an (albeit implicit) win for the respondent's party.

We can use these four conditions to distinguish our theoretical accounts. Our theoretical perspective suggests that respondents will be more accepting of policies implemented through Copartisan Clearance than Outpartisan Contravention because respondents react to the latter's violation of the rule of law rather than the former's partisan cues. Because the Partisan Prioritization account reverses that calculus, it suggests that acceptance is higher under Outpartisan Contravention than Copartisan Clearance. Both theoretical perspectives provide the same empirical implication for Copartisan Contravention (low level of acceptance) and Outpartisan Clearance (high level of acceptance); those two conditions are less useful to help us ajudicate between the two accounts.

Partisanship and Judicial Independence

Our discussion to this point has presumed one of the core constituent pieces of our Rule of Law account: judicial independence. As we have argued, the efficacy of judicial review is contingent upon a court's level of independence; courts with greater levels of real and perceived judicial independence are able to send more credible signals that help citizens resolve the monitoring and coordination challenges they face as they try to constrain the state. How are the predictions of the Partisan Prioritization account affected by the possibility that courts' levels of judicial independence differ? In the Partisan Prioritization account, it is *who* wins that matters, not whether the policy was implemented with (or without) judicial approval. This emphasis on partisan victory suggests that judicial independence should play little to no role in citizens' evaluations of executive policy in the aftermath of judicial review. When a copartisan wins in court, citizens should be just as pleased with the outcome if it comes from a highly independent court as if it were a low independence court issuing the decision. Conversely, displeasure toward an outpartisan legal victory is unlikely to be tempered by a recognition of the deciding court's independence. Therefore, the Partisan Prioritization account suggests little differentiation in citizens' responses to clearance and contravention according to courts' varying degrees of judicial independence.

In this respect, the Partisan Prioritization account presents a direct challenge to our Rule of Law account. Whereas we have emphasized the vital role of judicial independence throughout the book, we have yet to fully assess its resilience as a theoretical mechanism for judicial efficacy against the pressures brought on by partisanship. If it is the case that judicial signals can essentially be negated by the forces of partisanship, then our argument – and the promise of judicial efficacy – may be more promising in theory than in practice.

HYPOTHESES

Now that we have discussed how the two theoretical accounts relate to executive–judicial relationships in the face of abstract review, and outlined how the effects of judicial review and partisanship might vary across our cases, we can now articulate some testable hypotheses.

Our theoretical account suggests a contravention penalty (relative to clearance) that should be both negative and sizable when an executive ignores the ruling of an independent court. But, where judicial independence is lacking, the low credibility of judicial decisions weakens their ability to affect citizens' acceptance such that executives can defy low independence courts without suffering a loss of public support. Thus, just as we hypothesized in Chapter 5:

- H_{1ROL}: For courts with a high level of judicial independence, judicial contravention decreases acceptance of an executive's action.

The Partisan Prioritization account suggests that citizens' evaluations are driven by their partisan considerations; they are not concerned with how or from where partisan victories are gained. As a consequence, considerations like judicial independence are unlikely to affect their response to an executive's action. Therefore:

- $H_{1Partisan}$: Regardless of a court's level of judicial independence, judicial contravention neither increases nor decreases acceptance of an executive action.

Second, we have expectations related to the difference in acceptance according to the partisanship of the litigants. Our Rule of Law account anticipates that acceptance of a constitutionally dubious policy will not vary by litigant partisanship; citizens should judge executive actions that were cleared by a court after a copartisan challenge to the policy no different than they judge executive actions that implement a policy after the court endorsed an outpartisan challenge. The same is true for policies administered after contravention; our theoretical account predicts that respondents will be less likely to accept policies implemented through contravention, yet predicts no difference in acceptance according to the partisanship of the litigant's challenge that was ignored.

By contrast, the Partisan Prioritization account suggests that citizens' evaluations of a challenged policy will be based on the partisan value of the outcome. This account suggests that acceptance of an executive action will be higher when the executive implements a policy that has been challenged by an outpartisan (and is therefore more likely to be favored by the respondent's copartisans) than when the executive implements a policy that had been challenged by a copartisan. Thus, we have the following hypotheses:

- H_{2ROL}: Regardless of a court's level of judicial independence, acceptance of an executive's action challenged by a copartisan litigant is neither higher nor lower than an executive's action that is challenged by an outpartisan litigant.
- $H_{2Partisan}$: Regardless of a court's level of judicial independence, acceptance of an executive's action challenged by a copartisan litigant is lower than an executive's action that is challenged by an outpartisan litigant.

Finally, we turn to the extent to which the public's attachment to the rule of law conditions the magnitude of a contravention penalty. As we discussed earlier in the book, our theoretical perspective suggests that the size of such a penalty should grow with the public's support for the rule of law in countries that have high levels of judicial independence. On the other hand, where independence is low and therefore judicial efficacy is weakened, we should not expect to see the size of the contravention penalty vary according to the public's support for the rule of law. Therefore:

- H_{3ROL}: For courts with a high level of judicial independence, the penalty for contravening a court increases with support for the rule of law.

The Partisan Prioritization account suggests that rule of law compliance plays only a small role in citizens' acceptance calculations; instead, partisanship dominates. As our first hypothesis suggested, the Partisan Prioritization account suggests no average contravention penalty because citizens value outcomes over process. By this account, even those citizens with otherwise strong attachment to the rule of law should be expected to set those values aside when it conflicts with their partisan interests. Thus, this perspective suggests that the size of the contravention penalty is unrelated to public support for the rule of law.

- $H_{3Partisan}$: Regardless of a court's level of judicial independence, the penalty for contravening a court neither increases nor decreases with support for the rule of law.

RESEARCH DESIGN

We examine the effects of partisan litigation using a second experiment involving mandatory vaccine policies. To emphasize our focus on litigant partisanship and to distinguish it from the experiment analyzed in Chapter 7 (which used the same policy issue), we term this experiment the Abstract Review Experiment. Because the US Supreme Court has no power of abstract judicial review, we fielded this experiment in Germany, Hungary, and Poland.

The experiment asked all respondents to read about a mandatory vaccine policy announced by the national government. Respondents not assigned to the control condition then read about an abstract judicial review challenge to the constitutionality of the policy brought by one of two randomly assigned parties.[7] The second manipulation varied the constitutional court's ruling to either grant the government clearance or strike down the action as unconstitutional. As with all previous designs, respondents were told the government would implement the policy irrespective of the court's decision, either with the blessing of the constitutional authority or in direct defiance of it. Specifically, all respondents read the following text:

[7] The multiparty systems and coalition governments make clear identification of government and opposition challenging, especially in Germany and Hungary. As we detail below, we selected parties in each country that would have been focal representatives of the government coalition as well as credible and widely recognizable opponents to the official government stance.

> Imagine that the government announced a policy requiring all adults above the age of 18 to receive a coronavirus vaccine. Individuals who refuse the vaccination would be required to pay a substantial fine unless they receive an exemption for medical or religious reasons. The government contends that it is important to vaccinate all adults in order to improve the economy.

Then, respondents were divided into one of the following groups (using the Hungarian text as an example):

- *Control*: [No further text][8]
- *Contravention*: In response, a group of [PARTY] MPs who opposed the policy filed a challenge at the Hungarian Constitutional Court arguing that the policy violates citizens' constitutional rights. The Court agreed with the [PARTY] MPs and ordered the government to end the policy. Following the decision, the government announced that it would continue requiring all adults to get the vaccine, in defiance of the Court's decision.
- *Cleared*: In response, a group of [PARTY] MPs who opposed the policy filed a challenge at the Hungarian Constitutional Court arguing that the policy violates citizens' constitutional rights. The Court agreed with the government and allowed the government to continue the policy. Following the decision, the government announced that it would continue requiring all adults to get the vaccine, as permitted by the Court's decision.

In each country, two parties were assigned as litigants in the Cleared and Contravened arms of the experiment. In Germany, respondents were assigned to read either of a challenge by the Christian Democratic Union (CDU) or the Alternative for Germany (AfD). At the time of the survey, the longstanding German Chancellor (Angela Merkel) was a leader of the CDU; we therefore took this party as the core party of the coalition government. The AfD, a party widely known for its far-right policies and positions, represented a party with stark ideological differences with the ruling CDU party and was a highly visible political opponent of the government coalition and its policies.[9] To assign respondents as

[8] Because our sample sizes were bigger for the surveys on which we fielded the Abstract Review Experiment than the Mandatory Vaccine Experiment, we were able to include a control condition in this experiment, as we did in the Lockdown Experiment. However, deriving and testing separate hypotheses for the Clearance–Control and Contravention–Control differences would result in dozens of comparisons and would lead us to test a different quantity of interest than the Contravention–Clearance difference we analyzed in the previous chapter. Thus, in the interests of simplicity and comparability, we focus our discussion in this chapter on the same Contravention–Clearance difference we discussed in the previous chapter but include in the appendix results that include the control condition.

[9] At the time, the parliamentary opposition in German consisted of the Greens, the left-wing Die Linke, the fiscally conservative Free Democrats (FDP), and the AfD. Given this wide-ranging ideological nature of the opposition, our selection of the AfD was in part to provide the starkest contrast to the centrist governing grand coalition of the CDU/CSU and Social Democrats (SPD).

either copartisan or outpartisan to the challenge in Germany, we asked respondents, "If you were forced to choose in the next parliamentary election between the following two parties, which would you pick?" Here, respondents were more supportive of the CDU (78 percent of respondents) than the AfD (22 percent of respondents). Overall, 22 percent of German respondents were assigned to the control condition, 37 percent respondents read of a challenge by the party they did not select (an outpartisan challenge), and 40 percent of respondents read of a challenge made by the party they selected in response to that item (a copartisan challenge).[10]

In Hungary, those respondents assigned to a partisanship treatment read of a challenge to the law either by Fidesz or Hungarian Socialist Party (MSZP). At the time of the survey, Fidesz was the majority party in Hungary, and the party of Prime Minister Viktor Orbán. We selected the MSZP as the opposition party for two related reasons. First, although the party had joined with other parties before the April 2022 parliamentary elections to form a "United Opposition," opposition members of parliament at the time were still technically affiliated with their respective parties. As such, we wanted to maintain the realism of our vignette by having the opposition appeal come from a specific party with parliamentary representation. Second, we chose MSZP because the last non-Fidesz Prime Minister had come from the MSZP (in 2009), and it was the second largest opposition party in parliament with pronounced ideological distance from Fidesz.[11]

To identify copartisanship in Hungary, we asked respondents the following question: "As you may know, there is a national parliamentary election scheduled for next spring. Competing in this election will be Fidesz and the United Opposition, which is a coalition of several opposition political parties including Jobbik, MSZP, Momentum Mozgalom and Demokratikus Koalíció. If this election were held next week, which party would you be most likely to vote for?" Thirty-one percent of respondents indicated they would vote for Fidesz, 49 percent of respondents said they would vote for the United Opposition, and the remaining 20 percent of respondents said that they would vote for another party. We code respondents who indicated a preference for Fidesz as copartisan to the Fidesz litigant (and outpartisan to the MSZP challenger), and treat respondents who suggested they would vote for the United Opposition as copartisan to MSZP (and outpartisan to Fidesz).[12] Overall, 401 respondents in Hungary were assigned to the control

[10] Overall, the sizes of the treatment groups range from 210 (Clear-Outpartisan) to 268 (Control).

[11] The largest opposition party by seat share was Jobbik, which has generally been seen as a right-wing party (Pirro and Róna 2019), and is therefore ideologically adjacent to the ruling party of Fidesz.

[12] To further limit the number of respondents who must be excluded from the analysis because they selected an "Other" option to the parliamentary election, we coded respondents as copartisan to Fidesz if they answered Fidesz as their most liked party on the previous survey item; if the respondents could not be classified based on their answer to the parliamentary elections question but selected any of the United Opposition parties as their most liked party,

condition, 675 read of a challenge made by an outpartisan, and 639 respondents read of a copartisan challenge to the mandatory vaccine policy.[13]

In Poland, respondents read of a challenge by MPs from one of the two dominant parties, the governing Prawo i Sprawiedliwość (PiS) or opposition Platforma Obywatelska (PO).[14] To code copartisanship, we asked the same question as used in Germany, providing these two parties as options. Thirty-seven percent of the respondents indicated they would vote for a PiS candidate and 63 percent of the respondents responded that they would support the PO candidate. Overall, 21 percent of the respondents in Poland were assigned to the control group, 39 percent read of a challenge by an outpartisan candidate, and 40 percent read of a challenge by a copartisan.[15]

We selected three items to use in our outcome variable with the aim of measuring the same concepts used in our other experiments First, we asked the respondents, "To what extent do you support or oppose the government's decision to move forward with requiring all adults to get the vaccine?" On a four-point scale, 49 percent of Germans, 41 percent of Hungarians, and 44 percent of Poles said they at least "somewhat" support the national government's action. Second, we asked respondents, "Do you believe the government's decision to move forward with requiring all adults to get the vaccine is an appropriate exercise of power?" Forty-six percent of the German respondents, 37 percent of the Hungarian respondents, and 45 percent of the Polish respondents gave an affirmative answer. Finally, we asked respondents, "Thinking about this governmental policy, if an unvaccinated friend asked you whether he should get vaccinated, what would you tell him?" Respondents' answers could range on a four-point scale from "I would tell him to definitely get the vaccine" to "I would tell him to definitely not get the vaccine." 79 percent of Germans, 68 percent of Hungarians, and 67 percent of Polish respondents would encourage their friend to get the vaccine.[16]

These three items scale well in all three countries: in Germany, $\alpha = 0.88$ and the average factor loading is 0.83; in Hungary, $\alpha = 0.87$ and the average factor loading is 0.81; and in Poland, $\alpha = 0.91$ and the average factor loading is 0.86. In all three

we code them as copartisan with MSZP. Because we are unable to assign the remaining respondents as supporters of either Fidesz or MSZP's coalition, those respondents are excluded from the analysis that follows.

[13] The number of respondents per condition ranges from 313 in the Cleared-Copartisan condition to 401 in the Control condition.

[14] These parties are known by their English translations: Law and Justice and the Civic Platform.

[15] The treatment group sizes range from 365 (Clearance-Outpartisan) to 402 (Control).

[16] Although this is a new item to our battery of outcome variables, we opted to use this item to not probe respondents regarding a potentially sensitive question that would implicate their refusal to be vaccinated under a governmental regime of mandatory inoculations. Asking respondents instead the advice they might give to a friend allows us to gauge their reaction and acceptance of the policy without admitting to intentional noncompliance with a controversial government policy.

countries, the compliance item loads less well on the factor, though the factor loadings are above 0.65 in all three countries for all items. We rescale this variable to range from 0 to 1 with higher values indicating more acceptance of the government's decision.

One point about the experimental design and our analysis deserves additional discussion. Because we were interested in fielding the experiment in countries with varying degrees of judicial independence, we could not randomize the partisanship of the proposer as we did in the Mandatory Vaccine Experiment analyzed in Chapter 7, as neither Poland nor Hungary are federal systems. Thus, the proposer in this vignette is the national executive. This creates some "strange bedfellows" moments: respondents who are allied with the national executive but assigned to a condition in which a copartisan challenges their copartisan executive's policy. For this reason, we opt to conduct the bulk of the analysis of this experiment in a multivariate setting that allows us to control for respondents' support for the executive and for mandatory vaccine policies. The former measure was described in Chapter 4. Our measure of support for mandatory vaccine policies was asked as part of a battery used to measure vaccine skepticism. We asked respondents to rate their level of agreement with the following statement: "It is ok for the government to require citizens to get certain vaccines." Overall, 64 percent of Germans, 54 percent of Hungarians, and 43 percent of Poles gave an affirmative answer to that statement.[17]

RESULTS

We begin our analysis by examining the average effects of the experimental treatments in each country. The left-hand panels of Figure 8.2 plot the average value of Acceptance, by treatment, for each country.[18] Overall, the range of averages is small in each country. In Germany, as expected, Acceptance is highest in the Outpartisan Clearance condition and lowest in the Copartisan Contravention condition. Acceptance is also highest, as expected, in the Outpartisan Clearance condition among Hungarian respondents, while the other three conditions are nearly identical in size. Turning to Poland, the estimates are nearly identical across conditions, and we do not observe the expected ranking across conditions.

Before turning to our hypotheses, we pause to check the overall difference between the Contravention and Clearance conditions, pooling the partisan

[17] Though not analyzed in this chapter, 50 percent of Americans gave an affirmative answer to this question.

[18] Linear regression results underlying the analyses presented in this chapter, as well as a discussion of the robustness of our results to models including respondents' political and demographic characteristics, are provided in the Appendix.

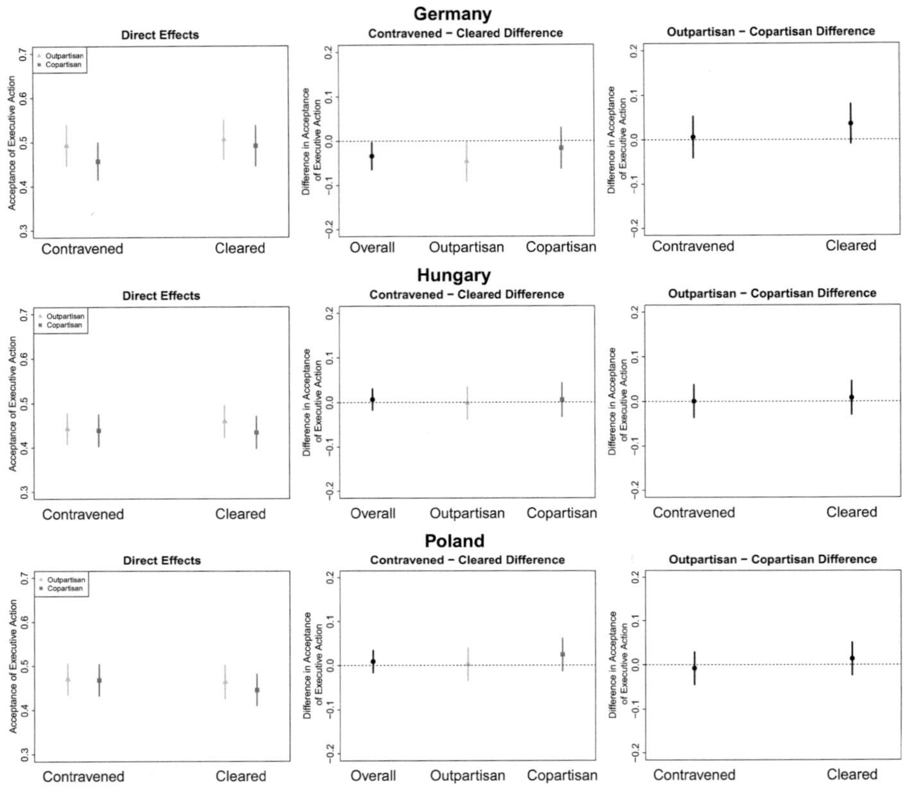

FIGURE 8.2 Direct effects of the Abstract Review Experiment. The left-hand panels plot the average value of acceptance of the executive's action, by condition. This variable has a range of 0–1; higher values of this variable indicate a greater level of acceptance. The middle- and right-hand panels illustrate the difference in means between experimental conditions. Positive values of the *y*-axis in these panels indicate an increase in acceptance, relative to the Cleared condition (middle panel) or the Outpartisan condition (right-hand panel). The estimates in these panels come from multivariate models controlling for support for the executive for mandatory vaccine policies; these models are reported in Tables 8.A1–8.A3 of the Appendix. The vertical lines in all three panels provide 95% confidence intervals.

conditions, to examine whether the general contravention penalty we observed in the Lockdown, Vaccine Approval, and Mandatory Vaccine Experiments is present in this experiment. Recall that our theoretical account suggests a negative and statistically significant contravention penalty in places with high levels of judicial independence, but no such effect in the two countries in our study with low judicial independence.

This contravention penalty – here, estimated from a multivariate model that controls for respondents' attitudes toward the executive and their opinion on mandatory vaccine policies, as discussed above – is plotted as the first point in the middle panels of Figure 8.2. In Germany, this effect ($\widehat{\beta} = -0.03$) is negative and statistically significant. It accounts for about 10 percent of a standard deviation shift in acceptance.[19] In both Poland and Hungary, as expected and consistent with evidence reported elsewhere in the book, we fail to observe difference between the Contravention and Clearance conditions. The estimated effect is 0.01 in both countries ($p = 0.58$ in Hungary and $p = 0.50$ in Poland). On average, respondents' levels of acceptance in these contexts do not depend on whether the mandatory vaccine policy is implemented with judicial approval or over the court's objection. This analysis therefore provides some initial support for the predictions of our theoretical account and provides evidence of the robustness of our conclusions from the book's previous chapters even in the face of direct partisan information in the experimental vignette.

Testing Hypothesis 1

Our first pair of hypotheses related to the contravention penalty: the difference in acceptance between actions implemented by contravening a constitutional court and those that received the endorsement of a constitutional court. Recall that our Rule of Law account suggested that we should observe a contravention penalty only in Germany while the Partisan Prioritization account in contrast predicted a null result in all three countries.

The second two point estimates in the middle panels of Figure 8.2 report the Contravention–Clearance difference by the partisanship of the litigant.[20] Turning first to the bottom two panels of the middle column, as both the Rule of Law and Partisan Prioritization accounts suggested, we observe no evidence of a contravention penalty in Hungary or Poland. In fact, most of the estimated effects in these two countries are *positive* (though never statistically significant).[21] The estimated effect for respondents who read of a challenge by an outpartisan litigant is –0.001 in Hungary ($p = 0.95$) and 0.002 in Poland ($p = 0.88$). For respondents who read of a challenge by a copartisan, the estimated contravention penalty is 0.01 in Hungary ($p = 0.76$) and 0.02 in Poland ($p = 0.20$). In the context of our first set of hypotheses, this finding suggests that decisions of low independence courts

[19] Were we to estimate this difference without controls, the difference is still –0.03 $p = 0.16$. If, as we discuss further in the Appendix, we define the contravention penalty as the difference between the Control and Contravention conditions (as we did in Chapters 5 and 6), the difference in means is –0.06; $p = 0.01$.

[20] Recall that "copartisan" and "outpartisan" refer to the respondent's congruence with the *challenge* not the *executive*.

[21] When looking at Figure 8.2, remember that the left-hand panels plot averages and the middle and right-hand panels plot regression coefficients from models that adjust for executive approval and support for mandatory vaccine policies: this is why differences in the left-hand panel are not exactly the same as the differences plotted in the other two panels.

continue to be ineffective at altering citizens' acceptance of constitutionally suspect executive actions.

The results from Germany enable us to better differentiate between the two theoretical perspectives we interrogate here. The estimated contravention penalty among respondents who read of a challenge by an outpartisan litigant is consistent with our Rule of Law account. Here, respondents withdrew support for policies carried out despite a court ruling in favor of the outpartisan's position. The estimated effect, $\hat{\beta} = -0.05$, accounts for about 13 percent of a standard deviation in acceptance. The same, however, does not hold for instances in which contravention means ignoring a copartisan's legal victory; the coefficient for this treatment (the right-most estimate in the middle figure) fails to reach statistical significance ($\hat{\beta} = -0.02$, $p = 0.50$). The divergence of results across shared partisanship – a statistically significant effect when the challenger is an outpartisan but not when the challenger is a copartisan – are consistent with the presence of a limited partisan effect, albeit not necessarily the one the Partisan Prioritization account anticipates. Here, we observe a slight bias *against* copartisans, as German respondents appear more willing to exact a penalty on the government for ignoring their political opponent's legal victory. Although not wholly consistent with our Rule of Law account either, that a contravention penalty exists for outpartisan legal victories is particularly remarkable when considering that for many respondents such a victory is being won by the AfD, a highly polarizing party in German politics that tends to elicit strong negative reactions from partisans across the political spectrum. That said, we are reluctant to read too much into this for a few reasons. For one, the coefficient for both copartisans and outpartisan treatments is negative and the estimated effects for copartisan and outpartisan challengers are so similar. Second, we suspect that the possibility of a "strange bedfellows" effect could be partially at work here. Given the mixed findings and these considerations, we turn to our other two hypotheses with the hope of better assessing the two competing accounts.

Testing Hypothesis 2

Next, we consider differences in Acceptance according to the partisanship of the litigant challenging the policy. Our Rule of Law perspective suggested that there should be no difference between policies implemented after copartisan (rather than outpartisan) challenges, accounting for the court's decision. The Partisan Prioritization account, by contrast, predicted that policies implemented after an outpartisan challenge should be accepted at higher levels than those implemented after a copartisan challenge (presumably because laws challenged by outpartisans are policies championed by a respondent's copartisan and vice-versa). Importantly, both theoretical perspectives suggest the same predictions regardless of a country's level of judicial independence.

The right-hand panels of Figure 8.2 plot these effects. With the exception of clearance in Poland, respondents accept policies challenged by outpartisans at higher levels than those challenged by copartisans. But, as our theoretical perspective suggested (and contrary to the predictions of the Partisan Prioritization account), none of these effects are statistically significant. Moreover, all of these effects – and especially those in Poland and Hungary – are small in size: four of the six estimates are less than 0.01 in size.[22] Thus, it's not for a lack of precision that these estimates fail to attain statistical significance despite being estimated from well-powered experimental designs. The results from the second hypothesis showing this consistent lack of partisan differences cut clearly in favor of our Rule of Law theoretical perspective.

Testing Hypothesis 3

Finally, we turn to the conditional effects of support for the rule of law. We start, as we did with the direct effects, by averaging across partisan conditions to see whether the results of this experiment mirror the results of the Lockdown Experiment. Recall that we found a contravention penalty that increased with support for the rule of law in countries with high levels of judicial independence in Chapter 6, but saw no such effect when judicial independence was lacking.

The left-hand panels of Figure 8.3 plot the Contravention–Clearance difference as support for the rule of law varies, pooling respondents across partisanship conditions. Comparing the three panels, we see the same pattern we reported in previous experiments: a contravention penalty that is statistically significant in Germany for respondents with high (but not low) support for the rule of law. For respondents in the highest tercile of support for the rule of law, the estimated penalty is –0.08. In Poland and Hungary, we observe no contravention penalty at any level of citizens' support for the rule of law. This null result is not due to imprecision; even the estimated contravention penalties for those with the highest support for the rule of law are small in size (–0.02 in Hungary and –0.01 in Poland).

The middle and right-hand panels of Figure 8.3 enable us to test Hypothesis 3 because they separately estimate the marginal effect for respondents who read about a challenge by an outpartisan (middle panels) or a copartisan (right-hand panels) litigant. Our theory suggested we should see a negative sloping line in both Germany panels with no difference in the slope of the line but no effect in Poland or Hungary; the Partisan Prioritization perspective suggested null effects for all three countries and both partisanship conditions.

22 The *p*-values for the estimates range from 0.47 to 0.97.

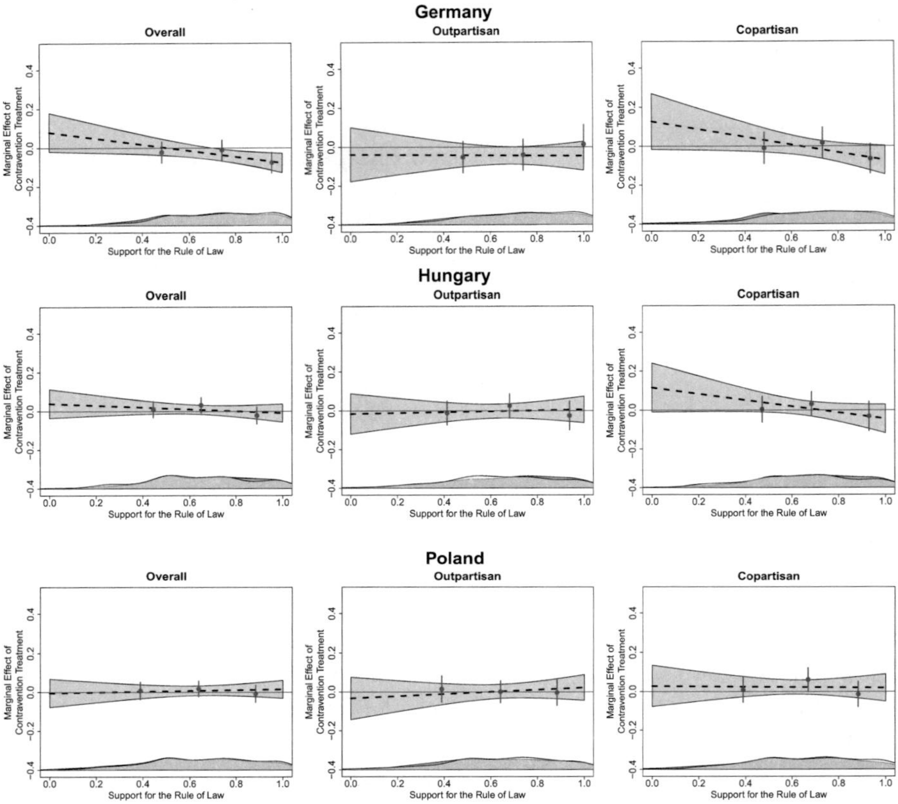

FIGURE 8.3 Conditional effects from the Abstract Review Experiment. Support for the Rule of Law increases with the *x*-axis. The shaded areas are 95% confidence intervals. The point estimates and associated confidence intervals are the Hainmueller, Mummolo, and Xu (2019) estimates of the marginal effect for each tercile of Support for the Rule of Law. The density plot shows the distribution for support for the rule of law by treatment; the darker density is the baseline group. The estimates in these panels come from a multivariate model controlling for support for the executive for mandatory vaccine policies. Full regression results are provided in Tables 8.A1–8.A3 of the Appendix. The baseline in all panels is Clearance.

Looking at the six panels, there is no statistically significant effect in any country, as predicted by the Partisan Prioritization account.[23] Moreover, looking at the Hainmueller, Mummolo, and Xu (2019) tercile estimates, the marginal effects do not appear to be linear, suggesting a lot of heterogeneity is at play. Nonetheless, we make two observations. First, we again see that the executive's congruence with the court's decision is inconsequential in the low judicial independence environments

[23] The results for Germany – where there is an effect for all respondents but not when the sample is split despite a clear negative trendline – suggest that a sample size issue may be at play.

of Hungary and Poland, irrespective of one's support for the rule of law. Second, we observe in Germany a weak (and not statistically significant) tendency to withdraw approval for policies challenged by copartisans among those with the highest tercile of support for the rule of law. Based on our analyses in Chapter 4, we suspect that this finding is at least in part a consequence of this set of respondents being particularly likely to prefer the CDU to the AfD. As such, they may be especially likely to have distaste for anything the AfD does, including winning at the Constitutional Court. This suggests that there may be something of a partisan double standard that takes the form of staunch supporters of the rule of law being vehemently opposed to an AfD party they view as antithetical to the rule of law.

Taken together, the results of the Abstract Review Experiment paint something of a mixed picture for our Rule of Law account vis-à-vis the Partisan Prioritization story. On the one hand, we found continued evidence in support for the book's core argument regarding judicial efficacy: citizens withdraw support for policies enacted in defiance of court rulings but only insofar as they support the rule of law and those rulings are issued by independent courts. Importantly, these findings come even with partisan cues provided to respondents in the vignette. On the other hand, we do, in fact, see some limited evidence of a partisan effect when we break the analyses down by copartisanship, specifically in Germany. Importantly, however, even this weak support for the Partisan Prioritization account is belied by German respondents' continued punishment for ignoring legal victories by both copartisans and outpartisans (albeit with the effect for the former lacking statistical significance). Critically, we see no evidence of respondents increasing their support for policies based on the partisanship of the winning litigant. All in all, then, it appears that those two core pillars of our theory – judicial independence and support for the rule of law – stand strong.

DISCUSSION

A vibrant body of research in recent years centers a concern for partisanship and polarization (Aarslew 2023; Carey et al. 2022; Simonovits, McCoy, and Littvay 2022; Svolik 2020). This research has raised serious concerns about how partisanship might threaten to tear apart the core fabric of society, the foundations of the separation of powers, and the vibrancy of democracy and the rule of law. We have spent the past two chapters developing and testing an alternative theoretical account, the Partisan Prioritization account, against the theoretical account we have advanced throughout this book. Our goal was to understand whether (and, if so, when) the efficacy of judicial review is imperiled by pernicious partisanship. We developed competing hypotheses from both theoretical accounts and tested them against each other in two different survey experiments.

Our theoretical and empirical account, which we acknowledge is surprising in the face of this strong body of extant evidence, suggests that partisan considerations play a limited role: citizens are committed to the rule of law and responsive to decisions by independent courts. Because judicial review by independent courts is an effective tool of state constraint, elites – regardless of partisanship – who flout the rule of law should face political consequences. In this way, independent courts can serve as a sort of beacon, lighting the way for citizens who might have difficulty discerning whether executives have acted illegally and providing a focal point around which they can coordinate. By our argument, independent courts retain this power even in the face of partisan ties that can cloud citizens' ability to monitor the state. Put simply, we expect judicial review by independent courts to be effective even as partisanship colors so much of citizens' political lives.

Just as partisanship-focused accounts have emphasized the possible willingness of citizens to forego punishing copartisan executives for breaches of constitutional obligations, we have considered the possibility that citizens may be more accepting of policy wins for their partisan allies than they are concerned about the legal means through which these victories come to be enacted. If such a form of partisan bias were the case, then judicial review may only provide a feeble means of state constraint.

Understanding the effects of partisanship is important for a second reason: it presents a difficult test for our theory. As we discussed in Chapter 2, strong partisan ties in the citizenry exacerbate the monitoring and coordination problems that citizens face as they try to constrain the state. When partisan bonds are strong, citizens might be willing to look the other way when they learn of illegal behavior by a copartisan, disrupting their ability to monitor the state. And, when a court alerts citizens that an executive has violated the rule of law, these partisan ties may make citizens unwilling or unable to coordinate their response in a way that can deter illegal behavior by elites. In this way, partisanship poses a salient threat to the efficacy of judicial review.

What have we learned? In this chapter, we evaluated this potential dynamic by leveraging the explicitly partisan identity of litigants in abstract judicial review proceedings like those found in Germany, Hungary, Poland, and many other countries. As in Chapter 7, the results we presented here suggest – at most – a limited effect of partisanship. We observed that in our low judicial independence cases, partisan differences in reactions to oversight decisions were negligible. This is a noteworthy finding given the highly contentious and polarized nature of partisan identity in both Hungary and Poland. And in Germany, we saw that even when the partisanship of those challenging a law is primed, the fundamental results we observed in the book's earlier experiments hold: citizens withdraw acceptance when independent courts are contravened. In short, the results from this pair of chapters are broadly consistent with our theoretical expectations both regarding differences across levels of judicial independence and the continued exacting of punishment for contravention in high judicial independence cases.

This is not to say, however, that partisanship plays no role. While we find no statistically differentiable results, we do see suggestive trends of a possible partisan double standard effect. We suspect this pattern of results may be a consequence of Germans, particularly those committed to the rule of law, having a particularly harsh reaction toward cases brought by specific party, the AfD. These results may therefore be reflective of a different means by which support for the rule of law might interact – and come into tension – with partisanship in high judicial independence contexts. Our experimental design put this directly to the test, with citizens asked whether they would accept rulings that were the result of challenges brought by the AfD, far-right party with weak commitment to the rule of law. In such instances, it is perhaps a reasonable question whether it is better for democracy that citizens enforce a court ruling that favors such a party, and thereby may legitimize them, or if it is instead better that the public continue to shun and ostracize the party so as to try and limit its success.

We close by noting two observations from the chapter's findings in combination with those of the preceding chapter. First, our argument through this book has been that institutions play a critical role in transforming support for the rule of law into a meaningful political constraint on executive power. As we have stated, though, the efficacy of institutions at fulfilling this role is predicated on the ability to do so independent of, rather than conditional on, partisanship. That we find evidence that comports with this view provides a significant counterpoint to the growing literature that emphasizes partisanship's broad-ranging destructive power. That is, our account and accompanying evidence are reminders that institutions can still matter, and that undermining judicial independence has serious consequences not only for the operation of interbranch politics but also for the linkages between citizens and their governments that are at the core of democratic accountability and ultimately democratic governance.

Second, that we find no clear influence of partisanship reinforces the value of courts to would-be authoritarians. If partisanship overwhelms the signaling capacity of institutions entirely, this weakens motivations to capture courts in the first place. Insofar as courts are useful for monitoring and facilitating coordination, they are thus useful targets for autocratic co-optation and capture. If instead, the public response to judicial contravention is overridden by partisanship, coopting a constitutional court may not pay the dividend it would otherwise. In this sense, the very capacity of courts to convey partisanship-resistant signals makes them all the more valuable to executives who seek to capture them.

Appendix

REGRESSION RESULTS AND ROBUSTNESS ANALYSIS

Tables 8.A1, 8.A2, and 8.A3 provide country-specific linear regression results that underlie the figures in the chapter. Models 1–6 estimate the contravention penalty for all respondents (Model 1), among those who read of an outpartisan proposer (Model 3), and among those who read of a copartisan proposer (Model 5), underlying the results shown in the middle panel of Figure 8.2. Models 2, 4, and 6 provide the results underlying Figure 8.3. The baseline reference category for the experimental manipulation of these models is the Cleared condition. Models 7 and 8 estimate the effect of the partisanship treatment, which is represented in the right-hand panel of Figure 8.2. Table 8.A1 reports the results for Germany. Table 8.A2 presents to the analyses from Hungary, and Table 8.A3 provides the experimental results from Poland.

In the online appendix, we report the results of additional analyses that account for respondents' political and demographic characteristics. With regard to Hypothesis 1, these analyses verify that our finding of a general contravention penalty holds in Germany (but not Hungary or Poland) when we account for additional respondent-level characteristics. However, the contravention penalty among outpartisans loses statistical significance at the .05 level when these additional variables are added to the linear regression model (the *p*-value rises from 0.048 to 0.074). Turning to Hypothesis 2, our results are entirely consistent regardless of whether we include additional respondent-level characteristics. As our theoretical account suggested, we find no evidence in any country that respondents react differently to clearance or contravention after learning the partisanship of the litigant who challenged the policy. Finally, looking at Hypothesis 3 and the conditional effect of contravention as respondents' support for the rule of law varies, the results of the pooled model are consistent with our theory and those findings reported in the other chapters of the book: averaging across the partisanship conditions, the effect of

TABLE 8.A1 *Linear regression results: Abstract Review Experiment (Germany). Models 1–6 estimate the contravention penalty across different respondent groups: Model 1 covers all respondents, Model 3 focuses on those who read about an outpartisan proposer, and Model 5 examines those who read about a copartisan proposer. These models correspond to the results presented in the middle panel of Figure 8.2. Models 2, 4, and 6 provide the data underlying Figure 8.3. In all these models, the reference category for the experimental manipulation is the Cleared condition. Finally, Models 7 and 8 assess the effect of the partisanship treatment, which supports the findings in the right-hand panel of Figure 8.2. The baseline category in these models is a copartisan litigant. The dependent variable in all models is acceptance of the Executive's Action; higher values indicate more acceptance. All variables are scaled to range from 0 to 1.*

	Overall		Outpartisan		Copartisan		Contravention	Clearance
	Model 1	Model 2	Model 3	Model 4	Model 5	Model 6	Model 7	Model 8
Contravention	−0.03*	0.08	−0.05*	−0.04	−0.02	0.13		
	(0.02)	(0.05)	(0.02)	(0.08)	(0.02)	(0.08)		
Support for the Rule of Law		−0.06		−0.09		−0.10		
		(0.05)		(0.07)		(0.08)		
Outpartisan Litigant							0.01	0.04
							(0.02)	(0.02)
Executive Approval	0.08*	0.08*	0.08*	0.08*	0.08	0.07	0.05	0.11*
	(0.03)	(0.03)	(0.04)	(0.04)	(0.04)	(0.04)	(0.04)	(0.04)
Mandatory Vaccine Opinion	0.62*	0.62*	0.66*	0.67*	0.61*	0.61*	0.60*	0.67*
	(0.02)	(0.02)	(0.03)	(0.03)	(0.04)	(0.03)	(0.04)	(0.03)
Contravention × Support for the Rule of Law		−0.16*		−0.01		−0.20		
		(0.07)		(0.10)		(0.11)		
Constant	0.07*	0.11*	0.06*	0.12*	0.06	0.14*	0.06*	0.01
	(0.02)	(0.04)	(0.03)	(0.05)	(0.03)	(0.06)	(0.03)	(0.03)
Observations	1,064	1,064	445	445	481	481	466	460
$R2$	0.48	0.49	0.51	0.52	0.46	0.48	0.45	0.53

Note: * $p < 0.05$.

TABLE 8.A2 *Linear regression results: Abstract Review Experiment (Hungary). Models 1–6 estimate the contravention penalty across different respondent groups: Model 1 covers all respondents, Model 3 focuses on those who read about an outpartisan proposer, and Model 5 examines those who read about a copartisan proposer. These models correspond to the results presented in the middle panel of Figure 8.2. Models 2, 4, and 6 provide the data underlying Figure 8.3. In all these models, the reference category for the experimental manipulation is the Cleared condition. Finally, Models 7 and 8 assess the effect of the partisanship treatment, which supports the findings in the right-hand panel of Figure 8.2. The baseline category in these models is a copartisan litigant. The dependent variable in all models is Acceptance of the Executive's Action; higher values indicate more acceptance. All variables are scaled to range from 0 to 1.*

	Overall		Outpartisan		Copartisan		Contravention	Clearance
	Model 1	Model 2	Model 3	Model 4	Model 5	Model 6	Model 7	Model 8
Contravention	0.01	0.04	−0.001	−0.02	0.01	0.12		
	(0.01)	(0.04)	(0.02)	(0.05)	(0.02)	(0.06)		
Support for the Rule of Law		0.06		−0.05		0.17*		
		(0.04)		(0.06)		(0.07)		
Outpartisan Litigant							0.001	0.01
							(0.02)	(0.02)
Executive Approval	0.20*	0.21*	0.19*	0.19*	0.25*	0.26*	0.24*	0.20*
	(0.02)	(0.02)	(0.03)	(0.03)	(0.03)	(0.03)	(0.03)	(0.03)
Mandatory Vaccine Opinion	0.53*	0.53*	0.56*	0.56*	0.50*	0.49*	0.49*	0.57*
	(0.02)	(0.02)	(0.03)	(0.03)	(0.03)	(0.03)	(0.03)	(0.03)
Contravention × Support for the Rule of Law		−0.05		0.02		−0.16		
		(0.05)		(0.08)		(0.09)		
Constant	0.06*	0.01	0.06*	0.09*	0.07*	−0.05	0.08*	0.04
	(0.01)	(0.03)	(0.02)	(0.04)	(0.02)	(0.05)	(0.02)	(0.02)
Observations	1,595	1,595	673	673	637	637	659	651
R2	0.47	0.47	0.48	0.48	0.47	0.47	0.47	0.48

Note: * $p < 0.05$.

TABLE 8.A3 *Linear regression results: Abstract Review Experiment (Poland). Models 1–6 estimate the contravention penalty across different respondent groups: Model 1 covers all respondents, Model 3 focuses on those who read about an outpartisan proposer, and Model 5 examines those who read about a copartisan proposer. These models correspond to the results presented in the middle panel of Figure 8.2. Models 2, 4, and 6 provide the data underlying Figure 8.3. In all these models, the reference category for the experimental manipulation is the Cleared condition. Finally, Models 7 and 8 assess the effect of the partisanship treatment, which supports the findings in the right-hand panel of Figure 8.2. The baseline category in these models is a copartisan litigant. The dependent variable in all models is Acceptance of the Executive's Action; higher values indicate more acceptance. All variables are scaled to range from 0 to 1.*

	Overall		Outpartisan		Copartisan		Contravention	Clearance
	Model 1	Model 2	Model 3	Model 4	Model 5	Model 6	Model 7	Model 8
Contravention	0.01	−0.01	0.003	−0.03	0.02	0.03		
	(0.01)	(0.04)	(0.02)	(0.05)	(0.02)	(0.06)		
Support for the Rule of Law		0.05		0.03		0.05		
		(0.04)		(0.05)		(0.06)		
Outpartisan Litigant							−0.01	0.01
							(0.02)	(0.02)
Executive Approval	0.08*	0.09*	0.10*	0.11*	0.04	0.04	0.05	0.09*
	(0.02)	(0.02)	(0.03)	(0.03)	(0.03)	(0.03)	(0.03)	(0.03)
Mandatory Vaccine Opinion	0.63*	0.63*	0.64*	0.64*	0.62*	0.62*	0.63*	0.63*
	(0.02)	(0.02)	(0.02)	(0.02)	(0.03)	(0.03)	(0.03)	(0.03)
Contravention × Support for the Rule of Law		0.02		0.06		−0.01		
		(0.05)		(0.08)		(0.08)		
Constant	0.13*	0.10*	0.13*	0.11*	0.14*	0.11*	0.16*	0.12*
	(0.01)	(0.03)	(0.02)	(0.04)	(0.02)	(0.04)	(0.02)	(0.02)
Observations	1,598	1,598	740	740	760	760	749	751
R2	0.48	0.48	0.49	0.50	0.45	0.45	0.46	0.48

Note: * $p < 0.05$.

contravention grows with support for the rule of law. However, – and as we saw in Figure 8.3 – we do not observe this effect once we divide the data by the copartisanship condition. In short, our results remain stable even after we account for a variety of different possible confounding variables.

INCLUDING THE CONTROL CONDITION

In the body of the chapter, we focused on the Contravene–Clearance difference in respondents' acceptance of the executive's response to an abstract review challenge. However, the Abstract Review Experiment also included a control condition as with the Lockdown Experiment. We can therefore examine separately the differences between the clearance and contravention conditions and the control condition to mirror our analyses in the Lockdown Experiment. Figure 8.A1 displays the average value of Acceptance, by condition, in the left-hand panel and the differences between the two judicial decisions and the control condition in the right-hand panel.[24] Additionally, for the sake of simplicity, we present all of the results in this appendix without any control variables to give readers a clearer sense of how the results we presented in the body of the chapter might look were we not to control for the respondent's level of executive approval and their support for mandatory vaccine policies.

As before, we first verify that we find the same effects as those we observed in the Lockdown Experiment in Chapter 5. Therefore, we expect to observe a statistically significant decrease in support among those who were told that the policy was implemented over the constitutional court's objection in Germany, but not in Poland and Hungary. As for the clearance condition, we expect to observe null results in all three countries.

This is indeed what we observe. Looking at the first solid black point estimate and confidence interval in the right-hand panel of Figure 8.A1, we find that average Acceptance among those in the contravention treatment is lower than those in the Control condition. As expected, this difference is only statistically significant in Germany, the country with a high level of judicial independence. To be precise, acceptance of the executive's proposal declines from an average of 0.53 (Control) to 0.47 in the contravention conditions. This difference is statistically significant from zero ($p = 0.04$).

Of particular note is the finding that the contravention penalty is significant here for respondents who read of a copartisan challenge, rather than an outpartisan challenge. This is the opposite of our finding presented in the chapter. However, as we discussed in the introduction to this Appendix, that result is not robust to the inclusion of additional demographic and political controls. This result, however,

24 Tables 8.A4 (Germany), 8.A5 (Hungary), and 8.A6 (Poland) provide linear regression results underlying the findings in this section.

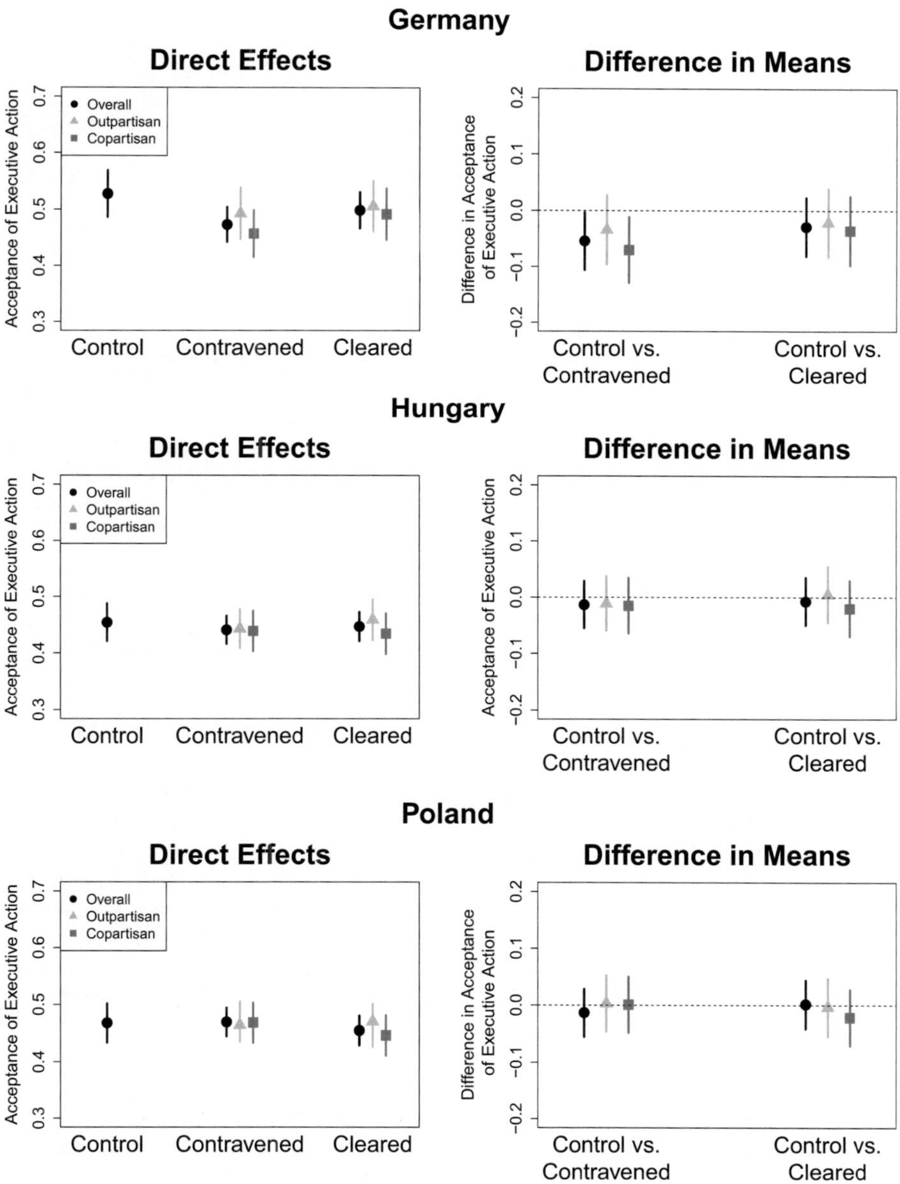

FIGURE 8.A1 Direct effects of the Abstract Review Experiment (with Control condition). The left-hand panels plot the average value of acceptance of the executive's action, by condition. This variable has a range of 0–1; higher values of this variable indicate a greater level of acceptance. The right-hand panels illustrate the difference in means between experimental conditions. Positive values of the *y*-axis in these panels indicate an increase in acceptance, relative to the Control condition. The vertical lines in both panels provide 95% confidence intervals.

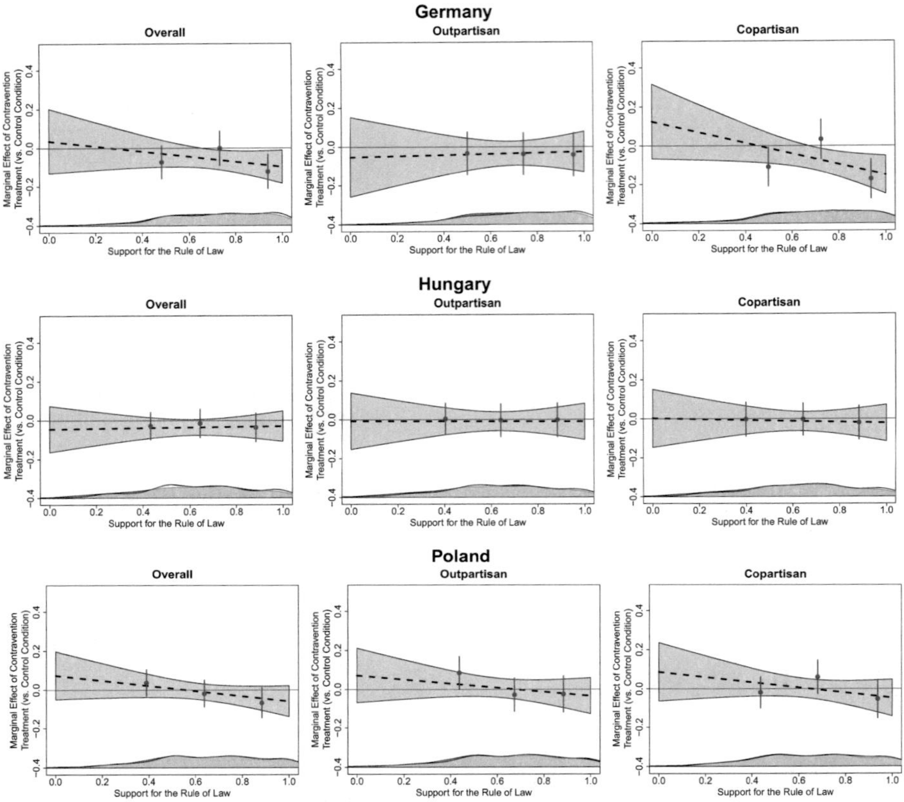

FIGURE 8.A2 Conditional effects from the Abstract Review Experiment (with Control condition). Support for the Rule of Law increases with the *x*-axis. The shaded areas are 95% confidence intervals. The point estimates and associated confidence intervals are the Hainmueller, Mummolo, and Xu (2019) estimates of the marginal effect for each tercile of Support for the Rule of Law. The density plot shows the distribution for support for the rule of law by treatment; the darker density is the baseline group. The panels plot the marginal effect of Contravention (left-hand panel) and Clearance (right-hand panel) relative to the Control condition, averaging across partisanship treatments.

does persist even as we control for additional respondent-specific characteristics. We are hesitant to make too much of either result: the one thing that is clear across both sets of results is that the difference in the difference for copartisan and outpartisan challenges is not itself statistically significant.

The results on this front in Hungary and Poland perform as we expect and are consistent with the findings we report elsewhere. The point estimates for the Contravention condition (0.44) are not statistically distinguishable from the Control condition (0.45, $p = 0.53$) in Hungary, and we similarly do not observe a statistically distinguishable difference in the Polish case. In Poland, the average level

TABLE 8.A4 *Linear regression results: Abstract Review Experiment (Germany, including control condition). The models estimate the contravention penalty (relative to the Control condition) for all respondents (Model 1), among those who read of an outpartisan proposer (Model 3), and among those who read of a copartisan proposer (Model 5), akin to the results shown in the right-hand panel of Figure 8.A1. Models 2, 4, and 6 provide the results underlying Figure 8.A2. The reference category for the experimental manipulation of these models is the Control condition. The dependent variable in all models is acceptance of the Executive's Action; higher values indicate more acceptance. All variables are scaled to range from 0 to 1.*

	Overall		Outpartisan		Copartisan	
	Model 1	Model 2	Model 3	Model 4	Model 5	Model 6
Contravention	−0.06*	0.04	−0.03	−0.05	−0.07*	0.12
	(0.03)	(0.09)	(0.03)	(0.10)	(0.03)	(0.10)
Clearance	−0.03	−0.06				
	(0.03)	(0.09)				
Support for the Rule of Law		−0.06		−0.06		−0.06
		(0.09)		(0.09)		(0.09)
Contravention × Support for the Rule of Law		−0.13		0.03		−0.27*
		(0.12)		(0.14)		(0.13)
Clearance × Support for the Rule of Law		0.04				
		(0.12)				
Constant	0.53*	0.57*	0.53*	0.57*	0.53*	0.57*
	(0.02)	(0.07)	(0.02)	(0.07)	(0.02)	(0.07)
Observations	1,332	1,332	478	478	524	524
R^2	0.004	0.01	0.003	0.004	0.01	0.03

Note: * $p < 0.05$.

TABLE 8.A5 *Linear regression results: Abstract Review Experiment (Hungary, including control condition). The models estimate the contravention penalty (relative to the Control condition) for all respondents (Model 1), among those who read of an outpartisan proposer (Model 3), and among those who read of a copartisan proposer (Model 5), akin to the results shown in the right-hand panel of Figure 8.A1. Models 2, 4, and 6 provide the results underlying Figure 8.A2. The reference category for the experimental manipulation of these models is the Control condition. The dependent variable in all models is acceptance of the Executive's Action; higher values indicate more acceptance. All variables are scaled to range from 0 to 1.*

	Overall		Outpartisan		Copartisan	
	Model 1	Model 2	Model 3	Model 4	Model 5	Model 6
Contravention	−0.04	−0.05	−0.02	−0.01	0.005	0.14
	(0.02)	(0.06)	(0.03)	(0.08)	(0.03)	(0.08)
Clearance	−0.04	−0.11				
	(0.02)	(0.06)				
Support for the Rule of Law		−0.06		−0.05		0.12
		(0.07)		(0.08)		(0.09)
Contravention × Support for the Rule of Law		0.02		−0.01		−0.21
		(0.09)		(0.11)		(0.12)
Clearance × Support for the Rule of Law		0.12				
		(0.09)				
Constant	0.45*	0.49*	0.46*	0.49*	0.43*	0.35*
	(0.02)	(0.05)	(0.02)	(0.05)	(0.02)	(0.06)
Observations	2,000	2,000	675	675	639	639
R^2	0.002	0.003	0.001	0.002	0.0001	0.005

Note: * $p < 0.05$.

TABLE 8.A6 *Linear regression results: Abstract Review Experiment (Poland, including control condition). The models estimate the contravention penalty (relative to the Control condition) for all respondents (Model 1), among those who read of an outpartisan proposer (Model 3), and among those who read of a copartisan proposer (Model 5), akin to the results shown in the right-hand panel of Figure 8.A1. Models 2, 4, and 6 provide the results underlying Figure 8.A2. The reference category for the experimental manipulation of these models is the Control condition. The dependent variable in all models is Acceptance of the Executive's Action; higher values indicate more acceptance. All variables are scaled to range from 0 to 1.*

	Overall		Outpartisan		Copartisan	
	Model 1	Model 2	Model 3	Model 4	Model 5	Model 6
Contravention	−0.01	0.07	0.01	−0.06	0.02	−0.03
	(0.02)	(0.06)	(0.03)	(0.07)	(0.03)	(0.07)
Clearance	−0.02	0.11				
	(0.02)	(0.06)				
Support for the Rule of Law		0.18*		−0.02		−0.03
		(0.08)		(0.08)		(0.07)
Contravention × Support for the Rule of Law		−0.13		0.10		0.08
		(0.09)		(0.11)		(0.11)
Clearance × Support for the Rule of Law		−0.20*				
		(0.09)				
Constant	0.47*	0.35*	0.46*	0.48*	0.45*	0.47*
	(0.02)	(0.05)	(0.02)	(0.05)	(0.02)	(0.05)
Observations	2,000	2,000	740	740	760	760
R^2	0.001	0.004	0.0001	0.002	0.001	0.002

Note: * $p < 0.05$.

of acceptance in the Contravention condition and the Control condition are essentially identical (0.47, $p = 0.93$).

Turning to Clearance, we observe the expected null result across all partisan categories. In Germany, this point estimate is slightly negative, but the confidence interval spans zero; in both Hungary and Poland the point estimates sit right at zero. As with the Lockdown and Mandatory Vaccine Experiments, this implies that we find no support for the direct effects of the clearance hypothesis in our Abstract Review experiment.[25]

Finally, Figure 8.A2 plots the contravention penalty as support for the rule of law varies and using the Control condition as the baseline. Here, we observe the same pattern of results as we did in Germany: a notably negative sloping marginal effect for all respondents and among those who read of a copartisan challenge. Of particular note, is the latter: here – but not in Figure 8.A2 – we see a contravention penalty that is distinguishable from zero for respondents who read of a copartisan challenge to the mandatory vaccine policy and are in the highest tercile of support for the rule of law. In Poland – and remarkably so in Hungary – we see null results across the board providing additional empirical support for the predictions of our theoretical account.

[25] In Germany, the average value of acceptance in the Cleared conditions is 0.50, which is not statistically distinguishable from the Control condition ($p = 0.28$). In Hungary, the average values of Acceptance in both the Cleared (0.45) is equal to that of the Control condition, with $p = 0.74$. As for Poland, the average Acceptance of the Cleared treatment is also equal to that of the Control condition, with $p = 0.93$.

9

The Prospects of Judicial Review

Countries around the globe have embraced constitutional courts and judicial review over the past century. One stated reason for judicial empowerment is to create an authority capable of reining in capricious executives. For courts to fulfill this promise, they must be *effective*. That is, they must be able to generate political penalties for elites whose actions transgress constitutional boundaries. Our goal in this book has been to understand the conditions under which courts are effective. What have we learned?

We argued that courts have the potential – more so than many other types of political and social institutions – to help constrain the state. Courts are uniquely positioned to ensure that incumbents face political consequences for their transgressions insofar as they can assist the public in monitoring state action and send a credible signal to the public regarding violations of the rule of law. At the same time, we suggested that, if existing theoretical accounts about the legitimizing capacity of judicial institutions were correct, courts might actually *weaken* constraints on executives by shaping public opinion in their favor, even when executives act outside the boundaries of their constitutional authority. Our theoretical account suggested that independent courts have the potential to do the former – to reduce citizens' acceptance of executive actions that they deem unconstitutional – but not the latter: courts, regardless of their independence, generally do not have the power to sway the public to their position after upholding a policy's constitutionality.

We focused our attention on one type of cost that courts might be able to generate and is likely to matter to incumbents: public acceptance of executive actions. Incumbents of all stripes – and in all political contexts – reap rewards for taking actions that citizens like; the likelihood that they lose office or political prestige often increases as they begin to raise public ire. By studying citizens' acceptance of executive action, we therefore examine how courts are able to shape the beginning of the process of political accountability. Before citizens decide to protest, to donate to a challenger, or to try to vote an incumbent out of office, they must first dislike what the incumbent has done and withhold their support.

Through a series of survey experiments fielded in the United States, Germany, Hungary, and Poland, we examined how citizens' acceptance changes in response to executive actions taken after constitutional courts use judicial review to evaluate the constitutionality of executive actions. We fielded these surveys during the COVID-19 pandemic, a time when threats to the rule of law were heightened as governments took extraordinary steps in the name of public health and safety. Our use of original survey experiments fielded across countries enables us to identify the causal effects of judicial review on citizens' attitudes while also allowing for variation in both individual values and institutional contexts. From here, we highlight four general conclusions from our research.

First, *we find robust and consistent evidence that judicial independence is a prerequisite to judicial efficacy*. Our key test of judicial efficacy was the presence (or absence) of a contravention penalty. That is, we looked to see whether acceptance declined in the face of noncompliance with a constitutional court compared to an experimental condition in which no court was ignored. In the United States and Germany, where judicial independence is high, we found evidence of judicial efficacy: in these cases, citizens punish executives for noncompliance with the judiciary. The implication of this finding is that independent courts can assist the public in imposing political penalties for constitutional transgressions. Independent courts can help citizens monitor executive actions by informing them when an executive action has violated the constitution. When executives move forward and defy the court by implementing those policies, the judicial ruling helps citizens coordinate a response, resulting in a lowered level of acceptance.

Our findings in Hungary and Poland, by contrast, underscore a key scope condition for judicial review to provide an efficacious constraint on executive power. Courts can help solve citizens' coordination problem when trying to constrain an overreaching incumbent, but the extent to which this is possible depends on the independence of the court and the credibility of its signal as a reliable judgment of constitutional authority. When executives ignore nonindependent courts, citizens' acceptance remains unchanged. These courts, it seems, are impotent to affect the public's response to executive actions, including those that directly violate judicial rulings.

Second, *judicial efficacy increases with the public's support for the rule of law*. We proposed a new measure of this important concept, presented data on the public's support for this norm from tens of thousands of survey interviews, and provided the most rigorous and systematic examination of the public's support for the rule of law to date. In the process, we demonstrated that the public's support for this norm in consolidated democracies was stable throughout the COVID-19 pandemic, a period when concerns about rule of law backsliding were pronounced. We demonstrated that the correlates and predictive validity of support for the rule of law are common across space and time, concluding that it is closely related to citizens' political sophistication and experience, as well as their broader attachment to democratic values.

More critically, however, support for the rule of law matters. Where courts can send effective signals that executives have violated the law, they activate citizens' attitudes about this norm such that those most committed to the rule of law impose especially punative penalties. By contrast, for those citizens who are not committed to the rule of law, a ruling from even the most independent court does not convince them to withdraw acceptance from rule of law defiant policy implementation. In this way, our results demonstrate that support for the rule of law and independent judicial review – attitudes and institutions – are symbiotic. State constraint requires both.

Third, *we find that these effects remain stable in the face of explicit partisan threats*. Despite loud and widespread concerns about the consequences of heightened partisanship for the rule of law, most notably due to fears that citizens prioritize partisanship above a commitment to democratic norms, we found only minimal and inconsistent evidence that copartisanship conditions the efficacy of independent courts as a mechanism of state constraint.

We observe in both the United States and Germany that respondents withhold support even for a copartisan-promoted policy when it is invalidated by those countries' respective high courts. In Germany, we find this contravention penalty to be most pronounced among those with strong support for the rule of law, although in the United States we somewhat surprisingly found this to be exclusively the case for copartisan executives. A central conclusion from our analyses in Chapter 7 was that what little partisan effect we did observe was *contrary* to what most partisan-centric theories would lead us to expect, in that the public imposed harsher penalties on copartisans, rather than members of an opposing party.

In Chapter 8, we probed how citizens might respond to learning the partisanship of litigants in a challenge to executive behavior. Here results were mixed. As expected, however, we continued to observe the inability of courts in our low judicial independence cases – Hungary and Poland – to shift citizens' reactions. Although we do not wish to overstate these results, our foremost conclusion is to suggest that partisanship appears to be, at most, a minimal threat to the ability of independent courts to animate the public to impose constraints on executives. The more general trends we theorize and report throughout the book hold in the face of partisanship.

Finally, *we find no evidence that courts' endorsements – regardless of their level of independence – increase acceptance of controversial policies*. For decades, scholars have argued, and made valiant attempts to demonstrate, that courts have the legitimizing powers that Dahl (1957) famously suggested they might. These investigations have persisted despite outright null, sometimes negligible, and otherwise conflicting empirical results, and other evidence suggesting that the ability of courts to achieve the sort of broad social change legitimizing theories would predict is scant (Rosenberg 2008).

We have provided a theory that explains why we should expect the legitimizing capacity of courts to be minimal. In short – incumbents do not get extra credit for doing the "right thing"; judicial assurances that executive actions comport with constitutional norms do not win hearts or minds. We tested this hypothesis in four countries, and our conclusions are both consistent and clear: in no country, in no experiment, and for no subgroup did we find evidence that judicial clearance increases the acceptance of executive's unconstitutional actions. For those who are distressed that courts might undermine state constraint through their legitimizing capacity, our results should assuage these concerns. For scholars of judicial institutions and public opinion, our results serve as a clarion call for more careful theorizing about the extent of any judicial legitimizing capacity in the first place.

IMPLICATIONS OF OUR ARGUMENT AND CONCLUSIONS

Our argument and analyses draw from a variety of areas of study in political science, law, and beyond. We hope that this book helps to push the research frontier in these areas forward and will spur new lines of research. Here, we try to connect our theory and findings back to these varied research traditions as a way to contextualize what we've learned.

The Concept of Judicial Efficacy

The idea of judicial efficacy is often invoked by political scientists and legal scholars, yet there is no commonly accepted conceptualization of the term. While scholars have poured efforts into defining and understanding concepts like judicial independence (Burbank and Friedman 2002; Ríos-Figueroa and Staton 2014; Tarr 2012; van Dijk 2024), compliance (Gonzalez-Ocantos and Dinas 2019; Hillebrecht 2024; Kapiszewski and Taylor 2013), and the rule of law (Carlin 2012; Gowder 2016; Tamanaha 2004; World Justice Project 2020), the question of judicial efficacy has not received this level of attention. This is surprising. We have argued throughout this book that judicial efficacy and independence are not synonymous nor is either one conterminous with the rule of law (Ríos-Figueroa 2007). One implication of our research is to highlight the importance of judicial efficacy as a concept; it should be elevated alongside these other notions as a concept that merits scrutiny and theorizing from legal scholars across methodological traditions. Thinking systematically about the ways in which the impacts of judicial decisions are felt, both inside and outside the courtroom, is a worthwhile objective for future scholarship.

Part of the path forward concerns an agreed-upon definition of the term. Our own conceptualization of judicial efficacy emphasizes the judiciary's effectiveness vis-à-vis the public. Other conceptualizations, which we reviewed in Chapter 1, take different tracks: some are normative, others linked to institutional design, and others equate efficacy with the ability of courts to secure implementation of their rulings. In this constellation of conceptualizations, our approach most closely comports with this latter tradition. By examining efficacy among the public, we test one mechanism through which effective courts are more likely to achieve implementation. It has long been assumed that, given sufficiently widespread support for judicial institutions, voluntary adherence to judicial decisions follows because there exist credible penalties for noncompliance that incentivize law-abiding behavior (e.g., Vanberg 2015). A major contribution of this book is focusing on the behavioral consequences of these theories and to test them experimentally in the court of public opinion.

By building a concrete conceptualization of judicial efficacy, scholars can begin to determine how it relates to other concepts like judicial independence, judicial power, and the rule of law. We have argued (and demonstrated) that judicial independence is a prerequisite to judicial efficacy, at least in terms of the effectiveness of courts vis-à-vis the public. Understanding the interrelationships between these core concepts in the study of law and courts is crucial.

Theories of Judicial Independence and Judicial Review

We provide ample and compelling empirical evidence that the public punishes executives for noncompliance with independent courts. Many formal theoretic models of interbranch relations explicitly suggest that incumbents face penalties when they defy judicial rulings (e.g., Krehbiel 2021c; Staton 2010; Vanberg 2015). Other accounts of judicial independence or power hinge implicitly on the presence of such costs. For example, accounts of courts as nonmajoritarian arbiters depend on those consequences as political cover (Graber 1993). Moreover, the value of courts as "insurance" or as a hegemonic preservation strategy hinge on these sorts of consequences for a new set of incumbents that defy the rulings of a constitutional court (Ginsburg 2003; Hirschl 2004). These theories also often imply that the costs of transgressing a court increase with the court's level of judicial independence.

Surprisingly, empirical evidence on this front has been scarce (but see Carlin et al. 2022; Driscoll, Çakir, and Schorpp 2024; Krehbiel 2021c). We provide robust evidence across multiple experiments of a contravention penalty in the public's willingness to accept policies achieved through ignoring an independent court compared to those that are either cleared by a court or adopted without judicial review. At the same time, we present evidence that such a penalty is not present when executives defy a low-independence constitutional court: the penalties for noncompliance are conditional on a court's level of judicial independence. Thus, our results provide some empirical evidence to underpin many prominent theories of judicial independence and power.

Additionally, scholars have long thought that judicial independence "matters," in part, because of what it might communicate to external audiences. This argument is perhaps best expressed through studies of judicial independence and credible commitment, which suggest that the presence of independent courts signals to external actors that property rights will be respected (e.g., Feld and Voigt 2003; LaPorta et al. 1998; North and Weingast 1989).

Our argument and findings extend this perspective to an additional but no less critical audience: the public. Our work suggests that judicial review has a powerful "second face": it informs the public about executive or legislative overreach and helps citizens monitor and coordinate their attempts to constrain the state. Not only can judicial review help to moderate policymaking (Tsebelis 2011; Vanberg 2001) and manage interelite bargains over time, but it can solve the public's coordination problem to enable state constraint. Moving forward, theories of judicial independence and power should consider public judgments of judicial institutions, as the signaling capacity of courts likely makes these institutions more powerful than previous account have fully appreciated.

There is more work to be done to understand the ability of low-independence courts to create political costs for elites. There are at least two reasons why the signaling capacity of courts and constitutional authorities is compromised in low-independence contexts. One possibility is that citizens simply cannot discern the content of the court's decision – they cannot tell whether it is a breach of the rule of law, merely a reflection of strategic behavior of the justices themselves, or something else entirely. In this context – where citizens can neither trust the court nor expect that judicial signals reflect rule of law (rather than partisan or some other) considerations – simply seeing the institution's decision is not informative, but rather a noisy signal that is difficult to decipher irrespective of one's support for the rule of law. Put differently, in these situations, citizens cannot trust the court to tell them whether an executive action is actually a violation of the law.

Alternatively, it may be that in these settings the court's decisions are simply received as reflections of the executive's will rather than verdicts on the rule of law. In this way, constitutional courts in places with low levels of judicial independence may actually amplify the partisan information that citizens receive about a particular policy's implementation, rather than signaling to citizens whether or not a policy is congruent with the rule of law. In these contexts, even strong support for the rule of law is not activated because citizens in those places do not perceive oversight as reflecting the rule of law but rather partisan interests. Although we find no evidence that low independence courts can alter citizens' acceptance of executive actions taken in response to judicial decisions, it is possible that the rulings of low independence courts might reinforce citizens' partisan perceptions about courts in other ways. This is a line of questioning ripe for future research.

This insight points to lessons not only for resisting democratic backsliding, but also for the interplay of institutions and political attitudes in polities that have already succumbed to autocratization. Both scholars and observers often point out that the judiciary is one of the first targets in democratic backsliding, with would-be autocrats seeking to make allies of erstwhile democratic guardrails that could legitimize anti-democratic policies (e.g., Ginsburg and Huq 2018; Levitsky and

Ziblatt 2018). Our findings in Hungary and Poland suggest that any such benefit of co-optation is squandered by the undermining of judicial independence that takes place to bring these institutions under the regime's control. Although it is plausible that courts retain their efficacy in the period immediately following their co-optation, especially if citizens are not able to update their beliefs about judicial independence, such a capacity is likely quickly lost as the public becomes aware of the judiciary's weakened state. With opposition politicians, international organizations, and other watchdogs well incentivized to make the public apprised of such threats to judicial independence, we suspect that the shelf life of judicial efficacy for even recently weakened courts is quite short.

We acknowledge that there may well be benefits to capture that we do not observe. For example, it is possible that institutional co-optation yields benefits to the regime in the immediate term, before citizens realize that the court has been captured. Perhaps at this very early stage of co-optation – before the public realizes that the court has been compromised – co-opted courts can work in ways that are beneficial to the regime. For this reason, understanding the dynamics of public perceptions of judicial independence, as well as the public's response to courts at various levels of co-optation, are also prime targets for additional research.

Courts and Public Opinion

Since at least Dahl (1957), political scientists and legal scholars have scoured survey data searching for evidence that courts are able to legitimize policies. We have carried out four experiments across four different countries and, like many studies before ours, we found no evidence – statistically or substantively – that constitutional courts legitimize the policies of the dominant coalition. Our suggestion to researchers is to think carefully about the conditions under which courts might legitimize policies and to be cognizant of the fact that even Dahl cautioned that this is likely a rare and tenuous power. Scholars are quick to quote (as we did, earlier in this book) Dahl's argument that "The main task of the Court is to confer legitimacy on the fundamental policies of the successful coalition" (294). But, in a passage that is not so often quoted from directly, Dahl went on to suggest that this power is likely circumscribed:

> There are times when the coalition is unstable with respect to certain key policies; at very great risk to its legitimacy powers, the Court can intervene in such cases and may even succeed in establishing policy. Probably in such cases it can succeed only if its action conforms to and reinforces a widespread set of explicit or implicit norms held by the political leadership; norms which are not strong enough or are not distributed in such a way as to ensure the existence of an effective lawmaking majority but are, nonetheless, sufficiently powerful to prevent any successful attack on the legitimacy powers of the court. This is probably the explanation for the relatively successful work of the Court in enlarging the freedom of Negroes to vote during the past three decades and in its famous school integration decisions (294).

Dahl is clear here – as research moving forward should be too – that a court's power to legitimize policies is likely rare, limited, and conditional. And, it does not escape our notice that the example Dahl gives of the Court legitimizing policy is one Rosenberg (2008) has persuasively shown to be a failure: public opinion about race relations and desegregation did not immediately shift following *Brown v. Board of Education*,[1] and schools did not begin to integrate until after Congress stepped in to coerce compliance with the Court's decision.

Second, scholars have deservedly spent decades understanding the determinants of judicial legitimacy (Bartels and Johnston 2013; Gibson and Caldeira 1992; Gibson, Caldeira, and Baird 1998; Gibson and Nelson 2014; Smyth 2024), and these studies have taught us much about how courts acquire and maintain public support. But, by and large, scholars have focused on judicial legitimacy to the exclusion of other legal attitudes. This has changed in recent years as scholars have begun to devote more attention to studies of Supreme Court approval (e.g., Ansolabehere and White 2020; Haglin et al. 2021), support for judicial power (e.g., Bartels, Horowitz, and Kramon 2021; Bartels and Johnston 2020; Bartels and Kramon 2020), and the family of related concepts.

Our focus on the public's support for the rule of law, which draws from the work of Gibson and Caldeira (1996), Reeves and Rogowski (2022a), and others, stands apart from this new wave of research. By focusing on a system-level attitude, rather than support for a particular institution, these studies – including ours – have provided new insights into the efficacy of political constraints on executive action. Further research on these attitudes, in addition to continued work on the legitimacy of constitutional courts (especially those outside of the United States), is essential as courts continue to play a vital role in polities around the globe.

Executive Orders and Constraint

Our research also points to an important pathway forward in the debate about the public's response to executive unilateral action. Some (e.g., Reeves and Rogowski 2022a) have argued that the public's evaluations of executive actions are grounded in constitutional considerations, like support for the rule of law, and have little relation to partisanship. Others (e.g., Christenson and Kriner 2017b; Braman 2023) have suggested that partisan and other political considerations overwhelmingly drive the public's response to unilateral action. While these studies focus nearly singlemindedly on responses to the US president's unilateral actions (but see Reeves and Rogowski 2023; Chu and Williamson 2025), we have examined the public's response to executive unilateral action in four countries, emphasizing how judicial review might shape the public's responses to such actions.

[1] Indeed, according to a May 1959 poll, "53% of Americans said the decision caused a lot more trouble than it was worth" (Carroll 2004).

Our conclusions largely coincide with the theoretical perspective that constitutional considerations matter. Like Reeves and Rogowski, we find limited evidence that partisan considerations color evaluations of executive action and instead find that the public's support for the rule of law provides a powerful pathway to state constraint. We have done so with experiments, unlike Reeves and Rogowski (but like Christenson and Kriner as well as Braman) that use concrete political controversies, and we have evaluated the public's responses to these actions with a broader conception of the outcome variable than any existing study. Our measure of acceptance blends both policy support and approval of the executive to provide a more holistic sense of the public's evaluation of policies adopted through executive action, one that future studies in this vein might adopt.

Further, our comparative research design provides an opportunity for future research that seeks to generalize these findings beyond the usual confines of a single North American case. Our case selection criteria focused, given our interest in judicial politics, on variable levels of judicial independence. But executives around the globe (and within countries) vary in their powers and their relative constitutional influence compared to the other branches of government (e.g., Bolton and Thrower 2021; Carey and Shugart 1998; Cheibub, Elkins, and Ginsburg 2014; Shugart and Carey 1992). Understanding the interplay between support for the rule of law and executive unilateralism in presidential and parliamentary systems, as well as within such systems, would promote a generalized understanding of the conditions under which independent judicial review, combined with support for the rule of law, can serve as an effective tool for state constraint.

On Partisanship

We end this section on a reassuring note. There has been much made – in academic journals and the popular press – about the threats pernicious partisanship poses to the rule of law, democratic stability, and survival (e.g., Carey et al. 2022; Graham and Svolik 2020; Kalmoe and Mason 2022). These accounts suggest that citizens care more about shared partisanship than democratic values and are thus often willing to sacrifice the latter for the former. Were this the case, then instrumentalism could accelerate democratic backsliding and raise the specter of authoritarianism.

We proposed a theory about how judicial review might be able to constrain the state by shaping citizens' opinions about executive actions that violate the law. We then tested this theory repeatedly in the context of experiments that explicitly prime partisan considerations. We cast a wide net, investigating both the prospect of partisan prioritization in a research context – the pandemic – where citizens faced real and immediate consequences from governments' actions. In this way, we set up a hard test for our theory: there were compelling reasons why citizens might prioritize partisan considerations over the rule of law across our study.

Yet the picture that emerges from our results is one that suggests the effect of partisanship has only muted effects. And, where we found them, they were surprising. In Chapters 6 and 7, for example, we found that partisanship might *help* constrain the state: Americans and Germans who approved highly of their executives punished them more for contravening a court than those citizens who held the executive in low regard. In this way, our results suggest one pathway through which partisanship might *assist*, rather than impede citizens' attempts to restrain the state.

From our results, an important question persists: why do we observe such limited effects of partisanship? The fact that our study focuses on courts suggests one possible answer. Courts judicialize political conflicts, taking them outside of the realm of "normal" political conflict in a way that changes how citizens evaluate policy conflicts. We have made this argument repeatedly throughout the book, though we acknowledge that we have done little to test this specific mechanism. Doing so – and understanding more broadly the consequences of populism and extreme partisanship for state constraint and the survival of the rule of law – is an essential topic for future research.

RESIDUAL PUZZLES

As with any project, we recognize that there remain important, yet unanswered, research questions beyond the scope of this book. As such, we end the book by discussing potential directions for further research suggested by our findings.

Judging Judicial Independence

Our theoretical argument suggests that, as levels of judicial independence increase, so too do the signaling capacity of judicial decisions and courts' ability to convey information to the public that might enable citizen coordination. We anticipated this relationship because we expected that with increased independence comes an enhanced capacity for trustworthiness and forthrightness, as established in Chapter 2. As we discussed in Chapter 3, the United States, Germany, Poland, and Hungary differ dramatically in their de facto level of judicial independence, as measured by V-Dem and others, and it was this broad conceptualization of judicial independence that guided our case selection. And as we demonstrated in Chapter 4, the largest differential in the public's support for the rule of law in the United States and Germany as opposed to Poland and Hungary centered on the public's expectations regarding institutions and institutional adherence to the constitutional foundations of law.

But, of course, the United States and Germany, on the one hand, and Poland and Hungary, on the other, differ on far more dimensions than just the level of judicial independence of their constitutional courts. Thus, there is much to be done both to verify that the differences we observe are, in fact, due to variation in judicial independence and also to test the underlying mechanisms that link judicial independence and signaling credibility.

One fruitful place to start would be to return to Figure 3.8, which plots the relationship between de facto levels of judicial independence in Europe along with a measure of *perceptions* of judicial independence. Countries like Spain, where actual and perceived levels of independence are misaligned would provide useful opportunities to test the foundations of our theory. It may be the case, for example, that citizens' perceptions of judicial independence, rather than actual levels of judicial independence, are the key driver of a court's source credibility. Other features of courts, such as their level of actual (Baum 2003) or perceived (Gadarian and Strother 2023; Gibson and Nelson 2017; Woodson 2015) levels of politicization, the extent to which their caseloads are judicialized, their institutional age (Gibson, Caldeira, and Baird 1998), or some other feature might also affect courts' signaling credibility. Similarly, citizens' lived experiences – for example, the mode of education they received – may color their views regarding judicial independence (Cheruvu 2023). Put broadly, understanding the foundations of judicial signaling credibility is an important path forward.

The Signaling Capacity of Other Institutions

We focused our investigation on the effects of judicial review by constitutional courts, arguing that judicial independence provides courts with credibility the public can rely upon to restrain the state. There are good reasons to expect that courts are favorably positioned for this type of task. As we have argued, courts imbue their decisions with an air of legality that might change how citizens evaluate policies by taking them out of the realm of "normal politics." Likewise, courts tend to be held in higher regard than other branches of government in a way that might enhance their credibility as a font of credible information (Bartels and Mutz 2009; Bishin et al. 2021; Driscoll and Nelson 2023a).

This trust in the courts, however, presents a double-edged sword. A co-opted or politically pressured court might uphold a suspect policy for strategic reasons (Epstein and Knight 1998). Yet, due to their faith in the process of apolitical judicial review, citizens might not recognize the court's calculation and instead view the decision as an impartial evaluation of the policy's constitutionality. This dynamic speaks to the motivations of would-be authoritarians to target the courts, as it highlights the potential value of silencing judicial fire alarms via institutional co-optation or capture. Our findings may also help explain why governments – including democratic ones – often fight so hard over appointments to apex courts (e.g., Spain, the United States, and many Eastern European countries in recent years). Control over who is on the court shifts the probability that courts will blow the whistle and alert the public to executive malfeasance. Such considerable potential impact speaks to the salience and significance of judicial appointments.

On a similar note, what are the prospects for state constraint in places where courts are too enfeebled by a lack of judicial independence to serve the role we have described? Might other judicial bodies pick up the reins? We think the most likely path forward in this vein concerns the role of international courts, like the European Court of Justice and the European Court of Human Rights. We suspect it is not happenstance that the global trend of increasingly frequent challenges to the rule of law has coincided with the increasing usage of international law and legal institutions as potential guardians of liberal democracy (Ginsburg 2021). Indeed, those European courts have been at the fore of publicizing and confronting the rule of law crisis in Hungary and Poland, issuing multiple rulings intended to stymie or otherwise curb the countries' retrocession away from democratic norms. Elsewhere in the world, we have similarly observed affronts to civil liberties and political rights being adjudicated in international courts. For instance, after a military in coup in Niger in 2023, the country's ousted president looked to that region's international court, the Economic Community of West African States (ECOWAS) Court of Justice, to order he be reinstated to his position (Asadu 2023).[2] While international courts face constraints on their power similar to those confronted by domestic courts (Staton and Moore 2011), which is compounded by the limitations inherent to the international legal system (Carrubba and Gabel 2015; Cheruvu 2019; Cheruvu and Krehbiel 2022; Voeten 2020), their detachment from domestic institutions and the typical diffusion of appointment power across multiple national governments may also help protect their judicial independence – to the extent they have independence in the first place (Voeten 2008) – and thus foster their source credibility. Moreover, many international legal systems grant domestic courts the power to become involved in the international legal process, which can help promote public acceptance of international law and by extension help domestic courts overcome political constraints (Cheruvu and Krehbiel 2024; Krehbiel and Cheruvu 2022).

That said, international courts are unlikely to be an immediate panacea. For one, they need cases to be brought to them, often by national governments or international institutions; if such litigants are unwilling to do so, international courts are left sitting quietly on the sidelines (Kelemen and Pavone 2023). A further key challenge for international courts – as it always is – is bringing political force to their rulings. Our account suggests that, at least when it comes to constraining the state, international courts are in some important respects better positioned to be effective than is typically expected. The critical conditions, then, may be if they have developed a positive reputation (Krehbiel 2021a) and the citizens to which they are speaking hold dear the rule of law.

[2] In a cautionary lesson for the efficacy of international courts, the military governments of three countries – Burkina Faso, Mali, and Niger – announced they were leaving the bloc, and thus the Court's jurisdiction, in response to rulings refusing to acknowledge the legitimacy of the coups that brought them to power.

Domestically, we wonder about the ability of other sorts of institutions to fulfill a function similar to the one we have discussed. We considered, in the appendix to Chapter 5, the possibility that legislatures might serve a similar role. Just as courts are empowered with judicial review, constitutions grant legislatures an independent basis of lawmaking authority and the power to oversee and investigate actions of the political executive. Yet, insofar as legislatures and parliaments are often unpopular for being the locus of overt politicking and partisan conflict (Hibbing and Theiss-Morse 1995, 2001), the greater antipathy held by the public toward legislatures (compared to courts) might undermine their ability to coordinate public sentiment to constrain executive transgressions. Our research suggests that legislatures are unlikely to fulfill the monitoring and coordination functions we have ascribed to courts through the power of judicial review. Yet, we view this as a fruitful point of departure and by no means the final say on this important claim.

Beyond legislatures, other sorts of institutions also present possibilities. After all, our argument is about a particular form of horizontal oversight – judicial review – and oversight of government takes many forms both inside and outside of the formal levers of government. Independent and free media might sound an alarm about executive overreach through investigative journalism or other careful reporting. So too might credible interest groups or other policy experts be able to provide citizens with information about potential executive malfeasance in a way that inspires citizens to adjust their views of an executive action. And, bureaucrats – especially civil servants or those that have strong nonpartisan bona fides – can play a classic whistleblower role to assist the public when executives are behaving badly. All of these possibilities are natural extensions of our theory, and each presents unique variation on the foundations of source credibility that might lead researchers to expect them to be more or less successful assistants to the public in maintaining state constraint.

The Rule of Law

We have provided the most comprehensive account, to date, of the public's support for the rule of law. Whereas most empirical accounts of the rule of law have focused on country-level measures and determinants of governments' respect for this norm (e.g., Carlin 2012; Nardulli, Peyton, and Bajjalieh 2013; World Justice Project 2020), we have charted a different path, examining the public's support for this essential democratic norm. Drawing on pathbreaking studies by Gibson and Caldeira (1996), Reeves and Rogowski (2022a), and others, we dedicated Chapter 4 to understanding the public's support for this vital democratic norm.

What did we learn? Just as its proponents contend, our findings suggest that the rule of law has the potential to be a powerful and stable force for democracy. Citizens' attachment to the rule of law appears steadfast both over time and even in the face of an unprecedented pandemic, trends that are reassuring especially in such challenging circumstances. But, at the same time, our study also highlights some of the weaknesses of democracy's exclusive reliance on this source of attitudinal support. While support for the rule of law is strong and largely stable in consolidated democracies, that its efficacy as a democratic guardrail depends on the signaling power of institutions emphasizes the potential fragility of democracy and the need for interlocking norms and institutions to promote its survival. Just as scholars have long recognized that institutions, constitutions, and statutory laws are only parchment barriers if they lack political will to give them effect (Carey 2000), our findings emphasize the importance of independent and trusted institutions for translating support for norms like the rule of law into meaningful action. In this sense, the book highlights the roles – sometimes complementary and at other times oppositional – of attitudes and institutions when it comes to sustaining a liberal democracy.

There are many other contexts where support for the rule of law might serve the salutary state constraint role that we have emphasized with respect to judicial review, and that Reeves and Rogowski (2022a) have demonstrated regarding unilateral executive action in the United States. Is support for the rule of law a generally useful tool for state constraint? Can it serve to constrain legislators and bureaucrats just as we have shown it can constrain executives?

Our findings, and those of Reeves and Rogowski (2022a), have demonstrated the power of this attitude primarily in established, industrialized democracies: the United States and Germany. Yet – concerns about democratic backsliding in these contexts aside – it might be the case that this norm is most effective in contexts where it is least useful. In Poland and Hungary, for example, where concerns about democratic backsliding and a decline in the rule of law are a clear and present danger, we uncover limited evidence that the public's support for the rule of law serves to constrain the state. By our theory, this happens because the courts in those countries cannot activate these attitudes, with judicial review failing to serve as an effective focal solution. When circumstances arise such as these, can other institutions step in to fill this void? Our results cry out for additional contextualization in order to uncover how support for the rule of law might assist with state constraint in places where a country's rule of law tradition is under fire, in retrocession, or in its nascent stage.

And, more broadly, we require additional data about the public's support for the rule of law. As we discussed in Chapter 4, this concept has been measured in a variety of different ways across major large-scale survey projects. Uniformity is needed, as is additional analysis about how support for the of law is built in democratizing contexts and why (or whether) this support is affected by autocratization and democratic backsliding. In regard to measurement, we discuss a distinction across our country pairs regarding items related to *individuals*' expectations about compliance and their beliefs that *governments* (institutions and elites) should also follow the law. While the former are similar across our country pairs, the latter are not. What is the mechanism that explains whether countries differ in this respect? And, given the importance of this norm for state constraint, how can support for the rule of law be fostered among citizens such that all citizens expect their governments to follow laws just as they expect their peers to do the same?

FINAL WORDS

This research teaches us that, while the ability of independent courts to serve as agents of state constraint is not a hollow hope, it is also not a guarantee. For generations, political scientists have sought to understand the conditions under which courts can play important and efficacious roles in political systems (e.g., Rosenberg 2008). These studies have taught us that, in many respects, courts are fundamentally weak institutions, lacking the power to implement their own decisions or to lead social change. Yet, the American framers reflecting on their experience with the Crown, the statesmen charged with state rebuilding in the aftermath of World War II, and the Eastern European patriots writing new constitutions after the fall of the Berlin Wall all put their faith in constitutional courts and judicial review as a powerful tool to ensure that their leaders and citizens alike would be bound by the rule of law.

We think this book tells us that their hope is not misplaced. We have found that independent courts are important tools of state constraint. Due to their credibility, independent courts can signal rule of law violations to the public through their use of judicial review, and citizens penalize executives who ignore these courts and press forward with policies courts have ruled as contrary to the constitution. In this way, independent courts do fulfill the promise that these framers hoped they would. Not only are they important partners in governance, they may become trusted authorities that monitor governments and alert citizens when elected officials breach their constitutional obligations. And, they can stand strong against partisan tides that can upend governments, wreak havoc among friends, and destabilize an otherwise steadfast regime.

But none of this is automatic. Judicial efficacy depends on judicial independence, and even independent courts are dependent upon citizens who value the rule of law. Without these two key features – institutional freedom to make the rulings they need to be able to make and a citizenry that is receptive to learning about violations of the rule of law – courts are the enfeebled institutions that political scientists and legal scholars have so often suggested they are. As such, it is important that efforts continue to defend independent courts against politicization and to educate citizens about the vital importance of the rule of law continue to. Without them, faith in courts to stand against tyranny is indeed hollow.

References

Aarslew, Laurits F. 2023. "Why Don't Partisans Sanction Electoral Malpractice?" *British Journal of Political Science* 53(2): 407–23.

Acemoglu, Daron, Simon Johnson, and James A. Robinson. 2001. "The Colonial Origins of Comparative Development: An Empirical Investigation." *American Economic Review* 91(5): 1369–1401.

Achen, Christopher H., and Larry Bartels. 2016. *Democracy for Realists: Why Elections Do Not Produce Responsive Government*. Princeton University Press.

Ackerman, Bruce. 1997. "The Rise of World Constitutionalism." *Virginia Law Review* 83(4): 771–97.

Adams-Cohen, Nicholas Joseph. 2020. "Policy Change and Public Opinion: Measuring Shifting Political Sentiment with Social Media Data." *American Politics Research* 48(5): 612–21.

Adolph, Christopher et al. 2022. "The Pandemic Policy U-Turn: Partisanship, Public Health, and Race in Decisions to Ease COVID-19 Social Distancing Policies in the United States." *Perspectives on Politics* 20(2): 595–617.

Ahlquist, John S., Nahomi Ichino, Jason Wittenberg, and Daniel Ziblatt. 2018. "How Do Voters Perceive Changes to the Rules of the Game? Evidence from the 2014 Hungarian Elections." *Journal of Comparative Economics* 46(4): 906–19.

Ahmed, Amel. 2023. "Is the American Public Really Turning Away from Democracy? Backsliding and the Conceptual Challenges of Understanding Public Attitudes." *Perspectives on Politics* 21(3): 967–78.

Albertus, Michael, and Guy Grossman. 2021. "The Americas: When Do Voters Support Power Grabs?" *Journal of Democracy* 32(2): 116–31.

Alivizatos, Nicos et al. 2020. *Interim Report on the Measures Taken in the EU Member States as a Result of the COVID-19 Crisis and Their Impact on Democracy, the Rule of Law and Fundamental Rights*. Council of Europe Venice Commission. Available at www.venice.coe.int/webforms/documents/?pdf = CDL-AD(2020)018-e.

Alizada, Nazifa et al. 2021. *Autocratization Turns Viral: Democracy Report 2021*. V-Dem; V-Dem Institute. Available at www.v-dem.net/static/website/files/dr/dr_2021.pdf.

Al Jazeera. 2020. "Thousands of Germans Protest against Merkel's Coronavirus Plans." *Al Jazeera* 18 November. Available at www.aljazeera.com/news/2020/11/18/thousands-of-germans-protest-against-merkels-coronavirus-plans.

Allen, Mark S., Dragos Iliescu, and Samuel Greiff. 2022. "Single Item Measures in Psychological Science." *European Journal of Psychological Assessment* 38(1): 1–5.

Almond, Gabriel A., and Sidney Verba. 1963. *The Civic Culture: Political Attitudes and Democracy in Five Nations*. Princeton University Press.

AmericasBarometer. 2006–2012. "Center for Global Democracy." LAPOP Lab. AmericasBarometer Dominican Republic, 2021, v1.2. Available at www.vanderbilt.edu/lapop.

Angenendt, Michael, and Lucy Kinski. 2022. "Germany: Political Developments and Data in 2021: The End of the Merkel Era." *European Journal of Political Research Political Data Yearbook* 61(1): 171–92.

Ansolabehere, Steven D., and Ariel White. 2020. "Policy, Politics, and Public Attitudes Toward the Supreme Court." *American Politics Research* 48(3): 365–76.

Arbatli, Ekim, and Dina Rosenberg. 2020. "United We Stand, Divided We Rule: How Political Polarization Erodes Democracy." *Democratization* 28(2): 285–307.

Ariely, Gal, and Eldad Davidov. 2012. "Assessment of Measurement Equivalence with Cross-National and Longitudinal Surveys in Political Science." *European Political Science* 11(3): 363–77.

Ariotti, Margaret, Simone Dietrich, and Joseph Wright. 2022. "Foreign Aid and Judicial Autonomy." *Review of International Organizations* 17: 691–715.

Armaly, Miles T. 2017. "Extra-Judicial Actor Induced Change in Supreme Court Legitimacy." *Political Research Quarterly* 71(4): 600–13.

Artiles, Alexandra, Martín Gandur, and Amanda Driscoll. 2021. "Los Estados (Des) unidos: Federalismo y Descentralizacion En Los Tiempos de Pandemia." In *Federalismo En Tiempos de COVID-19: Una Vision Comparada*, ed. Esteban Nader, Marie-Christine Fuchs, and Andres Villegas. Rule of Law Program for Konrad Adenauer Foundation; the Inter-American Institute of Parliamentary Law, pp. 278–317.

Asadu, Chinedu. 2023. "West Africa Court Refuses to Recognize Niger's Junta, Rejects Request to Lift Coup Sanctions." *AP News* 7 December. Available at https://apnews.com/article/niger-ecowas-coup-sanctions-court-abuja-9e168caebf71fa2c78a0f509b86cdb56.

Baird, Vanessa A. 2001. "Building Institutional Legitimacy: The Role of Procedural Justice." *Political Research Quarterly* 54(2): 333–54.

Baird, Vanessa A., and Debra Javeline. 2007. "The Persuasive Power of Russian Courts." *Political Research Quarterly* 60(3): 429–42.

Balogh, Eva. 2010. "A Legislative Proposal That Would Change the Composition of the Constitutional Court." *Hungarian Spectrum* 10 June. Available at https://hungarianspectrum.org/2010/06/10/a-legislative-proposal-that-would-change-the-composition-of-the-constitutional-court/.

Barabas, Jason, and Jennifer Jerit. 2010. "Are Survey Experiments Externally Valid?" *American Political Science Review* 104(2): 226–42.

Bárd, Petra. 2020. "The Rule of Law and Academic Freedom or the Lack of It in Hungary." *European Political Science* 19(1): 87–96.

Barrett, Andrew W., and Matthew Eshbaugh-Soha. 2007. "Presidential Success on the Substance of Legislation." *Political Research Quarterly* 60(1): 100–12.

Barro, Robert J. 1997. *Determinants of Economic Growth: A Cross-Country Empirical Study*. MIT Press.

Bartels, Brandon L., Jeremy Horowitz, and Eric Kramon. 2021. "Can Democratic Priniples Protect High Courts from Partisan Backlash? Public Reactions to the Kenyan Supreme Court's Role in the 2017 Election Crisis." *American Journal of Political Science* 67(3): 790–807.

Bartels, Brandon L., and Christopher D. Johnston. 2013. "On the Ideological Foundations of Supreme Court Legitimacy in the American Public." *American Journal of Political Science* 57(1): 184–99.

2020. *Curbing the Court: Why the Public Constrains Judicial Independence*. Cambridge University Press.

Bartels, Brandon L., and Eric Kramon. 2020. "Does Public Support for Judicial Power Depend on Who Is in Political Power? Testing a Theory of Partisan Alignment in Africa." *American Political Science Review* 114(1): 144–63.

Bartels, Brandon L., and Diana C. Mutz. 2009. "Explaining Processes of Institutional Opinion Leadership." *Journal of Politics* 71(1): 249–61.

Baum, Lawrence. 2003. "Judicial Elections and Judicial Independence: The Voter's Perspective." *Ohio State Law Journal* 64(1): 13–41.

2006. *Judges and Their Audiences: A Perspective on Judicial Behavior*. Princeton University Press.

Bayer, Lili. 2021. "Poland Lacks Judicial Independence Guarantees, Top EU Court Adviser Says." *Politico* 20 May. Available at www.politico.eu/article/poland-lacks-judicial-independence-eu-court-justice-advisor-says/.

BBC News. 2020. "SA Court Rules Lockdown Restrictions'Irrational'." *BBC News Online* 3 June. Available at www.bbc.com/news/world-africa-52904043.

2021a. "Poland Enforces Controversial Near-Total Abortion Ban." *BBC News Online* 28 January. Available at www.bbc.com/news/world-europe-55838210.

2021b. "COVID: Spain's Top Court Rules Lockdown Unconstitutional." *BBC News Online* 14 July. Available at www.bbc.com/news/world-europe-57838615.

Beardsley, Eleanor, and Rob Schmitz. 2021. "COVID-19 Surge Forces European Countries to Reintroduce Restrictions." *National Public Radio (NPR), Morning Edition* March 23. Available at www.npr.org/2021/03/23/980234512/covid-19-surge-forces-european-countries-to-reintroduce-restrictions.

Becher, Michael, and Sylvain Brouard. 2022. "Executive Accountability Beyond Outcomes: Experimental Evidence on Public Evaluations of Powerful Prime Ministers." *American Journal of Political Science* 66(1): 106–22.

Beim, Deborah, Alexander V. Hirsch, and Jonathan P. Kastellec. 2014. "Whistleblowing and Compliance in the Judicial Hierarchy." *American Journal of Political Science* 58(4): 904–18.

Benesh, Sara C. 2006. "Understanding Public Confidence in American Courts." *Journal of Politics* 68(3): 697–707.

Bennhold, Katrin, and Melissa Eddy. 2020. "Germany Bans Groups of More Than 2 to Stop Coronavirus as Merkel Self-Isolates." *New York Times* 22 March. Available at www.nytimes.com/2020/03/22/world/europe/germany-coronavirus-budget.html.

Bentsen, Henrik Litleré. 2019. "Dissent, Legitimacy, and Public Support for Court Decisions: Evidence from a Survey-Based Experiment." *Law & Society Review* 53(2): 588–610.

Bingham, Tom. 2011. *The Rule of Law*. Penguin Books.

Bishin, Benjamin G., Thomas J. Hayes, Matther B. Incantalupo, and Charles Anthony Smith. 2021. *Elite Led Mobilization and Gay Rights: Dispelling the Myth of Mass Opinion Backlash*. University of Michigan Press.

Boffey, Daniel, and Christian Davies. 2017. "Poland May Be Stripped of EU Voting Rights Over Judicial Independence." *The Guardian* 19 July. Available at www.theguardian.com/world/2017/jul/19/poland-may-lose-eu-voting-rights-over-judicial-independence.

Bolsen, Toby, and Thomas J. Leeper. 2013. "Self-Interest and Attention to News Among Issue Publics." *Political Communication* 30(3): 329–48.

Bolton, Alexander, and Sharece Thrower. 2021. *Checks in the Balance: Legislative Capacity and the Dynamics of Executive Power*. Princeton University Press.

Booth, John A., and Mitchell A. Seligson. 2009. *The Legitimacy Puzzle in Latin America: Political Support and Democracy in Eight Nations*. Cambridge University Press.

Bosen, Ralf, and Jens Thurau. 2021. "Chronology: How COVID Has Spread in Germany." *Deutsche Welle* 28 December. Available at www.dw.com/en/covid-how-germany-battles-the-pandemic-a-chronology/a-58026877.

Botero, Sandra. 2023. *Courts That Matter: Activists, Judges and the Politics of Rights*. Cambridge University Press.

Botero, Sandra, Daniel M. Brinks, and Ezequiel A. Gonzalez-Ocantos. 2022. *The Limits of Judicialization: From Progress to Backlash in Latin America*. Cambridge University Press.

Boudreaux, Donald J., and A. C. Pritchard. 1994. "Reassessing the Role of the Independent Judiciary in Enforcing Interest-Group Bargains." *Constitutional Political Economy* 5(1): 1–21.

Brady, Henry E., Sidney Verba, and Kay Lehman Schlozman. 1995. "Beyond SES: A Resource Model of Political Participation." *American Political Science Review* 89(2): 271–94.

Braman, Eileen. 2016. "Exploring Citizen Assessments of Unilateral Executive Authority." *Law & Society Review* 50(1): 189–223.

2021. "Thinking about Government Authority: Constitutional Rules and Political Context in Citizens' Assessments of Judicial, Legislative, and Executive Action." *American Journal of Political Science* 65(2): 389–404.

2023. *Constitutional Powers and Politics: How Citizens Think about Authority and Institutional Change*. University of Virginia Press.

Brecht, Arnold. 1949. "The New German Constitution." *Social Research* 16(4): 425–73.

Bricker, Benjamin. 2016. *Visions of Judicial Review: A Comparative Examination of Courts and Policy in Democracies*. ECPR Press.

2020. "The (Very) Political Dissent: Dissenting Opinions and the Polish Constitutional Crisis." *German Law Journal* 21(8): 1586–1605.

Brickman, Danette, and David A. M. Peterson. 2006. "Public Opinion Reaction to Repeated Events: Citizen Response to Multiple Supreme Court Abortion Decisions." *Political Behavior* 28(1): 87–112.

Brinks, Daniel M., and Abby Blass. 2018. *The DNA of Constitutional Justice in Latin America: Politics, Governance, and Judicial Design*. Cambridge University Press.

Broockman, David E., Joshua L. Kalla, and Sean J. Westwood. 2023. "Does Affective Polarization Undermine Democratic Norms or Accountability? Maybe Not." *American Journal of Political Science* 67(3): 808–28.

Brzozowski, Alexandra. 2019. "Human Rights Body Slams Poland for Lack of Judicial Independence." *Euractiv* 28 June. Available at www.euractiv.com/section/justice-home-affairs/news/human-rights-body-slams-poland-for-lack-of-judicial-independence/.

Burbank, Steven B., and Barry Friedman, eds. 2002. *Judicial Independence at the Crossroads: An Interdisciplinary Approach*. Sage Publications.

Burns, Nancy, Laura Evans, Gerald Gamm, and Corrine McConnaughy. 2008. "Pockets of Expertise: Institutional Capacity in Twentieth-Century State Legislatures." *Studies in American Political Development* 22(2): 229–48.

Butler, Daniel M., and Eleanor Neff Powell. 2014. "Understanding the Party Brand: Experimental Evidence on the Role of Valence." *Journal of Politics* 76(2): 492–505.

Çakir, Aylin Aydın. 2023. "The Varying Effects of Court Curbing: Evidence from Hungary and Poland." *Journal of European Public Policy* 31(5): 1179–1205.

Çakir, Aylin Aydın, and Eser Şekercioğlu. 2016. "Public Confidence in the Judiciary: the Interaction Between Political Awareness and Level of Democracy." *Democratization* 23(4): 634–56.

Caldeira, Gregory A. 1987. "Public Opinion and the U.S. Supreme Court: FDR's Court-Packing Plan." *American Political Science Review* 81(4): 1139–53.

Caldeira, Gregory A., and James L. Gibson. 1992. "The Etiology of Public Support for the Supreme Court." *American Journal of Political Science* 36(3): 635–64.

Calvert, Randall L. 1985. "The Value of Biased Information: A Rational Choice Model of Political Advice." *Journal of Politics* 47(2): 530–55.

Cameron, Charles M., and Sanford C. Gordon. 2023. "Fire Alarms and Democratic Accountability." In *Accountability Reconsidered: Voters, Interests, and Information in US Policymaking*, ed. Charles M. Cameron, Brandice Canes-Wrone, Sanford C. Gordon, and Gregory A. Huber. Cambridge University Press, pp. 221–41.

Canes-Wrone, Brandice, and Scott De Marchi. 2002. "Presidential Approval and Legislative Success." *Journal of Politics* 64(2): 491–509.

Cappelletti, Mauro. 1971. *Judicial Review in the Contemporary World*. Bobbs-Merrill Company.

Carey, John et al. 2022. "Who Will Defend Democracy? Evaluating Tradeoffs in Candidate Support Among Partisan Donors and Voters." *Journal of Elections, Public Opinion and Parties* 32(1): 230–45.

Carey, John M. 2000. "Parchment, Equilibria, and Institutions." *Comparative Political Studies* 33(6/7): 735–61.

Carey, John M. et al. 2019. "Party, Policy, Democracy and Candidate Choice in U.S. Elections." *Bright Line Watch*. Available at https://brightlinewatch.org/us-elections/.

Carey, John M., and Matthew Soberg Shugart, eds. 1998. *Executive Decree Authority*. Cambridge University Press.

Carlin, Ryan E. 2012. "Rule-of-Law Typologies in Contemporary Societies." *Justice System Journal* 33(2): 154–73.

Carlin, Ryan E., and Matthew M. Singer. 2011. "Support for Polyarchy in the Americas." *Comparative Political Studies* 44(11): 1500–26.

Carlin, Ryan E. et al. 2022. "Public Reactions to Noncompliance with Judicial Orders." *American Political Science Review* 116(1): 265–82.

Carnes, Nicholas. 2016. "Why Are There So Few Working-Class People in Political Office? Evidence from State Legislatures." *Politics, Groups, and Identities* 4(1): 84–109.

Carnes, Nicholas, and Noam Lupu. 2015. "What Good Is a College Degree? Education and Leader Quality Reconsidered." *Journal of Politics* 78(1): 35–49.

Carroll, Joseph. 2004. "Race and Education 50 Years After *Brown v. Board of Education*." *Gallup* 14 May. Available at https://news.gallup.com/poll/11686/race-education-years-after-brown-board-education.aspx.

Carrubba, Clifford J. 2005. "Courts and Compliance in International Regulatory Regimes." *Journal of Politics* 67(3): 669–89. Available at https://doi.org/10.1111/j.1468-2508.2005.00334.x.

2009. "A Model of the Endogenous Development of Judicial Institutions in Federal and International Systems." *Journal of Politics* 71(1): 55–69. Available at https://doi.org/10.1017/S002238160809004X.

Carrubba, Clifford J., and Matthew J. Gabel. 2015. *International Courts and the Performance of International Agreements: A General Theory with Evidence from the European Union*. Cambridge University Press.

Casper, Gerhard. 2001. "The Karlsruhe Republic – Keynote Address at the State Ceremony Celebrating the 50th Anniversary of the Federal Constitutional Court." *German Law*

Journal 2(18): E11. Available at www.germanlawjournal.com/index.php?pageID = 11& artID = 111.

Castro-Montero, José Luis, and Gijs Van Dijck. 2017. "Judicial Politics in Unconsolidated Democracies: An Empirical Analysis of the Ecuadorian Constitutional Court (2008–2016)." *Justice System Journal* 38(4): 380–98.

Centers for Disease Control and Prevention. 2021. "Delta Variant: What We Know about the Science." *National Center for Immunization and Respiratory Diseases. Division of Viral Diseases.* 6 August. Available at https://stacks.cdc.gov/view/cdc/108671.

Černušáková, Barbora. 2018. "Poland's Holocaust Law Is a Dangerous Threat to Free Speech." *Time* 3 March. Available at https://time.com/5193301/poland-holocaust-law-freedom-speech-amnesty/.

Cerulus, Laurens, and Adam Bouzi. 2021. "Court Orders Belgium to End Coronavirus Measures Due to Insufficient Legal Basis." *Politico* 31 March. Available at www.politico.eu/article/belgian-court-slaps-down-covid-19-measures-reports/.

Chávez, Rebecca Bill, John A. Ferejohn, and Barry R. Weingast. 2011. "A Theory of the Politically Independent Judiciary." In *Courts in Latin America*, ed. Gretchen Helmke and Julio Ríos-Figueroa. Cambridge University Press.

Cheibub, José Antonio, Zachary Elkins, and Tom Ginsburg. 2014. "Beyond Presidentialism and Parliamentarism." *British Journal of Political Science* 44(3): 515–44.

Chemerinsky, Erwin. 2001. "The Federalism Revolution." *New Mexico Law Review* 31(1): 7–30.

Cheruvu, Sivaram. 2019. "How Do Institutional Constraints Affect Judicial Decision-Making? The European Court of Justice's French Language Mandate." *European Union Politics* 20(4): 562–83.

2023. "Education, Public Support for Institutions, and the Separation of Powers." *Political Science Research and Methods* 11(3): 570–87.

Cheruvu, Sivaram, and Jay N. Krehbiel. 2022. "Delegation, Compliance, and Judicial Decision Making in the Court of Justice of the European Union." *Journal of Law and Courts* 10(1): 113–38.

2024. "Do Preliminary References Increase Public Support for European Law? Experimental Evidence from Germany." *International Organization* 78(1): 170–87.

Chewning, Taylor Kinsley, Bailey Johnson, Amanda Driscoll, Jay N. Krehbiel, and Michael J. Nelson. 2020. *COVID-19, Crises, and Public Support for the Rule of Law Teaching Modules.* Inter-University Consortium for Political and Social Research. Available at https://doi.org/10.3886/E120596V2.

Chewning, Taylor Kinsley, Amanda Driscoll, Martín Gandur, Jay N. Krehbiel, and Michael J. Nelson. 2025. "Preferences or Principles? The 'Noncompliance Penalty' and the Limits of Public Support for the Rule of Law." *Working Paper.* Available at http://bit.ly/3VVHEmC.

Chewning, Taylor Kinsley, Amanda Driscoll, Jay N. Krehbiel, and Michael J. Nelson. 2020. "Coronavirus Fatigue Is the Biggest Threat to Germany's Success Story in This Pandemic." *The Loop: ECPR's Political Science Blog.* Available at https://theloop.ecpr.eu/coronavirus-fatigue-is-the-biggest-threat-to-germanys-success-story-in-this-pandemic/.

Chiopri, Caterina, Monika Nalepa, and Georg Vanberg. 2023. "A Wolf in Sheep's Clothing: Citizen Uncertainty and Democratic Backsliding." Available at www.monikanalepa.com/uploads/6/6/3/1/66318923/chioprisnalepavanberg.pdf.

Christenson, Dino P., and David M. Glick. 2015a. "Chief Justice Roberts's Health Care Decision Disrobed: The Microfoundations of the Supreme Court's Legitimacy." *American Journal of Political Science* 59(2): 403–18.

2015b. "Issue-Specific Opinion Change: The Supreme Court and Health Care Reform." *Public Opinion Quarterly* 79(4): 881–905.

Christenson, Dino P., and Douglas L. Kriner. 2017a. "Constitutional Qualms or Politics as Usual? The Factors Shaping Public Support for Unilateral Action." *American Journal of Political Science* 61(2): 335–49.

2017b. "Mobilizing the Public Against the President: Congress and the Political Costs of Unilateral Action." *American Journal of Political Science* 61(4): 769–85.

2017c. "The Specter of Supreme Court Criticism: Public Opinion and Unilateral Action." *Presidential Studies Quarterly* 47(3): 471–94.

2019. "Does Public Opinion Constrain Presidential Unilateralism?" *American Political Science Review* 113(4): 1071–77.

2020a. "Beyond the Base: Presidents, Partisan Approval and the Political Economy of Unilateral Action." *Journal of Political Institutions and Political Economy* 1(1): 79–103.

2020b. *The Myth of the Imperial Presidency*. University of Chicago Press.

Chu, Jonathan A. and Scott Williamson. 2025. "Respect the Process: The Public Cost of Unilateral Action in Comparative Perspective." *Journal of Politics*. Available at https://doi.org/10.1086/730716.

Cienski, Jan. 2016. "Polish Judges Wrestle Warsaw Rulers." *Politico EU* 8 March. Available at www.politico.eu/article/polish-government-vs-judiciary-round-2/.

Claassen, Christopher. 2020. "Does Public Support Help Democracy Survive?" *American Journal of Political Science* 64(1): 118–34.

Clark, Chelsey S. et al. 2023. "Effects of a US Supreme Court Ruling to Restrict Abortion Rights." *Nature Human Behavior* 8(1): 63–71. Available at https://doi.org/10.1038/s41562-023-01708-4.

Clark, Tom S. 2009. "The Separation of Powers, Court Curbing, and Judicial Legitimacy." *American Journal of Political Science* 53(4): 971–89.

2010. *The Limits of Judicial Independence*. Cambridge University Press.

Clark, Tom S., and Jonathan P. Kastellec. 2015. "Source Cues and Public Support for the Supreme Court." *American Politics Research* 43(3): 504–35.

Clark, Tom S., Jeffrey K. Staton, Yu Wang, and Eugene Agichtein. 2018. "Using Twitter to Study Public Discourse in the Wake of Judicial Decisions: Public Reactions to the Supreme Court's Same-Sex-Marriage Cases." *Journal of Law and Courts* 6(1): 93–126.

Clark, Tom S., and Georg Vanberg. 2022. "Courts: A Historical Political Economy Perspective." In *The Oxford Handbook of Historical Political Economy*, ed. Jeffrey A. Jenkins and Jared Rubin. Oxford University Press, pp. C18S1–C18N6.

Clawson, Rosalee A., Elizabeth R. Kegler, and Eric N. Waltenburg. 2001. "The Legitimacy-Conferring Authority of the U.S. Supreme Court." *American Politics Research* 29(6): 566–91.

Clawson, Rosalee A., and Eric N. Waltenburg. 2009. *Legacy and Legitimacy: Black Americans and the Supreme Court*. Temple University Press.

Clayton, Katherine P. et al. 2021. "Elite Rhetoric Can Undermine Democratic Norms." *PNAS* 118(23): e2024125118. Available at https://doi.org/10.1073/pnas.2024125118.

Cohen, Mollie J., Amy Erica Smith, Mason W. Moseley, and Matthew L. Layton. 2023. "Winners' Consent? Citizen Commitment to Democracy When Illiberal Candidates Win Elections." *American Journal of Political Science* 67(2): 261–76.

Coleman, Justine. 2020. "All 50 States Under Disaster Declaration for the First Time in US History." *The Hill* 12 April. Available at https://thehill.com/policy/healthcare/public-global-health/492433-all-50-states-under-disaster-declaration-for-first.

Collings, Justin. 2015. *Democracy's Guardians: A History of the German Federal Constitutional Court 1951–2001*. Oxford University Press.

Collins, Paul M., Pamela C. Corley, and Jesse Hamner. 2015. "The Influence of Amicus Curiae Briefs on U.S. Supreme Court Opinion Content." *Law & Society Review* 49(4): 917–44.

Coppedge, Michael et al. 2023. "V-Dem Dataset V13." *Varieties of Democracy (V-Dem) Project*. Available at https://doi.org/10.23696/vdemds23.

Corder, Mike. 2021. "Dutch Govt Appeals Court Order to Scrap Coronavirus Curfew." *Associated Press* 16 February. Available at https://apnews.com/article/world-news-netherlands-coronavirus-pandemic-the-hague-92cf76ec9e318b6b5bd69954e2992b72.

Corrales, Javier. 2015. "The Authoritarian Resurgence: Autocratic Legalism in Venezuela." *Journal of Democracy* 26(2): 37–51.

Couloumbis, Angela, Jeremy Roebuck, Sarah Anne Hughes, and Justine McDaniel. 2020. "Wolf's COVID-19 Business Closures, Limit on Gatherings Unconstitutional, Federal Court Rules." *Philadelphia Inquirer* 14 September. Available at www.inquirer.com/health/coronavirus/spl/pa-coronavirus-business-closures-gathering-limits-unconstitutional-federal-court-20200914.html.

Council of Europe. 2016. "Opinion on Amendments to the Act of 25 June 2015 on the Constitutional Tribunal of Poland Adopted by the Venice Commission at Its 106th Plenary Session." Opinion No. 833/2015. Available at www.venice.coe.int/webforms/documents/?pdf=CDL-AD(2016)001-e.

Cruz, José Miguel. 2009. "Should Authorities Respect the Law When Fighting Crime." *AmericasBarometer Insights* 19: 1–8.

Dahl, Robert A. 1956. *A Preface to Democratic Theory*. University of Chicago Press.

1957. "Decision-Making in a Democracy: The Supreme Court as a National Policy-Maker." *Journal of Public Law* 6(Fall): 279–95.

Darmanin, Jules. 2021. "European Court Presses Poland to Take 'Rapid Action' on Judicial Independence." *Politico* 8 November. Available at www.politico.eu/article/poland-judicial-independence-european-court-human-rights-rapid-action/.

de Tocqueville, Alexis. 1835. *Democracy in America*. Trans. Henry Reeve. Saunders and Otley. Available at www.gutenberg.org/files/815/815-h/815-h.htm.

Denniston, Lyle. 2011. "Can the President Ignore Supreme Court Rulings?" *The Huffington Post* 18 December. Available at www.huffpost.com/entry/gingrich-supreme-court_b_1017418.

Desposato, Scott W. 2008. "Explaining Patterns of Oversight in Brazilian Subnational Governments." In *Legislative Oversight and Budgeting*, ed. Rick Stapenhurst, Riccardo Pelizzo, David M. Olson, and Lisa von Trapp. World Bank Institute, pp. 193–200.

Deutsche Welle. 2017. "Warsaw Takes Steps to Control NGO Funding." *Deutsche Welle* 16 September. Available at www.dw.com/en/polands-right-wing-government-takes-steps-to-control-ngo-funding/a-40535610.

Devlin, Kat, and Nicholas Kent. 2021. "As Pandemic Continues, More in U.S. and Europe Feel Major Impact on Their Lives." *Pew Research Report* 3 February. Available at www.pewresearch.org/global/2021/02/03/as-pandemic-continues-more-in-u-s-and-europe-feel-major-impact-on-their-lives/.

Diamantopoulos, Adamantios et al. 2012. "Guidelines for Choosing Between Multi-Item and Single-Item Scales for Construct Measurement: A Predictive Validity Perspective." *Journal of the Academy of Marketing Science* 40(3): 434–49.

Diamond, Larry. 2018. "The Liberal Democratic Order in Crisis." *The American Interest* 16 February. Available at www.the-american-interest.com/2018/02/16/liberal-democratic-order-crisis/.

Dressel, Björn. 2014. "Public Administration and the Rule of Law in Asia: Breadth Without Depth?" *Asia Pacific Journal of Public Administration* 36(1): 9–21.

Driscoll, Amanda, Aylin Aydın Çakir, and Susanne Schorpp. 2024. "Public (In)Tolerance of Government Non-Compliance with High Court Decisions." *Comparative Politics* 57(1): 71–90.

Driscoll, Amanda, and Martín Gandur. 2022. "Public Support and Compliance with High Courts Around the World." In *Research Handbook on Law and Political Systems*, ed. Robert Matthew Howard, Kirk Randazzo, and Rebecca Reid. Elgar Press, pp. 212–33.

Driscoll, Amanda, Jay N. Krehbiel, and Michael J. Nelson. 2020. "Once Lockdown Was over, Germans on Lower Incomes Went Out While Others Stayed at Home." *London School of Economics LSE COVID-19 Blog* 7 September. Available at https://blogs.lse.ac.uk/covid19/2020/09/07/once-lockdown-was-over-germans-on-lower-incomes-went-out-while-others-stayed-at-home/.

Driscoll, Amanda, Jay N. Krehbiel, Michael J. Nelson, and Sangyeon Kim. 2024. "The Consistency Principle: Crisis Perceptions, Partisanship and Public Support for Democratic Norms in Comparative Perspective." *European Journal of Political Research*. Available at https://doi.org/10.1111/1475-6765.12673.

Driscoll, Amanda, Jay N. Krehbiel, Michael J. Nelson, and Taran Samarth. 2023. "Evaluating Excuses: How the Public Judges Noncompliance." *Journal of Behavioral Public Administration* 6(1): 1–16. Available at https://doi.org/10.30636/jbpa.61.341.

Driscoll, Amanda, and Michael J. Nelson. 2012. "The 2011 Judicial Elections in Bolivia." *Electoral Studies* 31(3): 628–32.

2018a. "Democratic Values and Diffuse Support: Experimental Evidence from the United States." Paper Presented at the 2018 Meeting of the Southern Political Science Association, New Orleans, LA.

2018b. "There Is No Legitimacy Crisis: Support for Judicial Institutions in Modern Latin America." *Revista de la Sociedad Argentina de Análisis Político* 12(2): 361–77.

2019. "Chronicle of an Election Foretold: The 2017 Bolivian Judicial Elections." *Política y Gobierno* 26(1): 41–64.

2023a. "Are Courts 'Different?' Experimental Evidence on the Unique Costs of Attacking Courts." *Research & Politics* 10(3). Available at https://doi.org/10.1177/20531680231188302.

2023b. "The Costs of Court Curbing: Experimental Evidence from the United States." *Journal of Politics* 85(2): 609–24.

2024. "The Legibility of Court Reforms." Paper Presented at the 2024 Meeting of the Southern Political Science Association, New Orleans, LA.

Druckman, James N. 2001. "On the Limits of Framing Effects: Who Can Frame?" *Journal of Politics* 63(4): 1041–66.

Druckman, James N., and Arthur Lupia. 2000. "Preference Formation." *Annual Review of Political Science* 3: 1–24.

Dumenu, Mawusi Yaw, and Daniel Armah-Attoh. 2018. "Ghanaians Strongly Endorse Rule of Law but See Inequities in How Laws Are Applied." *AfroBarometer Dispatch* 194. Available at www.afrobarometer.org/publication/ad194-ghanaians-strongly-endorse-rule-law-see-inequities-how-laws-are-applied/.

Easton, David. 1953. *The Political System*. Alfred A. Knopf.

Easton, David, and Jack Dennis. 1969. *Children in the Political System: Origins of Political Legitimacy*. McGraw-Hill Book Company.

Eddy, Melissa. 2021. "Germany, Once a Model, Is Swamped Like Everyone Else by Pandemic's Second Wave." *New York Times* 2 February. Available at www.nytimes.com/2021/02/20/world/europe/germany-coronavirus-second-wave.html.

El Español. 2020. "Policías Negacionistas Convocan Una Protesta Contra Las Mascarillas y Las Restricciones Por El Virus." *El Español* 3 November. Available at www.elespanol.com/espana/20201103/policias-negacionistas-convocan-protesta-mascarillas-restricciones-virus/532948019_0.html.

Elkins, Zachary. 2010. "Diffusion and the Constitutionalization of Europe." *Comparative Political Studies* 43(8/9): 969–99.

Elkins, Zachary, and Tom Ginsburg. 2022. "Characteristics of National Constitutions, Version 4.0." *Comparative Constitutions Project*. Available at https://comparativeconstitutionsproject.org.

Elkins, Zachary, Tom Ginsburg, and James Melton. 2009. *The Endurance of National Constitutions*. Cambridge University Press.

Elkins, Zachary, and John Sides. 2007. "Can Institutions Build Unity in Multiethnic States?" *American Political Science Review* 101(4): 693–708.

Ellyat, Holly. 2021a. "Germany Considers a Full COVID Lockdown and Mandatory Vaccines." *CNBC.com* 24 November. Available at www.cnbc.com/2021/11/24/germany-considers-a-full-covid-lockdown-and-mandatory-vaccines.html.

2021b. "Germany's Vaccine Rollout Is Not Going to Plan, Frustrating Officials and Experts." *CNBC.com* 20 January. Available at www.cnbc.com/2021/01/19/germanys-vaccine-rollout-challenges-and-problems-in-vaccine-strategy.html.

Engst, Benjamin G. 2021. *The Two Faces of Judicial Power*. Springer.

Engst, Benjamin G., and Thomas Gschwend. 2021. "Citizens' Commitment to Judicial Independence: A Discrete Choice Experiment in Nine European Countries." Available at https://benjamin-engst.de/?p = 535.

Enyedi, Zsolt. 2018. "Democratic Backsliding and Academic Freedom in Hungary." *Perspectives on Politics* 16(4): 1067–74.

2022. "Academic Solidarity and the Culture War in Orbán's Hungary." *PS: Political Science & Politics* 55(3): 582–84.

Epp, Charles R. 1998. *The Rights Revolution: Lawyers, Activists and Supreme Courts in Comparative Perspective*. University of Chicago Press.

Epperly, Brad. 2019. *The Political Foundations of Judicial Independence in Dictatorship and Democracy*. Oxford University Press.

Epstein, Lee, Gunnar Grendstad, Urška Šadl, and Keren Weinshall. 2024. *Oxford Handbook of Comparative Judicial Behaviour*. Oxford University Press.

Epstein, Lee, and Jack Knight. 1998. *The Choices Justices Make*. CQ Press.

2018. "Efficacious Judging on Apex Courts." In *Comparative Judicial Review*, ed. Erin F. Delaney and Rosalind Dixon. Edgar Elgar Publishing, pp. 272–89.

Eurobarometer. 2023. "Standard Eurobarometer 98 – Winter 2022–2023." Available at https://europa.eu/eurobarometer/surveys/detail/2872.

European Parliament. 2022. "MEPs: Hungary Can No Longer Be Considered a Full Democracy." 15 September. Available at www.europarl.europa.eu/news/en/press-room/20220909IPR40137/meps-hungary-can-no-longer-be-considered-a-full-democracy.

Farganis, Dion. 2012. "Do Reasons Matter? The Impact of Opinion Content on Supreme Court Legitimacy." *Political Research Quarterly* 65(1): 206–16.

Fariss, Christopher J., and Geoff Dancy. 2017. "Measuring the Impact of Human Rights: Conceptual and Methodological Debates." *Annual Review of Law and Social Science* 13: 273–394.

Feld, Lars P., and Stefan Voigt. 2003. "Economic Growth and Judicial Independence: Cross-Country Evidence Using a New Set of Indicators." *European Journal of Political Economy* 19(3): 497–527.

Feldman, Noah. 2020. "Federal Judges Are Souring on Lockdown Orders." *Bloomberg Opinion* 16 September. Available at www.bloomberg.com/opinion/articles/2020-09-16/trump-appointed-judge-rules-covid-19-lockdown-unconstitutional.

Ferejohn, John A. 1998. "Independent Judges, Dependent Judiciary: Explaining Judicial Independence." *Southern California Law Review* 72(2/3): 353–384.

Ferejohn, John A., and Charles R. Shipan. 1990. "Congressional Influence on Bureaucracy." *Journal of Law, Economics, & Organization* 6: 1–20.

Fiedler, Tristan. 2022. "Liz Truss Now the Least-Popular UK Prime Minister in the History of Polling." *Politico.eu* 18 October. Available at www.politico.eu/article/uk-liz-truss-tories-least-popular-pm/.

Field, Oliver P. 1923. "Doctrine of Political Questions in the Federal Courts." *Minnesota Law Review* 8(6): 485–513.

Finkel, Jodi S. 2008. *Judicial Reform as Political Insurance: Argentina, Peru, and Mexico in the 1990s*. University of Notre Dame Press.

Fontana, David, and Donald Braman. 2012. "Judicial Backlash or Just Backlash? Evidence from a National Experiment." *Columbia Law Review* 112(4): 731–99.

Fontana, David, and Christopher N. Krewson. 2023. "The Costs of Policy Legitimation: A Test of the Political Capital Hypothesis." *Journal of Law and Courts* 11(2): 277–89.

Ford, Matt. 2018. "When the President Defies the Supreme Court." *The New Republic* 24 April. Available at https://newrepublic.com/article/148108/president-defies-supreme-court.

Fossati, Diego, Burhanuddin Muhtadi, and Eve Warburton. 2022. "Why Democrats Abandon Democracy: Evidence from Four Survey Experiments." *Party Politics* 28(3): 554–66.

Fox, Justin, and Matthew C. Stephenson. 2011. "Judicial Review as a Response to Political Posturing." *American Political Science Review* 105(2): 397–414.

Franklin, Charles H., and Liane C. Kosaki. 1989. "Republican Schoolmaster: The U.S. Supreme Court, Public Opinion and Abortion." *American Political Science Review* 83(3): 751–71.

Franzoi, Stephen L. 1996. *Social Psychology*. Brown & Benchmark.

Freedom House. 2021. "Poland: Freedom in the World 2021." Available at https://freedomhouse.org/country/poland/freedom-world/2021.

2023. *Freedom in the World 2023 the Annual Survey of Political Rights & Civil Liberties*. Freedom House. Available at https://freedomhouse.org/country/germany/freedom-world/2023.

Friedman, Barry. 2005. "The Politics of Judicial Review." *Texas Law Review* 84(2): 257–338.

Friedrich, Charles J. 1949. "Rebuilding the German Constitution, I." *The American Political Science Review* 43(3): 461–82.

Gadarian, Shana Kushner, Sara Wallace Goodman, and Thomas B. Pepinsky. 2022. *Pandemic Politics: The Deadly Toll of Partisanship in the Age of COVID*. Princeton University Press.

Gadarian, Shana Kushner, and Logan Strother. 2023. "Institutional Hybridity and Policy-Motivated Reasoning Structure Public Evaluations of the Supreme Court." *PLoS One* 18(11): e0294525. Available at https://doi.org/10.1371/journal.pone.0294525.

Gandhi, Jennifer. 2010. *Political Institutions Under Dictatorship*. Cambridge University Press.

Gandhi, Jennifer, and Adam Przworski. 2006. "Cooperation, Cooptation, and Rebellion Under Dictatorship." *Economics and Politics* 18(1): 1–26.

Gandur, Martín, Taylor Kinsley Chewning, and Amanda Driscoll. 2025. "Awareness of Executive Interference and Demand for Judicial Independence: Evidence from Four Constitutional Courts." *Journal of Law and Courts*. Forthcoming.

Gardbaum, Stephen. 2014. "Separation of Powers and the Growth of Judicial Review in Established Democracies (or Why Has the Model of Legislative Supremacy Motly Been Withdrawn from Sale?" *American Journal of Comparative Law* 62(3): 613–39.

Gárdos-Orosz, Fruzsina. 2012. "The Hungarian Constitutional Court in Transition – from Actio Popularis to Constitutional Complaint." *Acta Juridica Hungarica* 53(4): 302–15.

Garoupa, Nuno, and Tom Ginsburg. 2015. *Judicial Reputation: A Comparative Theory*. University of Chicago Press.

Garoupa, Nuno, Fernando Gomez-Pomar, and Veronica Grembi. 2013. "Judging Under Political Pressure: An Empirical Analysis of Constitutional Review Voting in the Spanish Constitutional Court." *The Journal of Law, Economics, & Organization* 29(3): 513–34.

Garoupa, Nuno, and Pedro C. Magalhães. 2021. "Public Trust in the European Legal Systems: Independence, Accountability and Awareness." *West European Politics* 44(3): 690–713.

Gash, Alison, and Michael H. Murakami. 2015. "Venue Effects: How State Policy Source Influences Policy Support." *Politics & Policy* 43(5): 679–722.

Gehrke, Laurenz. 2021a. "Citizens Blame EU and National Governments for Slow Coronavirus Vaccine Rollout: Poll." *Politico.com* 2 March. Available at www.politico.eu/article/coronavirus-vaccine-eu-slow-rollout-poll-kekst-cnc/.

2021b. "Coronavirus Restrictions Were Legal, German Top Court Rules." *Politico* 30 November. Available at www.politico.eu/article/coronavirus-rectrictions-legal-germany-top-court-rules/.

Gerber, Alan S., and Donald P. Green. 2012. *Field Experiments: Design, Analysis, and Interpretation*. W.W. Norton & Company.

German Constitutional Court. 2024. "The Court's Duties." Available at www.bundesverfassungsgericht.de/EN/Das-Gericht/Aufgaben/aufgaben_node.html.

German Ministry of Health. 2020. *National COVID-19 Vaccination Strategy: Strategy to Introduce and Evaluate a Vaccine Against Sars-CoV-2 in Germany*. Robert Koch Institute; Paul-Ehrlich Institute; Bundeszentrale fur gesundheitliche Aufklarung. Available at www.rki.de/EN/Content/infections/epidemiology/outbreaks/COVID-19/COVID-19_Vaccination_Strategy-Overview.pdf?__blob = publicationFile.

Gibler, Douglas M., and Kirk A. Randazzo. 2011. "Testing the Effects of Independent Judiciaries on the Likelihood of Democratic Backsliding." *American Journal of Political Science* 55(3): 696–709.

Gibson, James L. 1991. "Institutional Legitimacy, Procedural Justice, and Compliance with Supreme Court Decisions: A Question of Causality." *Law & Society Review* 25(3): 631–36.

2003. "Russian Attitudes Towards the Rule of Law: An Analysis of Survey Data." In *Law and Informal Practices: The Post-Communist Experience*, ed. Denis J. Galligan and Marina Kurkchiyan. Oxford University Press, pp. 77–91.

2007a. "Changes in American Veneration for the Rule of Law." *DePaul Law Review* 56(2): 593–614.

2007b. "The Legitimacy of the U.S. Supreme Court in a Polarized Polity." *Journal of Empirical Legal Studies* 4(3): 507–38.

2009. "'New-Style' Judicial Campaigns and the Legitimacy of State High Courts." *Journal of Politics* 71(4): 1285–1304.

Gibson, James L., and Gregory A. Caldeira. 1992. "Blacks and the United States Supreme Court: Models of Diffuse Support." *Journal of Politics* 54(4): 1120–45.

1995. "The Legitimacy of Transnational Legal Institutions: Compliance, Support, and the European Court of Justice." *American Journal of Political Science* 39(2): 459–89.

1996. "The Legal Cultures of Europe." *Law and Society Review* 30(1): 55–85.

2003. "Defenders of Democracy? Legitimacy, Popular Acceptance, and the South African Constitutional Court." *Journal of Politics* 65(1): 1–30.

2009. *Citizens Courts and Confirmations: Positivity Theory and the Judgments of the American People*. Princeton University Press.

Gibson, James L., Gregory A. Caldeira, and Vanessa A. Baird. 1998. "On the Legitimacy of National High Courts." *American Political Science Review* 92(2): 343–58.

Gibson, James L., Gregory A. Caldeira, and Lester Kenyatta Spence. 2003. "Measuring Attitudes Toward the United States Supreme Court." *American Journal of Political Science* 47(2): 354–67.

2005. "Why Do People Accept Public Politics They Oppose? Testing Legitimacy Theory with a Survey-Based Experiment." *Political Research Quarterly* 58(2): 187–201.

Gibson, James L., and Amanda Gouws. 1997. "Support for the Rule of Law in the Emerging South African Democracy." *International Social Science Journal* 58(2): 173–91.

Gibson, James L., Milton Lodge, and Benjamin Woodson. 2014. "Losing, But Accepting: Legitimacy, Positivity Theory, and the Symbols of Judicial Authority." *Law & Society Review* 48(4): 837–66.

Gibson, James L., and Michael J. Nelson. 2014. "The Legitimacy of the U.S. Supreme Court: Conventional Wisdoms, and Recent Challenges Thereto." *Annual Review of Law and Social Science* 10(1): 201–19.

2015. "Is the U.S. Supreme Court's Legitimacy Grounded in Performance Satisfaction and Ideology?" *American Journal of Political Science* 59(1): 162–74.

2017. "Reconsidering Positivity Theory: What Roles Do Politicization, Ideological Disagreement, and Legal Realism Play in Shaping U.S. Supreme Court Legitimacy?" *Journal of Empirical Legal Studies* 14(3): 592–617.

2018. *Black and Blue: How African Americans Judge the U.S. Legal System*. Oxford University Press.

2021. *Judging Inequality: State Supreme Courts and the Inequality Crisis*. Russell Sage Foundation.

Gibson, James L., Jeffrey Sonis, and Sokhom Hean. 2010. "Cambodians' Support for the Rule of Law on the Eve of the Khmer Rouge Trials." *International Journal of Transitional Justice* 4(3): 377–96.

Gidengil, Elisabeth, Dietlind Stolle, and Olivier Bergeron-Boutin. 2022. "The Partisan Nature of Support for Democratic Backsliding: A Comparative Perspective." *European Journal of Political Research* 61(4): 901–29.

Ginsburg, Tom. 2003. *Judicial Review in New Democracies: Constitutional Courts in Asian Cases*. Cambridge University Press.

2008. "The Global Spread of Constitutional Review." In *The Oxford Handbook of Law and Politics*, ed. Keith Whittington, R. Daniel Kelemen, and Keith E. Whittington. Oxford University Press, pp. 81–98.

2021. *Democracies and International Law*. Cambridge University Press.

Ginsburg, Tom, and Aziz Z. Huq. 2018. *How to Save a Constitutional Democracy*. University of Chicago Press.

Ginsburg, Tom, Aziz Z. Huq, and Mila Versteeg. 2018. "The Coming Demise of Liberal Constitutionalism." *University of Chicago Law Review* 85(2): 239–56.

Ginsburg, Tom, and Mila Versteeg. 2014. "Why Do Countries Adopt Constitutional Review?" *Journal of Law, Economics, & Organization* 30(3): 587–622.

2024. "Models of Constitutional Review." In *The Oxford Handbook of Comparative Judicial Behaviour*, ed. Lee Epstein, Gunnar Grendstad, Urška Šadl, and Keren Weinshall. Oxford Academic. Available at https://doi.org/10.1093/oxfordhb/9780192898579.013.2.

Glasser, Susan B. 2020. "Bob Woodward Finally Got Trump to Tell the Truth about COVID-19." *The New Yorker* 10 September. Available at www.newyorker.com/news/letter-from-trumps-washington/bob-woodward-finally-got-trump-to-tell-the-truth-about-covid-19.

González-Ocantos, Ezequiel, and Elias Dinas. 2019. "Compensation and Compliance: Sources of Public Acceptance of the U.K. Supreme Court's Brexit Decision." *Law & Society Review* 53(3): 889–919.

Gordon, Sanford C., and Gregory A. Huber. 2007. "The Effect of Electoral Competitiveness on Incumbent Behavior." *Quarterly Journal of Political Science* 2(2): 107–38.

Gowder, Paul. 2016. *The Rule of Law in the Real World*. Cambridge University Press.

Graber, Mark A. 1993. "The Nonmajoritarian Difficulty: Legislative Deference to the Judiciary." *Studies in American Political Development* 7(1): 35–73.

2004. "Resolving Political Questions Into Judicial Questions: Tocqueville's Thesis Revisited." *Constitutional Commentary* 21(2): 485–545.

Graham, Matthew H., and Milan W. Svolik. 2020. "Democracy in America? Partisanship, Polarization, and the Robustness of Support for Democracy in the United States." *American Political Science Review* 114(2): 392–409.

Grillo, Edoardo, and Carlo Prato. 2023. "Reference Points and Democratic Backsliding." *American Journal of Political Science* 67(1): 71–88.

Grosskopf, Anke, and Jeffrey J. Mondak. 1998. "Do Attitudes Toward Specific Supreme Court Decisions Matter? The Impact of *Webster* and *Texas v. Johnson* on Public Confidence in the Supreme Court." *Political Research Quarterly* 51(3): 633–54.

Grote, Rainer. 2014. "The German Rechtsstaat in a Comparative Perspective." In *The Legal Doctrines of the Rule of Law and the Legal State (Rechtsstaat)*, ed. James R. Silkenat, James E. Hickey Jr., and Peter D. Barenboim. Springer, pp. 193–207.

Grove, Tara Leigh. 2015. "The Lost History of the Political Question Doctrine." *New York University Law Review* 90(6): 1908–74.

Haggard, Stephan, Andrew MacIntyre, and Lydia Tiede. 2008. "The Rule of Law and Economic Development." *Annual Review of Political Science* 11: 205–34.

Haggard, Stephan, and Lydia Tiede. 2014. "The Rule of Law in Post-Conflict Settings: The Empirical Record." *International Studies Quarterly* 58(2): 405–17.

Haglin, Kathryn M., Soren Jordan, Alison Higgins Merrill, and Joseph Daniel Ura. 2021. "Ideology and Public Support for the Supreme Court." *Political Research Quarterly* 74(4): 955–69.

Hainmueller, Jens, Jonathan Mummolo, and Yiqing Xu. 2019. "How Much Should We Trust Estimates from Multiplicative Interaction Models? Simple Tools to Improve Empirical Practice." *Political Analysis* 27(2): 163–92.

Hamilton, Alexander, James Madison, and John Jay. 1787/1788. *The Federalist Papers*. Oxford University Press.

Hanley, John, Michael Salamone, and Matthew Wright. 2012. "Reviving the Schoolmaster: Reevaluating Public Opinion in the Wake of *Roe v. Wade*." *Political Research Quarterly* 65(2): 408–21.

Harding, Andrew, Peter Leyland, and Tania Groppi. 2008. "Constitutional Courts: Forms, Functions and Practice in Comparative Perspective." *Journal of Comparative Law* 3(1): 1–21.

Harvey, Cole J. 2022. "Can Courts in Nondemocracies Deter Election Fraud? De Jure Judicial Independence, Political Competition, and Election Integrity." *American Political Science Review* 116(4): 1325–39.

Hazelton, Morgan L. W., and Rachael K. Hinkle. 2022. *The Significance of Briefs in Judicial Decision-Making*. University of Kansas Press.

Hazelton, Morgan L. W., Rachael K. Hinkle, and Michael J. Nelson. 2023. *The Elevator Effect: Contact and Collegiality in the American Judiciary*. Oxford University Press.

Helmke, Gretchen. 2005. *Courts Under Constraints: Judges, Generals and Presidents*. Cambridge University Press.

2010a. "Public Support and Judicial Crises in Latin America." *University of Pennsylvania Journal of Constitutional Law* 13(2): 397–411.

2010b. "The Origins of Institutional Crises in Latin America." *American Journal of Political Science* 54(3): 737–50.

Helmke, Gretchen, Mary Kroeger, and Jack Paine. 2022. "Democracy by Deterrence: Norms, Constitutions, and Electoral Tilting." *American Journal of Political Science* 66(2): 434–50.

Helsinki Foundation for Human Rights. 2020. "Coronavirus COVID-19 Outbreak in the EU Fundamental Rights Implications: Poland." *European Union Agency for Fundamental Rights (FRA)* 8 April. Available at http://fra.europa.eu/sites/default/files/fra_uploads/poland-report-covid-19-april-2020_en.pdf.

Hestermeyer, Holger. 2020. "Coronavirus Lockdown-Measures Before the German Constitutional Court." *CounstitutionNet* 30 April. Available at https://constitutionnet.org/news/coronavirus-lockdown-measures-german-constitutional-court.

Hibbing, John R., and Elizabeth Theiss-Morse. 1995. *Congress as Public Enemy: Public Attitudes Toward American Political Institutions*. Cambridge University Press.

2001. "Process Preferences and American Politics: What the People Want Government to Be." *American Political Science Review* 95(1): 145–53.

Hillebrecht, Courtney. 2024. "Compliance with Judicial Decisions." In *The Oxford Handbook of Comparative Judicial Behaviour*, ed. Lee Epstein, Gunnar Grendstad, Urška Šadl, and Keren Weinshall. Oxford Academic, pp. 849–68. Available at https://doi.org/10.1093/oxfordhb/9780192898579.013.41.

Hirschl, Ran. 2004. *Towards Juristocracy: The Origins and Consequences of the New Constitutionalism*. Harvard University Press.

2008. "The Judicialization of Politics." In *The Oxford Handbook of Law and Politics*, ed. Keith E. Whittington, R. Daniel Kelemen, and Gregory A. Caldeira. Oxford University Press, pp. 119–41.

2024. "The Global Expansion of Judicial Power." In *The Oxford Handbook of Comparative Judicial Behaviour*, ed. Lee Epstein, Gunnar Grendstad, Urška Šadl, and Keren Weinshall. Oxford Academic. Available at https://doi.org/10.1093/oxfordhb/9780192898579.013.3.

Hoekstra, Valerie J. 1995. "The Supreme Court and Opinion Change: An Experimental Study of the Court's Ability to Change Opinion." *American Politics Quarterly* 23(1): 109–29.

Horowitz, Donald L. 2006. "Constitutional Courts: A Primer for Decision Makers." *Journal of Democracy* 17(4): 125–37.

Hovland, Carl Iver, and Walter Weiss. 1953. "The Influence of Source Credibility on Communication Effectiveness." *Public Opinion Quarterly* 15(4): 635–50.

Howard-Williams, Mara et al. 2022. "Association Between State-Issued COVID-19 Vaccine Mandates and Vaccine Administration Rates in 12 US States and the District of Columbia." *JAMA Health Forum* 3(10): e223810.

Howell, William G. 2003. *Power Without Persuasion: The Politics of Direct Presidential Action*. Princeton University Press.

Huber, John D. 1996. "The Vote of Confidence in Parliamentary Democracies." *American Political Science Review* 90(2): 269–82.

Hume, Robert J. 2012. "State Courts and Policy Legitimation: An Experimental Study of the Ability of State Courts to Change Opinion." *Publius* 42(2): 211–33.

Hutchings, Vincent L. 2005. *Public Opinion and Democratic Accountability: How Citizens Learn About Politics*. Princeton University Press.

Iaryczower, Matías, Pablo T. Spiller, and Mariano Tommasi. 2002. "Judicial Independence in Unstable Environments, Argentina 1935–1998." *American Journal of Political Science* 46(4): 699–716.

International Monetary Fund. 2023. "Israel: Staff Concluding Statement of the 2023 Article IV Mission." *International Monetary Fund* 10 May. Available at www.imf.org/en/News/Articles/2023/05/10/israel-staff-concluding-statement-of-the-2023-article-iv-mission.

Iyengar, Shanto et al. 2019. "The Origins and Consequences of Affective Polarization in the United States." *Annual Review of Political Science* 22: 129–46.

Iyengar, Shanto, and Donald R. Kinder. 1987. *News That Matters: Television and American Opinion*. University of Chicago Press.

Jackman, Robert W. 1985. "Cross-National Statistical Research and the Study of Comparative Politics." *American Journal of Political Science* 29(1): 161–82.

Jaschke, Philipp, Sekou Keita, Ehsan Vallizadeh, and Simon Kühne. 2023. "Satisfaction with Pandemic Management and Compliance with Public Health Measures: Evidence from a German Household Survey on the COVID-19 Crisis." *PLoS One* 18(2): e0281893.

Jasiewicz, Krzysztof, and Agnieszk Jasiewicz-Betkiewicz. 2022. "Poland: Political Developments and Data in 2021: The Democratic Backsliding Continues." *European Journal of Political Research Political Data Yearbook* 61(1): 362–73.

Jedrzejak, Piotr. 2022. "Heads Roll in Poland but Problems Remain as Flagship Tax Reform Falls Flat." *Emerging Europe* 16 February. Available at https://emerging-europe.com/news/heads-roll-in-poland-but-problems-remain-as-flagship-tax-reform-falls-flat/.

Johnson, Benjamin, and Keith E. Whittington. 2018. "Why Does the Supreme Court Uphold So Many Laws?" *University of Illinois Law School* 2018(3): 1001–48.

Johnson, Timothy R., and Andrew D. Martin. 1998. "The Public's Conditional Response to Supreme Court Decisions." *American Political Science Review* 92(2): 299–309.

Johnson, Timothy R., Paul J. Wahlbeck, and James F. Spriggs. 2006. "The Influence of Oral Arguments on the U.S. Supreme Court." *American Political Science Review* 100(1): 99–113.

Jordans, Frank. 2022. "Germany Says Pandemic Not over as Court OKs Vaccine Mandate." *AP News* 19 May. Available at https://apnews.com/article/covid-politics-health-germany-8b3412463cfbe9c2b48694e36372021c.

Kafura, Craig et al. 2020. "Global Public Opinion Shows Fear, Caution as COVID-19 Lockdowns Renew." *The Chicago Council on Global Affairs Blog* 12 November. Available at https://globalaffairs.org/commentary-and-analysis/blogs/global-public-opinion-shows-fear-caution-covid-19-lockdowns-renew.

Kalmoe, Nathan P., and Lilliana Mason. 2022. *Radical American Partisanship: Mapping Violent Hostility, Its Causes, and the Consequences for Democracy*. University of Chicago Press.

Kantorowicz, Jarosław, and Nuno Garoupa. 2016. "An Empirical Analysis of Constitutional Review Voting in the Polish Constitutional Tribunal, 2003–2014." *Constitutional Political Economy* 27(1): 66–92.

Kapiszewski, Diana, and Matthew M. Taylor. 2013. "Compliance: Conceptualizing, Measuring, and Explaining Adherence to Judicial Rulings." *Law & Social Inquiry* 38(4): 803–35.

Karnitschnig, Matthew. 2020. "Germans Being Germans About Coronavirus." *Politico EU* 29 April. Available at www.npr.org/2021/03/23/980234512/covid-19-surge-forces-european-countries-to-reintroduce-restrictions.

Karp, Paul. 2020. "High Court Rejects Legal Challenge Against Victoria's COVID Lockdown." *The Guardian* 5 November. Available at www.theguardian.com/law/2020/nov/06/high-court-rejects-legal-challenge-against-victorias-covid-lockdown.

Keith, Linda Camp. 2002. "Judicial Independence and Human Rights Protection Around the World." *Judicature* 85(4): 195–200.

Kelemen, R. Daniel, and Tommaso Pavone. 2023. "Where Have the Guardians Gone? Law Enforcement and the Politics of Supranational Forbearance in the European Union." *World Politics* 75(4): 779–825.

Kim, Dongwook, and Paul Nolette. 2024. "The Institutional Foundations of the Uneven Global Spread of Constitutional Courts." *Perspective on Politics* 22(1): 294–311.

Kommers, Donald P. 1994. "The Federal Constitutional Court in the German Political System." *Comparative Political Studies* 26(4): 470–91.

Kommers, Donald P., and Russell A. Miller. 2012. *The Constitutional Jurisprudence of the Federal Republic of Germany*. Duke University Press.

2008. "Das Bundesverfassungsgericht: Procedure, Practice and Policy of the German Federal Constitutional Court." *Journal of Comparative Law* 3(2): 194–211.

Kornai, János. 2015. "Hungary's U-Turn: Retreating from Democracy." *Journal of Democracy* 26(3): 34.

Kosar, David, and Katarina Sipulova. 2020. "How to Fight Court Packing?" *Constitutional Studies* 6(1): 133–64.

Kość, Wojciech. 2021. "Poles in Legal Jeopardy for Insulting President Duda." *Politico EU* 24 March. Available at www.politico.eu/article/poles-legal-jeopardy-insulting-president-andrzej-duda-poland-moron/.

Kotkamp, Lukas. 2021. "On Judicial Independence, Poland Slips Furthest in Global Ranking." *Politico* 18 November. Available at www.politico.eu/article/judicial-independence-poland-global-ranking/.

Kousser, Thad. 2005. *Term Limits and the Dismantling of State Legislative Professionalism*. Cambridge University Press.

Kovács, Kriszta. 2021. "Hungary and the Pandemic: A Pretext for Expanding Power." *Verfassungsblog* 11 March. Available at https://verfassungsblog.de/hungary-and-the-pandemic-a-pretext-for-expanding-power/.

Kovács, Kriszta, and Kim Lane Scheppele. 2018. "The Fragility of an Independent Judiciary: Lessons from Hungary and Poland – and the European Union." *Communist and Post-Communist Studies* 51(3): 189–200.

Krehbiel, Jay. 2019. "Elections, Public Awareness, and the Efficacy of Constitutional Review." *Journal of Law and Courts* 7(1): 53–79.

Krehbiel, Jay N. 2016. "The Politics of Judicial Procedures: the Role of Public Oral Hearings in the German Constitutional Court." *American Journal of Political Science* 60(4): 900–1005.

2021a. "Public Awareness and the Behavior of Unpopular Courts." *British Journal of Political Science* 51(4): 1601–19.

2021b. "Strategic Delay and the Use of Incompatibility Rulings at the German Constitutional Court." *The Journal of Politics* 83(3): 821–33.

2021c. "Do Voters Punish Noncompliance with High Courts? A Cross-National Analysis." *Politics* 41(2): 156–72.

Krehbiel, Jay N., and Sivaram Cheruvu. 2021. "The COVID-19 Pandemic and Public Support for European Integration: Evidence from Germany." *Journal of Political Institutions and Political Economy* 2(1): 63–80.

2022. "Can International Courts Enhance Domestic Judicial Review? Separation of Powers and the European Court of Justice." *The Journal of Politics* 84(1): 258–75.

Krehbiel, Keith. 1998. *Pivotal Politics: A Theory of U.S. Lawmaking*. University of Chicago Press.

Kreitzer, Rebecca J., Allison J. Hamilton, and Caroline J. Tolbert. 2014. "Does Policy Adoption Change Opinions on Minority Rights? The Effects of Legalizing Same-Sex Marriage." *Political Research Quarterly* 67(4): 795–808.

Krekó, Péter, and Zsolt Enyedi. 2018. "Orbán's Laboratory of Illiberalism." *Journal of Democracy* 29(3): 39–51.

Krewson, Christopher N., and Jean R. Schroedel. 2023. "The Gender Gap in Supreme Court Legitimacy." *American Politics Research* 51(6): 781–96.

Krishnarajan, Suthan. 2023. "Rationalizing Democracy: The Perceptual Bias and (Un) Democratic Behavior." *American Political Science Review* 117(2): 474–96.

Landau, David. 2012. "The Reality of Social Rights Enforcement." *Harvard International Law Journal* 53(1): 189–247.

Landes, William M., and Richard A. Posner. 1975. "The Independent Judiciary in an Interest-Group Perspective." *Journal of Law and Economics* 18(3): 875–901.

Landfried, Christine. 1992. "Judicial Policy-Making in Germany: The Federal Constitutional Court." *West European Politics* 15(3): 50–67.

LaPorta, Rafael, Florencio Lopez-de-Silanes, Andrej Shleifer, and Robert W. Vishny. 1998. "Law and Finance." *Journal of Political Economy* 106(6): 1–25.

Laurent, Pech, and Kim Lane Scheppele. 2017. "Illiberalism Within: Rule of Law Backsliding in the EU." *Cambridge Yearbook of European Legal Studies* 19: 3–47.

Lenz, Gabriel S. 2009. "Learning and Opinion Change, Not Priming: Reconsidering the Priming Hypothesis." *American Journal of Political Science* 53(4): 821–37.

2012. *Follow the Leader? How Voters Respond to Politicians' Policies and Performance*. University of Chicago Press.

Levitsky, Steven, and Daniel Ziblatt. 2018. *How Democracies Die*. Crown.

Lewis, David E. 2003. *Presidents and the Politics of Agency Design*. Stanford University Press.

Lijphart, Arend. 1999. *Patterns of Democracy*. Yale University Press.

Linz, Juan J. 1990. "The Perils of Presidentialism." *Journal of Democracy* 1(1): 51–69.

Linzer, Drew A., and Jeffrey K. Staton. 2015. "A Global Measure of Judicial Independence, 1948–2012." *Journal of Law and Courts* 3(2): 223–56.

Lipset, Seymour Martin. 1959. "Some Social Requisites of Democracy: Economic Development and Political Legitimacy." *American Political Science Review* 53(1): 69–105.

1963. *Political Man: The Social Basis of Politics*. Anchor Books.

Lipset, Seymour Martin, and William Schneider. 1987. *The Confidence Gap: Business, Labor, and Government in the Public Mind*. Revised Edition. JHU Press.

Liptak, Adam. 2020. "Splitting 5 to 4, Supreme Court Backs Religious Challenge to Cuomo's Virus Shutdown Order." *New York Times* 26 November. Available at www.nytimes.com/2020/11/26/us/supreme-court-coronavirus-religion-new-york.html.

Little, Eric, and Carolyn Logan. 2009. *The Quality of Democracy and Governance in Africa: New Results from Afrobarometer Round 4*. AfroBarometer.

Lupia, Arthur. 2002. "Who Can Persuade Whom? Implications from the Nexus of Psychology and Rational Choice Theory." In *Thinking About Political Psychology*, ed. James H. Kuklinski. Cambridge University Press, pp. 51–88.

2016. *Uninformed: Why People Know So Little About Politics and What We Can Do About It*. Oxford University Press.
Lupia, Arthur, and Mathew D. McCubbins. 1998. *The Democratic Dilemma: Can Citizens Learn What They Need to Know?* Cambridge University Press.
Lutig, Doreen, and J. H. H. Weiler. 2018. "Judicial Review in the Contemporary World – Retrospective and Prospective." *International Journal of Constitutional Law* 16(2): 315–72.
Madsen, Mikael Rask, Juan A. Mayoral, Anton Strezhnev, and Erik Voeten. 2022. "Sovereignty, Substance, and Public Support for European Courts' Human Rights Rulings." *American Political Science Review* 116(2): 419–38.
Maeda, Ko. 2010. "Two Modes of Democratic Breakdown: A Competing Risks Analysis of Democratic Durability." *Journal of Politics* 72(4): 1129–43.
Magalhães, Pedro C., and Nuno Garoupa. 2020. "Judicial Performance and Trust in Legal Systems: Findings from a Decade of Surveys in Over 20 European Countries." *Social Science Quarterly* 101(5): 1743–60.
Maier, Clara. 2019. "The Weimar Origins of the West German *Rechtsstaat*, 1919–1969." *The Historical Journal* 62(4): 1069–91.
Makowski, Marcin. 2022. "The Polish Deal: How a Landmark Tax Reform Has Turned Into a PR Disaster for the Government." *Notes from Poland* 23 January. Available at https://notesfrompoland.com/2022/01/23/the-polish-deal-how-a-landmark-tax-reform-has-turned-into-a-pr-disaster-for-the-government/.
Malleson, Kate, and Peter H. Russell, eds. 2006. *Appointing Judges in an Age of Judicial Power*. University of Toronto Press.
Malone, Mary Fran T. 2011. "Does Dirty Harry Have the Answer? Citizen Support for the Rule of Law in Central America." *Public Integrity* 13(1): 59–80.
Marshall, Thomas R. 1989. *Public Opinion and the Supreme Court*. Unwin Hyman.
Martin, Michelle. 2020. "German Institute Says Coronavirus Vaccinations Could Start in Early 2021." *Reuters.com* 19 August. Available at www.reuters.com/article/us-health-coronavirus-germany-vaccine/german-institute-says-coronavirus-vaccinations-could-start-in-early-2021-idUSKCN25F0HA.
Matějka, Filip, and Guido Tabellini. 2021. "Electoral Competition with Rationally Inattentive Voters." *Journal of the European Economic Association* 19(3): 1899–1935.
Matthews, Donald R. 1954. *The Social Background of Political Decision-Makers*. Random House.
Mavčič, Arne Marjan. 2018. *Constitutional Review Systems Around the World*. Concourts.net: European Law School to the New University of Ljubljana, Slovenia.
Mazepus, Honorata, and Dimiter Toshkov. 2022. "Standing up for Democracy? Explaining Citizens' Support for Democratic Checks and Balances." *Comparative Political Studies* 55(8): 1271–97.
McAllister, Jordan H., and Keith E. Schakenberg. 2022. "Designing the Optimal International Climate Agreement with Variability in Commitments." *International Organization* 76(2): 469–86.
McCann, Michael W. 1994. *Rights at Work: Pay Equity Reform and the Politics of Legal Mobilization*. University of Chicago Press.
McCoy, Jennifer, and Murat Somer. 2021. "Overcoming Polarization." *Journal of Democracy* 32(1): 6–21.
McCubbins, Mathew D., Roger G. Noll, and Barry R. Weingast. 1987. "Administrative Procedures as Instruments of Political Control." *Journal of Law, Economics, & Organization* 3(2): 243–77.

McCubbins, Mathew D., D. Rodriguez, and Barry R. Weingast. 2010. "The Rule of Law Unplugged." *Emory Law Journal* 59(6): 1455–94.

McCubbins, Mathew D., and Thomas Schwartz. 1984. "Congressional Oversight Overlooked: Police Patrols Versus Fire Alarms." *American Journal of Political Science* 28(1): 165–79.

McGuire, Kevin. 2004. "The Institutionalization of the U.S. Supreme Court." *Political Annalysis* 12(2): 128–42.

McMahon, Patrice. 2023. "Young, Female Voters Were the Key to Defeating Populists in Poland's Election – Providing a Blueprint to Reverse Democracy's Decline." *The Conversation* 31 October. Available at https://theconversation.com/young-female-voters-were-the-key-to-defeating-populists-in-polands-election-providing-a-blueprint-to-reverse-democracys-decline-216397.

Melton, James, and Tom Ginsburg. 2014. "Does de Jure Judicial Independence Really Matter? A Reevaluation of Explanations for Judicial Independence." *Journal of Law and Courts* 2(2): 187–217.

Meng, Anne, Jack Paine, and Robert Powell. 2023. "Authoritarian Power Sharing: Concepts, Mechanisms, and Strategies." *Annual Review of Political Science* 26: 153–73.

Miller, Gary J. 1992. *Managerial Dilemmas: The Political Economy of Hierarchy*. Cambridge University Press.

2005. "The Political Evolution of Principal-Agent Models." *Annual Review of Political Science* 8: 203–25.

Mok, Kenny, and Eric A. Posner. 2022. "Constitutional Challenges to Public Health Orders in Federal Courts During the COVID-19 Pandemic." *Boston University Law Review* 102(6): 1730–85.

Møller, Jørgen, and Svend-Erik Skaaning. 2012. "Systematizing Thin and Thick Conceptions of the Rule of Law." *Justice System Journal* 33(2): 174–94.

Mondak, Jeffrey J. 1992. "Institutional Legitimacy, Policy Legitimacy and the Supreme Court." *American Politics Quarterly* 20(4): 457–77.

1993. "Source Cues and Policy Approval." *American Journal of Political Science* 37(1): 186–212.

1994. "Policy Legitimacy and the Supreme Court: The Sources and Contexts of Legitimation." *Political Research Quarterly* 47(3): 675–92.

Mondak, Jeffrey J., and Shannon Ishiyama Smithey. 1997. "The Dynamics of Public Support for the Supreme Court." *Journal of Politics* 59(4): 1114–42.

Mooney, Christopher Z. 1995. "Citizens, Structures, and Sister States: Influences on State Legislative Professionalism." *Legislative Studies Quarterly* 20(1): 47–67.

Morris, Loveday, Luisa Beck, and Rick Noack. 2020. "Merkel Says Caronavirus Presents Gravest Crisis Since WWII." *Washington Post* 18 March. Available at www.washingtonpost.com/world/europe/germany-coronavirus-merkel/2020/03/18/9f34f2aa-6880-11ea-b199-3a9799c54512_story.html.

Moustafa, Tamir. 2007. *The Struggle for Constitutional Power: Law, Politics and Economic Development in Egypt*. Cambridge University Press.

2014. "Law and Courts in Authoritarian Regimes." *Annual Review of Law and Social Science* 10: 281–99.

Moustafa, Tamir, and Tom Ginsburg. 2008. "Introduction: The Functions of Courts in Authoritarian Politics." In *Rule by Law: The Politics of Courts in Authoritarian Regimes*, ed. Tom Ginsburg and Tamir Moustafa. Cambridge University Press, pp. 1–22.

Mummolo, Jonathan, and Erik Peterson. 2019. "Demand Effects in Survey Experiments: An Empirical Assessment." *American Political Science Review* 113(2): 517–29.

Mutz, Diana C. 2011. *Population-Based Survey Experiments*. Princeton University Press.

Nardulli, Peter F., Buddy Peyton, and Joseph Bajjalieh. 2013. "Conceptualizing and Measuring Rule of Law Constructs, 1850–2010." *Journal of Law and Courts* 1(1): 139–92.

Near, Janet P., and Marcia P. Miceli. 1995. "Effective Whistle-Blowing." *Academy of Management Review* 20(3): 679–708.

Nelson, Michael J., and Michael Burnham. 2024. "Judicial Elections and Judicial Behaviour." In *The Oxford Handbook of Comparative Judicial Behaviour*, ed. Lee Epstein, Gunnar Grendstad, Urška Šadl, and Keren Weinshall. Oxford Academic, pp. 371–96. Available at https://doi.org/10.1093/oxfordhb/9780192898579.013.19.

Nelson, Michael J., and Amanda Driscoll. 2023. "Accountability for Court Packing." *Journal of Law and Courts* 11(2): 290–311.

Nelson, Michael J., and Lee Epstein. 2022. "Human Capital in Court: The Role of Attorney Experience in US Supreme Court Litigation." *Journal of Law and Courts* 10(1): 61–85.

Nelson, Michael J., and James L. Gibson. 2019. "How Does Hyper-Politicized Rhetoric Affect the US Supreme Court's Legitimacy?" *Journal of Politics* 81(4): 1512–16.

Nelson, Michael J., Morgan L. W. Hazelton, and Rachael K. Hinkle. 2022. "How Interpersonal Contacts Affects Appellate Review." *Journal of Politics* 84(1): 573–77.

Nelson, Michael J., and Patrick Tucker. 2021. "The Stability and Durability of the U.S. Supreme Court's Legitimacy." *Journal of Politics* 83(2): 767–71.

Nelson, Michael J., and Alicia Uribe-McGuire. 2017. "Opportunity and Overrides: The Effect of Institutional Public Support on Congressional Overrides of Supreme Court Decisions." *Political Research Quarterly* 70(3): 632–43.

New York Times. 2023. "Tracking Abortion Bans Across the Country." *The New York Times* June 5 (Update). Available at www.nytimes.com/interactive/2022/us/abortion-laws-roe-v-wade.html.

Ngendakumana, Pierre Emmanuel. 2023. "Polish Abortion Verdict Violated Rights of Pregnant Woman, Human Rights Court Rules Polish Abortion Verdict Violated Rights of Pregnant Woman, Human Rights Court Rules." *Politico EU* 14 December. Available at www.politico.eu/article/poland-abortion-european-court-of-human-rights-verdict-fetal-anomaly/.

Nicholson, Stephen P., and Thomas G. Hansford. 2014. "Partisans in Robes: Party Cues and Public Acceptance of Supreme Court Decisions." *American Journal of Political Science* 58(3): 620–36.

Nienaber, Michael. 2021. "Germany's Top Court Upholds Night Curfews in COVID-19 Fight." *Reuters* 5 May. Available at www.reuters.com/world/europe/germany-looks-loosening-lockdown-covid-19-cases-fall-2021-05-05/.

North, Douglass C. 1990. *Institutions, Institutional Change and Economic Performance*. Cambridge University Press.

North, Douglass C., and Barry R. Weingast. 1989. "Constitutions and Commitment: The Evolution of Institutional Governing Public Choice in Seventeenth-Century England." *The Journal of Economic History* 49(4): 803–32.

Notes from Poland. 2021. "Poland Accelerates Timetable for Removing COVID Restrictions." *Notes from Poland* 12 May. Available at https://notesfrompoland.com/2021/05/12/poland-accelerates-timetable-for-removing-covid-restrictions/.

Organization for Security and Co-operation in Europe Office for Democratic Institutions and Human Rights. 2020. *Republic of Poland Presidential Election 28 June and 12 July 2020 ODIHR Special Election Assessment Mission Final Report*. Available at www.osce.org/files/f/documents/6/2/464601.pdf.

Orhan, Yunus Emre. 2022. "The Relationship Between Affective Polarization and Democratic Backsliding: Comparative Evidence." *Democratization* 29(4): 714–35.

Över, Defne. 2021. "Democratic Backsliding and the Media: The Convergence of News Narratives in Turkey." *Media, Culture, & Society* 43(2): 343–58.

Page, Benjamin I., Robert Y. Shapiro, and Glenn Dempsey. 1987. "What Moves Public Opinion?" *American Political Science Review* 81(1): 23–44.

Pancevski, Bojan. 2021. "COVID-19 Surge Prompts Renewed Lockdown in Parts of Europe." *Wall Street Journal* 18 November. Available at www.wsj.com/articles/covid-19-surge-prompts-renewed-lockdown-in-parts-of-europe-11637267293.

Parmet, Wendy, and Faith Khalik. 2023. "Judicial Review of Public Health Powers Since the Start of the COVID-19 Pandemic: Trends and Implications." *American Journal of Public Health* 113(3): 280–87.

Pavone, Tommaso, and Øyvind Stiansen. 2022. "The Shadow Effect of Courts: Judicial Review and the Politics of Preemptive Reform." *American Political Science Review* 116(1): 322–36.

Pech, Laurent, and R. Daniel Kelemen. 2020. "If You Think the U.S. Is Having a Constitutional Crisis, You Should See What Is Happening in Poland: Poland's Government and Supreme Court Are Engaged in an Epic Battle." *The Monkey Cage* 25 January. Available at www.washingtonpost.com/politics/2020/01/25/if-you-think-us-is-having-constitutional-crisis-you-should-see-what-is-happening-poland/.

Pepinsky, Thomas B. 2019. "The Return of the Single-Country Study." *Annual Review of Political Science* 22: 187–203.

Peréz-Liñán, Anibal, and Andrea Castagnola. 2009. "Presidential Control of High Courts in Latin America: A Long Term View." *Journal of Politics in Latin America* 1(2): 87–114.

2024. "Judicial Tenure and Retirements." In *The Oxford Handbook of Comparative Judicial Behaviour*, ed. Lee Epstein, Gunnar Grendstad, Urška Šadl, and Keren Weinshall. Oxford Academic. Available at https://doi.org/10.1093/oxfordhb/9780192898579.013.20.

Picheta, Rob, and Ivana Kottasová. 2020. "'You Don't Belong Here' in Poland's 'LGBT-Free Zones,' Existing Is an Act of Defiance." *CNN* 15 October. Available at www.cnn.com/interactive/2020/10/world/lgbt-free-poland-intl-scli-cnnphotos/.

Pirro, Andrea L. P., and Dániel Róna. 2019. "Far-Right Activism in Hungary: Youth Participation in Jobbik and Its Network." *European Societies* 21(4): 603–26.

Polish Government. 2020. "Kolejne Kroki w Walce z Koronawirusem – w Sklepie Mniej Osób, Ograniczenia w Poruszaniu Nieletnich, a Parki, Plaże i Bulwary Zamknięte." *gov.pl* 31 March. Available at https://archive.ph/20200331105508/https://www.gov.pl/web/koronawirus/kolejne-kroki.

Polish Helsinki Foundation for Human Rights. 2019. "HFHR Report: Poland Threatening Human Rights Protections." *Civil Liberties Union for Europe* 21 October. Available at www.liberties.eu/en/stories/hfhr-report-poland-threatening-human-rights-protections/17781.

Polsby, Nelson W. 1968. "The Institutionalization of the U.S. House of Representatives." *American Political Science Review* 62(1): 114–68.

Popkin, Samuel L. 1994. *The Reasoning Voter: Communication and Persuasion in Presidential Campaigns*, 2nd ed. University of Chicago Press.

Potter, Philip B. K., and Matthew A. Baum. 2014. "Looking for Audience Costs in All the Wrong Places: Electoral Institutions, Media Access, and Democratic Constraint." *Journal of Politics* 76(1): 167–81.

Powell, Emilia J., and Jeffrey K. Staton. 2009. "Domestic Judicial Institutions and Human Rights Treaty Violation." *International Studies Quarterly* 53(1): 148–74.

Powell Jr, G. Bingham. 2004. "The Chain of Responsiveness." *Journal of Democracy* 15(4): 91–105.

Pozen, David E., and Kim Lane Scheppele. 2020. "Executive Underreach, in Pandemics and Otherwise." *American Journal of International Law* 114(4): 608–17.

Putnam, Robert. 1993. *Making Democracy Work*. Princeton University Press.

Raifman, Julia et al. 2020. "COVID-19 US State Policy Database." *Inter-University Consortium for Political and Social Research* 15 September. Available at https://doi.org/10.3886/E119446V30.

Rakove, Jack. 1997. *Original Meanings*. Vintage Press.

Ramseyer, J. Mark. 1994. "The Puzzling (In)dependence of Courts: A Comparative Approach." *Journal of Legal Studies* 23(2): 721.

Reenock, Christopher, Jeffrey K. Staton, and Marius Radean. 2013. "Legal Institutions and Democratic Survival." *Journal of Politics* 75(2): 491–505.

Reeves, Andrew, and Jon C. Rogowski. 2015. "Public Opinion Toward Presidential Power." *Presidential Studies Quarterly* 45(4): 742–59.

2016. "Unilateral Powers, Public Opinion, and the Presidency." *Journal of Politics* 78(1): 137–51. Available at https://doi.org/10.1086/683433.

2018. "The Public Cost of Unilateral Action." *American Journal of Political Science* 62(2): 424–40.

2022a. *No Blank Check: The Origins and Consequences of Public Antipathy Towards Presidential Power*. Cambridge University Press.

2022b. "Unilateral Inaction: Congressional Gridlock, Interbranch Conflict, and Public Evaluations of Executive Power." *Legislative Studies Quarterly* 47(2): 427–57.

2023. "Democratic Values and Support for Executive Power." *Presidential Studies Quarterly* 53(2): 293–312.

Reuters. 2020. "Polish Government Considers Law Forcing NGOs to Declare Foreign Funding." *Reuters* 11 May. Available at www.reuters.com/article/poland-ngos-idUSL8N2CT53C.

Reuters Staff. 2020a. "Court Overturns Local Lockdown on German Slaughterhouse Town." *Reuters* 6 July. Available at www.reuters.com/article/us-health-coronavirus-germany-meat-guete/court-overturns-local-lockdown-on-german-slaughterhouse-town-idUSKBN2472BW.

2020b. "Poland's Coronavirus Restrictions Extend Towards Election Date." *Reuters* 9 April. Available at www.reuters.com/article/us-health-coronavirus-poland-restriction/polands-coronavirus-restrictions-extended-towards-election-date-idUSKCN21R1SQ.

2023. "German Foreign Minister Concerned about Judicial Independence in Israel." *Reuters* 28 February. Available at www.reuters.com/world/german-foreign-minister-concerned-about-judicial-independence-israel-2023-02-28/.

Ríos-Figueroa, Julio. 2007. "Fragmentation of Power and the Emergence of an Effective Judiciary in Mexico, 1994–2002." *Latin American Politics and Society* 49(1): 31–57.

Ríos-Figueroa, Julio, and Jeffrey K. Staton. 2009. "Summary: Unpacking the Rule of Law." *Comparative Politics Newsletter* 20(1): 22–26.

2014. "An Evaluation of Cross-National Measures of Judicial Independence." *Journal of Law, Economics & Organization* 30(1): 104–34.

Rogers, James R. 2001. "Information and Judicial Review: A Signaling Game of Legislative-Judicial Interaction." *American Journal of Political Science* 45(1): 84–99.

Romeu, Francisco Ramos. 2006. "The Establishment of Constitutional Courts: A Study of 128 Democratic Constitutions. *Review of Law and Economics* 2(1): 103–35.
Rose-Ackerman, Susan. 2010. "The Law and Economics of Bribery and Extortion." *Annual Review of Law and Social Science* 6: 217–38.
Rosenberg, Gerald N. 2008. *The Hollow Hope: Can Courts Bring about Social Change?* 2nd ed. University of Chicago Press.
Rueters. 2020. "Poland Tightens Public Life Restrictions Against Coronavirus." *Reuters.com* 30 March. Available at www.reuters.com/article/health-coronavirus-poland-restrictions/refile-poland-tightens-public-life-restrictions-against-coronavirus-idUKW8N2AY01F.
Sadurski, Wojciech. 2019. "Polish Constitutional Tribunal Under PiS: From an Activist Court, to a Paralysed Tribunal, to a Governmental Enabler." *Hague Journal on the Rule of Law* 11(1): 63–84.
Saikkonen, Inga A.-L., and Henrik Serup Christensen. 2022. "Guardians of Democracy or Passive Bystanders? A Conjoint Experiment on Elite Transgressions of Democratic Norms." *Political Research Quarterly* 76(1): 127–42.
Sances, Michael W. 2017. "Attribution Errors in Federalist Systems: When Voters Punish the President for Local Tax Increases." *Journal of Politics* 79(4): 1286–1301.
Şaşmaz, Aytuğ, Alper H. Yagci, and Daniel Ziblatt. 2022. "How Voters Respond to Presidential Assaults on Checks and Balances: Evidence from a Survey Experiment in Turkey." *Comparative Political Studies* 55(11): 1947–80.
Scheer, Steven. 2023. "Israel's Cenbank Urges Judicial Independence, Sees More Rate Hikes." *Reuters* 15 March. Available at www.reuters.com/world/middle-east/israels-cenbank-chief-sees-more-rate-hikes-critical-judicial-reforms-2023-03-15/.
Schelling, Thomas C. 1960. *The Strategy of Conflict*. Harvard University Press.
Scheppele, Kim Lane, Miklos Bankuti, and Gabor Halmai. 2012. "Hungary's Illiberal Turn: Disabling the Constitution." *Journal of Democracy* 23(3): 138–46.
Schepple, Kim Lane. 2018. "Autocratic Legalism." *The University of Chicago Law Review* 85(2): 545–84.
Schmitter, Philippe C. 2009. "The Nature and Future of Comparative Politics." *European Political Science Review* 1(1): 33–61.
Schroeder, Phillipp. 2022. "Pushing Boundaries: How Lawmakers Shape Judicial Decision-Making." *Comparative Political Studies* 55(14): 2447–79.
Schuetze, Christopher. 2022. "A German State Is Last in Almost Everything. But It's No. 1 in Vaccines." *New York Times* 12 April. Available at www.nytimes.com/2022/04/12/world/europe/germany-covid-vaccine-strategy.html.
Schwartz, Alex. 2024. "Threats to Judicial Independence." In *The Oxford Handbook of Comparative Judicial Behaviour*, ed. Lee Epstein, Gunnar Grendstad, Urška Šadl, and Keren Weinshall. Oxford Academic. Available at https://doi.org/10.1093/oxfordhb/9780192898579.013.47.
Schwartz, Herman. 2000. *The Struggle for Constitutional Justice in Post-Communist Europe*. University of Chicago Press.
Sears, David O. 1986. "College Sophomores in the Laboratory: Influences of a Narrow Data Base on Social Psychology's View of Human Nature." *Journal of Personality and Social Psychology* 51(3): 515–30.
Shapiro, Martin M. 1988. *Who Guards the Guardians? Judicial Control of Administration*. University of Georgia Press.
1999. "The Success of Judicial Review." In *Constitutional Dialogues in Comparative Perspective*, ed. S. Kenny, W. Wieseinger, and J. Reitz. St. Martin's Press.

Shipan, Charles R. 2000. "Legislative Design of Judicial Review." *Journal of Theoretical Politics* 12(3): 269–304.
Shklar, Judith N. 1998. *Political Thought and Political Thinkers*. University of Chicago Press.
Shugart, Matthew Soberg, and John M. Carey. 1992. *Presidents and Assemblies: Constitutional Design and Electoral Dynamics*. Cambridge University Press.
Simonovits, Gabor, Jennifer McCoy, and Levente Littvay. 2022. "Democratic Hypocrisy and Out-Group Threat: Explaining Citizen Support for Democratic Erosion." *Journal of Politics* 84(3): 1806–11.
Singh, Shane P., and Ryan E. Carlin. 2015. "Happy Medium, Happy Citizens: Presidential Power and Democratic Regime Support." *Political Research Quarterly* 68(1): 3–17.
Smith, Mitch, and Ava Sasani. 2022. "Michigan, California and Vermont Affirm Abortion Rights in Ballot Proposals." *New York Times* 10 November. Available at www.nytimes.com/2022/11/09/us/abortion-rights-ballot-proposals.html.
Smithey, Shannon I., and Mary Fran T. Malone. 2013. "Crime and Public Support for the Rule of Law in Latin America and Africa." *African Journal of Legal Studies* 6(2–3): 153–69.
Smithey, Shannon Ishiyama, and John Ishiyama. 2000. "Judicious Choices: Designing Courts in Postcommunist Politics." *Communist and Post-Communist Studies* 33(2): 163–82.
Smyth, Russell. 2024. "Public Opinion and Legitimacy." In *The Oxford Handbook of Comparative Judicial Behaviour*, ed. Lee Epstein, Gunnar Grendstad, Urška Šadl, and Keren Weinshall. Oxford Academic, pp. 803–28. Available at https://doi.org/10.1093/oxfordhb/9780192898579.013.39.
Sólyom, László. 2003. "The Role of Constitutional Courts in the Transition to Democracy: With Special Reference to Hungary." *International Sociology* 18(1): 133–61.
Spring, Marianna. 2021. "COVID-19: How Did a Volunteer Panel React When We Showed Them an Anti-Vax Video?" *BBC News Online* 14 February. Available at www.bbc.com/news/blogs-trending-56047409.
Squire, Peverill. 1992. "Legislative Professionalization and Membership Diversity in State Legislatures." *Legislative Studies Quarterly* 17(1): 69–79.
2008. "Measuring the Professionalization of U.S. State Courts of Last Resort." *State Politics & Policy Quarterly* 8(3): 223–38.
Staton, Jeffery K. 2004. "Judicial Policy Implementation in Mexico City and Mérida." *Comparative Politics* 37(1): 41–60.
2006. "Constitutional Review and the Selective Promotion of Case Results." *American Journal of Political Science* 50(1): 98–112.
2010. *Judicial Power and Strategic Communication in Mexico*. Cambridge University Press.
Staton, Jeffery K., and Georg Vanberg. 2008. "The Value of Vagueness: Delegation, Defiance, and Judicial Opinions." *American Journal of Political Science* 52(3): 504–19.
Staton, Jeffrey K., and Will H. Moore. 2011. "Judicial Power in Domestic and International Politics." *International Organization* 65(3): 553–87.
Staton, Jeffrey K., Christopher Reenock, and Jordan Holsinger. 2022. *Can Courts Be Bulwarks of Democracy? Judges and the Politics of Prudence*. Cambridge University Press.
Stephenson, Matthew C. 2003. "'When the Devil Turns…': The Political Foundations of Independent Judicial Review." *The Journal of Legal Studies* 32(1): 59–89.
2004. "Court of Public Opinion: Government Accountability and Judicial Independence." *Journal of Law, Economics, & Organization* 20(2): 379–99.
Sternberg, Sebastian, Sylvain Brouard, and Christoph Hönnige. 2021. "The Legitimacy-Conferring Capacity of Constitutional Courts: Evidence from a Comparative Survey Experiment." *European Journal of Political Research* 61(4): 973–96.

Stiers, Dieter. 2021. "Political Information and Retrospective Voting." *West European Politics* 44(2): 275–98.

Stone, Alec. 1992. *The Birth of Judicial Politics in France: The Constitutional Council in Comparative Perspective*. Oxford University Press.

Stone Sweet, Alec. 1998. "A Comment on Vanberg: Rules, Dispute Resolution, and Strategic Behavior." *Journal of Theoretical Politics* 10(3): 327–38.

2012. "Constitutional Courts." In *Oxford Handbook of Comparative Constitutional Law*, ed. Michel Rosenfeld and András Sajó, pp. 816–30.

Stoutenborough, James W., Donald P. Haider-Markel, and Mahalley D. Allen. 2006. "Re-Assessing the Impact of Supreme Court Decisions on Public Opinion: Gay Civil Rights Cases." *Political Research Quarterly* 59(3): 419–33.

Sunstein, Cass. 1989. "On the Costs and Benefits of Aggressive Judicial Review of Agency Action." *Duke Law Journal* 1989(3): 522–37.

Sutter, Daniel. 1997. "Enforcing Constitutional Constraints." *Constitutional Political Economy* 8(2): 139–50.

Svolik, Milan. 2012. *The Politics of Authoritarian Rule*. Cambridge University Press.

2019. "Polarization Versus Democracy." *Journal of Democracy* 30(3): 20–32.

2020. "When Polarization Trumps Civic Virtue: Partisan Conflict and the Subversion of Democracy by Incumbents." *Quarterly Journal of Political Science* 15(1): 3–31.

Taiwo, Olufemi. 1999. "The Rule of Law: The New Leviathan?" *Canadian Journal of Law & Jurisprudence* 12(1): 151–68.

Tamanaha, Brian Z. 2004. *On the Rule of Law: History, Politics, Theory*. Cambridge University Press.

Tarr, G. Alan. 2012. *Without Fear or Favor: Judicial Independence and Judicial Accountability in the States*. Stanford University Press.

Tavits, Margit. 2007. "Clarity of Responsibility and Corruption." *American Journal of Political Science* 51(1): 218–29.

Terrel, Raúl. 2020. "Froilán Se Salta a La Torera Las Medidas Contra El COVID-19." *El Periódico* 4 November. Available at www.elperiodico.com/es/gente/20201104/froilan-pasea-amigos-sin-mascarilla-incumple-medidas-sanitarias-contra-covid-8189167.

Than, Krisztina, and Marton Dunai. 2013. "Hungary, Defying EU, Limits Power of Top Court." *Reuters* 12 March. Available at www.reuters.com/article/idUSBRE92B0ON/.

Tharoor, Ishaan. 2020. "Poland's Narrow Election Has Big Consequences for Its Democratic Future." *Washington Post* 15 July. Available at www.washingtonpost.com/world/2020/07/15/poland-election-duda-trump/.

Thompson, Jack. 2022. "Attitudes Towards LGBT Individuals After *Bostock v. Clayton County*: Evidence from a Quasi Experiment." *Political Research Quarterly* 75(4): 1374–85.

Thurau, Jens. 2022. "Vaccine Mandate: A Political Disaster." *Deutsche Welle* 10 April. Available at www.dw.com/en/opinion-germanys-vaccine-mandate-was-a-disaster-in-the-making/a-61421424.

Tiede, Lydia Brashear. 2022. *Judicial Vetoes Decision-Making on Mixed Selection Constitutional Courts*. Cambridge University Press.

2024. "Selecting Judges." In *The Oxford Handbook of Comparative Judicial Behaviour*, ed. Lee Epstein, Gunnar Grendstad, Urška Šadl, and Keren Weinshall. Oxford Academic, pp. 347–70. Available at https://doi.org/10.1093/oxfordhb/9780192898579.013.18.

Tilles, Daniel. 2021. "Ban on Gatherings During Pandemic Was Unlawful, Rules Polish Supreme Court." *Notes from Poland* 6 July. Available at https://notesfrompoland.com/2021/07/06/ban-on-gatherings-during-pandemic-was-unlawful-rules-polish-supreme-court/.

Tóth, Csaba. 2014. "Full Text of Viktor Orbán's Speech at băile Tuşnad (Tusnádfürdő) of 26 July 2014." *The Budapest Beacon*. Available at https://budapestbeacon.com/full-text-of-viktor-orbans-speech-at-baile-tusnad-tusnadfurdo-of-26-july-2014/.

Tsebelis, George. 2011. *Veto Players*. Princeton University Press.

Türk, Volker. 2023. "Comment by UN Human Rights Chief Volker Türk on Recent Developments in Israel." *United Nations Office of the High Commissioner for Human Rights* 27 July. Available at www.ohchr.org/en/statements-and-speeches/2023/07/comment-un-human-rights-chief-volker-turk-recent-developments.

Turner, Ian R. 2017. "Working Smart and Hard? Agency Effort, Judicial Review and Policy Precision." *Journal of Theoretical Politics* 29(1): 69–96.

Tyler, Tom R. 1988. "What Is Procedural Justice? Criteria Used by Citizens to Assess the Fairness of Legal Procedures." *Law & Society Review* 22(1): 103–35.

2003. "Procedural Justice, Legitimacy, and the Effective Rule of Law." *Crime and Justice* 30: 283–357.

Ura, Joseph Daniel. 2014. "Backlash and Legitimation: Macro Political Responses to Supreme Court Decisions." *American Journal of Political Science* 58(1): 110–26.

Vallinder, Torbjörn, and Chester Neal Tate. 1995. *The Global Expansion of Judicial Power*. New York University Press.

van Dijk, Frans. 2024. "Conceptualizing and Measuring Judicial Independence." In *The Oxford Handbook of Comparative Judicial Behaviour*, ed. Lee Epstein, Gunnar Grendstad, Urška Šadl, and Keren Weinshall. Oxford Academic, pp. 775–800. Available at https://doi.org/10.1093/oxfordhb/9780192898579.013.38.

Vanberg, Georg. 1998a. "Abstract Judicial Review, Legislative Bargaining, and Policy Compromise." *Journal of Theoretical Politics* 10(3): 299.

1998b. "Reply to Stone Sweet." *Journal of Theoretical Politics* 10(3): 339–46.

2000. "Establishing Judicial Independence in Western Europe: The Impact of Opinion Leadership and the Separation of Powers." *Comparative Politics* 32(3): 333–53.

2001. "Legislative-Judicial Relations: A Game-Theoretic Approach to Constitutional Review." *American Journal of Political Science* 45(2): 346–61.

2005. *The Politics of Constitutional Review in Germany*. Cambridge University Press.

2008. "Establishing and Maintaining Judicial Independence." In *The Oxford Handbook of Law and Politics*, ed. Gregory A. Caldeira, R. Daniel Kelemen, and Keith E. Whittington. Oxford University Press, pp. 99–118.

2011. "Substance vs. Procedure: Constitutional Enforcement and Constitutional Choice." *Journal of Economic Behavior & Organization* 80: 309–18.

2015. "Constitutional Courts in Comparative Perspective: A Theoretical Assessment." *Annual Review of Political Science* 18: 167–85.

2020. "Judicialization and the Political Executive." In *The Oxford Handbook of Political Executives*, ed. Rudy B. Andeweg et al. Oxford University Press, pp. 566–87.

Várnagy, Réka. 2022. "Hungary: Political Developments and Data in 2021." *European Journal of Political Research Political Data Yearbook* 61(1): 206–13.

Varol, Ozan. 2015. "Stealth Authoritarianism." *Iowa Law Review* 100(4): 1673–1742.

Vigdor, Neil. 2020. "Wisconsin Supreme Court Strikes down Stay-at-Home Order." *New York Times* 13 May. Available at www.nytimes.com/2020/05/13/us/coronavirus-wisconsin-supreme-court.html.

Voeten, Erik. 2008. "The Impartiality of International Judges: Evidence from the European Court of Human Rights." *American Political Science Review* 102(4): 417–33.

2020. "Populism and Backlashes Against International Courts." *Perspectives on Politics* 18(2): 407–22.

Volcansek, Mary L. 1994. "Political Power and Judicial Review in Italy." *Comparative Political Studies* 26(4): 492–509.

Vuković, Danilo, and Slobodan Cvejić. 2014. "Legal Culture in Contemporary Serbia: Structural Analysis of Attitudes Towards the Rule of Law." *Početna* 62(3): 52–73.

Walker, Lee Demetrius. 2009. "Delegative Democratic Attitudes and Institutional Support in Central America." *Comparative Politics* 44(1): 83–101.

2016. "A Multi-Level Explanation of Mass Support for the Judiciary." *Justice System Journal* 37(3): 194–210.

Walker, Shawn. 2020. "Pro-Choice Protesters March in Polish Cities Amid Abortion Ban Anger." *The Guardian* 23 October. Available at www.theguardian.com/world/2020/oct/23/poland-braced-for-more-protests-over-abortion-ban-ruling.

Ward, Dalston G., and Matthew Gabel. 2019. "Judicial Review Timing and Legislative Posturing: Reconsidering the Moral Hazard Problem." *Journal of Politics* 81(2): 681–85.

Weingast, Barry R. 1997. "The Political Foundations of Democracy and the Rule of Law." *American Political Science Review* 91(2): 245–63.

Whittington, Keith E. 2005. "'Interpose Your Friendly Hand': Political Supports for the Exercise of Judicial Review by the United States Supreme Court." *American Political Science Review* 99(4): 583–96.

Williams, Daniel K. 2023. "Post-Dobbs Climate Has Exposed Longstanding GOP Divisions on Abortion." *The Washington Post* 19 May. Available at www.washingtonpost.com/made-by-history/2023/05/19/abortion-republicans/.

Wlodarczak-semczuk, Anna. 2021. "Leading Polish Government Critic Should Leave Ombudsman Role, Says Court." *Reuters* 15 April. Available at www.reuters.com/world/europe/leading-polish-government-critic-should-leave-ombudsman-role-says-court-2021-04-15/.

Woodson, Benjamin. 2015. "Politicization and the Two Modes of Evaluating Judicial Decisions." *Journal of Law and Courts* 3(2): 110–26.

2019. "The Causes of the Legitimacy-Conferring and Republican Schoolmaster Capabilities of Courts." *Journal of Law and Courts* 7(2): 281–303.

World Justice Project. 2020. *World Justice Project Rule of Law Index 2020*. World Justice Project. Available at https://worldjusticeproject.org/our-work/publications/rule-law-index-reports/wjp-rule-law-index-2020.

Wright, George. 2020. "Coronavirus: Berlin Ad Sticks Middle Finger to Mask Rule Breakers." *BBC News Online* 14 October. Available at www.bbc.com/news/world-europe-54537519.

Wu, Fn et al. 2020. "A New Coronavirus Associated with Human Respiratory Disease in China." *Nature* 579(7798): 265–69.

Yadav, Vineeta, and Bumba Mukherjee. 2014. *Democracy, Electoral Systems, and Judicial Empowerment in Developing Countries*. University of Michigan Press.

Zaller, John R. 1992. *The Nature and Origins of Mass Opinion*. Cambridge University Press.

Zhou, Peng et al. 2020. "A Pneumonia Outbreak Associated with a New Coronavirus of Probable Bat Origin." *Nature* 579(7798): 270–73.

Zilis, Michael A. 2015. *The Limits of Legitimacy: Dissenting Opinions, Media Coverage, and Public Responses to Supreme Court Decisions*. University of Michigan Press.

2021. *The Rights Paradox: How Group Attitudes Shape US Supreme Court Legitimacy*. Cambridge University Press.

Zink, James R., James F. Spriggs, and John T. Scott. 2009. "Courting the Public: The Influence of Decision Attributes on Individuals' Views of Court Opinions." *Journal of Politics* 71(3): 909–25.

Index

abstract review, 208–10
Abstract Review Experiment, 215–32
autolimitation, 22, 47, 209

Basic Law, 1, 83
Bundesverfassungsgericht, 1–2, 83, 140–1, 193. *See also* German Federal Constitutional Court (GFCC)

capacity, 37, 51
  of federal government, 85
  institutional, 2, 16, 21, 28, 36, 40, 52, 168
  judicial, 52, 80, 158, 162, 186–7, 208
  of judicial review, 137
  professional, 38
  public, 173
  of U.S. Supreme Court, 81
careerism, 37, 51
clearance, 170
  copartisan, 190–1, 196, 212
  institutional, 43–5
  judicial, 12, 54–5, 136, 139, 151, 155, 174–5, 242
  outpartisan, 190–1, 196, 212
  and partisanship, 189
  and support for rule of law, 162–3
Comparative Constitutions Project, 3, 5–6
compliance, 7, 45–7, 129, 151
constitutional courts, 8, 23, 37–8, 140, 239
  and judicial review, 2–7, 35, 136, 253
  and public opinion, 67, 245–6
constitutional review, 3, 9, 22, 40, 48. *See also* judicial review
  in Germany, 83–4
contravention, 25–6, 45, 54, 159, 170
  consequences of, 43, 202
  copartisan, 189–91, 196, 212
  definition of, 42
  in Hungary, 42
  institutional, 42–3
  outpartisan, 190–1, 196, 212
  and partisanship, 189–91
  in Poland, 42
  and support for rule of law, 159, 161–2
coordination, 31–5, 40, 57, 138, 160, 169, 226, 240
copartisans, 187, 191, 193, 195, 198, 211
copartisanship, 198, 211, 241
  and institutional signals, 189–91. *See also* partisanship
Covid-19 pandemic, 24, 59, 63, 74–6. *See also* countries by name; research design

executive action, 5, 11, 23, 34, 40–1, 51, 58–9, 81, 87, 136–51, 165, 170
  and clearance, 43–5
  compliance as, 151–5
  and constraint, 246–7
  and judicial review, 53, 136, 161
  and legislatures, 179
  legitimization of, 44
  public acceptance of, 15–16, 136, 142, 155, 158, 172, 239
  public evaluation of, 16–18
  self-restraint as, 14
executive-judicial interactions, 40–1, 141, 212–13
experimental design. *See* research design: experimental
expertise, 35, 51
  institutional, 36–8, 51

forthrightness. *See* trustworthiness

German Federal Constitutional Court (GFCC), 1–2, 83, 148, 196. *See also* Bundesverfassungsgericht
Germany, 63–72, 83, 195
  Covid-19 pandemic in, 84–5
  and GFCC, 1–2, 83–4
  July 2021 in, 85–6
  partisanship in, 226
  Vaccine Approval experiment in, 140
Grundgesetz. *See* Basic Law

Hungary, 63–72, 86, 241, 250
  contravention in, 42
  Covid-19 pandemic in, 88–9
  and executive action, 181
  and Hungarian Constitutional Court, 42, 86–8
  judicial review in, 240
  July 2021 in, 89

institutional independence, 29
international courts, 250

judicial efficacy, 7–12, 18–22, 42, 136, 240, 242
  definition of, 9, 11
  and judicial independence, 10, 23, 25–6, 136, 240, 253
  and public attitudes, 53
judicial independence, 17, 23–6, 28, 47–53, 70–1, 94, 200, 243–5
  definition of, 48
  and executive action, 150
  expert judgments of, 64–6, 72
  future of, 248–9
  perceptions of, 49–53, 59, 249
  in Poland, 50
  public perceptions of, 66–74
  and research design, 64
  and source credibility, 51, 138, 249
  variation in, 61
judicial legitimacy, 117–18
judicial reform, 50–1, 93
judicial review, 28–9, 33–40, 45, 47, 239, 243–5
  centralized, 5–6, 209
  and citizen attitudes, 62
  decentralized, 5
  efficacy of, 138–40, 159, 173–4
  and executive action, 53, 136, 155, 161
  and litigant partisanship, 210–13
  public response to use of, 77, 159
  rise of, 3, 6–7
  shaping attitudes, 138
  and support for rule of law, 53–5, 62–3, 160–1
  types of, 5

legitimization
  capacity of courts, 151, 242
  effect of judicial clearance, 174–5
  of executive action, 44
  power of courts, 136, 241
  theories, 241
Lockdown Experiment, 145–51, 159, 165–70, 193, 195

Mandatory Vaccine Experiment, 192, 196, 200
monitoring, 15, 29–31, 34, 40, 57, 138, 160, 226
  of executives, 55, 240

noncompliance, 8, 11, 15, 54
  costs of, 42–3
  of executives, 160, 240
  institutional, 43
nonimplementation, 11, 15
nonmajoritarian theories, 20–2, 243

outpartisans, 187, 191, 193, 195, 198, 211

partisan prioritization, 247
Partisan Prioritization account, 26, 185–6, 190–3, 198–9, 202, 207, 211–15, 221–5
partisanship, 26, 28–9, 32, 55–7, 172, 185–7, 225–7, 241, 247–8
  and institutional signals, 192–6
  and prioritization, 56, 187–9
Poland, 63–72, 89–90, 241, 250
  contravention in, 42
  Covid-19 pandemic in, 74–6
  and executive action, 181
  judicial review in, 240
  July 2021 in, 93–4
  and Polish Constitutional Tribunal, 90–2
polarization, 24, 156, 175, 185–7, 225
  affective, 188
  partisan, 189
political consequences, 8–9, 12, 33, 47, 57, 226, 239
political costs, 28–33, 42, 62, 84, 94, 158–60, 163, 186, 244
  citizen driven, 29, 56
political penalties, 6, 9, 11–12, 16, 19, 22, 24, 174, 239–40
  citizen-driven, 14–15
  elite-driven, 12–14
professionalism, 37
  institutional, 51–2

research design, 59–61, 99, 215
  and Covid-19 pandemic, 74–8, 94
  and data types, 78–80

experimental, 44, 59, 61, 85, 148, 169–70, 187, 193, 195–6, 219, 223, 227
item selection, 108–10
rule of law, 63, 250
conceptualization of, 103–6
definitions of, 103–5
enforcement of, 7, 160
future of, 251–3
influence of, 163–4
and state constraint, 160
support for, 25, 28–9, 40, 54–5, 100–3, 158, 169
and clearance, 162–3
comparative, 110–11
conditional effects of, 161, 181
and contravention, 161–2
during Covid-19 pandemic, 60, 240
executive, 169–73
and executive action, 54–5
and judicial efficacy, 80, 160–1, 240
and judicial review, 54–5, 63, 129
measuring, 103–5
stability of, 111–16
and universalism-particularism, 101, 103–4, 106–8
validating, 101, 105, 116–29
violation of, 12–19, 21, 24–5, 28–33, 35, 40, 136, 173, 188, 200, 253
Rule of Law account, 185–7, 189–92, 197–202, 207–8, 211, 213–14, 225

self-constraint, 45–7
signaling capacity
of courts, 78, 246
institutional, 53, 58, 227, 249–51
of judicial decisions, 248
signaling credibility
of courts, 139
and judicial independence, 53, 240
signaling power
of courts, 29, 78
and judicial independence, 49
of judicial review, 33–6
of legislatures, 179
signals
credible, 35–6, 51
institutional, 38, 40, 58, 188
judicial, 62
public reception of, 62
source credibility, 35–6
of independent courts, 51–3, 62, 138
state constraint, 3, 19, 33–40, 46, 57, 161, 242
and Covid-19 pandemic, 76–7
judicial, 10, 186, 239, 250, 253
and judicial review, 21, 28, 138, 185, 188, 226, 241
by public, 15, 23
and rule of law, 160
state restraint, 31–2
symbols, institutional, 39–40

trustworthiness, 35–6, 38–40, 51–3, 248

US Supreme Court, 31, 42, 44, 46, 67, 81
United States, 63–72, 80–1, 195
Covid-19 pandemic in, 81–2
July 2021 in, 82–3
universalism and particularism. *See* rule of law, support for

Vaccine Approval Experiment, 140–5, 151, 164–5, 195
validity
convergent and discriminant, 116–17, 119, 135
of case selection, 94
of experimental design, 148
external, 147, 195–6
of findings, 61
of hypotheses, 74
of item selection, 108
predictive, 25, 126–9, 240
and reliability, 134–5
Varieties of Democracy (V-Dem) project, 64–6

Printed by Integrated Books International,
United States of America